D0378940

A theory of efficient cooperation and competition

A theory of efficient cooperation and competition

LESTER G. TELSER
University of Chicago

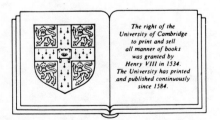

The right of the
University of Cambridge
to print and sell
all manner of books
was granted by
Henry VIII in 1534.
The University has printed
and published continuously
since 1584.

CAMBRIDGE UNIVERSITY PRESS

Cambridge
New York   New Rochelle   Melbourne   Sydney

Published by the Press Syndicate of the University of Cambridge
The Pitt Building, Trumpington Street, Cambridge CB2 1RP
32 East 57th Street, New York, NY 10022, USA
10 Stamford Road, Oakleigh, Melbourne 3166, Australia

First published 1987

Printed in the United States of America

Library of Congress Cataloging-in-Publication Data
Telser, Lester G., 1931–
A theory of efficient cooperation and competition.
Bibliography: p.
Includes index.
1. Competition – Mathematical models.   I. Title.
HD41.T43   1987   338.6′042′0724   87–5114

British Library Cataloguing in Publication Data
Telser, Lester G.
A theory of efficient cooperation and
competition.
1. Competition   2. Cooperation
I. Title
338.6   HD41

ISBN 0 521 30619 1

Contents

Contents

Tables

ix

Preface

Preliminary versions of some parts of this book came out in various articles published between 1982 and 1985. This holds true for parts of Chapters 2, 7, and 8 (Telser 1984a, 1984b, and 1982a). The material in Chapter 3 is based on a paper presented at a conference at the Hoover Institution in September, 1984, which was published in the conference proceedings (Telser 1985). I presented Chapter 2 at another conference at the Hoover Institution in February, 1986. Chapter 6 is a substantial revision of Telser (1980). Part 1 of Chapter 4 draws on some ideas in Telser (1982b) and corrects some errors therein.

Propositions and lemmas are numbered sequentially in each chapter starting with 1, and by part in each chapter with more than one part. Corollaries are numbered sequentially starting with 1 by proposition or lemma. Equations are numbered sequentially starting with 1 by section.

Sheldon Kimmel has been my most attentive and faithful critic. He has read preliminary versions of almost everything in this book and has saved me from many errors and obscurities. Howard Marvel carefully read preliminary versions of Chapters 2 and 3. George Bittlingmayer and David Haddock read these and some other chapters and gave me many useful comments and suggestions. I am also grateful to Frank Easterbrook, David Galenson, John Hause, Roger Noll, and Daniel Spulber for their helpful comments on various parts of this book. Two of my former students, Stephen Craig Pirrong and the late Yuichiro Hamada, deserve thanks for finding errors and ambiguities in some of the technical material. I also wish to thank Ken Judd, William Lynk, Menahem Speigel, Hod Thornber, and Robert Topel for their helpful comments on Chapter 8, Part 2.

I wish to thank the Lilly Endowment, Inc., and the Foundation for Research in Economics and Education for their support of some of the research reported in Chapter 2. I also wish to thank the Hoover Institution, Stanford University, Stanford, California, for supporting me as a Visiting Scholar during the final stages of writing this book in the Winter Quarter, 1986.

The most important person who has constantly encouraged me, listened to me, read my attempts at explaining things in plain English, and tried to make me coherent is my wife Sylvia. I doubt whether this book would have been written without her.

Finally, I wish to thank Jaffer Qumar and Greg Pelnar for their help in proofreading.

CHAPTER 1

Prologue

1 Introduction

This book has three main divisions. The first introduces the major themes, the second studies the conditions under which an efficient equilibrium exists, and the third examines the consequences of rivalry.

The basic tenet is that an efficient equilibrium requires an appropriate combination of both cooperation and rivalry. Under the cost conditions typical of many industries in a modern free-enterprise economy, it is not possible to have efficient results unless there are areas of cooperation among firms and among customers as well as rivalry. This was not fully understood in the last half of the nineteenth century in the United States and is still hotly debated. The purpose of Chapter 2 is to place the debate in its historical setting by discussing the events preceding and following the passage of two major legislative acts, the Interstate Commerce Commission Act of 1887 and the Sherman Antitrust Act of 1890. The proposition that an equilibrium may not exist unless firms are allowed to cooperate in some areas would probably not have been accepted by the supporters of antitrust legislation and railroad regulation even if they had been aware of it. Many proponents of this legislation considered competition as good under all circumstances and did not recognize the complications arising from the new technology: capital intensive methods of manufacturing, mass production and the use of interchangeable parts, improvements in communication and transportation, and so on. Chapter 3 is a theoretical analysis of some of these issues using models of these new technologies. It shows that even the simplest models present very difficult practical problems for firms and their customers.

Efficient cooperation is the main theme of the second division (Chapters 4 and 5). The studies of efficient cooperation apply the theory of the core. Chapter 4, in three parts, describes conditions under which a stable coalition exists. A coalition is stable if none of its members wishes to secede and form subcoalitions. Each member believes he is better off in the given coalition than in some other coalition. The first part of Chapter 4 studies semiprivate goods. These are goods that belong to all members of the coalition and are such that each member gets the same quantity of each semiprivate good. In addition, the members can prevent outsiders from deriving any benefits from these goods. The latter assumption explains why "private" and the former why "semi" join together in the name of these goods. Semiprivate goods are between private and public goods and share some features with both extremes. Private goods do not require each person to obtain the same quantity, whereas semiprivate and public goods do. No one can be excluded from the benefits of public goods, but this is not true of semiprivate goods. There are two different kinds of semiprivate and public goods. In the first kind individuals can contribute to the total on their own. Knowledge is the leading example of such public goods. Each individual can contribute to total knowledge and, we may say, the total is accessible to all as a public good. For the second kind of public goods, individuals cannot affect the quantity on their own. Instead it is necessary for them all to agree on some procedure for choosing the common quantity. An aircraft carrier is an example of this. Individuals do not have their own aircraft carriers as part of the public good, national defense. Public goods of the second kind raise both political and economic problems. The political problems refer to the nature of the mechanisms used to decide what and how much of these public goods to have. Semiprivate goods pose similar problems to some degree for the coalitions that can choose them. Part 2 of Chapter 4 studies private goods and gives necessary and sufficient conditions for a nonempty core in terms of the nature of the cost functions. It is shown that the core is nonempty if and only if there are nondecreasing returns to scale, that is, either constant or increasing returns to scale. The last part of Chapter 4 gives sufficient conditions for a nonempty core in an economy that has both private and semiprivate goods.

Chapter 5 describes in detail a situation for which no competitive equilibrium exists. It does so for a case in which there are many firms, each in a different location, that can ship their outputs to spatially separated markets. The cost function of each firm is the sum of two components: an avoidable cost and a shipping cost. Its avoidable cost depends on its capacity. This cost is positive only if the firm is active. If the firm is not active it can avoid this cost, hence the term *avoidable cost*. The other component of its cost is the transportation cost, which is proportional to distance and quantity shipped. The chapter describes an integer programming algorithm for finding the optimal allocation of outputs among the firms for given demand conditions. It also shows that there exists a set of upper bounds on firm output rates that, of course, cannot exceed the capacity installed in the firm's plants such that subject to these constraints an efficient equilibrium exists that can satisfy the given demand conditions. There does not exist a set of lower bounds on prices that can give an efficient equilibrium. Therefore, upper bounds on outputs are not equivalent to lower bounds on prices in this case. The results illustrate how an appropriate combination of cooperation and competition can give an efficient equilibrium.

The remaining division of the book (Chapters 6–8) discusses various forms of rivalry. It opens with the theory of self-enforcing agreements in Chapter 6. This theory applies when those who wish to have an agreement cannot rely on outsiders to enforce it. If they are unable to have a self-enforcing agreement, then the result is a noncooperative equilibrium, not enforcement of an agreement by a third party. The latter is often a more costly and a less beneficial arrangement. The chapter describes four situations in order to display a broad range of circumstances for which a self-enforcing agreement may be pertinent. It shows when it is and when it is not possible to have a self-enforcing agreement. One situation, the Prisoners' Dilemma, applies to cartels. The alternative to a cartel is a noncooperative equilibrium. The theory shows when firms can gain from collusion even though a single firm could obtain a temporary gain from a violation of the cartel agreement. Chapter 7 examines duopoly in detail. Duopoly applies when the firms cannot collude either via a self-enforcing agreement or via enforcement by a third party. This chapter gives a complete enough description of the strategies available to the firms so that a computer would have enough information to play it as a game. In so doing the implicit assumptions of Cournot, Bertrand, and Edgeworth rise to the surface and new results emerge.

Rivalry by innovation is the topic of the last chapter. It pursues a line of argument first proposed most vigorously by Schumpeter. To him competition is not the impersonal abstract version popular in beginning economics texts. It is instead analogous to a sporting contest with winners and losers. When there is competition by means of innovation, the successful firms can obtain large profits that may last for a long time despite the efforts of others to emulate them. Firms enter an industry when they believe they are not at a disadvantage relative to the incumbent firms. Entry stops and the industry is mature when innovation by any firm in that industry is no longer expected to be profitable. The theory explains differences in merger rates among industries, the distribution of firm sizes in an industry, the dynamic pattern of prices and outputs by industry, and why there is so little trafficking in patent rights so that royalty receipts are a relatively unimportant source of income even for firms actively engaged in research.

2   Guide for the reader

Although the theory of the core has a pedigree going back to Edgeworth's famous book *Mathematical Psychics* (1881), it is a newcomer to the economist's toolkit. It is therefore desirable to describe how this theory fits together with the more familiar tools of economics. My intention is to furnish a simple description of the relations among the pertinent parts of economic theory. It is not to describe the real economy and its social setting. The framework for this purpose uses two basic concepts: the status of contracting among the economic actors and the status of the core.

Contracting may be restricted or unrestricted. It is unrestricted if the economic actors may make any contracts they please among themselves without hindrance from outsiders. In short there is freedom of contracting. The status of contracting may be restricted. The restrictions take the form of constraints that set limits on the terms of the contracts and determine who may enter contracts. There are two states of the core, empty or not empty. The core is not empty if there is a feasible set of imputations acceptable to all of the participants and all coalitions of participants. A nonempty core combines an optimal mixture of competition and cooperation. The degree of cooperation implicit in a nonempty core is self-enforcing because no one can gain by rejecting the return received as a member of the grand coalition and instead going off independently outside that coalition. The core is said to be empty if for any feasible imputation there is at least one coalition that would do better on its own. Putting together these two basic concepts and the two possible states for each gives four categories. These four categories supply a framework for describing the relation between economic applications of the theory of the core and received economic theory. The contents of these four categories constitute the guide for the reader.

Received economic theory implicitly assumes the core is always nonempty and does not recognize the possibility of an empty core. Inquiry into the conditions that can bring about an empty core simply does not arise. Assume along with the received theory that the core is not empty. In terms of the preceding framework, there are two cases – freedom of contracting and restrictions on contracting. Take the category of unrestricted contracting and a nonempty core. This category includes the neoclassical perfectly competitive equilibrium. It includes the anal-

ysis by Edgeworth of pure exchange among traders with convex preference sets who have given initial endowments of goods. Edgeworth's
analysis is the origin of the theory of the core. The extension to en-
compass production under conditions of constant returns to scale is
the culmination of the neoclassical theory of perfect competition. Freedom of contracting in the presence of a nonempty core for an economy
with constant returns to scale results in an efficient equilibrium.

While still assuming there is a nonempty core, let there be restrictions
on contracting. The latter cause departures from perfect competition
and become the subject of various theories of imperfect competition
in the received economic theory. The simplest case in this category is
monopoly. Cournot (1838) was the first to present a formal analysis of
monopoly. The next important advance in the theory of monopoly,
Alfred Marshall's concept of natural monopoly (1890), is not always
in this category because a natural monopoly does not always have a
nonempty core. When there is a nonempty core and restrictions on the
freedom of contracting, then monopoly causes contrived scarcity and
an inefficient equilibrium. This begs the question of what led to the
monopoly. A facile reply blames government. Even if government is
the source of the monopoly and enforces it, the reply is unsatisfactory
because the actions of government are themselves a necessary and a
proper subject of economic inquiry not a given on a par with the natural
environment. Remember that economics used to be called political
economy. A cartel is another example of restrictions on contracting.
It is a form of monopoly and may produce the same result as a profit-
maximizing monopoly. A noncooperative equilibrium may also fall into
this category. The individual firms in the industry each act on their
own and choose their strategies independently. In this theory, since
the only legal coalitions are singletons, which are coalitions each with
a single member, the effect is to impose restrictions on contracting
because the theory assumes coalitions cannot have as many members
as they please. The Cournot–Nash equilibrium for an oligopoly is usually inefficient. Still another case that fits into this category is the monopolistic competition of Chamberlin. This is a noncooperative equilibrium combined with free entry. It does not reduce to a competitive
equilibrium for reasons apparently plain to Chamberlin but not to his
critics such as Kaldor (1935) and Demsetz (1968).

Given a nonempty core and restrictions on contracting, there is the
question of what sustains the restrictions. It may be a third party. For
instance, in Imperial Germany a cartel agreement was legal, and there
was a special cartel court to which the parties to a cartel agreement
could bring their disputes. Although the members of the cartel could

fashion their own terms, the legality of these terms could be tested by bringing suit in the cartel court. In England the courts would not enforce a collusive agreement nor could firms who made such agreements be confident of immunity from prosecution by the crown. England had ancient common law against monopoly, and the crown could bring suit against a party for its monopolistic practices. These precedents of English common law also applied in the United States so that collusive agreements would not be enforceable in any U.S. court even before there was antitrust legislation. It was the federal system of the United States and the growth of large firms engaged in interstate commerce that partly explain the birth of federal antimonopoly laws. States and local governments do not have jurisdiction over transactions going beyond their political boundaries. If there was to be a national policy against collusion and monopoly, it would require federal legislation. Although in the United States cartel agreements are illegal according to the various antitrust laws, there are, however, numerous exceptions and circumstances under which the U.S. government does enforce monopolistic restrictions on contracting. Nor is this all. Illegal acts do occur. Even in the United States where price-fixing agreements are generally illegal, firms make such agreements. These may persist for a long time as self-enforcing agreements (see Chapter 6). Restrictions on contracting can endure because the parties to the restrictions individually may gain from them even after taking into account what they would obtain from violations of such agreements.

A large fraction of received economic theory explored various parts of the territory encompassed by the joint category of a nonempty core and the two states of contracting, unrestricted and restricted. When the core is not empty, unrestricted contracting yields an efficient equilibrium. Given a nonempty core, restricted contracting is a fall from grace that causes an inefficient equilibrium. The circumstances that may create an empty core, though not wholly unrecognized, met with considerable skepticism from most professional economists.

The conjunction of an empty core with the two states of contracting, unrestricted and restricted, is new terrain. Here several problems in formal economic theory were known to be troublesome such as nonconvexities, indivisibilities, and externalities. For the most part, the main body of economic theory ignored these topics. As we shall see, these are often the source of an empty core. Businessmen complaining of excessive or chaotic competition are sometimes in situations that an impartial economic observer would describe as an empty core. It is hard for many economists to accept the proposition that competition may be excessive because the received theory regards competition as always good, and the more there is, the better. The claim that unrestricted contracting combined with an empty core means no equilibrium is possible encounters disbelief. There are two common objections. The first denies there are circumstances that can lead to an empty core. The second asks for observable symptoms of an empty core.

To say there is chaos when the core is empty suggests that seeing chaos is to see the observable symptoms of an empty core. What is chaos? It does not mean that people run aimlessly in circles wringing their hands in despair. It does mean that under the existing rules and practices what happens is undesirable for nearly everyone. Unless there are new rules or changes in the existing ones, nearly everyone will suffer. It would be out of place here to dwell on the issues in greater detail, but something more must be said. There is chaos when price cutting is extreme, most firms in the industry are losing money, and yet it is plain that buyers want the product and are willing to pay higher prices than those currently prevailing. The state of the domestic passenger airline industry since 1980 may illustrate such chaos. A century ago, the railroad industry was in a similar state, and it remains in precarious health to this day. There are episodes in the history of the steel industry that seem consistent with the view that chaos can occur. A well-documented case occurred between 1920 and 1921 when there was a breakdown of the Pittsburgh-Plus basing point system. Periods of drastic price cutting coupled with large losses have also occurred in the cement industry. Merely to deny the possibility that conditions can exist that result in an empty core is a position that should have no claim to serious consideration. Yet it requires an answer. A way of doing so starts with the construction of a model consistent with plausible assumptions about cost and demand conditions. One can then show when, how, and why there is no efficient equilibrium.

While still assuming the core is empty, restrictions on contracting become necessary in order to restore an equilibrium. Whether or not it is an efficient equilibrium depends on the nature of the restrictions. The main point is that restrictions of some sort are essential; the alternative is chaos. Thus we are led to examine the nature of the restrictions.

It is possible to have restrictions that give an inefficient equilibrium. Monopoly or a cartel behaving like a monopoly illustrates such restrictions. Although in either case the result is an equilibrium, it may be an inefficient one. Let us examine the contrast between this case and one where the core is not empty. With a nonempty core a monopoly or cartel is not necessary for an equilibrium since competition in the form of unrestricted contracting can yield an efficient equilibrium. With an empty core some restrictions on the freedom of contracting are necessary in order to have an equilibrium. The Cournot–Nash (Nash 1950 and 1951) assumptions illustrate the kind of constraints on contracting that can produce an equilibrium. Monopolistic restrictions can also produce an equilibrium. But in neither case will the equilibrium always be efficient.

Buyers and sellers may agree on restrictions that not only furnish an equilibrium but also one that is efficient. For instance, there may be complete vertical integration. An example is a railroad and a coal mine. Merger of the two serves their interest best as well as the interest of downstream customers such as a public utility generating electricity that buys coal from the mine that is shipped by rail. A long-term contract between the buyer and the seller is another alternative. They may prefer this to vertical integration that would interfere with their other activities. Two-part prices are another restriction that can give an efficient equilibrium. Some recognition or distinction between long-term and spot or casual customers is necessary for the success of such prices. A seller may offer lower prices to regular or loyal customers provided they agree to render him their exclusive patronage. Though this practice impedes entry and thereby restricts competition, it can result in an efficient equilibrium. Indeed, under the hypothesis of an empty core, unrestricted contracting, that is, unhindered competition, would not result in an equilibrium at all, either efficient or inefficient. Deferred rebates furnish still another example. These are common in ocean shipping. A shipper can obtain a lower cost by remaining loyal to the members of a shipping conference for a stipulated period of time because they give him a discount in return for his loyalty. A coalition of sellers, a cartel if you like, that imposes output quotas on its members may result in an efficient equilibrium. On the other side of the market, a coalition of buyers that places input quotas on its members may give an efficient equilibrium. In all of these cases, given the circumstances that lead to an empty core, some restriction on contracting is necessary for an equilibrium. Not only are there restrictions that can supply an equilibrium but also, if chosen well, it will be an efficient equilibrium.

It is fair to ask what conditions can lead to an empty core. Take the case of private goods. These are goods such that each person can choose on his own how much to buy or sell. Assume that the goods are continuously divisible and that each individual's preferences satisfy the usual assumptions. Chapter 4 shows that there is an implication of a nonempty core if and only if there are constant or increasing returns to scale. Consequently, under any other cost conditions the core is empty. For instance, in an industry where individual firms have identical U-shaped average cost curves and increasing marginal cost curves, called Viner industries (Telser 1978, Chapter 3), the core is empty. However, even in the latter case, if the optimal output rate of each firm is small relative to the total demand for the product, then there is an approximation to constant returns and consequently an approximation to a nonempty core.

Economic applications of the theory of the core also give results for semiprivate goods as well as the more complicated case when there are both private and semiprivate goods. A semiprivate good is one that must be available in the same quantity for each member of a coalition. It is in contrast to private goods for which each member of a coalition can decide for himself how much he wants. When there are both private and semiprivate goods, the core is nonempty if there are constant or increasing returns to scale in the production of these goods. No conditions that are both necessary and sufficient for a nonempty core are known for the case with private and semiprivate goods.

Reconsider a situation where there are only private goods and the core is empty. Restrictions on contracting are necessary to have an equilibrium. If contracting were unrestricted, then some coalition must accept a return below the amount it can assure itself were it to secede from the whole group and go off on its own. It is this coalition that stands to gain the most by leaving the whole group. The theory thereby predicts not only when cooperation breaks down – it is when the core is empty, an event that occurs when demand is low – but it also predicts which coalition can gain the most by evading the prevailing rules that restrict contracting. At high levels of demand restrictions on contracting in the form of cooperation are unnecessary because then the core is not empty. Consequently, given the cost conditions that imply an empty core, the theory predicts that the status of the core depends on the level of demand. At high levels of demand there can be a nonempty core because then there can be an efficient equilibrium without restrictions on contracting. But at low levels of demand, the core is empty so that some restrictions on contracting become necessary to have an equilibrium at all. Hence cartels are more likely to arise when demand is low or falling than when it is high or rising. Recessions are conducive to the formation of cartels and declining industries are likely candidates for collusion.

CHAPTER 2

Perceptions and reality: the genesis of the Sherman act

1   Introduction

The actions people take depend on what they believe is true. But what they believe is true, that is, their perceptions, may be only partly true or even wholly false. Even so, these perceptions of reality, not reality itself, affect their behavior. The effects of their actions do depend on reality and may in turn cause changes in their perceptions. People's knowledge is surely incomplete and partly wrong. Learning is the process of expanding and correcting the stock of knowledge. As there is learning so perceptions change. A theory of behavior that assumes there is a difference between what is true and what people believe to be true can make better predictions of what they will do than a theory assuming omniscience. As an illustration consider the problem of explaining which trade routes were used by merchants. By taking into account people's belief that the world was flat, we could make better predictions of the actual trade routes that were used until the beginning of the sixteenth century than by assuming that people knew the true shape of the earth. Only those who believe the earth is round would be willing to sail west in order to go to the Far East.

The better theory of behavior not only distinguishes between perception and reality but it also explains how and when people reduce the discrepancy between them. If an individual cannot change reality, then the theory must describe the conditions leading him to change his beliefs. You are willing to learn if you expect more benefit than cost from your learning. Learning occurs to the extent that it is expected to yield a net gain to the learner. The gains from learning depend on many things. A learner may acquire a skill, revise a stock of knowledge because changes in the situation require it, or look for something. Learning how to play the piano illustrates the first, making a weather forecast illustrates the second, and prospecting for gold is an example of the third.

So far I refer to learning by an individual. Our problem also concerns the actions and beliefs of a group so that the theory ought to explain how the members of the group learn. Perhaps those who are the first to learn teach the others so that we may say the group contains students and teachers. Now the difficulty lies not only in describing how knowledge diffuses among the members of the group but also perhaps how some may gain from deceiving others. It is naive to believe that all people seek to perfect their knowledge. Moreover, reality itself is not entirely a given. By changing the rules (or laws) of society, people can change some aspects of their environment and thereby affect their behavior. These considerations complicate the task of constructing a theory that purports to explain how a group changes its perceptions and in response modifies its behavior.

Individuals have different stocks of knowledge and different costs of learning. They do not all derive the same benefits from increasing and improving their knowledge. Proposed actions will not affect them all in the same way. When the group can make rules that will affect everyone so that anyone who violates the rules may be subject to the penalties that the rules provide, then there are apparent costs of making and revising rules. Consequently, new rules will not often be made, given that members of the group differ with respect to their beliefs and gains from the proposed changes. These considerations are relevant in order to understand the extraordinary new laws that Congress enacted between 1885 and 1914.

By the latter part of the nineteenth century nearly everyone in the United States was becoming aware that thanks to the discovery and use of new technology the standard of living was rising rapidly. Among the reasons for this was the application of steam power in transportation and in factories. Expanding from local to national and international markets made possible the gains from greater specialization. There was a revolution in communications as well. The invention of the telegraph and telephone lowered the cost of communication so that men of great ability could control bigger enterprises than ever before. By 1880 electricity was moving from the laboratory to the community, first as a source of illumination and then as a new form of power. It would be easy to give numerous other examples. Never before had there been so rapid an exploitation of new knowledge in commerce and industry. The enormous benefits would not seem cause for complaint. It would seem reasonable that the inventors themselves or those who could apply and improve their inventions would become wealthy. But it was surprising to many that a few could accumulate great wealth though these few had apparently little direct involvement with these technological advances. This was a source of concern. What could explain such wealth? People were accustomed to see wealthy rulers and aris-

tocrats. That some bankers and merchants who served the rulers and
nobility could become wealthy as a result was also a long familiar
observation. Before the Civil War, even the United States had a
wealthy class in the South like the European aristocracies. It was in
the South that one could find the largest fortunes in the United States
(Jones 1980). By the 1870s Americans saw something new. Ordinary
men, not princes or dukes, acquired great wealth in oil, railroads, and
steel. Jay Gould, a railroad financier, left an estate of $73 million, an
amount comparable to about $1 billion in 1985. It is estimated that the
Morgans, Astors, Goulds, and Rockefellers had aggregate wealth of
about $600 million by the end of the nineteenth century (Myers 1909).
How did they become so rich? None was an inventor. Though some
famous inventors were rich, such as Edison, Bell, McCormick, and
Singer, none was so spectacularly rich as Astor, Gould, Morgan, or
Rockefeller. The popular view could supply only three explanations of
these great fortunes. It was held that such great wealth could not be
acquired honestly. It must come from some kind of chicanery, im-
morality, or dishonesty – paying workers low wages, selling products
at monopoly prices, or destroying competitors with predatory tactics.
It was believed that the foundation of a great fortune must rest on
exploitation of the worker, cheating the consumer, destroying small
competitors, or any combination of these.

   Accepting this as the perception of most people, certain consequences follow. One is popular support for an income tax levied on
the richest members of society. Congress did enact an income tax in
1894 as part of the Tariff Act. Second, the abuses of the railroads must
be corrected. Congress enacted the Interstate Commerce Act in 1887.
Third, monopolies must be curbed. The Sherman Antitrust Act became
law in 1890. The adulteration of products must be stopped. Congress
passed the Pure Food and Drug Act in 1906. To protect labor there
were new laws controlling hours of work and conditions of employment
enacted by Congress during the 1890s.

   The framework sketched above explains some of the laws passed by
Congress during this period. This is owing to the gap between the real
economic world and people's perception of it. The fact is that relative
prices of the goods made and sold by the so-called trusts fell during
the 20 years preceding the enactment of the Sherman Antitrust Act in
1890. Reality did not support the belief that there was a monopoly
problem. To explain the perception of a monopoly problem requires
looking in areas unrelated to symptoms of monopoly that would be
present according to economic theory.

   Another case, Prohibition, though outside this area of interest is nevertheless instructive. Examination of the evidence shows no rise in consumption of alcohol per capita in the United States during the fourscore years preceding adoption of the Eighteenth Amendment of the Constitution. Though per capita beer consumption rose, it was offset by the decline in per capita consumption of other alcoholic beverages. It would appear that, although the total number of alcoholics was rising, the relative number in the population was constant. To argue that drunkenness was becoming an increasingly serious problem, one must show that the cost of treating and handling the consequences of alcoholism was placing an increasing burden on the nation. It is doubtful that the proponents of Prohibition could make this case convincingly. I claim that the reality did not support the perception of an increasingly severe problem arising from consumption of alcoholic beverages. In fact, in two countries, France and Italy, alcohol consumption per capita had always been much higher than in the United States and yet there was no serious effort to control its consumption. Nevertheless, from 1920 until 1933 when there was repeal of Prohibition, the production and sale of alcoholic beverages in the United States was forbidden by federal law. Repeal was the result of widespread learning on the basis of experience that the costs of Prohibition seemed to exceed the benefits by a wide margin (Warburton 1932).

2   Reality: the legacy from the past

Nothing is more difficult than to imagine what things were like in the past. Speaking for myself, events that occurred before I was 10 years old seem very remote and far less real than those in my adult life. There is a strong tendency to believe that what is has always been and will remain. It is hard to comprehend that many things now so familiar are actually very new and did not exist at all even a short time ago. It is true not only of material things such as computers, television, radio, automobiles, airplanes, electrical power, nuclear energy, and antibiotics but it is also true of economic institutions. The latter do not enter our daily lives in the same obtrusive way as material things, and yet these institutions have very important effects. Our present circumstances owe much to innovations creating new economic institutions and changes in existing ones. The corporation is a leading example. It is sobering to realize that many familiar aspects of corporations are in fact quite recent phenomena. Trade in shares of stock on the New York Stock Exchange did not exceed the volume of bond trading until close to the end of the nineteenth century. Only 52 industrial and public utility stocks were traded on the New York Stock Exchange between

1861 and 1870. In 1866, the peak trading year of that decade, only 38 of these stocks were traded and of these only 8 were traded in each month of the year. In 1871 the market value of all companies whose stocks were traded on the New York Stock Exchange constituted about 2 percent of the wealth of the nation at that time (Cowles 1938, pp. 4–5). The oldest surviving organized futures market in the United States is the Chicago Board of Trade, which was incorporated in 1848. Railroads did not exist before 1820. The problems of financing, constructing, and operating them explain the development of many of the new economic organizations. The subject of economics itself is a new discipline, and the period of its most rapid development coincides with the changing economic environment. In order to understand the reasons for the passage of the Sherman act of 1890 and its closely related and equally important predecessor, the Interstate Commerce Act of 1887, we must try to imagine what the economy was like in the nineteenth century. Our purpose at this point is to understand the reality and not how it was perceived.

Although modern forms of business organization started in Renaissance Italy and in the Netherlands, for our purposes Elizabethan England is the best starting point. It was then that the joint-stock companies under royal charter were born in order to trade with distant regions. The Russia Company, the Turkey Company, Hudson's Bay Company, the East India Company, and the Africa Company are the leading examples. The owners of these companies invested their capital by purchasing shares of stock in them. Under prescribed conditions they could sell their shares to whomever they pleased without the consent of their fellow shareholders. The owners had limited liability and got the profits and the losses. It does not seem possible to explain the origin of these companies solely as the result of innovation in ships and shipbuilding, though these were both necessary and important. Trade over long distances to remote areas was risky. Partly to limit their risk, individuals were loath to put more than a fraction of their wealth in such trading ventures. Joint-stock companies should be viewed primarily as devices for accommodating the preferences of investors with respect to risk while raising the capital necessary to promise a reasonable chance of gain. Merchants joining together in order to finance voyages for profit was not new. But such ventures would dissolve at the conclusion of the voyage. What was new about the joint-stock companies was their intention to remain in business forever. Indeed, one of them, Hudson's Bay Company, exists to this day. Some joint-stock companies became the focus of notorious scandals; recall the South Sea Bubble and John Law's Mississippi Scheme (Mackay 1852).

Two centuries after the Elizabethan age Adam Smith (1776) wrote with deep suspicion of joint-stock companies. He regarded them as inefficient, avenues of monopoly profit, easily turned into schemes for defrauding investors, and subject to abuse to serve political ends. He pointed out the conflict of interest between the owners and their employees who ran the companies. He did not believe that owners could have adequate protection against fraud, incompetence, and lack of diligence save in those businesses that were routine and did not require managers to act with energy and initiative. Yet even as Adam Smith wrote, the joint-stock company stood at the start of its most significant development, which continues to the present day.

By the end of the seventeenth century there were important joint-stock companies in banking and insurance in addition to the trading companies. The Bank of England, a private joint-stock company was founded in the 1690s during the reign of William and Mary. It was then that the debts of the government of England were consolidated and trade began in the new financial instruments called consols. At the same time there was also the reform of the coinage of England, including the introduction of milled coins. The reform was under the direction of John Locke and Isaac Newton, who, as Master of the Mint, was knighted for his services (and not for his contributions to physics). This era saw the beginning of the insurance companies. The men who insured ships met at Lloyd's Coffee House in London. Companies were formed to write life insurance and still others offered fire insurance. The latter also furnished their clients with fire-fighting service. This combination did not prosper and the city of London itself undertook fire protection at the time of Adam Smith, who gave various interesting reasons for the failure of private fire-fighting companies.

During this period each joint-stock company needed its own charter from Parliament. It was no routine affair to obtain a charter. Parliament had to approve each specific instance. It was not until 1844 that Parliament enacted general requirements by which a joint-stock company could be formed (Haney 1914, p. 104).

Being English possessions until 1776, the American colonies were subject to English law. Divergence did not occur until after 1789, the birth year of the United States. Early U.S. corporations built and operated canals and toll roads. Like the English companies, there were U.S. corporations in insurance and banking. In all of these cases, however, the authority to form the companies came from specific acts of a state legislature. No state had general enabling legislation permitting incorporations until shortly after the passage of such a law by Parliament. With few exceptions, notably the First and Second Bank of the United States, the U.S. Congress did not grant charters to joint-stock companies. The timing of the legislation that reduced the cost of forming a corporation is noteworthy. It coincides with the rising importance of railroads.

The invention of the steam engine in the latter part of the eighteenth century originated in attempts to lower the cost of pumping water out of mines. It was to have far-reaching consequences. By the 1820s locomotives powered by steam engines and pulling trains of cars had appeared first in England and then in the United States. The railroad was on the scene. It was soon to become the largest commercial enterprise in the private sector of the economy. Prior to it the largest enterprises were creations of the state, often temporary organizations formed during time of war. In both England and the United States, it was not government that planned, financed, built, and ran railroads. It was private corporations formed by individuals who encountered vast new problems typical of the new industries that were to emerge in that century.

The railroad industry exhibits the problem of obtaining the maximum efficiency by means of an optimal balance between cooperation and rivalry. For instance, there is the choice of the width of the railroad tracks. Initially, each railroad chose its own width. When a shipment had to pass from one railroad line to another, it was necessary to unload the freight from one train and reload it on the other. The savings that would accrue by having a common gauge were soon apparent. It took conscious cooperation and agreement among the railroads to decide on a common width for their tracks, and even so this did not occur in the mountainous regions in the western United States. Even with a common gauge the railroads had the problem of how to share the revenue from a shipment of goods that went over the tracks of a series of connected railroads. A rail shipment is a joint product of complementary inputs composed of sequences of starting and ending points from the origin to the final destination. Nor is this all. Except on the most heavily traveled lines, there is only a single track. One train can pass another only at places where there are sidings. Coordination is necessary to schedule trains over a common route so that the faster trains, such as passenger trains, do not interfere with the slower ones. Empty boxcars pose another problem. More freight goes from west to east than in the reverse direction. Hence empty cars must go from east to west. Who should bear the cost of moving the empty cars? All shippers benefit from the use of the common track. How should they share its cost? The signaling system and the freight sorting yards are common to all. How should their costs be allocated among the shippers? Some shippers want occasional service, whereas others can guarantee a steady volume of shipments at regular intervals. These impose different costs that the railroad may wish to have reflected in the freight rates. It would be an error to suppose that these were peculiar problems of railroads. On the contrary they were the first examples of what were to become the predominant kinds of problems characteristic of a technologically sophisticated economy made up of highly specialized industries.

This brief historical survey would be seriously deficient if it did not mention the rise of the factory system in the New England textile industry before the Civil War. Water power, and not the steam engine, together with the inventions in this industry, explain the aggregation of the looms under one roof. These factories were still small enough so that the necessary capital could be obtained from investors who knew personally the major owners who ran their own companies.

It was also in New England that there began the sequence of innovations leading a century later to the assembly line and mass production. The first step in this sequence was the problem of making interchangeable parts. The demand came initially from the U.S. Army, which wanted its muskets made from interchangeable parts, though this would greatly increase the cost of these weapons. Machinists learned how to do this at the Springfield and Harper's Ferry armories. Some left to start their own machine shop companies, and so there grew around the Connecticut River the first machine tool industry in the United States. Hounshell (1984) traces in detail the spread and improvement of this knowledge from its origins in the musket industry in 1800 to other industries – sewing machines, reapers, bicycles, and on to the Ford Motor Company where between 1908 and 1910 the Model T Ford became the first mass-produced commodity using interchangable parts manufactured on an assembly line.

An assembly line is an important feature of a modern economy. On an assembly line goods are manufactured at a constant rate using components made available at prescribed sites on the line. At each of these sites are men, machines, and the parts that come together to operate on the object moving along the assembly line and contribute to its completion. The parts must be interchangeable so that no costly hand-fitting is required to attach a part to the main product. It is necessary to design the operation of the line allowing it to run at a steady pace. This requires careful planning so that inventories of parts are available at the right time and place and so that each operation can occur at just the right pace, neither too quickly nor too slowly, thereby preventing bottlenecks at any point on the line. The workers must do their jobs at the rate set by the assembly line. Each assembly line has a large team of workers and their supervisors. An assembly line may have subassembly lines where some components are made. It is efficient to create a subassembly line for those components for which the least-cost solution requires a very different rate of operation than the main assembly line. Differences in the optimal rates of operation among subassembly and main assembly lines pose scheduling problems whose solutions require the holding of inventories and the shipment of batches of components from the subassembly to the main assembly. Subassembly lines may be located far from the main assembly lines. This poses formidable problems of planning and communication. The firms that own and operate the subassembly lines are not always the same as those who have the main lines. This by itself raises difficult and important questions about the nature of the firm. Viewing an assembly line in this abstract way suggests some appropriate ways of representing the cost conditions in an economic theory. We should remember this when we consider how the people perceived these new technologies.

3   Perceptions about the economy after the end of the Civil War

This section presents evidence showing the various perceptions about the economy held by different groups and influential individuals. Then, as always, there was no consensus. Recall, for example, that Congress did not pass unanimously its declaration of war on Japan on December 8, 1941. Different kinds of evidence reveal the nature of prevailing views. These include direct measures of opinion as expressed in publications and by the content of and votes on the acts of Congress. Even when acts are passed nearly unanimously, as is true of the Sherman Antitrust Act of 1890, the percentage of the membership not voting is a significant indicator of divergence of views. An interpretation of congressional votes is complicated by vote trading. A congressman successfully represents the interests of his constituents to the extent that he is reelected. Since his constituents are not alike and have divergent views and interests, he faces the necessity of taking those positions in Congress that will best accommodate their views so that he can return to his seat again and again. For example, there is a bill that is supported by a bare majority of his constituents. It may be difficult for him to calculate precisely how much support it has in his district. Say he believes a bare majority of his constituents support it. He may vote in its favor at an earlier stage, counting on the fact that, as is often true, it will go into conference. After it returns to the floor from the conference committee for another vote, he has three choices: Vote the same way as he did before, vote against the bill, or abstain. In case the division of opinion is narrow in his district, his most prudent strategy would seem to be not to vote at all. For these reasons representative government offers opportunities for observing and interpreting the effects of public opinion that can aid our understanding of perceptions. It is not quite so simple owing to the diverse bills coming before Congress that present complicated patterns of gains and losses for individuals. A congressman may support one bill that would harm his constituents as part of a bargain to gain votes for another on an entirely different matter for which their benefit would outweigh their loss from the first bill. This is the well-known process called logrolling.

Thanks to the research of Galambos (1975), there is now a solid basis for assertions about some aspects of the state of public opinion toward big business from 1880 to 1940. His work is based on analysis of newspapers catering to special audiences. His research assumes that the opinions expressed in these publications reflect the attitudes of their readers. A plausible argument supports this assumption. Newspapers cannot survive unless their receipts are tolerably close to the costs of publication. They depend, therefore, on sales to an interested audience and must furnish this audience with a product it is willing to buy. It is not so much that the writers of the publication shape the opinion of their readers as it is that they reflect it or, perhaps more accurately, make it more articulate. Galambos studies the content of publications aimed at what he considers three middle-class groups: professional men consisting primarily of engineers and clergymen; farmers, treated as two separate groups by region (the South and the Midwest); and organized labor. By noting how the publications he analyzed describe big business and business leaders, one can draw plausible inferences about the attitudes of the readers of these publications.

The findings of Galambos are interesting and, perhaps, surprising. Contrary to some widely held views, he concludes there was less hostility toward big business for the period from 1880 to 1892 than there was for the period from 1893 to 1900 (pp. 78, 112). It was in the former period, however, that Congress enacted two major laws, the Interstate Commerce Commission Act of 1887 and the Sherman Antitrust Act of 1890. The McKinley Tariff of 1890, hardly a piece of antibusiness legislation, was enacted by Congress only three months after the Sherman act. Even this seems to confirm Galambos's findings. The fourth important legislation in my analysis, the federal income tax, was part of the Tariff Act of 1894. It is in the second period that the groups studied by Galambos display a significant change in their attitudes, and in his words "this decade witnessed a major crisis in American life" (p. 112). For both periods organized labor tended in general to express consistently greater hostility toward big business than did the other groups studied, as is shown by the percentage of pejoratives used when referring to big business (Galambos 1975, Table 5.8, p. 155).

It was in the latter part of the nineteenth century that a political movement partly reflecting anti–big business feelings became important – the Granger or Populist movement. Indeed it became sufficiently so that William Jennings Bryan, a leader esteemed by those sympathetic to the Populists, was twice the Democratic candidate for president of the United States, in 1896 and again in 1900. In 1896 Bryan received 47.8 percent of the total vote cast for the Republican and Democratic candidates and lost to McKinley, the Republican, 176 electoral votes to McKinley's 271. In 1900 Bryan's share of the popular vote dropped slightly to 46.8 percent of the Democratic plus Republican total while his electoral votes fell to 155 against McKinley's 292. Bryan plainly had much political support. This is not to say that hostility toward big business was the only source of his popular appeal, though few would deny it was an important part of it. It seems almost to belabor the obvious to assert that this adds to the evidence of a sizable group that was hostile to big business.

The results of presidential elections are not the only evidence for this hypothesis. The nature of the legislation introduced and enacted by Congress furnishes more evidence. The Interstate Commerce Commission Act (ICCA) of 1887 was passed during the administration of Grover Cleveland, a conservative Democrat. In the Senate, 36 voted aye, 12 nay, and 28 did not vote. Although the ICCA passed the Senate by 75 percent of those voting, this was only 47 percent of the membership of the Senate. In the House, controlled by the Democrats, only 41 congressmen voted against the ICCA, while 219 voted for it, and 65 did not vote. The act passed the House by 67.4 percent of the total membership. The House of the 50th Congress had 169 Democrats and 152 Republicans. Therefore, a substantial number of Republicans must also have voted in favor of the ICCA. Even in the Senate where the Republicans had 39 seats to 37 seats of the Democrats, there plainly was Republican support for the ICCA. Some would argue that these results do not necessarily reflect an antirailroad bias. Instead of regarding the ICCA as merely reflecting public sentiment against railroad abuses, Kolko (1965) and MacAvoy (1965) interpret it as favored by the railroads themselves so they could harness the power of government to enforce their cartels. There are several reasons for doubting this interpretation. Anticipating my more detailed argument given below, these are, first, that the act itself did not give the Interstate Commerce Commission (ICC) the power to enforce the rules needed by a railroad cartel even if the commission was inclined to accommodate it; second, the railroad cartels antedated the ICCA; and, third, the individual railroads had divergent interests with respect to the effects of the ICCA and would not all have welcomed ICC-sponsored cartels.

The Sherman Antitrust Act became law in July, 1890, during the term of Benjamin Harrison, a Republican. No member of the House voted against it, 85 members did not vote at all, and 242 voted for it. Only one senator voted against the Sherman act, 52 voted for it, and 23 did not vote. As is the case for the ICCA, and despite the overwhelming vote for the Sherman act, one need not regard this as a bill to make the modern economists' notion of perfect competition the law of the land. It is even plausible to argue that anticompetitive interests would welcome the Sherman act. In this instance the welcomers are those small business firms who under competitive pressure from the "trusts" would favor antitrust legislation since it would inhibit competition by preserving their existence as (inefficient) competitors.[1]

Only three months after the Sherman Antitrust Act became law, on October 1, 1890, Congress enacted the McKinley Tariff Act of 1890, which it would be accurate to describe as a probusiness measure. In its original form the House passed the bill by 164 to 142 with 19 not voting, and the Senate passed a different version by 40 to 29 with 7 not voting. The final vote after the bill was reported out by the conference committee was 151 to 81 in the House with 93 not voting and 33 to 27 in the Senate with 16 not voting. This shows a drop in the number voting in both chambers, an especially large one in the House. Notice in particular the decrease in the number voting against it in the House. Obviously, there must have been many representatives and senators who voted in favor of both the Sherman Antitrust Act and the McKinley tariff. This tariff act, which brought about a sizable rise in tariff rates, comes after a well-known slogan, "Tariffs are the mother of Trusts," started during the debate on the Sherman bill, had echoed

[1] There have been many studies of the origins of the U.S. antitrust policy. Among the better known are Thorelli (1955), Letwin (1965), Bork (1978), and Stigler (1985). Canadian antitrust legislation, though actually preceding the United States by one year, was cosmetic (Reynolds 1940). The Senate document (1903), which has the major speeches, furnishes useful insights into the motives of Congress for enacting antitrust laws.

from one end of the land to the other. As an aside, it is a puzzling slogan because the only commodity manufactured by a trust subject to a high tariff was sugar. Why would the makers of refined sugar benefit from a higher tariff on their main raw material? It is tempting to regard the combination of the two acts as the result of logrolling. The conjunction of the two acts is also consistent with the findings of Galambos that the antibusiness sentiments were far from a consensus.

Surely deserving our attention are the views of the leading American economists. The professional economists of that time most highly regarded today were young when Congress was debating the Sherman act – in 1890 J. B. Clark was 43, Richard Ely was 36, Taussig was 31, E. R. A. Seligman was 29, and Irving Fisher was 23. Their comparative youth may explain their lack of influence, but it is also fair to say that although they were aware of the problems arising in the debates about trusts, monopoly, and big business, only Richard Ely viewed these with the same alarm as some of the popular writers. One prominent economist of that time, David A. Wells, may even have been sympathetic to cartels. Wells, who was 62 in 1890, was a member of a Board of Arbitrators to adjudicate the disputes among the firms in a leading railroad cartel, known as the Joint Executive Committee, consisting of the largest railroads going between Chicago and the Eastern seaboard, for which Wells received an annual fee of $10,000 at a time when annual average family income was about $500 (Ulen 1983, p. 129).

Let one of these economists, Taussig, perhaps one of the wisest, speak to us as a contemporary observer of these events. His statement, published in the 1896 edition of his classic *Tariff History of the United States,* summarizing some of his conclusions about the Tariff Act of 1894 is as follows:

No doubt the strong feeling which the surrender to the sugar monopoly aroused rested largely on a blind opposition to combinations in general, and to the corporations which are supposed, rightly or wrongly, to have a monopoly position. Whether the tendency to combination is to be welcomed or regretted, has not often been soberly considered by the American public. The usual assumption is that it is an unquestionable evil, to be fought in every way by legislation. That disposition which shows itself, both among the welcomers of socialism and among many critical economists, to accept combinations and consolidations and to use them as instruments of social reform, finds hardly an echo in the United States. Doubtless the popular instinct here is right. The drift to consolidation and monopoly presents problems with which a democratic community can deal only under great disadvantages. To regulate it, to use it, to secure from it the possible benefits, requires a degree of nicety and consistency in legislation which our American communities could reach only by slow and arduous steps. Legislation to check consolidation may be unwise, and probably is futile; but legislation to encourage it, still more legislation to augment the profits of a monopoly, is surely of the worst.

The revulsion against the extreme protective system which showed itself in the elections of 1890 and 1892 was probably in a large degree a consequence of the popular feeling just described. While the essential question as to protective duties is comparatively simple, the intricate reasoning which is needed to follow the effects of such duties into all ramifications of international and domestic trade can have but little effect on the average citizen. He reasons from few premises, and is affected by simple catch-words. The outcry against trusts and monopolies, though in fact it describes an exception rather than the normal working of protective duties, was probably the most effective in bringing about the public verdict against the McKinley Act [of 1890]. It is expressive of the general feeling of unrest as to the power of great corporations, the growth of plutocracy, the gulf between the few very rich and the masses of comparatively poor, which is becoming a stronger and stronger political force, and is destined in the future to have a larger and larger effect on legislation. (pp. 316–17, 4th ed., 1898)

Of the popular writers perhaps the most influential on these topics was Henry Demarest Lloyd. His book, *Wealth and Commonwealth* (1894), vividly summarizes the views he had previously published in newspapers and magazines. Lloyd believed that competition leads inevitably to monopoly. His hostility toward business, the profit motive, and what he regarded as monopolistic abuses give his writing the fervor of an Old Testament prophet. He was an especially harsh critic of the oil trust. Lloyd did not believe that regulation, legislation such as the antitrust laws, or a return to competition would solve the economic problems of America. In Lloyd's view big business creates a new aristocracy that would destroy democratic government. As the Founding Fathers abolished hereditary aristocracy, Lloyd sought equally wise men who would solve the problems of economic aristocracy. Lloyd's voice added to the critical volume but not to practical proposals for reform.

Another congressional act reveals much about the public perception toward economic problems. In late 1892 a severe recession was beginning. Perhaps partly because of this, in the 1892 elections the Democrats won a sizable majority in the House and Cleveland defeated Harrison for president. A reduction of tariffs was a major plank in the Democratic platform. Debate began on new tariff legislation. The result, the Tariff Act of 1894, is important for my analysis because it contains the first peace time income tax in U.S. history. During the Civil War both sides had an income tax. The one in the North was allowed to expire in 1872. As Seligman put it: "For some years a progressive income tax was one of the chief planks in the platform, not only of the Populists and of the Anti-Monopolists, but of the farmers' convention throughout the length and breadth of the land'' (1914, p. 495). The Southern and Midwestern congressmen joined forces and were strong enough to have an income tax made part of the Tariff Act of 1894. Although the tax rate was only 2 percent of the excess of individual income above $4,000, so that only a relatively few individuals would be subject to the tax and not much revenue would be raised, it is a direct attempt to affect the distribution of income and is important for this reason alone. That only a small number would have to pay the tax is shown by the figures on who paid the old Civil War income tax in its last year, 1872. That tax exempted all incomes below $2,000, and there were only 72,949 taxpayers (Seligman 1914, p. 524). Though the population in 1894 was larger than in 1872, the exemption was twice as high so it is reasonable to conclude that at most one percent of the population would be subject to the tax. It is important to note that corporations and companies would also be subject to an income tax under this law. The act passed the House by 204 to 140 with 12 not voting. The vote in the Senate was much closer, 39 to 34 with 12 not voting. Had Cleveland vetoed the bill, it seems likely his veto would have been sustained. Instead, he allowed it to become law without his signature. The Supreme Court found the income tax unconstitutional. It was nearly two decades before there was a constitutional amendment meeting the objections raised by the Supreme Court decision so that in 1913 Congress could enact the direct ancestor of the present federal income tax.[2]

Acting through the instrument of government, society sanctions the levels of individual and family income and wealth. It affects wealth directly through taxes on property. The 1894 federal income tax would only have applied to the very highest income recipients in America. Federal property taxes were levied only on estates and, therefore, on the transmission of wealth from one generation to the next. At the state and local levels of government in addition to estate and inheritance taxes there were direct taxes on the property held by the living owners. In the nineteenth century some states such as Massachusetts did also tax income. All of these taxes, on income and on wealth, partly depend on society's perception about how high income and large wealth are obtained and on how they are used and spent. The justification for such taxation does not rely only on whether in the view of society a recipient owes his present circumstances to a fair, moral, and ethical process but also on how he spends his income and uses his wealth. A society judges this implicitly. It reveals its judgment by the nature of the tax-

---

[2] It is also interesting to note that the first study of the distribution of income and wealth in the United States was published in 1896 by Spahr.

ation of income and wealth. The perception that influences this judgment also involves beliefs about what are the acceptable forms of consumption. One writer is particularly important for my argument, perhaps not so much for his direct influence on the laws as for reflecting contemporary society's perception about the mode of life of the wealthy. He is Thorstein Veblen and the book is *The Theory of the Leisure Class* (1899). It was not only a considerable financial success for its publisher, which is a measure of its popularity, but also some of its phrases, such as conspicuous consumption, are part of the English language. Recall that Veblen's book appeared and was read while Congress debated and passed the constitutional amendment that would enable the federal income tax that was enacted in 1913. Veblen's acerbic attack on the forms of consumption of the rich is an erudite reflection of perception if not a direct influence on the debate. Another widely read book, Gustavus Myers's *History of the Great American Fortunes* appeared in 1909. His recounting how Consuelo Vanderbilt's father in effect spent $5 million so that she could marry the Duke of Marlborough and become the Duchess would not enhance the popular esteem for the wealthy. It is also worth remembering the point Sherlock Holmes made about the dog that did not bark. There were few contemporary widely read defenses of the trusts, great wealth, the free-enterprise system, and so on. The famous books Upton Sinclair's *The Jungle* and Ida Tarbell's *History of the Standard Oil Company* (1904), the novels of Dreiser, and more were all on the other side of the debate.

4 State of the U.S. economy during the last third of the nineteenth century

One of the first and simplest things to do is to look at the prices of goods in order to see whether those produced and sold by the firms thought to face less competition were high and rising relative to prices of goods in the more competitive sectors of the economy. Price and output data are available for broad sectors of the economy from 1869 to the present. In addition we shall look more closely at the situation in two areas where monopoly was believed to be a serious problem – railroads and oil. I shall then discuss four important antitrust cases of the 1890s: E. C. Knight, Trans-Missouri, Joint Traffic, and Addyston Pipe. The section concludes with an analysis of the great merger wave that began around 1897 and ended in 1904.

At the outset it is necessary to see how large the U.S. economy was in the nineteenth century. Even as early as 1840, it was a relatively big economy. According to Gallman's figures (1966), as measured by the gross national product (GNP) in 1950 prices, the United States in 1840 was about as big as the United Kingdom while France was between 23 and 56 percent larger than the United States. By 1950, more than a century later, the GNP of the United Kingdom was about one fifth as large as that of the United States and that of France was about one seventh the size of the U.S. GNP. In 1840 real per capita GNP in the United States was about the same as that of the United Kingdom or perhaps a bit larger while per capita real GNP in France was between 42 and 53 percent that of the United States. In 11 decades, real GNP per capita had grown much more rapidly in the United States than in the United Kingdom or France. The decenniel growth rate of real per capita GNP in the United States was 16 percent during these 110 years, a period that included several turbulent events. An annual growth rate of real per capita GNP of nearly 1.6 percent over so long a period of time may be without precedent in world history. Moreover, and this is the important point for my argument, the decade following the end of the Civil War had one of the highest growth rates of real per capita GNP in the whole U.S. history, perhaps second only to the decade growth rates for 1934 to 1943, and 1944 to 1953.

It is also instructive to look at the growth rate of real output by sector for the period from 1869 to 1953 (see Table 2.1). Real GNP grew at an

Table 2.1. *Percentage annual growth rate for selected industries, 1869–1953*

Industry	Growth rate
Farming	1.61
Fisheries	1.39
Mining	4.01
Gonstruction	3.26
Manufacturing	4.30
Trade	3.97
Communications and public utilities	7.31
Post office	5.23
Financial services	4.91
Railroads	3.90
Telephone and telegraph (1879–1953)	7.07
Real GNP	3.88

Source: Kendrick 1961, Table A-IV.

annual rate of nearly 3.9 percent per year during this 84-year period. The most rapidly growing sectors were communications and public utilities. These two sectors had growth rates nearly double that of the economy as a whole. Farming and fisheries had the lowest growth rates. Notice that transportation and the post office had high growth rates. Think of the economy as analogous to a living organism. Then it is accurate to describe the changes in the economy as developing the nervous system relative to the rest of the organism. Against this background of the long-term trends that show a growing and increasingly prosperous U.S. economy after the end of the Civil War the main complaint of some Americans between 1870 and 1900 was the declining price level. Prices fell by about 30 percent during this time. Debtors, especially farmers, who had borrowed when the price level was higher, found themselves with an increasingly heavier burden of real debt over this period.

Wholesale prices of manufactured goods fell nearly 6 percent in the decade 1880–90 and by almost 9 percent in the next decade (see Table 2.2). The biggest price decline in 1880–90 was in petroleum refining

Table 2.2. *Percentage change in wholesale prices and real output by selected industry for 1880–90 and 1890–1900*

Industry	Wholesale prices[a]		Output (1929 prices)[b]	
	1880–90	1890–1900	1880–90	1890–1900
All manufacturing	−5.99	−8.92	73.18	51.77
Food	−7.31	−18.90	63.70	69.26
Textiles	−2.98	−17.15	54.70	54.78
Leather	−10.75	−1.69	29.32	19.77
Rubber	45.11	28.54	23.53	76.19
Forest prods	7.30	−7.59	70.21	26.45
Paper, pulp	0.00	−34.36	48.89	149.25
Printing	2.27	−21.44	169.33	59.24
Chemicals	−8.29	−17.69	69.58	70.93
Petroleum refining	−61.06	16.56	392.86	25.36
Stone, clay, glass	14.29	−18.14	86.70	55.84
Iron, steel	−21.13	9.34	130.50	35.54
Nonferrous	−2.20	−19.50	71.25	192.34
Machinery excluding transportation	−21.57	7.92	67.83	63.00
Transportation equipment	−16.28	15.34	327.45	41.74
Miscellaneous	−5.45	−9.01	101.18	26.90

[a] Creamer 1960, Table A-12.
[b] Creamer 1960, Table A-10.

products, a decrease of more than 61 percent, more than 10 times as large as the price decline for all manufacturing goods in this decade! The rise in output of refined petroleum products was equally spectacular, 393 percent, almost 6 times as large as the rise in output of the whole manufacturing sector. The iron and steel industry, also popularly regarded as noncompetitive, had a 21 percent decline of prices and a 130 percent rise of output for this decade. It was at the end of this decade in 1890 that Congress enacted the Sherman Antitrust Act. It was only after it had become the law of the land that real prices of refined petroleum products rose by 7.5 percent while output went up by 25 percent. In that same decade the real price of iron and steel products also rose slightly while the output of these products went up by more than 35 percent. In both these industries the output rose less than the growth rates of all manufacturing for the decade 1890–1900. These facts do not support the view that the actual performance of the oil, iron, and steel industries explains the discontent leading to the passage of the Sherman Antitrust Act of 1890.

The facts for railroads are similar. Between 1882 and 1890, railroad passenger revenue per mile decreased by more than 11 percent and railroad freight revenue per ton-mile fell by 25 percent. Since the time period is shorter, it is desirable to calculate the annual average price change. For rail passengers, the decrease is 1.3 percent and for freight it is 3.1 percent. These are bigger price declines than for all manufacturing. The actual performance of the railroad industry could not explain why Congress passed the Interstate Commerce Commission Act of 1887. That some contemporary observers knew the truth about railroads is shown by the statement of Senator Cullom, chairman of the Senate committee that presented the Cullom Report leading to the ICCA. On April 14, 1886, Senator Cullom spoke in the Senate as follows:

An examination of the report and testimony will not show that railroad corporations are making too much money, or that the average rates of transportation are too high. On the other hand they have been in the main unprofitable, and transportation between competing points in America is the cheapest in the world. The complaints of the people is [sic] of discrimination, uncertainty, and secret injury. (17th Cong. Record, p. 3477)

The study of the issues leading to the ICCA by Seligman (1887) is not only important for the support it gives to my arguments but also because it furnishes a contemporary analysis by one of America's leading economists.

To complete our survey of prices, consider sugar. The first major antitrust case was against the sugar trust (E. C. Knight). Between 1880 and 1890, the price of refined sugar products fell by more than 18 percent and between 1890 and 1900 by more than 28 percent. Real prices of refined sugar were lower in both decades. This is not behavior one would expect of monopoly.

The facts about relative prices do not support the rhetoric that a serious monopoly problem was present in the United States during the last third of the nineteenth century. Let us now look at railroads and oil in greater detail.

Several quantitative studies of railroad cartels are available covering the period before the ICCA of 1887: MacAvoy (1965), Ulen (1979), and Porter (1983). MacAvoy claims there was much cheating by the members of the railroad cartels, in my opinion a position consistent with the facts. However, his methods of analysis are vulnerable to several damaging criticisms as Ulen points out. Two are important. First, MacAvoy uses a measure of market share stability to indicate adherence to the cartel agreement that fails to take adequate account of the effects of random forces on freight shipments of individual railroads. The cartel itself, aware of these forces, had rules for this. Second, MacAvoy has no direct estimates of the rail rates, and his indirect estimates reflect many factors other than those of primary interest to students of the cartel. For these reasons I rely on Ulen's own findings on the cartel studied by MacAvoy and him. Porter's study gives useful independent corroboration of the accuracy of Ulen's measure of cartel loyalty.

Starting in June, 1879, railroads in the Midwest operating between the Mississippi River and the Eastern seaboard fashioned an elaborate organization that some modern economists would call a cartel. It applied to eastbound freight. It had been preceded in July, 1877, by a pool of five leading railroads for westbound freight, and it is thought that the success of this earlier arrangement inspired the attempt to form one for the eastbound freight (MacAvoy 1965, pp. 51–3). All the railroads between Chicago and St. Louis in the west and New York and Baltimore in the east became members of the new organization called the Joint Executive Committee. It had complicated rules governing its members. It set rates and assigned output quotas to its members. It had a board of arbitration to revise the allotments. The allotments and actual shipments were published in the *Railroad Review, Railway Age,* and the *Chicago Tribune.* There were six revisions of the allotments during the sample period of nearly seven years according to Ulen's study. It arranged for railroads with shipments under quota to get more business from those whose actual shipments were above their assigned quotas. It took good-faith deposits from its members that would be forfeited if a firm was found in violation of its rules. It had a committee that heard complaints from its members and made decisions to resolve them and to impose penalties for violations of its rules. It is difficult to think of anything a cartel would need that was overlooked.

A cartel is a hypothesis, not a fact. One must determine whether the behavior of the organization is consistent with the hypothesis of a cartel or with something else – a competitive industry. The leading question at the outset, therefore, is this. How often did cheating occur? In a competitive industry with given supply conditions, prices are lower when demand is low and are higher when demand is high. Is this true for the railroads? If so, it is consistent with competition and does not necessarily indicate the presence of a weak cartel beset with frequent cheating by its members. There is a more subtle question to ask about a cartel. Although, as in the present instance, the cartel had mechanisms to detect and punish violations of its rules, these required complicated and costly proceedings before an arbitration board. A cartel is more likely to begin and survive as a self-enforcing agreement among its members than as an organization relying on third-party enforcement by an arbitration board. The latter is more likely to enter the scene only for major violations. In a self-enforcing cartel each firm adheres to the rules and refrains from price cutting despite the short-run profits it can get from rule violations. Each is loyal to the cartel because this yields the largest expected present value of profits for each firm in the cartel. The self-interest of each cartel member enables the cartel to survive. Cheating by one member of the cartel evokes punishment by the other members in the form of lower prices. Therefore, the probability of adherence to the cartel is lower after price cutting has taken place and higher after there has been loyalty to the cartel rules. In fact, as we shall see, just the reverse is true for the so-called railroad cartel on eastbound freight.

Using weekly data for the period from January, 1880, to April, 1886, 328 consecutive weeks, Ulen does an elaborate econometric study of the cartel. Although price data are unavailable, each week four publications reported whether or not the railroads were cheating on the cartel agreement. Ulen sets a dummy variable equal to 1 if there is no report of cheating by any of the four sources during a given week and sets it equal to 0 if even a single source reports cheating occurred during that week. He asserts contradictions among the four sources occurred fewer than 10 times for the 328 weeks in the sample. Ulen's measure of cheating can be taken as a proxy for actual railroad freight rates. Rates are lower when cheating is reported and higher when it is not reported. Ulen's regression results confirm this interpretation. He calculates an equation that estimates what he calls the probability of adherence to the cartel by its members as a function of the total tonnage shipped, whether or not the Great Lakes are open, a measure of deviations between actual and assigned rail shipments, and a certain interaction term that requires a fuller explanation owing to my interpretation of his results.

The simplest fact to ascertain about the cartel is the frequency of cheating. According to Ulen's own figures, it varied considerably. In its first year of operation (1880) adherence was perfect. In the very next year there was adherence only one third of the time. Adherence rose again in 1882 and 1883 to over 90 percent, but then it fell to 42 percent in 1884 and on down to 23 percent in 1885. For the whole sample of 328 consecutive weeks, there was adherence to the cartel 63 percent of the time. More than one third of the weeks had cheating. This is not evidence of a strong cartel.

Here is another simple fact. Rail freight rates were lower when the Great Lakes were open to shipping than during the winter months when the lakes were closed. At first blush it would seem, therefore, that when there was more competition from lake shipping the response of the cartel was to have lower rates. However, there is another explanation for higher rail rates when the lakes were closed. Shipping is more costly in the winter months than at other times of the year. Even in a competitive industry one would expect higher freight rates as a consequence. Hence the facts about the seasonal variations of rail freight rates are also consistent with competition among railroads.

A third piece of evidence refers to the fact that the cartel that controlled the westbound shipments from the eastern seaboard apparently met with more success than the one that attempted to control the eastbound freight from the Midwest. Since more freight went from west to east, there were more empty than full freight cars to send from east to west. This means that relative to the demand, the available freight capacity was greater for the freight moving east to west. Consequently, one would expect more price-cutting pressures on the westbound than on the eastbound freight. A cartel, therefore, would have even more incentive to control the east to west movements, where the temptation to cut freight rates would be greater than for the eastbound freight. In fact, the westbound pool concentrated in New York where a single office handled all the business (Ulen 1979, p. 224). That the cartel for the east–west freight was more successful than the west–east one is consistent with the evidence that the cost conditions in railroads prevented the existence of a competitive equilibrium so that the core was empty. Chapter 5 explains the reasons in detail. A brief summary of these results must suffice here.

Since there is usually more capacity available to carry freight from east to west than in the reverse direction, some railroad would always be tempted to lower rates in order to attract business for its empty cars that must in any case travel to the west in order to pick up the usual eastbound shipments. Without an agreement among the westbound railroads, no equilibrium could exist because the core is empty. The situation is different for the west–east market where excess capacity is not the normal state. For the freight going from west to east it is not always true that a competitive equilibrium fails to exist. It is only when the demand is unusually low that the theory predicts there would not be a competitive equilibrium. At high levels of demand, a competitive equilibrium would exist for eastbound shipments and the core is then not empty. Therefore, the theory of the core would predict breakdowns of competitive equilibria for eastbound traffic when the demand is low but not when it is high. On the westbound freight from the Atlantic seaboard, the theory would predict that a departure from competition is always necessary since otherwise given the large capacity relative to the normal level of demand, no competitive equilibrium can exist. Therefore, the difference in the success of the two cartels, the eastbound versus the westbound, is confirmation of the theory of the core as applied to these railroads.

Consider the more formal aspects of the quantitative analysis of the cartel. Let $P(A)$ denote the probability of adherence to the cartel rules by its members in the current week as a function of the state of adherence, A, in the preceding week. $A = 1$ means adherence in the preceding week and $A = 0$ means cheating took place in the preceding week. The explanatory variables in Ulen's equation using his notation are given as follows:

x_6 = total tonnage of freight shipped east by the members of the cartel in the preceding week;

x_7 = an interaction term, the state of the cartel in the preceding week, 1 for adherence, 0 for cheating, multiplied by the total number of tons below allotment in that week;

x_8 = dummy variable equal to 1 if the lakes were open that week and equal to 0 otherwise;

x_9 = sum of all (absolute) deviations in tonnage during week $t - 1$ divided by the mean tonnage of flour and grain shipped east by the cartel during the past month.

The equation has the following form:

$$P(A) = 1/\{1 + \exp[-f(x)]\}, \tag{1}$$

where

$$f(x) = g_0 + \sum_{i=6}^{9} g_i x_i. \tag{2}$$

We shall need $\partial P(A)/\partial x_i$ given as follows:

$$\frac{\partial P(A)}{\partial x_i} = P(A)[1 - P(A)] \frac{\partial f}{\partial x_i}. \tag{3}$$

A variable that has a positive partial derivative has a positive effect on the probability of adherence to the cartel, while one with a negative partial has a negative effect on the probability of adherence. The estimates of the regression coefficients and related statistics are as follows:

Variable	Coefficient	t-ratio
Constant	7.534	6.111
x_6	7.030	4.104
x_7	−0.033	3.141
x_8	0.055	1.775
x_9	−14.044	4.556

The fit measured by R^2 is 0.886 and the Durbin–Watson statistic is 1.813 (Ulen 1979, Table 2, Eq. 2).

It follows from these regression coefficients that the probability of adherence to the cartel is

> Higher, the greater the total tonnage
> Lower, if there was adherence in the preceding week for given tonnage in that week
> Higher, if the Great Lakes are open
> Lower, the greater the absolute deviations from allotments

Curiously, there is no direct estimate of the effect of adherence in the previous week on the probability of adherence in the current week. Only the indirect effect via the interaction term x_7 is in the regression.

There is a difficulty at the outset. A cartel in which cheating is frequent enough is a contradiction in terms. Anyone who remains in such a cartel is made worse off as a victim of cheating than he would be without a cartel under a noncooperative equilibrium. Even if cheating is not so frequent so that the expected return to the victims is above their return in a noncooperative equilibrium, it is always more profitable to cheat than to be cheated (see Chapter 6, Section 5). But then who is willing to be the victim? Putting aside these objections, damaging though they are to the very hypothesis that this railroad organization could be fairly described as constituting a cartel, let us suppose there was a cartel. If a cartel is plagued by cheating, then the probability of adherence to the cartel is higher if there was adherence in the preceding week and it is lower if there was cheating in the previous week. This is because the members of the cartel are inclined to punish cheating in the preceding week by their own temporary departure from the cartel agreement. It is implicit in this argument that a viable cartel is self-enforcing so that the usual form of punishment for cheating by one or more members is price cutting by most of them. The cartel is most likely to remain in force when there has been adherence to the cartel rules in the preceding week. The question, therefore, is whether the estimates of the coefficients given above are consistent with this model of a cartel. As we shall see, they are not consistent.

Since the coefficient of x_7 is negative, the probability of adherence to the cartel is lower if there was adherence in the previous week and it is higher if there was cheating in the previous week. This is the opposite of what we would expect of a cartel. Ulen regards the negative coefficient as consistent with the hypothesis that there was a cartel. I regard it as inconsistent with that hypothesis. Surely one would not expect a cartel to reward disloyalty in one week with loyalty in the next. On the contrary, loyalty should follow loyalty and disloyalty should follow disloyalty. These empirical results are consistent with another view. The railroads were grappling with the forces of competition under new technological conditions that they did not yet fully understand nor to which they were able to adapt.

The sign of another regression coefficient is consistent with the hypothesis of competition, the positive coefficient of x_6, the tonnage variable. It implies rates are lower when tonnage is higher, which is consistent with competition if the demand curve is relatively more stable than the supply curve.

Unfortunately, comparable data to study the period after 1887 when the Interstate Commerce Commission Act became law are unavailable. This prevents a comparison of the behavior of the cartel before and after the ICCA. That the act did little or nothing to aid the railroads' attempts to solve the new kinds of economic problems posed by the technological conditions in the industry is shown by two considerations; first, the actual language of the act and, second, the effects of the Sherman Antitrust Act.

Six major provisions of the act are pertinent. The act prohibits unreasonable or extortionate charges, but it does not give the commission power to establish maximum rates. Indeed, it gives the commission no power to set rates. Second, a railroad may not produce the commodities it carries. This meant there could be no merger between a railroad and the shippers of goods. Third, there could be no personal discrimination. The railroads could not strike private bargains with individual shippers. Fourth, there could be no unreasonable discrimination between local and through traffic. This referred to the frequent complaint that rates were lower on long-haul than on short-haul shipments. Fifth, there could be no pooling of freights or their aggregates or net earnings. This provision outlawed the most successful form of cooperation that the railroads were able to work out by themselves. It can hardly be taken as evidence that Congress sought to encourage railroad cartels. On the contrary, this provision would supply railroads with incentive for merger. Sixth, rates must be posted and may not be changed without sufficient prior notice. This is the provision cited by those who argue that the commission would aid the enforcement of cartels because it made secret price cutting unlawful.

There are two significant omissions from the act. Congress did not mention oil shipments by pipeline nor any water traffic. Since pipelines and shipment by water are both competitors for railroads, these omissions are stumbling blocks for those who argue that the Interstate Commerce Commission was intended to promote and strengthen railroad cartels.

The commission had been in existence for only about three years when the Sherman act became law. A question arose about the relations between the two laws. The commission did nothing affecting cooperation among the railroads notwithstanding the antipooling provision of the ICCA. It seemed to await actions by the Justice Department and the federal courts. Two major antitrust cases directly raising the issue of cooperation among competing railroads eventually reached the Supreme Court, Trans-Missouri and Joint Traffic. In both cases the Court found in favor of the government. It asserted that the Sherman act did apply to railroads and that the ICCA did not exempt them from the Sherman act. Congress saw otherwise and moved to remedy this. In 1903 it passed the Elkin Act, which legalized pooling and gave the Interstate Commerce Commission the power to set railroad rates. Starting with this act the government in the form of the commission was to become an increasingly potent regulator of the railroads.

In the meantime many railroads took the merger route to cooperation as a substitute for pooling. Railroad merger was an explicit issue in the Northern Securities case decided by the Supreme Court in 1904. The government won the case, and the merger in the form of a holding company was struck down. The railroads could not be sure of solving their problems by merging.

It would be hard to decide which was the more common object of criticism and attack by the antimonopolists – the oil trust or the railroads. To the educated public of that time Henry Demarest Lloyd (1894) and later Ida Tarbell (1904) were the best known critics. The critic I propose to rescue from obscurity is a professor of economics, C. J. Bullock, who wrote in his survey of the antitrust problem in the *Quarterly Journal of Economics* (1901) as follows:

Partisans of the trusts follow generally one of two methods when presenting statistics of prices. Sometimes they naively quote merely the prices of refined oil from 1872 to the present, and claim for the trust the credit of the reduction. . . . In other cases, they exhibit tables showing the margin between the prices of crude and refined oil from 1871 down to the time of writing, and claim for the trust the credit of the decline. Here they carefully avoid comparing the margin before the formation of the trust in 1882 with the margin since that date. . . . Comment upon any of these performances is needless. (1901, p. 185)

In the text for which the preceding appears as a footnote, Bullock (1901) asserts:

Therefore, we are not surprised to learn that the most reliable investigation into prices shows that, in almost every case combinations have managed to increase the margin between the cost of materials and the price of the finished product for considerable periods of time.

In fact, an empirical investigation of the relation between the refined and the crude price of oil better supports those who are the subject of Bullock's scorn than his own position as we shall see.

Bullock's suggestion that there may be a difference in the price pattern before and after the establishment of the oil trust is a good one. There were several attempts to organize the oil industry before the formation of the oil trust in January, 1882. Some of these are as follows:

May 6, 1871	South Improvement Company starts
Dec. 19, 1872	Agreement between Petroleum Producers' Association and Petroleum Refiners' Association of which John D. Rockefeller was president
Jan. 29, 1880	Standard Oil Co. and Petroleum Producers' Union agreement
Jan. 2, 1882	Formation of the oil trust[3]
July 1, 1892	de jure dissolution of the oil trust but not its de facto existence

[3] The text of the oil trust is given by Tarbell (1904, vol. 2, pp. 364–73). Its official name was the Standard Trust, but it is more popularly known as the oil trust. One must bear in mind that this trust is an actual legal entity and not some sub rosa conspiracy. I would regard it as a predecessor to a holding company.

There was a fairly well-organized market for crude oil in Oil City, Pennsylvania, the heart of the producing area at that time, and an active market in refined oil at New York City. *Derrick's Handbook of Petroleum* (1898) furnishes a reliable source of monthly prices covering the period from 1874 to 1895. It gives the monthly high, low, and average crude oil price together with the monthly average refined oil price. In view of the history of the several attempts to organize the oil industry starting in 1871, it is reasonable to begin by studying the behavior of monthly prices for the longest period for which this is possible – January, 1874, to December, 1895. The following regression relates the monthly average refined price in dollars per gallon (there are 42 gallons per barrel) to the monthly average crude price in dollars per barrel and two trend terms, denoted by T and T^2:

1. RefAvgPrice = 0.067082 + 0.047308 CruAvgPrice
    (t-ratios)   18.567   34.404

$$-\ 0.0027042T\ +\ 0.00000034727T^2$$
$$15.491\qquad\qquad 5.743$$

$R^2 = 0.91525$; S.E. $= 6.65578$ E-004;

$$n\ =\ 264;\ \text{F-stat}\ =\ 935.98$$

According to this regression, the refined price fell relative to the crude price but at a decreasing rate. Therefore, over the whole 22-year period there was a downward trend of the margin between the refined and the crude price. Now we wish to see if the relation between the refined and crude oil price is different before than after the formation of the oil trust. Let D denote a dummy variable equal to 1 from January, 1874, to December, 1881, the pretrust era, and equal to 0 from January, 1882, to December, 1895, the trust era. The regression estimating the effect of the oil trust on the monthly average refined price is as follows:

2. RefAvgPrice = 0.030956 + 0.030464 CruAvgPrice
    (t-ratios)   11.273   34.724

$+\ \ 0.041215D\ +\ \ 0.00033187T\ -\ \ 0.0000013135\text{-}T^2$
    30.988   37.752   31.857

$+\ D\times(0.021621\ \text{CruAvgPrice}\ -\ \ \ 0.0011746T$
          27.505   121.11

$+\ \ 0.0000064680T^2)$
    80.730

$R^2 = 0.94076$; S.E. $= 5.60802$E-004; F-stat $= 580.77$

Regression 2 fits the data better than regression 1 judging by the R^2. The coefficients involving the dummy variable D that represent the pretrust era give a collective partial r^2 of 0.30. Note that in regression 2 all of the coefficients interacting with the dummy variable have high statistical significance as meaured by the t-ratios. Since the regression includes the average crude price as an independent explanatory variable, the coefficients of the various trend terms show how the refined price behaves relative to the crude price over time, assuming the oil trust did not affect the crude price itself. According to regression 2, before the oil trust, dummy $= 1$, given the pattern of crude prices, the refined price reached a minimum in October, 1880. That is, from January, 1874, to October, 1880, the refined price fell relative to the crude price. It rose relative to the crude price from October, 1880, until December, 1881, the last month before the oil trust began. The regression does show an upward jump in the refined price relative to the crude price in January, 1882, when the oil trust officially started. During the period of existence of the oil trust, the refined price attains its maximum relative to the crude price between June and July of 1884. After July, 1884, until the end of the sample period, more than a decade later, the refined price fell relative to the crude price and so continues falling until December, 1895. Consequently, contrary to Professor Bullock, the margin of the refined to crude price did not remain higher after the formation of the oil trust.

There is another revealing way of looking at the regression results. By setting the dummy equal to 1 in each month, we can compute what the refined oil price would have been had there been no trust. Similarly, by setting the value of the dummy variable equal to 0 in every month, we can calculate what the refined price would have been had the oil trust existed throughout the period. In this fashion we can compute the incremental effect on the refined price in the hypothetical absence and presence of the oil trust, assuming the actual pattern of the crude price is the same in both cases. The numerical results for selected dates are shown in Table 2.3.

Figure 2.1 shows the estimated monthly average refined prices predicted on the basis of the trend coefficients of regression 2. This graph underlies the figures shown in the second column of Table 2.3. The hypothesis maintained in Table 2.3 is that the historical pattern of the crude oil prices is the same whether or not there is an oil trust. The defense for this hypothesis is that the oil trust did not then engage in crude production to any significant extent, and producers of crude could and did sell their product in a competitive international market, especially to European importers. Critics of the oil trust, aware of the

Table 2.3. *Incremental effect on the refined oil price in cents per gallon predicted by the trend coefficients of regression (2), given the actual pattern of crude oil prices*

Date	Trust from Jan, 1882	No trust $D = 1$	Trust $D = 0$	Comment
Jan. 1874	7.133	7.133	3.129	
Nov. 1877	4.376	4.376	4.376	Common price
Oct. 1880	3.773	3.773	4.931	Minimum before trust
Dec. 1881	3.877	3.877	5.071	End of pretrust era
Jan. 1882	5.079	3.892	5.079	Trust begins
July 1884	5.192	4.797	5.192	Maximum after trust begins
Dec. 1885	5.184	5.184	5.184	Common price
July 1890	4.479	10.980	4.479	Sherman act
Dec. 1895	2.702	20.894	2.702	Sample end

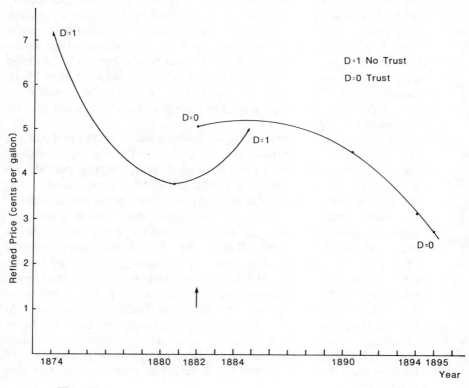

Figure 2.1

declining crude price, denied that the decline of the refined price was the result of any actions taken by the trust and instead attributed it to the effect of the crude price on the refined price. We are, therefore, justified in focusing our attention on what the refined price would have been with and without the trust given the actual time series of crude oil prices. The second column in Table 2.3 shows the predicted incremental effect on the monthly average refined price using the trend coefficients and assuming the oil trust began on January, 1882, as it did. Hence the figures in this column are the same as those in the third column from January, 1874, to December, 1881. From January, 1882, until December, 1895, the figures in the second column are the same as those in the fourth column. In the third column the figures from January, 1882, until the sample ends show what the refined price would have been in the absence of the oil trust, assuming the crude prices were the same as they actually were (but see below). The figures in the fourth column show what the refined prices would have been in the period before the oil trust between January, 1874, and December, 1881. Had there been no trust, these calculations show that the margin would have been higher starting in December, 1885, while in the period preceding the actual formation of the trust, the refined price would have been higher from January, 1874, until November, 1877. Had the trust begun in January, 1874, the refined prices would have been lower than they were! Had there not been a trust, refined prices would have been higher than they were from December, 1885, until the sample end in December, 1895!

These calculations are actually upward-biased estimates of the effect of the oil trust on the refined price because, as the regression shows, the coefficient of the crude price is smaller during the trust period than during the pretrust period. The coefficient of the average crude price shows how much the average refined price changes per unit change in the average crude price. This effect is bigger before than after the trust began. Stated differently, the regression shows that a change in the crude price had a smaller effect on the refined price after January, 1882, than it had before. Consequently, assuming the oil trust had no effect on the crude price, it follows from these results that the refined price predicted by the regression is lower following the formation of the oil trust than is shown by the figures in Table 2.3 for the column $D = 0$. (See Figure 2.1.) Hence the above results are biased in favor of the critics of the oil trust and even so do not show that the trust raised the refined price relative to the crude price or put an upward trend in the refined price relative to the crude price after it came into existence.

These empirical results are not the implications of a hypothesis of monopoly pricing by the oil trust. One important point must not be overlooked: the yield of refined oil per barrel of crude. The margin between the refined and the crude price depends on this yield. The higher the yield, the lower the response of the refined price to a unit change in the crude price. Obviously, the size of the margin itself depends on the cost of refining crude oil. This depends not only on the state of technology but also on the characteristics of the crude oil. That the yield varied over time is plain from statistics showing total production of refined oil and crude oil. Between 1873 and 1875 the yield reached a maximum that it nearly attained again in the period from 1883 to 1885. Thereafter, the refined yield is lower and fluctuating. Thus the margin between the refined and the crude price depends on the cost of refining crude oil and not merely on the monopoly power of the trust.

Since the trust did sell 90 percent of U.S. refined oil, the usual monopoly theory asserts it had the power to raise the refined oil price to a monopoly level. I propose to turn the argument around. The oil trust did not charge high prices because it had 90 percent of the market. It got 90 percent of the refined oil market by charging low prices. This is the way of competition, and it was hard on the rivals of the Standard Oil Company (cf. McGee 1958).

Among the first cases brought by the government under the Sherman act included that against the sugar trust (the E. C. Knight case in 1895), two against railroad associations (the Trans-Missouri case in 1892 and the Joint Traffic case in 1896), and a fourth against a cartel of some producers of cast-iron pipe (the Addyston case in 1897). The issue relevant for my analysis that might have arisen in the Knight case concerns the structure of corporations.[4]

Corporations were evolving during the nineteenth century as it became necessary to devise new ways of organizing business enterprises to enable them to obtain large amounts of capital from investors who sought to limit both their risk and their involvement in these enterprises. Because great potential for abuse and fraud was present, judging from the lessons of past experience with corporations, legislation to allow changes in their structure was enacted at long intervals. General laws permitting a company to become a corporation by satisfying prescribed conditions date from the 1840s in the United States. Corporations were made subject to many restrictions in order to protect both investors and the public (Haney 1914).

---

[4] Letwin (1965) and Bork (1978) contain excellent discussions of these and other major antitrust cases.

One law in particular prohibited a corporation from owning stock in another corporation without the explicit permission in the form of special legislation enacted by the legislature of the state in which it was incorporated. This made it very difficult for corporations to form co-operative ventures unless they actually merged into a single corporation. Under the existing laws and depending on the states in which a company was incorporated and wished to carry on business, such mergers might have created difficulties owing to the legal restrictions imposed by the various states. Economic reasons as well made a merger a less attractive alternative than a cartel. As separate firms in a cartel each individual company would have more incentive to maximize its own profits than it would have as a part of a joint venture. The consolidated company determines a distribution of the total profit when it decides on the proportion of the total shares of stock that goes to each of the companies that combine in the merger. This creates a free-rider problem because each dollar of profit generated by one company is shared among them all in proportion to the stock that each owns. If the profit were a certain and unambiguous residual, then, in principle, it would be possible to solve the free-rider problems, but these qualifications merely beg the question. It might be possible to solve these problems by issuing distinct classes of stock for each component company of the merger, but this solution would require special legislation. There is also the question of how much autonomy an individual company may have. A loose alliance gives each more independence than a merger, where one person or a committee has the power to make decisions. With separate and distinct companies the alliance has more entrepreneurial talent than it would have in the single company formed by merger.

The existing legal restrictions on the corporate structure were among the chief reasons for the device of a trust. Mr. Dodd, the general counsel of the Standard Oil Company of Ohio, invented the trust in 1879 as a possible solution that seemed to conform to the prevailing laws. The trust was a well-known device used to manage estates on behalf of the heirs. It would therefore seem possible to use it to form a legal alliance among corporations that did not wish to consolidate into a single corporation and yet wanted to cooperate in some areas of mutual interest. However, as trusts came under increasing attack in many states an alternative became necessary. The state of New Jersey supplied one alternative when in 1888 it passed a law that allowed firms incorporated in New Jersey to own stock and other assets in separate corporations, a type of corporate structure called a *holding company*. This act, amended in the following year, became known as the New

Jersey Holding Company Act and several trusts took advantage of it. These included the cottonseed oil trust, which became the American Cotton Oil Company, incorporated in New Jersey, the lead trust, which became the National Lead and Oil Company of New Jersey, and in 1891, the sugar trust, which became the American Sugar Refining Company.

A corporation in the form of a holding company can more easily solve a free-rider problem among its subsidiaries than one in the form of a merger of the same constituent companies where the constituents lose their separate existence. The holding company owns a controlling interest in each of its subsidiaries, and they may still have outstanding publicly traded stock. Those who own stock in the subsidiary may also own stock in the holding company. A given company as part of a merger may be discouraged from some undertaking because other companies in the merger may reap where it has sown so that it cannot obtain the full benefit of its efforts. As a subsidiary of a holding company this need not be true. With the choice of an appropriate structure, the holding company can instill enough incentive and have enough entrepreneurial input among its subsidiaries as will secure an optimal combination of cooperation and competition.

The Supreme Court decided the E. C. Knight case in 1895. The main point in its decision relevant for my analysis is that the American Sugar Refining Company, the defendant in the case, was a holding company incorporated under the New Jersey act. The issue of whether this state act was in violation of the federal Sherman act did not arise in the case and so the Court had to remain silent on it. Implicit in the silence was a new avenue for forming alliances among firms. Until the consistency between the New Jersey act and the Sherman act became an explicit issue introduced in a case by a federal prosecutor, a lawful way now existed for companies to make more or less loose alliances by forming a holding company, which they were unable to do by forming a trust. The issue of the legality of a corporation as a holding company is distinct from the question of which actions are lawful for the holding company or its constituent companies. (The same is true for a partnership or any other joint venture.) The Sherman act declared that separate companies may not collude by setting prices jointly. But if separate companies were to merge into a single concern, a holding company, then that concern could do what the Sherman act prevented the original companies from doing as separate and independent entities. It would appear that merger in the form of a holding company could accomplish what was forbidden by the Sherman act.

The issues that arose in the two railroad cases and in the Addyston

Pipe case directly concern competition. The courts had to wrestle with
the question of whether unrestricted competition was always necessarily good and whether all forms of collusion were necessarily bad
under the Sherman Antitrust Act. The railroads argued that circumstances peculiar to their industry meant competition was not always
good and made some restraints on competition not always bad. The
decisions of the Supreme Court in these railroad cases rejected these
arguments although they were accepted by the lower courts. Among
other reasons the Supreme Court asserted its reluctance to become a
forum for deciding whether the prices that result from collusion among
the railroads are reasonable or not. A similar issue arose in the Addyston case. Many buyers of cast-iron pipe testified that they believed
they had paid reasonable prices, though it was clear from the description of the facts presented by the government that the prices paid were
not the outcome of a competitive process. These facts are of unusual
interest and it is instructive to examine them.

In the Addyston case the product was high-pressure cast-iron pipe
for water purchased by state and local governmental bodies in sealed
bid auctions, who announced their needs and solicited bids from the
manufacturers. The winner of the contract was the firm who submitted
the lowest bid. The cartel had six member firms including Addyston
Pipe. On an occasion when the cartel decided to submit a sealed bid,
a chairman called a meeting of the six firms and announced the price
that would be submitted. This price had to take into account competition from cast-iron pipe producers who were not members of the
Addyston cartel. Prior to the official sealed bid auction, the six firms
meeting together held an unofficial auction like an English auction. The
firm with the lowest bid won the right to submit the sealed bid as set
by the chairman to the subsequent official sealed bid auction. The other
five firms could submit higher sealed bids that would not, of course,
be successful. If the cartel member's sealed bid did win the contract,
then it would pay an amount into a fund equal to the difference between
its winning bid in the private meeting of the six firms and the price
chosen by the chairman. At periodic intervals the funds accumulated
in this way were divided among the six firms according to a formula
based on their capacities. It follows that in the private meeting of the
six firms where they were openly bidding for business each firm would
know how much of the difference between the chairman's price and
its bid price it could expect to receive should it win the governmental
contract in the later official sealed bid auction.

These are the essential facts in the Addyston case. It would seem
at first blush that the cartel must have raised the price of cast-iron pipe

above the competitive level. Thus, if the six firms had not met privately before the sealed bid auction, each would have submitted their sealed bids independently to the municipality. The firm that had made the lowest bid in the private meeting of the cartel would presumably have been willing to submit the same bid sealed to the municipality. Does it not then follow that the effect of the cartel must have been to raise the price? The answer is no. In the private meeting the firms were holding an auction that actually determined a two-part price: One part was their bid for the contract, and the other part was in the form of the rebate they would receive from the accumulated funds. The proceeds of the latter would defray overhead costs. Had there been no cartel, the firms would not have submitted the same bids as they did in the private meeting. They would have submitted higher bids in order to cover their fixed costs. Indeed, the bids in the private auction reflect the marginal costs of the orders to the firms, whereas the difference between the chairman's price and these bids reflects overhead costs. A firm might submit a bid in the prior auction that was below its marginal cost owing to the fact that it would receive back a portion of the difference between its bid price and the cartel price as its share of the proceeds from the pool. It was even possible for one firm to be the lowest bidder in the prior unofficial private auction though its marginal cost was above that of the other firms, provided its share of the pool was high enough. It is safe to conclude that the procedure used by the six firms in the cartel to determine which one would be its bidder in the subsequent official auction was more conducive to an efficient outcome than was the official sealed bid auction, given the nature of the cost conditions for making cast-iron pipe. These cost conditions lead to an empty core. Without some form of cooperation among the firms, there would have been no equilibrium, and prices would have been driven to ruinously low levels.[5]

The problems in these cases arose from the nature of the underlying economic forces. The courts had to grapple with these problems on the basis of the statutes and the precedents. The courts and the country were learning the characteristics of a modern economy – a slow and difficult process.

It is now useful to discuss these underlying economic issues. Competition is a means to an end, not an end in itself. In my view a proper end is an efficient equilibrium. In such an equilibrium changes are not possible that would make someone better off without making at least one other person worse off. Were this not true it would show that the

[5] For a detailed analysis of the Addyston case, see Bittlingmayer (1981 and 1982).

original situation was inefficient. Therefore, the problem is to learn when competition can give an efficient equilibrium. A central thesis of my argument is that competition does not always result in an equilibrium. It can lead to chaos. The railroads claimed this but the Court rejected their argument. Most of the contemporary economists sided with the Court and against the railroads. Admittedly, the arguments of the railroads are self-serving, and we are rightly skeptical of them. But to conclude that self-serving arguments are necessarily wrong is an error. To assess the validity of an argument requires examination of its merits and not the credentials of those who advance it. There are rigorous models that furnish a reasonably good approximation to the cost conditions for industries like railroads and cast-iron pipe such that a competitive equilibrium does not exist. I describe them in later chapters. When conditions prevent the existence of a competitive equilibrium, people will modify the conditions so that not only can a stable equilibrium emerge but it will also be an efficient one. Their self-interest leads to these changes. When the Court uses language such as the rule of reason or ancillary constraints (as in the Addyston case referring to constraints that reduce competition but not as their primary purpose, whatever that may mean), the Court implicitly recognizes the complicated nature of the possible conflict between competition as an end in itself and efficiency in a modern economy.

Decisions of the Supreme Court reflect a learning process as well as interpretations of statutes and previous cases. Outright reversals of previous decisions though rare do happen. It is illuminating to interpret decisions as the result of then current understanding about the desirability of various forms of competition. For instance, the 1904 decision in the Northern Securities case did contain explicitly the issue of using a holding company for a merger of railroads. In this case the Court found in favor of the government. In the earlier Knight case the same economic issue was actually present, but it was not explicitly raised in the case so the Court could say nothing about it. Since the Court found in favor of the government and against the railroads in Northern Securities, it cast a chill on the merger movement that had been underway for the preceding 7 years, a movement on a scale without precedent then or since.

There is, of course, the valid argument that monopoly can and does result in an inefficient equilibrium under some conditions. This happens when competition would give an efficient equilibrium. When unrestricted competition can result in a stable equilibrium, it is also one that is efficient. A departure from competition in the form of monopoly then gives a stable but inefficient equilibrium. This is the classic argument against monopoly. It raises two questions. First, under what conditions can there be a stable competitive equilibrium? Second, given such conditions, what explains the presence of monopoly? The analysis given in the following chapters derives necessary conditions in terms of the properties of the cost functions for the existence of a competitive equilibrium.

After the decision by the Court of Appeals in February, 1898, in favor of the government in the Addyston case, which was upheld by the Supreme Court in November, 1899, a new firm was formed by merger of the six defendants in the case together with five other cast-iron pipe producers who were not defendants in that case. Soon after, with the addition of another nondefendant firm, the result of all these mergers was the U.S. Cast Iron Pipe and Foundry Company, which had 68 percent of total U.S. melting capacity by 1900, which was 30 percentage points more than the capacity of the six original defendants in 1900 (Bittlingmayer 1981, Table 3.5). As a result of this merger of 12 firms, the new company could do what the 12 separate firms could not do, make joint decisions on prices.

A very large number of mergers then took place between 1897 and 1904 especially in the iron and steel industry. The timing and the content of the Supreme Court decisions in E. C. Knight, Addyston, and Northern Security furnish strong circumstantial evidence that these decisions were the motive for many of the mergers. Mergers swept through the railroad industry as well as many others. Chandler (1977, p. 172) points out that between July, 1899, and December, 1900, 25,000 miles of track, one-eighth of the total U.S. mileage, was brought in one way or another under the control of other lines. Chandler attributes the merger wave to these Supreme Court decisions. Bittlingmayer's evidence (1985) supporting this hypothesis is much more convincing than Nelson's earlier skeptical remarks on this explanation of the merger wave (1959, p. 135). Hence the Sherman act and the decisions in the cases I discussed led to many mergers. It is not possible to explain them all as the result of the Court's rulings. Some mergers have intrinsic reasons independent of the state of the law. These are especially important for firms that obtain new knowledge from their research. Therefore, they become attractive acquisitions for other firms that wish to embark on the new ventures opened up by this new knowledge. We shall consider this important motive for merger in more detail in Chapter 8 on rivalry via research and development.

CHAPTER 3

Competition, cooperation, and efficiency

1   Introduction

In a contest to name the words most often used by economists, *supply, demand, market,* and *competition* would be among the leading contenders. These words represent complex and subtle concepts. I choose them intentionally because they are all intertwined. The relations among them would interest few outside the circle of professional economists were it not that beginning in 1890 with the passage of the Sherman act, the policy of the United States seems to have embarked on a course never before seen among nations. This course was to preserve competition. It developed in a series of additional laws, prosecutions, court decisions, opinions of the attorney general, orders of the Federal Trade Commission, and so on. It has become a potent source of regulation over every part of the economy with many practical consequences. Yet the protection and promotion of competition is not always the motive or the effect of all this activity. Things are not what they seem on the surface. It may be that the results of antitrust policy are explained better by the forces affecting Congress than by economic analysis confined to facts and theoretical reasoning. An example may help clarify my point. Hardly any economist favors tariffs or import quotas. Yet the United States has many of these. Similarly, it is the exception not the rule when Congress makes antitrust legislation on the basis of high principles of welfare economics. The influence of constituents is more important. The congressional debaters may often appeal to these high principles of welfare economics, but such appeals are more often the cloak under which hides naked economic self-interest.

Nevertheless, I shall present my analysis of the relations among cooperation, competition, and efficiency using the tools of economics. Even so the analysis may help explain the direction of antitrust policies. As we shall see, competition may require some cooperation in order to obtain efficiency. Some of my analysis stems from theories of very distinguished economists including Edgeworth (1881), Böhm-Bawerk

(1889), Alfred Marshall (1890), F. H. Knight (1921), and J. M. Clark (1923). I take the argument farther than they did partly because since their time the economy has moved clearly in directions that support the relevance of my theoretical analysis. These ideas are not fads or idiosyncrasies. They come from the mainstream of economic theory and help us understand the modern economy.

It is important to recall some basic facts about economic history. Until the coming of the railroad in the 1820s, all large-scale enterprise was the creation of government. Yet it was only in time of war that governments created large organizations. Large private enterprises are a recent phenomenon. This is not to say that Adam Smith described a simple economy in 1776. Raw materials came from the four corners of the earth to his island. After many stages of processing, manufacturing, and distribution, the goods came to the hands of the final consumers. Think of tea and coffee as examples. No private large-scale enterprises were under the control of a single management. Railroads marked the beginning of a new era. Building and running a railroad created new problems an order of magnitude more difficult than any ever seen before. Other industries, some old and some new, also posed new problems of coordination and competition like those of the railroads. By the late nineteenth century there were private companies larger than some of the smallest nations in Europe and Latin America. Some private firms borrowed larger sums than did some of these governments. The legal forms of business enterprise changed in response to the new technology. The corporation with its limited liability became the leading form of private business enterprise. The past century and a half saw these new events. These changes in the economy create puzzles to challenge economic science. Among the puzzles is the nature of competition in a modern economy.

2 Competition in pure exchange

Competition refers to the nature of the conditions under which individuals may trade property rights. It assumes a definition of these rights and describes a trading process consistent with competition. A private property right is one that an individual can trade at his own discretion without the necessity of obtaining the consent of anyone else. The nature of private property rights is far from simple. It depends on a body of law, and it changes as the laws and court decisions change. When Edgeworth and Marshall presented their theory of exchange using nuts and apples as the objects of trade, they took a very simple example. Brand name apples and California walnuts are less simple.

Still less simple are the property rights conferred on inventors and originators of other kinds of intellectual goods. A private property right is analogous to a fence around a piece of land. It intends to prevent encroachment and trespassing by others and to allow the owner to use the land in lawful ways. The definition of property rights circumscribes the extent of limitation. Again using the analogy of land, it determines how closely one neighbor can approach another without that neighbor's consent. Let a group of neighbors build a swimming pool. How and when can they prevent others from using their pool? Property rights define the extent of possible free-rider problems. A free rider is someone who gets a benefit from something without bearing the burden of its cost. Free riding is costly to prevent. Individuals themselves try to do this, and sometimes they can enlist the services of the state for this purpose. Patents and copyrights are examples of the latter. Keeping new knowledge secret illustrates the former. There are many other ways to reduce the amount of free riding. Under some conditions resale price maintenance is one of these (Telser 1960).

A competitive equilibrium is the outcome of a competitive process. Its very existence may depend on the nature of the property rights. Since a property right is one that can exclude and restrict, it can be mistaken for a monopolistic restriction. Theoretical analyses of market exchange sometimes overlook how much the results depend on the nature of the definition and assignment of property rights. Some of the pertinent issues emerge most clearly in the simplest situation – pure exchange.

In this situation traders have initial endowments of commodities. Each individual derives utility only from his own bundle of commodities. The utility does not depend on the holdings of other individuals. Each person treats his holdings as private property that he can trade without requiring the consent of anyone else. He can make and accept bids and offers on his own. He can reject the bids and offers of others on his own initiative. The theory assumes that each individual seeks to advance his own interest as well as he can. It follows that he will not leave the market with a bundle of goods that he regards as inferior to his initial holdings. Edgeworth's analysis of this situation, published in 1881, hardly needs improvement. He invented the ingenious theoretical device of recontracting so that he could study the essential aspects of competition while sidestepping some extraneous problems arising from the nature of the actual dynamic path leading to the final outcome. Consider a subset of traders who make a tentative agreement among themselves on a set of trades. It is a potential contract among them. Each of the traders in this subset is at liberty to seek other traders who may be willing to offer better terms. The final outcome of all this bargaining must be acceptable to each trader and each coalition of traders. Hence it is not susceptible to improvement by any subset of traders. As a result, the acceptable final allocations of goods belong to what we now call the Edgeworth contract surface. These are efficient allocations. Efficiency means there are no unexploited opportunities for improvement. Put differently, it is not possible to make anyone better off by changing his final allocation without making at least one other person worse off. The outcome of the trading process is a reassignment of the initial allocations of the goods among the traders so that the final allocations place them in the hands of those who value most what they get. The modern terminology calls the set of final assignments of goods acceptable to all traders and subsets of traders the core of the market. In view of the nature of the process leading to allocations in the core, I believe it represents the set of competitive equilibria. I am confident that Edgeworth would share this view.

Several important conclusions follow from this analysis. First, the competitive process gives an efficient equilibrium. The process is valuable because of this result and not for its own sake. Although the precise details of how to organize a competitive market is an important topic for economic analysis deserving much attention, it would not command the interest of economists were it not that a competitive market can attain an efficient equilibrium. Second, the theoretical representation of competition in the theory of the core seems to capture the main features of competition. Therefore, it deserves serious attention as a tool of analysis. Third, when the theory of the core is applied to the problems posed by classical economics, it gives the same answers as the classical analysis. It thereby passes the first test of a new theory that intends to operate in a new terrain where the old tools will fail. I do not wish to give the impression that nothing really new emerges from an application of the theory of the core to market exchange. A central question is whether an equilibrium exists and under what conditions. The most powerful approach for answering these questions uses the core theory.

Despite the importance of Edgeworth's work and its wide acceptance, the new territory of economics he discovered attracted few explorers. Nor did a warmer reception greet the related work of Böhm-Bawerk, an Austrian contemporary of Edgeworth. For more than 70 years this topic seems to have been regarded as closed and to be one in which there was little more to be done. Revival of interest was to spring from the theory of a market as presented by Böhm-Bawerk. His treatise on capital theory gives a detailed account of market exchange.

In this market each trader either wishes to buy or to sell one unit of a commodity. The seller has a minimal acceptable price and the buyer a maximal acceptable price. The market supply schedule ranks the sellers from the most to the least eager so that the seller with the lowest minimal acceptable price is the most eager and so on up to the one with the highest acceptable price who is the least eager. Similarly, there is a ranking of the buyers from the most eager, the one who is willing to pay the highest price, down to the one with the lowest maximal acceptable price. The upwardly sloping supply curve reflects the ranking of sellers according to their eagerness to sell as measured by their minimally acceptable prices; the downwardly sloping demand curve likewise reflects the ranking of the buyers from the most to the least eager as measured by their maximally acceptable prices. There is a market clearing price such that each actual buyer pays and each actual seller gets this price per unit. The result is a transfer of the goods from some of the initial owners, the sellers, to some of the initial nonowners, the buyers, such that the final owners all value the goods more than those of the initial owners who sold it. Like Edgeworth's analysis, Böhm-Bawerk's shows that the competitive process results in a final allocation of the goods that is efficient.

Almost 50 years were to pass before this analysis came to life again in a chapter of Neumann and Morgenstern's *Theory of Games* (1944). Morgenstern, the Austrian economist, was the link between his predecessor, Böhm-Bawerk, and his collaborator, the mathematician Neumann. Martin Shubik (1959), 15 years later, made the connection between the theory of the core and Edgeworth's theory of market exchange.

For the sake of simplifying the exposition, my examples follow Böhm-Bawerk instead of Edgeworth. This enables the use of simple algebra and arithmetic instead of calculus. One feature of Böhm-Bawerk's approach relates closely to Marshall's theory. Think of the area under the demand curve as a measure of the benefit that consumers derive from the good. The demand price corresponds to the marginal benefit. The area under the supply curve measures the total cost, and the supply price is the marginal cost. At the equilibrium quantity traded, the marginal benefit equals the marginal cost. The net benefit is the total benefit minus the total cost. Marshall shows that if the marginal net benefit is a decreasing function of the quantity, then the net benefit is a maximum at the point where the marginal net benefit is zero. Therefore, the market clearing price, which equilibrates the quantity demanded to the quantity supplied, yields the maximal net benefit. The marginal net benefit is a decreasing function of the quantity if the mar-

ginal benefit decreases more rapidly than the marginal cost. Given a
negatively sloped demand curve so that more is demanded, the lower
the price, Marshall's theory can give the conclusion that the equilibrium
price maximizes the net benefit even for a downward-sloping supply
curve, provided the demand price is a more rapidly decreasing function
of the quantity than is the supply price. This conclusion together with
Marshall's well-known statement that a seller might not lower his price
"for fear of spoiling the market" is strong evidence of his sophisticated
comprehension of the nature of a competitive equilibrium.

The supply conditions being complications in their train. The theory
of the core, proven on the testing ground of pure exchange, is well
made for the study of these complications. The bulk of these complications arises from the fact that costs are lower if producers make commitments in advance of the revenue they expect to receive. This is to
say that they choose inputs of capital equipment, finance these inputs,
hire labor, arrange the marketing of the outputs, decide what and how
much to produce, and many other things before the outputs are ready
for actual sale. Having done all of this, the producers have incurred
fixed costs and other kinds of costs that do not necessarily rise
smoothly and continuously with their actual rates of output. Marshall's
awareness of negatively sloped supply schedules and his analysis of
natural monopoly is one of the earliest recognitions in economic theory
of some of the implications of the new technology coming into existence
in the nineteenth century. By choosing production methods capable of
making complicated articles at low cost, provided the means of production are ready before the appearance of the actual demand, producers become hostages of the vagaries of uncertain future demand.
This may create opportunities for the buyers to drive hard bargains.
In this way the buyers can get short-term gains, but they may also
sacrifice the longer-term gains coming from the use of better methods
of production. Sellers will not willingly make long-term commitments
without some assurance of recouping the costs of their investments.
Both buyers and producers face the practical problem of devising mutually satisfactory terms among themselves so that they can share the
gains from lower costs made possible by the new technology. I assume
that people seek to advance their own interests as well as they can.
Their actions form the subject of economic theory. Changes in their
environment resulting from new scientific and engineering knowledge
cause adaptations of economic institutions. These pose new challenges
to economic theory. The theory of the core can meet these challenges.

I propose to defend these assertions by working through an example.
It has the main features that explain the complicated nature of the

supply response. Yet it is simple enough to avoid distracting technical details.

3   Description of the example

Assume there are identical potential customers each of whom is willing to pay at most an amount b per unit of the good. It means they derive a benefit of at least b per unit of the good. The actual number of customers who want to obtain the good at any instant behaves like a random variable. We may think of a store where customers arrive by a process like a sequence of independent random events. If the good is available, then a customer can satisfy his demand without delay. Otherwise, if the store is out of stock, the customer cannot obtain the good, which imposes a loss on him of t per unit. As a result, the net benefit to the customer is lower when the store is out of stock than when the inventory is ample enough to satisfy the demand.

The store determines the size of its inventory before the customers arrive. It must not only decide how much of the commodity to stock but it must also determine in advance how much space to make available for storing the inventory. Say the good arrives at the store early in the morning before it is open for business. It starts with an inventory y and continues to satisfy the demand of the customers as they appear until its inventory is exhausted. If the store decides to have no inventory of the good at all, then it would incur no cost of inventory. If it decides to have an inventory of the good, then it incurs an inventory cost $C(y)$, which depends on the size of its inventory. Because the inventory cost is zero if y is zero and is $C(y) > 0$ if $y > 0$, the cost of the inventory is an avoidable cost. The term *avoidable* reminds us that the cost is avoidable if the inventory is zero. There may also be costs of serving an individual customer. These costs vary with the number of customers and with the actual sales of the store. Hence these are the variable costs. Presumably, it would not pay to satisfy the demand of an individual customer unless he were willing to pay at least the cost of doing so. Even this simple point raises an interesting problem owing to the possibility that the customer may wish information about the product before deciding whether or not to buy it. In case the nature of the information inclines the customer against buying the product, the store may be unable to obtain remuneration from the customer in compensation for the cost of the information it provides him (Telser 1960). For the sake of keeping the example simple, I shall assume each customer is willing to buy the product if it is available at a price not above b. There is no demand for information about the product from the seller by the customer because each already knows enough to have decided on a purchase.

Since stores usually sell many different products, there is another complication to consider. Some customers buy some of the products but none buys all of them. Each product type imposes its own cost. There are also costs common to all of the products. These raise the question of how to divide the common costs among the customers. It is usual to pose this question by asking how overhead costs are allocated among the different products. Again in the interest of having a simple example, I assume the store carries only one commodity. In a more general theory this would be the first step. Thus, imagine initially there are many stores each with only one product. The general theory would describe conditions under which it would be advantageous for which types of stores to merge.

Given that the store holds an inventory, there is the question of whether its unsold stocks are subsequently available for sale. This would mean that later sales are a substitute for current sales. Depending on the nature of the costs of storing the good, the seller could convert the avoidable cost into a variable cost. That is, he would have the alternative of selling one unit now or selling it later. The incremental cost of the latter would be the cost of storing the good. Including this alternative would merely complicate the analysis without contributing any essential new features to it. Therefore, I assume the good is available for sale in only one period. A daily newspaper is an example. If the good is perishable, meaning it is prohibitively expensive to store for more than some given period of time, then, under these conditions as well, there would be no storage for more than one period.

On the basis of these assumptions we can derive the level of inventories that would maximize the expected net benefit of the consumers. Let x denote the quantity demanded per unit of time. It is a random variable with a probability density function given by $f(x)$. Let β denote the benefit.

$$\beta = \begin{cases} bx & \text{if } x \leq y, \\ by - t(x - y) & \text{if } x > y. \end{cases} \tag{1}$$

If the quantity demanded, x, does not exceed the inventory, y, then the total benefit is bx. However, if the quantity demanded does exceed the available supply, then the total benefit is lower by the excess demand, $x - y$, multiplied by the positive constant t. Therefore, in case the inventory is inadequate, the total benefit is lower by the loss from the failure to satisfy the entire demand. The expected benefit, denote it by $E(\beta)$, is as follows:

$$E(\beta) = \int_0^y bxf(x)\, dx + \int_y^\infty [by - t(x - y)]f(x)\, dx. \qquad (2)$$

The actual benefit is a random variable depending on the rate of demand x, which is a random variable. Hence the expected value of the benefit depends on the probabilities of the two events, a rate of demand below the available stock and one above it.

The total cost of the inventory y is $C(y)$. It does not depend on a random event so it is deterministic. The expected net benefit of an inventory level y is

$$E(\beta) - C(y). \qquad (3)$$

The inventory giving the maximal expected net benefit must satisfy the equation as follows:

$$\frac{\partial E(\beta)}{\partial y} = \frac{\partial C}{\partial y} \qquad (4)$$

so that the marginal expected benefit of an inventory level y equals its marginal cost. It is instructive to calculate the explicit form of the marginal expected net benefit, which is as follows:

$$\frac{\partial E(\beta)}{\partial y} = (b + t)[1 - F(y)], \qquad (5)$$

where $1 - F(y)$ is the probability that the rate of demand exceeds the inventory y, the stock-out probability, so that,

$$1 - F(y) = \int_y^\infty f(x)\, dx. \qquad (6)$$

It is natural to interpret the marginal expected net benefit as the ex ante demand for the inventory y and the marginal cost of the inventory as the ex ante supply of the inventory. The marginal expected benefit is a decreasing function of y so that the larger the stock, the lower the marginal expected benefit. Figure 3.1 illustrates the situation. The curve DD' shows the ex ante demand for stocks, which is the marginal expected benefit. When stocks are zero, $F(0) = 0$, because it is certain that a positive quantity is demanded. Therefore, the ordinate of the point D is $b + t$. The larger the inventory, the less likely is a rate of demand in excess of the available stock. Hence $1 - F(y)$ is a decreasing function of y, which approaches 0 as y increases. The curve SS' is the ex ante supply of stocks. It shows the marginal cost of holding stocks. The supply curve in Figure 3.1 assumes the marginal cost is an increasing convex function of y. The optimal level of stocks, y_0, is de-

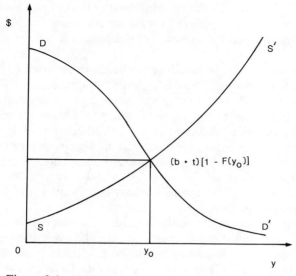

Figure 3.1

termined by the intersection of the ex ante supply and the ex ante demand curves. Note that the ex ante demand is greater the larger are b and t. It is also true that the expected quantity is less than y_0 corresponding to the intersection of the ex ante supply and demand curves. This means it is optimal to have more stocks on hand than are expected to be sold. A proof is instructive. Let q denote the quantity sold, which is a random variable.

$$q = \begin{cases} x & \text{if } x \leq y, \\ y & \text{if } x > y. \end{cases}$$

Hence the expected sales, $E(q)$, is given by

$$E(q) = \int_0^y xf(x)\, dx + y \int_y^\infty f(x)\, dx.$$

$$E(q) - y = \int_0^y (x - y)f(x)\, dx + (y - y) \int_y^\infty f(x)\, dx$$

$$= \int_0^y (x - y)f(x)\, dx < 0,$$

as asserted.

Since the optimal level of inventories satisfies the equation

$$(b + t)[1 - F(y_0)] = C_y(y_0), \tag{7}$$

it follows that $b + t$ exceeds the marginal cost of the optimal inventory. Although this formulation gives the necessary condition for the optimal inventory, it leaves open the question of what arrangements can attain the optimum.

The point is this. There is no adversary relation between customers and their suppliers. Instead there is a gain for them to share. The expected value of this gain is the difference between the expected benefit and the cost. By choosing the value of that y that gives the maximal net benefit, the suppliers and their customers obtain the greatest gain they can share among themselves. It is as if the customers own the stores and the managers of the stores were their agents. There would still remain the problem of devising appropriate terms between the customers and their agent-suppliers that would induce the latter to choose the optimal inventory.

Reconsider the nature of the demand conditions. Since the customers bear a loss of t per unit if the demand exceeds the available supply, it follows that they would would be willing to pay up to $b + t$ per unit when $x > y$. It would therefore seem possible to have two prices, p_1 and p_2 such that

$$p = \begin{cases} p_1 & \text{if } x \leqq y, \\ p_1 + p_2 & \text{if } x > y. \end{cases} \tag{8}$$

This scheme makes the price a random variable dependent on the state of demand. The expected price, $E(p)$, satisfies

$$E(p) = p_1 + p_2 \int_y^\infty f(x) \, dx \tag{9}$$
$$= p_1 + p_2[1 - F(y)].$$

This expected price would equal the marginal expected benefit of the stocks if

$$(b + t)[1 - F(y)] = p_1 + p_2[1 - F(y)].$$

Rearranging terms, this becomes

$$p_1 = [(b + t) - p_2][1 - F(y)]. \tag{10}$$

Any pair of prices, p_1, p_2, satisfying (10) would equate the expected price to the expected marginal benefit of the stocks. Hence it passes the first test necessary to induce holding the optimal inventory. A second test requires examination of the revenue this scheme would generate.

Let r denote the revenue that is a random variable via the random nature of the demand.

$$r = \begin{cases} p_1 x & \text{if } x \leqq y, \\ (p_1 + p_2)y & \text{if } x > y. \end{cases} \tag{11}$$

Call $E(r)$ the expected value of the revenue.

$$\begin{aligned} E(r) &= \int_0^y p_1 x f(x)\, dx + \int_y^\infty (p_1 + p_2)y f(x)\, dx \\ &= \int_0^y p_1 x f(x)\, dx + (p_1 + p_2)y[1 - F(y)]. \end{aligned} \tag{12}$$

Assume the prices p_1, p_2 satisfy (10) so that they equate the expected price to the marginal expected benefit of the optimal inventory, y_0. It is an implication of (7) and (10) that

$$(p_1 + p_2)[1 - F(y_0)] = C_y^0 - p_1 F(y_0). \tag{13}$$

where $C_y^0 = \partial C(y_0)/\partial y$. Substituting (13) into (12) gives the following result:

$$E(r) - C(y_0) = p_1 \int_0^{y_0} (x - y_0) f(x)\, dx + y_0 C_y^0 - C(y_0). \tag{14}$$

This relation is important for seeing whether the pricing scheme can generate enough receipts on average to cover the total cost of the inventory.

Now $x - y_0 \leqq 0$ so the first term on the right-hand side of (14) is nonpositive. Consider the second term. If the average cost of inventories is always greater than the marginal cost owing to economies of scale in the holding of inventories, then this term is always negative. If so, the expected revenue would always be less than the total cost, and the pricing scheme would fail to yield enough receipts to cover the cost of the optimal inventory. Suppose, however, that the marginal cost of holding inventories eventually rises above the average cost. At some level, say y^*, the average cost of holding inventories is a minimum.

$$\frac{C(y^*)}{y^*} \leqq \frac{C(y)}{y} \quad \text{for all } y \geqq 0 \quad \text{and} \quad C_y(y^*) = C(y^*)/y^*. \tag{15}$$

If $C(y)/y$ had a U-shape, then (15) would be true.

$$y_0 C_y(y_0) - C(y_0) < 0 \quad \text{if } y_0 < y^*, \tag{16}$$
$$y_0 C_y(y_0) - C(y_0) > 0 \quad \text{if } y_0 > y^*.$$

For the two-price system to work it is necessary that

$$E(r) - C(y_0) \geqq 0,$$

and this can be true only if the second inequality of (16) is true. The latter in turn is true only if the optimal inventory is above the inventory level giving the minimal average cost. Nothing in the situation assures this. The value of y^* giving the minimal average cost of holding inventories depends solely on the cost conditions, whereas the optimal inventory depends on both the demand and the cost conditions. It would be a lucky coincidence if it were to turn out that the second inequality of (16) is true.

Take the special case where the inventory cost is linearly proportional to y so that

$$C(y) = cy. \tag{17}$$

Now

$$yC_y - C = 0 \quad \text{for all } y. \tag{18}$$

In this case it would be possible to satisfy the condition that expected receipts equal total cost by setting $p_1 = 0$. This creates a new problem, fraud, or, as is fashionable to describe it nowadays, moral hazard. Customers could receive the good for free if the total demand is below the available supply and according to equation (10) would pay a price equal to $b + t$, the maximum they are willing to pay, if there is excess demand. Plainly, there would be nothing to stop customers from taking as much as they want when there is excess supply, and the suppliers would get a positive payment only when there is excess demand. With this pricing scheme it is reasonable to suppose suppliers would always hold less than the optimal stocks at the outset since only by so doing would they obtain positive receipts.

As an alternative consider the proposal where suppliers pay a penalty to customers when the quantity demanded is above the supply and customers pay a positive amount to suppliers when the supply is excessive. It would seem at first blush to furnish suppliers with an adequate incentive to begin with the optimal inventory. However, this scheme is also subject to abuse. As soon as it were known that a supplier is out of stock, some people posing as customers could appear and demand payment in compensation for being unable to get the good.

To prevent this, service could be confined to regular customers so that casual passersby could receive no payment. A moral hazard problem still remains. A regular customer could claim payment for a quantiy larger than he had actually planned to buy, and it would be difficult to verify his claim. To prevent this, suppliers might restrict the total payment to an upper bound and set a limit to the maximum number of units they would sell to a regular customer. This proposal begins to resemble a kind of insurance contract between the supplier and regular customers.

A flexible price arrangement depending on the state of demand is vulnerable to criticism since it requires knowledge about the demand state before it can go into effect. That is, the price depends on the state of demand, which may be costly to ascertain. There are in addition the two criticisms that it may fail to generate enough revenue to cover total cost and that it invites fraud, which would be costly to deter. A single price needs no advance knowledge about the state of demand, and it is less vulnerable to fraud so it is worth considering.

To satisfy the condition for an optimal inventory level, the single price p must equal the marginal expected benefit so it must satisfy the following equation:

$$p = (b + t) [1 - F(y_0)]. \tag{19}$$

The revenue r that a single price would generate remains a random variable.

$$r = \begin{cases} px & \text{if } x < y, \\ py & \text{if } x \geq y. \end{cases}$$

The expected revenue $E(r)$ is defined as follows:

$$E(r) = p \left[\int_0^y xf(x)\, dx + \int_y^\infty yf(x)\, dx \right],$$

which is equivalent to

$$E(r) = p \int_0^y xf(x)\, dx + py[1 - F(y)]. \tag{20}$$

It is understood in these formulas that y equals the optimal value y_0. Since the price equals the marginal cost of the optimal inventory as well as the marginal expected benefit, there is the implication that

$$E(r) - C(y) = p \int_0^y xf(x)\, dx + yC_y[1 - F(y)] - C(y). \tag{21}$$

Nothing ensures that expected receipts will cover the total cost of the optimal inventory. The special case where the inventory cost is linearly proportional to the amount of inventories is again instructive. Now $C(y) = yC_y$ and (21) becomes

$$E(r) - C(y) = p \int_0^y xf(x) \, dx - F(y)yC_y$$

$$= C_y \int_0^y (x - y)f(x) \, dx < 0.$$

Thus with a constant marginal cost of inventory set equal to the price as required by the condition for the optimal inventory level, expected receipts would fall short of the total cost of the inventory. The single price fails to yield enough receipts to cover the total cost. Moreover, depending on the demand conditions and on the shape of the total cost curve, a single price can give either profits or losses on average at the optimal inventory level. If there were profits on average, it would create incentives to hold more than the optimal amount of inventories. If there were losses on average, it would create incentives to hold less than the optimal inventory level. Although it is easy to calculate a single price that would satisfy the necessary conditions for optimality, namely, one that equates the marginal cost to the marginal expected benefit, it is not easy to maintain the optimal level of inventories. Explicit agreement between suppliers and their customers on the inventory level, the price per unit, and a provision for sharing the difference between expected receipts and total cost in the form of long-term contracts could give a mutually acceptable arrangement among all of the parties that would be efficient.

4   Analysis of competition for the example

The model described in the preceding section focuses on the factors determining the optimal level of inventories, which depend on the cost and demand conditions. It gives no explicit treatment of competition. The purpose of this section is to remedy this neglect. For the sake of confining the analysis to arithmetic and algebra, in contrast to the preceding section where the demand is a continuous variable, which requires using calculus, here the demand comes in discrete units, like the theory of Böhm-Bawerk.

Assume four firms hold inventories and that their combined capacity is at the optimal level as determined by the cost and demand conditions. Let k_i denote the capacity of firm A_i, $i = 1, \ldots, 4$. Each firm incurs a cost when it is open for business that it can avoid by not opening. Let a_i denote this avoidable cost of A_i. It depends on the capacity of A_i but not on its actual sales. The following figures give the capacities and avoidable costs of the four firms:

Firm	k_i	a_i
A_1	1	5
A_2	2	8
A_3	4	12
A_4	8	16

Firm A_2 has a capacity of 2 units and an avoidable cost of 8. It would not open for business without getting receipts of at least 8. Note that integer combinations of the four firms make it possible to satisfy any rate of demand up to 15 units. This means the optimal level of inventories is 15 and the expected rate of demand is below 15 units. The actual value of the expected rate of demand does not enter this analysis and so it does not concern us here. Also, in this example a_i/k_i, the avoidable cost per unit of capacity, is a decreasing function of capacity. It is plausible to assume this for several reasons. If the avoidable cost were a linear or an increasing nonlinear function of capacity, then it would be optimal to have many small firms, each, say, with a capacity of one unit. The main consideration against this would be fixed costs. The total fixed cost of many small firms may exceed the total fixed cost of a few large ones. By explicitly assuming there are scale economies in terms of the avoidable cost, one can avoid implicit assumptions about fixed costs that do not directly affect the analysis of competition.

As in the preceding section, assume all customers are identical so that each is willing to pay the same maximal amount per unit. To be specific, let this be five per unit. The difference between the maximal amount a customer is willing to pay and the actual amount he does pay is his gain. Since all customers are alike, the gain per unit must be the same for each one. Let s denote this gain per unit. Each customer can refuse to buy and thereby assure himself a gain of zero. Therefore, s must be nonnegative. This corresponds to Edgeworth's assumption that no trader accepts a bundle of goods that would make him worse off than he was initially. Here it is convenient, though it would not be necessary for the validity of the analysis in a more general model, to assume each customer wants at most one unit of the good.

Let r_i denote the gain of firm A_i. Since firms differ by virtue of their different capacities and avoidable costs, it is not generally true that each firm gets the same gain. The subscript on r_i indicates this. Each firm has the alternative of remaining closed and selling nothing, thereby assuring itself a gain of zero. It follows that r_i must be nonnegative.

Let B denote a buyer so that mB denotes m buyers. A coalition of m buyers and firm A_i can be certain of getting a combined net gain equal to the maximum amount the buyers are willing to pay minus the avoidable cost of the firm. This gain corresponds to Marshall's consumer surplus. It turns out that the only types of coalitions it is necessary to consider are those between a firm and the maximal number of customers it can accommodate. The surpluses for these coalitions of buyers and firms operating at their respective capacities are as follows:

$$\Pi(1B, A_1) = \max\{0, 5 - 5\} = 0,$$

$$\Pi(2B, A_2) = \max\{0, 10 - 8\} = 2,$$

$$\Pi(4B, A_3) = \max\{0, 20 - 12\} = 8,$$

$$\Pi(8B, A_4) = \max\{0, 40 - 16\} = 24.$$

For example, A_4 has a capacity of 8 so it can sell 8 units to potential buyers. The buyers are each willing to pay at most 5 per unit and the avoidable cost of A_4 is 16. Consequently, the consumer surplus for a coalition of 8 buyers and A_4 is $5 \times 8 - 16 = 24$.

Assume that individual firms and buyers may act on their own, each seeking the best possible terms for themselves. Whatever is the gain of the individual firms and buyers in the whole market, it must be at least as large as that for any coalition composed of a firm and a group of customers. Such a coalition can confine trade to its own members and on the basis of a mutually acceptable bargain among its own members, it can assure them a total gain equal to the maximal consumer surplus of the coalition. To see this in more detail, assume there are at least eight potential customers in the market. Any one of these can make a tentative contract with A_1, any two can do so with A_2, any four with A_3 and all eight can make a tentative contract with A_4. As a result of all these feasible contracts, the gains of individual buyers and sellers must satisfy the following inequalities:

$$s + r_1 \geqq \Pi(B, A_1) = 0,$$

$$2s + r_2 \geqq \Pi(2B, A_2) = 2,$$

$$4s + r_3 \geqq \Pi(4B, A_3) = 8,$$

$$8s + r_4 \geqq \Pi(8B, A_4) = 24.$$

(1)

Since s is the buyer's gain per unit, which is the maximum price less the actual price, given that 5 is the maximum price per unit any buyer is willing to pay, the actual price that would be capable of satisfying the constraints imposed by the forces of competition is readily found from the equation $p = 5 - s$.

There are several points to note about this analysis. First, the individual buyers and the firms who make tentative agreements among themselves do not consider the interest of those outside their own group. Second, no coalition has the power to affect directly the bargains that can be struck by mutual consent among traders who are outside its own coalition. Third, the traders seek to advance their individual interests as much as they can by forming coalitions. Individuals are free to join any coalition they please and coalitions are at liberty to attract anyone they please for membership. Inside the coalition is cooperation and among the coalitions, competition. The formal analysis represents this competition by means of inequalities that set lower bounds on the gains of coalitions.

A constraint applies to the whole group. It gives the maximum consumer surplus available for distribution among all of the traders. The analysis of the preceding section finds the inventory level giving the maximum gain as a function of the demand and cost conditions. That analysis determines the optimal total capacity of the firms. Now there is the problem of finding the optimal assignment of buyers to firms that can attain this maximum consumer surplus. The main question is: Can the forces of competition as represented by the constraints imposed by the lower bounds attainable by the coalitions, the inequalities (1), bring about an optimal assignment that can realize the globally maximal consumer surplus? The separate coalitions seek to advance their local interests. A competitive equilibrium can resolve the collisions among the local interests and attain the global optimum under certain conditions. What are these conditions?

The answers to these questions depend on the number of potential customers in the market. Following the notation in the preceding section, let x denote the number of units demanded. It is convenient to assume $x \geqq 8$ so that there are enough customers to enable each of the four firms to operate at its capacity. For given x, solve the following linear programming problem:

$$\min z, \quad \text{where } z = xs + \sum_{i=1}^{4} r_i,$$

with respect to s and r_i nonnegative and subject to the inequalities (1) that represent the constraints imposed by the alternatives available to the various coalitions. They show how competition constrains the outcome. The value of z giving the solution shows the smallest sum of the gains that would be acceptable to each of the x buyers and each of the four firms.

For all x such that $8 \leqq x < 13$, the solution of these problems is as follows:

$$s = 2, \qquad r_1 = r_2 = r_3 = 0, \qquad r_4 = 8, \qquad z = 2x + 8.$$

It is instructive to see why this is the solution. First, assume $x = 8$. Firm A_4 could accommodate the whole demand and the consumer surplus from a contract between A_4 and the eight customers would be $\Pi(8B, A_4) = 24$. However, A_3 could make a deal with any four of these customers. The largest gain that A_3 could offer any set of four customers would give each buyer $s = 2$. This would mean that A_3 would get a return of zero, $r_3 = 0$, the least it would be willing to accept. These terms would satisfy the third inequality of (1). However, A_4 can meet the price implicit in this offer by A_3 (the price would be 3), and A_4 would then get a gain of 8 ($r_4 = 8$). This would satisfy all the constraints. Nor is this all. The global maximum of the consumer surplus occurs by assigning the eight buyers to A_4. Consequently, the global maximum is 24. Therefore, with eight buyers the forces of competition produce a price and returns to the sellers that are both locally and globally optimal. There is an implication of a nonempty core. The entries in the first row of Table 3.1 refer to this case.

Next assume a larger demand, say, $x = 9$. Clearly, it is still globally optimal for A_4 to satisfy the demand of eight out of the nine potential buyers and not to satisfy one unit of demand. It is still true that A_3 could accommodate any four out of the nine potential buyers and offer each one of the four a gain of 2. This competing offer from A_3 sets an upper bound on the price equivalent to a lower bound on the gain of any customer. The minimally acceptable total gain for the whole group is $(9 \times 2) + 8$, but this is above the globally maximal consumer surplus, which is 24. It is therefore impossible to satisfy all of the constraints within the bounds set by the maximal consumer surplus. It follows there is an implication of an empty core. This means there is no equilibrium if $x = 9$.

Next, assume the quantity demanded is 10. Now the global optimum requires A_2 and A_4 to be active, and the maximal consumer surplus of the whole group is $2 + 24$. However, A_3 offers a competitive alternative. Although A_3 ought to remain idle according to the requirement of the global optimum, it can still offer any four buyers terms that would

Table 3.1. *Quantity demanded, maximum consumer surplus, minimal acceptable gains, and optimal supply response* [a]

Quantity demanded x	Maximum consumer surplus	Minimum acceptable gains = z	Optimal supply response
8	24	24	A_4
9	24	26	A_4
10	26	28	A_4, A_2
11	27	30	A_4, A_3
12	32	32	A_4, A_3
13	32	33	A_4, A_3
14	34	34	A_4, A_3, A_2
15	34	34	A_4, A_3, A_2, A_1

[a] For rates of demand between 8 and 12, $s = 2$, $r_4 = 8$, $r_1 = r_2 = r_3 = 0$ is the solution of the problem giving the minimally acceptable total gains. For a rate of demand equal to 13, $s = 1$, $r_4 = 16$, $r_3 = 4$, $r_1 = r_2 = 0$. For rates of demand equal to 14 or 15, $s = 0$, so that buyers pay the maximal price, $r_4 = 24$, $r_3 = 8$, $r_2 = 2$, and $r_1 = 0$.

allow them to obtain a gain of 8. This can force the price to an upper bound of 3 so each customer would gain at least 2. The minimal acceptable gain of the whole group would be $(10 \times 2) + 8$, which is above 26, the global maximum of the consumer surplus. It is impossible to satisfy the individual gains resulting from unfettered competition so the core is empty. Observe that in contrast to the preceding case with a rate of demand of 9, in the present case with $x = 10$, the optimal assignment requires each customer to get 1 unit of the good so there would be no demand unsatisfied. With $x = 9$ the optimal assignment leaves one unit of demand unsatisfied. But the forces of competition give to each customer a gain of 2. Therefore, the one customer who does not get the good must instead receive in compensation a payment of 2. In this fashion that customer gains as much as each of the eight who do receive one unit of the good and pay a price of 3 per unit. For a rate of demand equal to 9, it would be necessary for the supplier to pay the one customer whose demand would not be satisfied the compensatory amount of 2. It is impossible to do this because the total consumer surplus under the optimal assignment is too small to satisfy the requirements imposed by the minimal acceptable gains resulting from unrestricted competition.

It is not globally optimal for A_3 to become active until the rate of demand reaches 11. Nevertheless, even at this rate of demand the core is empty. Although the optimal assignment requires A_3 to be active and to satisfy 3 units of demand, it can satisfy up to 4 units, which is its capacity. Nothing can prevent A_3 from offering a price low enough to attract a fourth customer. The price goes down to 3 and the gain of every buyer goes up to 2. As a result the minimally acceptable value of z becomes $(11 \times 2) + 8$, a figure above the value of the maximal consumer surplus at $x = 11$. This surplus is 27, composed of 24 from the coalition of A_4 with 8 customers and 3 from A_3 with 3 customers $[3 = (5 \times 3) - 12]$.

At a level of demand equal to 13, the most efficient of the inactive firms is A_2. It can make mutually advantageous bargains with sets of two buyers by offering each customer a price of at most 4 so each buyer would gain 1. The resulting value of z equals 13×1 plus $r_3 = 4$ plus $r_4 = 16$, which sums to 33. However, the global maximum of the consumer surplus is 32, and so there is an implication of an empty core.

At levels of demand equal to 14 or 15, competition among the buyers drives the price up to the maximum each is willing to pay, and each buyer gets a gain of zero ($s = 0$). For A_2, $r_2 = 2$, A_3 gets 8 and A_4 gets 24. This makes $z = 34$, which is also the value of the global maximum consumer surplus. Hence, at these levels of demand, the maximum consumer surplus is big enough to satisfy the requirements imposed by the minimal gain that would be acceptable to the buyers and sellers as a result of the forces of competition.

Since by hypothesis the actual rate of demand behaves like a random variable, any of the values of x can occur. Unrestricted competition among buyers and sellers would not result in an equilibrium at each rate of demand. It is only at some rates of demand that unrestricted competition can give an equilibrium, and in these cases it is efficient. To have an efficient supply response for arbitrary rates of demand requires cooperation among the participants. In the general class of cases where each firm has an avoidable cost depending on its capacity but not on its actual rates of sales, there is a form of cooperation that can give an efficient equilibrium. It is this. Let each firm get a sales quota imposing an upper bound on the quantity it may sell. These upper bounds depend on the total quantity demanded as well as on the cost conditions of the individual firms – the capacities and the avoidable costs. The assigned quotas may be below the actual firm capacities. Subject only to these upper bounds on their rates of sale, let the firms compete for buyers so there are no restrictions on prices. It can be shown that there exists a set of output quotas, one for each firm, such that subject to the constraint that no firm can sell more than its quota allows, an efficient equilibrium exists that is compatible with the given demand conditions.

Chapter 5 contains a rigorous demonstration of these results. Here using one of the above examples, it is possible to explain the main idea. Recall that the solution of the linear programming problem gives the gain to each person so that no trader or group of traders would be worse off by accepting this outcome than with any of the feasible alternatives. Each constraint of the linear programming problem sets a lower bound on the sum of the gains that the members of the coalition, corresponding to that constraint, are willing to accept. It is a lower bound because the members of the given coalition can assure themselves a consumer surplus equal to this amount using only their own resources. However, each coalition ignores the effects of its actions on the other coalitions. Moreover, each coalition explicitly takes into account only those factors that directly concern its own members. Hence each seeks its own local optimum without regard to the global one. The consequence is an infeasible set of required gains whenever the global optimum cannot generate a big enough total surplus to satisfy the gains required by each individual. These gains required by the individuals are the result of the coalitions they can form. The following example where the rate of demand is 10 well illustrates the nature of the problem.

With $x = 10$, the maximum consumer surplus available to the group as a whole is 26. The sum of the gains that would be minimally acceptable to the members of the whole group resulting from the forces of competition is 28. In order to attain the global maximum, firms A_2 and A_4 should be active while A_1 and A_3 should be inactive. Since the capacity of A_2 is 2 and of A_4 is 8, these two firms have just enough capacity to satisfy the total demand. However, A_3 with a capacity of 4 and an avoidable cost of 12 can generate a consumer surplus of 8 if it can attract 4 customers. The total benefit of the 4 customers would be 5×4, and the avoidable cost of satisfying their demand would be 12 so the consumer surplus would be 8. The lowest price A_3 would be willing to offer is 3, which would give each customer a gain of 2. Hence if A_3 is at liberty to compete freely for customers it could give each one a gain of 2. Firm A_4 can generate a consumer surplus of 24 and by giving each of its 8 customers a gain of 2, the coalition formed by A_4 and 8 customers obtains 24, which is minimally acceptable to them. But the total number of customers is 10, not 12 as would be required in order that both A_3 and A_4 fully use their available capacities. The competition for customers by these two independent firms results in a value of z equal to $8 + (10 \times 2)$. The global optimum does take into account the fact that the total quantity demanded is 10 and that the maximal global consumer surplus is 26. It is generally true that the sum of the minimally acceptable gains is never less than the globally maximal consumer surplus. In order to get an efficient allocation in this case with $x = 10$, the quantity that A_3 is allowed to sell should be lowered to 2. Giving a sales quota of 2 to A_3, its avoidable cost remaining the same since this depends on its actual capacity but not on its rate of sales, competition in the new situation results in a set of gains that sum to the true globally maximal consumer surplus. To see why this is so, consider the dual linear programming problem for $x = 10$.

The dual linear programming problem is defined as follows:

$$\max(0\delta_1 + 2\delta_2 + 8\delta_3 + 24\delta_4)$$

with respect to $\delta_j \geqq 0$ subject to

$$\delta_1 + 2\delta_2 + 4\delta_3 + 8\delta_4 \leqq 10, \tag{2}$$

and

$$\delta_j \leqq 1, \quad j = 1, \ldots, 4. \tag{3}$$

The coefficient of δ_j in the objective function is $\Pi(k_j B, A_j)$. The coefficient of δ_j in the demand constraint (2) is k_j. The solution of this dual linear programming problem is as follows:

$$\delta_1 = \delta_2 = 0, \quad \delta_3 = \tfrac{1}{2}, \quad \delta_4 = 1.$$

Although constraint (2) expresses the fact that the total quantity offered, shown on the left-hand side of the inequality, should not exceed the total quantity demanded, 10, which is shown on the right-hand side of the inequality, a difficulty appears. It is that δ_3 is a positive fraction. It can be shown that there is an implication of a nonempty core if and only if the solution of the dual linear programming problem gives values of δ_j that are either 0 or 1. Equivalently, the core is empty if and only if any δ_j appearing as part of the solution of the dual problem is a positive fraction (Proposition 2, Chapter 5). In case some δ_j is a positive fraction, then the sales quota of that firm A_j is

$$k_j' = (1 - \delta_j)k_j. \tag{4}$$

Applying this result to A_3 gives $k_3' = (1 - 0.5) \times 4 = 2$. Corresponding to the value of this sales quota is a new value of $\Pi(\cdot)$ for A_3:

$$\Pi(k_3'B, A_3) = \max\{0, 2 \times 5 - 12\} = 0.$$

Hence the following constraint (5) replaces the constraint for A_3 given by the third inequality of (1):

$$2s + r_3 \geqq 0, \tag{5}$$

which, in view of the nonnegativity constraints, is, of course, redundant. It can be shown that with this replacement, the resulting solutions of the primal and dual linear programming problems imply minimally acceptable gains that are globally feasible because they sum to the globally maximal consumer surplus.

It usually takes more than one but always a finite number of iterations of the linear programming problems to find the sales quotas that yield minimally acceptable gains that are globally optimal. The imposition of sales quotas according to this procedure lowers the excess supply in an optimal fashion. Cooperation among the firms with respect to these reductions is necessary to attain an efficient equilibrium.

For the purpose of explaining the general principles without introducing distracting complications, these examples assume the firms have avoidable but no variable costs. Variable costs depend on the actual output rates of the firms. If there were also variable costs, then the sales quotas would depend on these as well as on the avoidable costs. Though it would complicate the analysis, the general conclusion that properly chosen sales quotas can give an efficient equilibrium remains true. It is owing to the presence of avoidable costs that efficiency is attainable via upper bounds on rates of sale but not via lower bounds on prices. Moreover, price floors could not yield an efficient allocation. Given the proper sales quotas, a form of cooperation, firms may compete and the result is an efficient equilibrium. For this reason there is the conclusion that efficiency requires an optimal combination of cooperation and competition.

Some may concede that sales quotas will accomplish this purpose but only because of the two restrictive assumptions in this model: that each firm has a definite capacity and an avoidable cost. This is incorrect. Chapter 5 studies much more general models and derives similar results as those given here. Nor are the assumptions of this simple model unduly restrictive. In the inventory example the capacity represents the stocks on hand that the firm must order in advance before knowing its actual sales. The assumption of a definite firm capacity approximates a more general situation where average variable cost rises sharply at output rates that are high relative to the one at which average variable cost is a minimum. Thus capacity represents the practical upper bound on the output rate. Avoidable cost also approximates a more general case. Say the firm has an output rate below which it is prohibitively expensive to operate. Therefore, it would become an active producer only at output rates above this minimum. The avoidable cost represents this situation.

Together the two assumptions of an avoidable cost and a definite capacity are a source of indivisibilities. This is to say that the optimal supply response to changes in the rate of demand has jumps in total cost as a result of changes in which firms are active. Indivisibilities are important in industries where the capacities of the smallest yet efficient firms are large relative to the total quantity demanded. When the minimally efficient sizes are small relative to the equilibrium quantity demanded, the supply response is nearly continuous and indivisibilities have little practical effect. However, there are many circumstances where indivisibilities are important because they enable use of the least-cost methods of production. Auto production is a good example.

Despite the fact that annual auto production is millions of cars, indivisibilities are important. Underlying these indivisibilities are the factors that enable manufacture of this complicated machine at the lowest cost possible. An assembly plant is the final stage of production. The basic unit of output in an assembly plant is an assembly line. It operates at a given rate, say, 60 cars per hour. It must be fed with enough components at each point so that the line can move smoothly at the planned rate. Bottlenecks and excessive stocks must be prevented. It is very costly to change the hourly output rate of an assembly line so this seldom happens. When it does, the change is within a very narrow range. An assembly plant may have two assembly lines. Changes in the output rate take the form of opening or closing one assembly line for a five-day, eight-hour per day shift. Smaller adjustments take the form of adding overtime in an eight-hour shift on Saturday. If the plant has two assembly lines, it is usually cheaper to run them both simultaneously than to operate only one of them for two eight-hour shifts. A plant may be opened or closed for one or more weeks. The shortest time interval for this decision is one week. More than one plant may make the same mix of car models. If so, the output response has additional flexibility by taking various combinations of plants and their component assembly lines. The result makes the output rate an integer combination of assembly lines working weekly full eight-hour shifts. Opening or closing an assembly line constitutes a substantial change in the output rate relative to the demand for the mix of models assembled on that line. It is also worth noting that auto firms attempt to work for advance orders and do not usually make cars for inventory.

The auto industry is the leading example of indivisibilities, but it is only one member of a numerous species. Indivisibilities are present and important throughout manufacturing industries. Transportation, gas pipelines, and more are other major examples of this phenomenon.

5   Conclusion

Under the cost conditions described in the preceding section, there is no equilibrium without an appropriate combination of cooperation and competition. Cooperation takes the form of suitable upper bounds on the quantities each firm may sell. Provided firms do not exceed their sales quotas, each may compete freely for customers. Given the appropriate sales quotas, buyers and sellers can reach an efficient equilibrium as a result of the forces of competition.

To say that unrestricted competition can have no equilibrium at all strikes against strongly held beliefs of some economists. Surely, say these economists, a price must always exist that can clear the market. It is not so. Existence of an equilibrium in a market depends on the nature of the property rights that the participants are allowed to have. Thus, if the sellers have avoidable costs, then, depending on the demand conditions, a seller and some buyers can have a mutually acceptable agreement among themselves resulting in a price that destroys the possibility of an equilibrium for the market as a whole. Only by suitably restraining competition among the firms can there be an equilibrium. The restraints on competition take the form of sales quotas. If these are well chosen, the result is an efficient equilibrium. This supplies part of the solution to the puzzle about the nature of competition in a modern economy.

CHAPTER 4

Stable coalitions

PART 1. STABLE COALITIONS WHOSE RETURNS ARE CONVEX FUNCTIONS

1 Introduction

In many important economic applications the return to a coalition is given by a convex function. For this reason the theory given here has two purposes. First, it explains which coalitions can form and survive when the return to a coalition is a convex function of its size and composition. Second, it describes the nature of the imputation of the returns to the coalition.

The size and composition of a coalition are represented by a vector in the nonnegative orthant of R^n. Let t denote such a vector. Its ith coordinate shows how many members of type i belong to the coalition represented by the vector t. Since the coordinates of t are nonnegative numbers, t_i measures the size of type i membership in t. Think of a very large number of participants so that one individual is a very small fraction of the total number like him. A subcoalition of t is a vector s with $0 \leq s \leq t$. Such a subcoalition will secede from t if it can get more doing this than by remaining in the grand coalition. Let the function $f(s)$ denote the return to a subcoalition s so that $f(t)$ represents the return to the whole group. The latter can divide the total return among its members so that each one of the same type i gets x_i and together all members of this type get $x_i t_i$. Thus, all members of the same type divide their total imputation equally among themselves. The imputation of the total return is given by a vector x in R^n whose ith coordinate, x_i, shows how much goes to each member of type i. The total imputation is subject to the constraint that it cannot exceed the maximum return available to the whole group. Therefore, the imputation of the total return, which is $\sum_{i=1}^{n} x_i t_i$, must satisfy the inequality as follows:

$$\sum_{i=1}^{n} x_i t_i \leq f(t). \tag{1}$$

In order to simplify the notation, denote the sum $\sum x_i t_i$ by the scalar

74

product xt. With this notation the imputation of the total return going to the subcoalition s becomes the scalar product xs if it joins the grand coalition t or it can obtain $f(s)$ by remaining separate. It joins or not depending on which alternative yields the larger return. Let $\pi(s)$ denote the maximal return of the coalition s. Consequently,

$$\pi(s) = \max\{xs, f(s)\}. \tag{2}$$

If there is an imputation x such that for all s with $0 \leqq s \leqq t$, it is true that

$$\pi(s) = xs, s \neq t, \text{ and } f(t) = xt, \tag{3}$$

then call t a stable coalition. It is appropriate to describe t as a stable coalition under these circumstances because the return to t, which is given by $f(t)$, is big enough to satisfy all legitimate demands of any subcoalition. Therefore, t can survive. When (3) is true, no subcoalition of t can do better on its own than as a member of the grand coalition. Note that (3) applies to the grand coalition itself. For a stable grand coalition (1) must hold with equality. Therefore, a necessary and sufficient condition for the stability of t is the existence of an imputation x satisfying (1) with equality such that for all $s: 0 \leqq s \leqq t, s \neq t$, x can also satisfy

$$xs \geqq f(s). \tag{4}$$

This is to say that t is a stable coalition if and only if the function f admits a nonempty core.

Though it is important to study conditions implying a nonempty core, it is at least as important to analyze situations for which the core is empty. When the core is empty, the grand coalition is unstable thereby raising the question of what is then likely to happen. We shall study these problems on the hypothesis that $f(t)$ is a convex function of t on the whole nonnegative orthant of R^n. Interest in convex functions is explained by the fact that in many significant economic applications, the return to a coalition is a convex function of its size and composition. A leading example follows.

Assume there are n types of participants such that the benefit each type i person derives from a bundle of m goods is given by the concave function, $B^i(q)$, where q is a vector in R^m. Each member of the coalition s gets the same quantity of each of the m goods. The goods are called semiprivate if the coalition can prevent nonmembers from getting them. If everyone can get the same quantities of the goods whether or not they belong to the given coalition, then the goods are called public goods. For now the important point is that each person gets the same

q. Let $C(q)$ denote the total cost of q. Define the net benefit to a coalition s as follows:

$$\sum_i s_i B^i(q) - C(q) = sB(q) - C(q).$$

Assume the coalition s can choose q in order to maximize its net benefit. This means the goods are semiprivate. If the goods were public, it would raise questions about how the coalition can determine q without consulting those outside the coalition who are affected by its choice of q. These complications are absent for semiprivate goods. Even so analysis of the simpler situation for semiprivate goods is very rewarding.

$$f(s) = \max_q [sB(q) - C(q)] \tag{5}$$

defines the return to s. If $C(q)$ is convex and strictly increasing, a maximum exists that is unique if each $B^i(q)$ is strictly concave. This formulation makes q an implicit function of s. In Section 6 it is shown that $f(s)$ is a convex function of s. Assume the core is not empty for this f. Let x_i denote the imputation of the total return going to a type i person. Write

$$\Theta_i = \alpha_i \bigg/ \sum_i t_i \alpha_i$$

so that

$$x_i = B^i(q) - \Theta_i C(q).$$

Consequently, the imputation x_i determines the fraction of the total cost, Θ_i, borne by a type i individual. According to this interpretation, each person pays enough to cover the total cost of the bundle q that is optimal for the grand coalition. Since the core is not empty by hypothesis, each person and each coalition is at least as well off by remaining in the grand coalition as by leaving it.

There are other examples of semiprivate goods for which it is better to define a somewhat different f. To be specific, consider a publication such as a magazine that covers m related topics. An example is *Scientific American*. Each issue contains articles on some of the topics it covers regularly. Let q_j denote the number of articles on topic j during a year. Let $B^i(q)$ define the benefit to a type i reader from the collection of articles represented by the m-vector q. All readers have access to the same articles so q does represent a semiprivate good. All readers do not necessarily derive the same benefit from the articles on a given topic. The theory reflects this by putting the superscript i on individual i's benefit function. Even though there is a diversity of interest among the readers, nevertheless all types can gain from a single publication owing to the saving of common costs made possible by their implicit cooperation. Let s_i denote the number of type i readers. The total cost to a coalition depends on its size and composition as well as on the number of articles published during a year. Let $G(s)$ denote the cost of printing and distributing the publication to the members of s and let $C(q)$ denote the cost of publishing the collection of articles q. The total cost is the sum of these two components. Define the net benefit as follows:

$$sB(q) - G(s) - C(q).$$

Assume a coalition s chooses that q which gives the maximal net benefit.

$$f(s) = \max_q [sB(q) - G(s) - C(q)]. \tag{6}$$

The presence of the term $G(s)$ affects the shape of f. In contrast to (5), this f is not necessarily convex in s. It would be if $G(s)$ were a concave function of s. For instance, if $G(s)$ were a linear function of s because the cost of printing and distributing the publication were a linear function of s, then f would be a convex function of s.

In this example a coalition may choose articles more closely related to the interests of its members than would the grand coalition. Thus, suppose the coalition s had much interest in astronomy. They would prefer a magazine with articles closely related to astronomy. Another coalition might prefer articles on botany. Together the two coalitions would reduce the number of specialized articles in each category in favor of less specialized articles on both topics.

Semiprivate goods fall between the two extremes of private and public goods. A coalition of two or more persons can choose the common quantities of semiprivate goods and prevent anyone from using them without their consent. Some may wish to regard semiprivate goods as a general category on a continuum that has private goods at one extreme and public goods at the other. It is better to preserve explicit distinctions among private, semiprivate, and public goods. A public good must have two attributes; first, it is prohibitively expensive to prevent anyone in the grand coalition from being affected by such a good and, second, an increase in the consumption of the services of such a good by any individual or group does not reduce the services another can obtain from the same good. Semiprivate goods have the second attribute but do not have the first because a coalition can confine the benefits from its semiprivate goods to its own members. If all individuals can agree on the common quantities of semiprivate goods, then these can become the universal choice and are thereby induced to become public goods. This is in contrast to autonomous public goods for which it is wholly impractical to prevent their effects on any given individual or coalition of individuals. A swimming pool is a semiprivate good. A public official is an autonomous public good. A magazine that everyone reads is an example of an induced public good since it is a semiprivate good that the grand coalition chooses. A loaf of bread is a private good in most places. As is well known, one cannot both have and eat a loaf of bread, and what one person eats becomes unavailable for another. This may not be true of a magazine article if it does not diminish the supply of the article when one person reads it.

Another factor distinguishes private from other goods: There are two kinds of semiprivate and public goods. The first kind somewhat resembles private goods. It is such that any individual or coalition can choose independently the quantity of goods of this kind, and the total quantity available to the grand coalition is the sum of these individual amounts. Think of knowledge. Each person can add to total knowledge so that the whole stock of knowledge is a semiprivate or public good depending on the nature of the property rights that society allows for intellectual goods. The second kind of semiprivate or public good is sharply different from private goods. Individuals and subcoalitions cannot make their own contributions to this kind. They must collectively agree on the total. Certain governmental activities seem to fall in this class such as defense and police powers. Some political process is used to determine the quantities of the second kind of semiprivate and public goods. For semiprivate goods the process is within the coalition while for public goods it is for the grand coalition. For the purpose of studying semiprivate goods, we may draw a veil over the political process because competition among coalitions is the dominating influence over the decision. For public goods of the second kind politics is of the essence. Since the analysis here refers to semiprivate goods, it becomes unnecessary to distinguish between these two kinds.

2   Definitions and basic properties

We shall study a class of certain convex functions whose domain is the nonnegative orthant of R^n, which is denoted by Ω^n. We shall need in addition the closed, bounded convex set $T(t)$ defined as follows:

$$T(t) = \{s: s \leqq t, t \geqq 0 \text{ and } s \in \Omega^n\}. \tag{1}$$

The vector t is a fixed semipositive point in Ω^n that represents the grand coalition while s is a subcoalition. A function f is convex if

$$f[\theta r + (1 - \theta)s] \leq \theta f(r) + (1 - \theta)f(s) \tag{2}$$

is true for all θ with $0 \leq \theta \leq 1$ and for all r and s in the domain of f. We shall confine our attention to the class of convex functions that have finite subgradients. A subgradient of f at a point s is an n-vector, denote it $f^*(s)$, such that for all s and $s + \Delta s$ in the domain of f, it is true that

$$f(s + \Delta s) - f(s) \geq f^*(s) \, \Delta s. \tag{3}$$

In fact, this property (3) can be used as an alternative definition of a convex function since f is convex only if it satisfies (3). In case f has first-order partial derivatives, the coordinates of f^* are these derivatives. Note that Δs need not be nonnegative. The definition of a subgradient only requires that $s + \Delta s$ be in the domain of f. Some or even all of the coordinates of Δs may be negative.

Two coalitions can gain by joining together if the function describing their returns is superadditive. A coalition can raise its return by expanding its size without changing the relative composition of its membership if the function describing its return is superhomogeneous. Formally, the definitions of superadditivity and superhomogeneity are as follows.

Definition: A function $g(\cdot)$ is superadditive if

$$g(r + s) \geq g(r) + g(s) \tag{4}$$

is true for all points in the domain of g. It is superhomogeneous if for all $\alpha > 1$,

$$g(\alpha s) \geq \alpha g(s). \tag{5}$$

In the analysis below it will be important to distinguish between convex functions that are superadditive on the whole nonnegative orthant and those that have this property on only some subset of Ω^n. However, for present purposes, this distinction is not necessary, and it suffices to assume there is some subset of Ω^n on which the function is superadditive.

Lemma 1: Let f be convex and superadditive. Then for all r, $s \geqq 0$,

$$f^*(r + s)s \geq f(s). \tag{6}$$

Proof: Using (3) and the hypothesis of superadditivity,

$$f^*(r + s)s \geq f(r + s) - f(r) \geq f(s) \qquad\blacksquare$$

Lemma 2: *Let f be convex.*

$$f(0) \leq 0; \tag{7}$$

$$f(\alpha s) \geq \alpha f(s) \quad \text{for all } \alpha \geq 1; \tag{8}$$

$$f^*(\alpha s)s > f(s) \quad \text{for all } \alpha > 1. \tag{9}$$

Then (7) $\Leftrightarrow$ (8) $\Leftrightarrow$ (9).

Proof: (7) $\Rightarrow$ (8). By convexity, $0 \leq \theta \leq 1$,

$$f[\theta s + (1 - \theta)0] \leq \theta f(s) + (1 - \theta)f(0) \leq \theta f(s).$$

Take $r = \theta s$ so that $s = \alpha r$ with $\alpha = 1/\theta \geq 1$. Consequently,

$$f(r) \leq (1/\alpha)f(\alpha r) \Rightarrow \alpha f(r) \leq f(\alpha r) \quad \text{for all } \alpha \geq 1.$$

(8) $\Rightarrow$ (9). Using (3) [or (6)] and (8),

$$f^*(\alpha s)(\alpha s - s) \geq f(\alpha s) - f(s) \geq \alpha f(s) - f(s)$$

$$\Rightarrow (\alpha - 1)f^*(\alpha s)s \geq (\alpha - 1)f(s). \tag{10}$$

Since $\alpha - 1 > 0$, (9) is an implication of (10).

(9) $\Rightarrow$ (7). Set $s = 0$ in (9). $\qquad\blacksquare$

Corollary: *If $\lim f^*(\alpha s)s$ exists as $\alpha \to 1^+$ and $f(0) \leq 0$, then*

$$f^*(s)s \geq f(s). \tag{11}$$

Proof: Immediate from (9). $\qquad\blacksquare$

Lemma 2 gives three equivalent conditions for superhomogeneity of a convex function. The next result shows that every superadditive convex function must also be superhomogeneous. Hence superadditivity is sufficient for superhomogeneity of a convex function and superhomogeneity is necessary for superadditivity of a convex function.

Lemma 3: *Let f satisfy the hypotheses of Lemma 1. Then f is superhomogeneous.*

Proof: $f(0 + s) \geq f(0) + f(s) \Rightarrow f(0) \leq 0$ and the desired conclusion follows from Lemma 2. ∎

Summarizing, every convex superadditive function must satisfy (6), and every convex function satisfying (6) must also be superhomogeneous. Thus, (6) alone without the additional hypothesis of superadditivity implies that a convex function must be superhomogeneous. Although (6) is necessary for superadditivity of a convex function, it is not sufficient. It is useful to study the relation between (6) and superadditivity more generally. To this end consider Lemma 4.

Lemma 4: Let f be convex and satisfy (6). It follows that

$$f(r + s) \geq f(r) + f(s) \tag{12}$$

provided that either $s \leq r$ or that $r \leq s$.

Proof: $f^*(r + s)(r + s) - f(r) \geq f(r + s) - f(r) \geq f^*(r)s \geq f(s)$ is true if $s \leq r$. A similar argument applies if $r \leq s$. ∎

Given that f is convex and satisfies (6), this lemma shows there are pairs for which (12) is true. Consequently, f is not superadditive only if there is a pair r, s for which

$$f(r + s) = f(r) + f(s) \tag{13}$$

and some other pair, say p and q, such that

$$f(p + q) < f(p) + f(q). \tag{14}$$

Therefore, given s, the right side of (13) must rise more rapidly in some direction r_i than does the left side. This means that the ith coordinate of $f^*(r + s)$ is less than the ith coordinate of $f^*(r)$. This remark completes the proof of:

Corollary 1: If f is convex and for all r, $s \in \Omega^n$ it is true that: $f^*(r + s)(r + s) \geq f(r + s)$, then f is not superadditive only if there is a pair r, s such that $f^*(r + s) \not\geq f^*(r)$.

In case f has second-order partial derivatives, Corollary 1 yields a useful result in terms of a local condition involving these.

Corollary 2: In addition to the hypotheses of Corollary 1, as-

sume f has second-order partial derivatives. It follows that f is not superadditive only if there is a point in the domain of f at which

$$\partial^2 f(t)/\partial^2 t_i\, \partial^2 t_j < 0, \qquad i \neq j.$$

When the hypotheses of Corollary 2 are true, it means that adding members of type j to a coalition t would lower the marginal return to the type i members of that coalition.

There is an important reason for dwelling on whether the function f is superadditive. Only superadditive functions can have a nonempty core. This assertion is true not only for convex functions but also more generally for any function describing the return of a coalition. This deserves a formal statement and proof given as follows.

> **Proposition 1:** Let the function g with domain $T(t)$ represent the return to a coalition $s \in T$. If g has a nonempty core on T, then it must be superadditive on T.

Proof: By hypothesis, g admits a nonempty core on T so there is a vector x giving the imputation of the total return to each type of participant that can satisfy all constraints as follows:

$$xt = g(t) \quad \text{and} \quad xs \geq g(s) \quad \text{for all } s \in T.$$

If g were not superadditive, then there would be a pair $r, s \in T$ such that

$$g(r + s) < g(r) + g(s). \tag{15}$$

Let y be an imputation such that

$$y(r + s) = g(r + s).$$

The core consists of all undominated imputations so that y cannot dominate x. It follows that

$$yr > g(r) \quad \text{and} \quad ys \geq g(s).$$

Consequently,

$$g(r + s) = y(r + s) > g(r) + g(s) \tag{16}$$

giving a contradiction of (15).   ∎

3   Extreme coalitions

This section shows how to simplify the analysis of the status of the core when the return to a coalition is a convex function. A convex function can admit a nonempty core if it can satisfy the demands of certain extreme coalitions. These extreme coalitions correspond to the verteces of the convex polyhedron, $T(t)$ defined in (2.1), that represents the set of all possible coalitions. Owing to this fact, it is unnecessary to consider the demands of all of the coalitions represented by the points in $T(t)$. It suffices instead to consider the demands of a finite number of them – those represented by the verteces of $T(t)$. Of course, this is a large number since $T(t)$ has 2^n verteces. Even so, there is another advantage because the reduction to a finite number of alternatives given by the verteces of $T(t)$ allows the use of linear programming to study the status of the core.

> **Definition:** *The ith coordinate of a vertex of T is either zero or t_i. An interior vector of T has no coordinate equal to zero or t_i. A semiextreme vector of T has at least one coordinate between zero and t_i and all of its remaining coordinates are either zero or t_i. Hence at least one and at most $n - 1$ coordinates of a semiextreme vector of T equal zero or t_i.*

A coalition corresponding to a vertex of T includes either none or all of the individuals of a given type i. These are the coalitions whose demands must be satisfied in order to have a nonempty core. If an imputation is capable of doing so, then it can satisfy the demands of all other coalitions in T.

> **Proposition 2:** *Let f be strictly convex and have a nonempty core on T.*
>
> (i) *No core constraint for an interior vector of T can be satisfied with equality.*
> (ii) *No core constraint for a semiextreme vector of T can be satisfied with equality.*

Proof: (i) By contradiction. Let s be an interior vector of T and let x be an imputation satisfying all of the core constraints. Suppose that

$$xs = f(s). \tag{1}$$

There is an $\alpha > 1$ such that $\alpha s \le t$. Since f is strictly convex and has a nonempty core, it must be superadditive by Proposition 1. This in turn implies it must be strictly superhomogeneous by Lemma 3. Hence by Lemma 2, if $\alpha > 1$, $f(\alpha s) > \alpha f(s)$. Then it would follow from (1) that

$$x(\alpha s) = \alpha f(s) < f(\alpha s). \tag{2}$$

But $\alpha s \in T$ so that (2) would give a contradiction of the hypothesis that x satisfies all core constraints. Hence there cannot be equality in (1) for any x in the core and any interior s in T.

(ii) By contradiction. Suppose (1) were true for a coalition s that is neither a vertex nor an interior point of T. This would mean that

$$s = \langle s_1, s_2, \ldots, s_m, t_{m+1}, \ldots, t_n \rangle$$

and at least one $s_i > 0$. Write

$$s = q + r \tag{3}$$

where q is a vertex and r includes all positive coordinates of s that are less than the corresponding coordinates of t. Since x is in the core by hypothesis,

$$xq \geq f(q) \quad \text{and} \quad x(r + \Delta r + q) \geq f(r + \Delta r + q).$$

There is no loss of generality by assuming $s_i > 0$ if $i = 1, \ldots, m$ so that

$$q = \langle 0, 0, \ldots, 0, t_{m+1}, \ldots, t_n \rangle,$$
$$r = \langle s_1, s_2, \ldots, s_m, 0, \ldots, 0 \rangle.$$

Observe that q and r are orthogonal so that $qr = 0$. There are Δr_i with

$$0 < \Delta r_i < t_i - r_i, \qquad i = 1, \ldots, m, \tag{4}$$

and θ with $0 < \theta < 1$ such that

$$s_i = (1 - \theta)(s_i + \Delta r_i). \tag{5}$$

This is to say that it is possible to choose Δr_i to satisfy (4) and (5) and find θ inside the unit interval to satisfy (5). Consequently, θ and Δr satisfy

$$r = (1 - \theta)(r + \Delta r). \tag{6}$$

If f is strictly convex,

$$\theta f(q) + (1 - \theta)f(r + \Delta r + q)$$

$$> f(q + (1 - \theta)(r + \Delta r)). \quad (7)$$

Appealing to (6),

$$\theta f(q) + (1 - \theta)f(r + \Delta r + q) > f(q + r) = f(s). \quad (8)$$

Since x is in the core,

$$xq \geq f(q) \quad \text{and} \quad x(r + \Delta r + q) \geq f(r + \Delta r + q). \quad (9)$$

It is an implication of (9) that

$$x[\theta q + (1 - \theta)(r + \Delta r + q)] \geq \theta f(q)$$

$$+ (1 - \theta)f(r + \Delta r + q). \quad (10)$$

From (10) it would follow that

$$xs = f(s) > f(s),$$

which is a contradiction. ∎

In contrast with what has gone before, Proposition 2 assumes a strictly convex f. Now a convex function is not strictly convex if and only if it is piecewise linear or is homogeneous of degree 1. In the latter case it is subadditive unless it is actually linear. Hence a nonlinear convex function that is not strictly convex must have an empty core because it would fail to satisfy a necessary condition for a nonempty core, namely, superadditivity. A linear function always has a nonempty core, but this is a trivial case since there is no incentive to form coalitions. We may conclude that the proposition fails to cover a superadditive, piecewise linear convex function.

The reduction to consideration of extreme coalitions uses the following important result.

> **Lemma 5:** *Let f be strictly convex and have a nonempty core on T. Let x be any imputation in the core. Then*
>
> $$x \leq f^*(t), \quad (11)$$
>
> *where $f^*(t)$ denotes a subgradient of f at t.*

Proof: Define the function

$$h(s) = f(s) - xs, \quad (12)$$

which is strictly convex and superadditive because f has these attributes. Moreover, since x is in the core, $h(s) \leq 0$ and $h(t) = 0$. Hence, for all $s \in T$,

$$0 \geq h(s) - h(t) \geq h^*(t)(s - t) \tag{13}$$

and $s - t \leq 0$. Consequently,

$$h^*(t) = f^*(t) - x \geq 0. \qquad \blacksquare$$

It follows from this result that in case f has a nonempty core, the imputation of no participant can exceed the marginal contribution of that type to the grand coalition.

With the aid of these results we can derive a finite number of linear constraints such that any imputation of the total return capable of satisfying these constraints is in the core. Define the imputation of a type i participant as follows:

$$x_i = f_i^*(T^N) - a_i/t_i, \tag{14}$$

where T^N is the vertex of T that includes all participants of every type and $a_i \geq 0$ gives the excess of the marginal contribution over the imputation for type i participants. According to (14), the excess is shared equally among the participants of the same type. Let T^S denote a vertex of T where S is the set of positive coordinates in the vertex. The imputation x is in the core if and only if it can satisfy the inequalities as follows:

$$\sum x_i t_i = \sum f_i^*(T^N) t_i - \sum a_i \leq f(T^N),$$

$$\sum_{i \in S} x_i t_i = \sum f_i^*(T^N) t_i - \sum a_i \geq f(T^S). \tag{15}$$

In order to have a more concise notation, introduce the indicator function of a set S, $\phi(S)$, so that $\phi(S)$ is an n-vector whose ith coordinate is 1 if the ith coordinate of T^S is t_i and is 0 if the ith coordinate of T^S is 0. Using this convenient notation, we can write (15) in the shape as follows:

$$\phi(N)x = f^*(T^N)T^N - \phi(N)a \leq f(T^N), \tag{16}$$

$$\phi(S)x = f^*(T^N)T^S - \phi(S)a \geq f(T^S). \tag{17}$$

Next, define $F(S)$ so that for all $S \subseteq N$,

$$F(S) = f^*(T^N)T^S - f(T^S). \tag{18}$$

The core is not empty if and only if there is an n-vector $a \geq 0$ such that

$$\phi(N)a \geq F(N), \tag{19}$$

$$\phi(S)a \leq F(S) \quad \text{for all } S \subset N. \tag{20}$$

As we shall see, a systematic study of the status of the core and its properties can proceed by an analysis of the finite system of linear inequalities in (19) and (20). This analysis relies on a crucial fact con-, tained in the following result.

Lemma 6: *Let f be strictly convex and superadditive;*

$$0 < F(S) < F(N) \tag{21}$$

is true for all $S \subseteq N$.

Proof: The hypotheses allow us to apply Lemma 1, and strict convexity gives

$$f^*(r + s)s > f(s).$$

Since $T^S \leq T^N$ for all $S \subseteq N$,

$$F(S) = f^*(T^N)T^S - f(T^S) > 0.$$

By strict convexity,

$$f^*(T^N)(T^N - T^S) > f(T^N) - f(T^S).$$

Rearranging terms,

$$F(N) = f^*(T^N)T^N - f(T^N) > f^*(T^N)T^S - f(T^S) = F(S). \quad \blacksquare$$

4 Properties of the imputations for a superadditive, strictly convex function

A nonnegative solution of the system of linear inequalities (3.19 and 3.20) must be in the core. However, even when $f(\cdot)$ is superadditive and strictly convex, it is not necessarily true that this system of linear inequalities does have a nonnegative solution. A more general approach is desirable – one that yields a point in the core when the core is not empty and that yields a point as close as possible to satisfying the core constraints when the core is empty.

At the outset consider the implications of an empty core. We require that each type of participant gets an imputation that does not exceed the marginal contribution of that type to the grand coalition. When the core is empty, it means that for any $a \geqq 0$ satisfying $\phi(N)a = F(N)$, there is at least one coalition S such that $\phi(S)a > F(S)$. This in turn means that the coalition S would receive an imputation below the return $f(T^S)$ that it could receive on its own. It would, therefore, have an objection to such an imputation and its objection is measured by the size of the difference between $f(T^S)$ and the imputation of the total return that it would obtain from the grand coalition. Given an empty core, for any $a \geqq 0$ with $\phi(N)a = F(N)$, there is at least one coalition S with an objection to a.

We can imagine at least two ways of handling the situation arising when the core is empty. One is to separate the participants into distinct coalitions that will not affect each other. Sometimes this is possible by an appropriate definition of property rights and the means of enforcing these rights. The creation of semiprivate goods is sometimes such a means. However, depending on the particular application, it may not be possible to create such semiprivate goods because the nature of the choices available to the grand coalition has unavoidable effects on individuals and subcoalitions of individuals. For example, it is hard to imagine how someone can be deprived of the benefit of national defense. A second alternative suggests itself as a consequence of the very situation giving an empty core: Choose an imputation of the total return that gives the minimum of the maximum difference between the return of a coalition and its imputation of the total return from the grand coalition. This procedure minimizes the maximum objection by any coalition. Imputations with this property are solutions of a linear programming problem that constitute the subject of this section.

Consider the following linear programming problem. (I shall use the convention that lowercase Greek letters denote scalars.)

Primal: *min* β *with respect to* $a \geqq 0, \beta \geq 0$

subject to

$$-\phi(N)a + F(N) \leq 0, \qquad \delta_N \geq 0, \tag{1}$$

$$\phi(S)a - F(S) - \beta \leq 0, \qquad \delta_S \geq 0. \tag{2}$$

Dual: *max*$[\delta_N F(N) - \sum \delta_S F(S)]$

with respect to $\delta_N, \delta_S \geq 0$

subject to

$$1 - \sum \delta_S \geq 0, \qquad \beta \geq 0, \tag{3}$$

$$\sum \delta_S \phi(S) - \delta_N \phi(N) \geq 0, \qquad a \geqq 0. \tag{4}$$

We first show the constraints are feasible. On the one hand, if the core is not empty, then the primal constraints have a solution with $\beta = 0$ and $a \geqq 0$; on the other hand, if the core is empty, they have a solution with $a \geqq 0$ and β positive and large enough. The dual constraints are always feasible – take $\delta_N = \delta_S = 0$. Since both the dual and primal constraints always have feasible solutions, the duality theorem of linear programming applies, and we may conclude that

$$\min \beta = \max[\delta_N F(N) - \sum \delta_S F(S)]. \tag{5}$$

The core is not empty if and only if $\min \beta = 0$. If f is strictly convex and superadditive, then by Lemma 6,

$$F(N) > F(S) > 0.$$

Consequently, $\sum \delta_S F(S) \geq 0$ so that

$$\min \beta > 0 \Rightarrow \delta_N > 0 \Rightarrow -\phi(N)a + F(N) = 0.$$

This completes the proof of:

> **Lemma 7:** Let f be strictly convex and superadditive. If the core is empty so that $\min \beta > 0$, then (1) must be satisfied with equality.

Next we prove:

> **Lemma 8:** $\delta_N \leq 1$.

Proof: Since $\phi(S)$ is the indicator function of a proper subset of N, it follows that $\phi(S) \leq \phi(N)$. This in turn implies that $\delta_S \phi(S) \leq \delta_S \phi(N)$. Summing gives

$$\sum \delta_S \phi(S) \leq (\sum \delta_S) \phi(N). \tag{6}$$

But $\sum \delta_S \leq 1$ from (3), and (6) in conjunction with (4) implies that

$$0 \leq \delta_N \phi(N) \leq \sum \delta_S \phi(S) \leq (\sum \delta_S) \phi(N) \leq \phi(N)$$

from which we have the desired conclusion. ∎

> **Lemma 9:** If the core is not empty, then the solution of the primal problem gives $a_i > 0$ for all i.

Proof: Assume a nonempty core so that $\min \beta = 0$. Suppose that some $a_i = 0$. Let $S = \{a_i: a_i > 0\}$ so that $\bar{S} = N - S \neq \emptyset$. It would follow that

$$F(S) < F(N) \le \phi(N)a = \phi(S)a \le F(S)$$

giving a contradiction.   ∎

Summarizing, min β = 0 implies $a > 0$ and min $\beta > 0$ is consistent with $a \ge 0$ so that one or more a_i may be zero. As we shall see, there is a sharper result for an empty core. To get this result, we need the following lemma.

Lemma 10: *If the core is empty, then $\delta_N = 1$.*

Proof: In the proof of Lemma 7 we see that min $\beta > 0$ implies $\delta_N > 0$. Dividing through by $\delta_N > 0$ in (5) gives

$$F(N) - \sum (\delta_S/\delta_N)F(S) = \beta/\delta_N > \beta \qquad (7)$$

if $\delta_N < 1$. Now δ_S/δ_N satisfies the dual constraints (4) so that (7) would imply

$$F(N) - \sum (\delta_S/\delta_N)F(S) > \max[\delta_N F(N) - \sum \delta_S F(S)] = \beta,$$

which is impossible.   ∎

The next result we shall prove is the converse of Lemma 9. To do so let us recall some facts about solutions of linear programming problems. The solutions are on a convex polyhedron, a figure that has a finite number of verteces. In the present application each vertex has $n + 1$ coordinates, n for a, which is in R^n, and one for β, which is in R^1. The $n + 1$ coordinates of a vertex are the unique solution of $n + 1$ linearly independent equations from among the constraints of the primal problem, (1) and (2).

Lemma 11: $a > 0 \Rightarrow \beta = 0$.

Proof: By contradiction. Assume $a > 0$ and suppose that $\beta > 0$. It would follow from Lemma 10 that $\delta_N = 1$ on every vertex containing the solutions so that the coordinates of a vertex would satisfy

$$\phi(N)a = F(N),$$

$$\phi(S_i)a = F(S_i) + \beta, \qquad i = 1, \ldots, n.$$

Therefore,

$$\phi(N - S_i)a = F(N) - F(S_i) - \beta > 0$$

because $a > 0$ by hypothesis. Hence

$$\beta < F(N) - F(S_i),$$

and since $\sum \delta_{S_i} = 1$ because we suppose $\beta > 0$, it would follow that

$$\beta = \sum \delta_{S_i}\beta < \sum \delta_{S_i}[F(N) - F(S_i)] = F(N) - \sum \delta_{S_i}F(S_i).$$

But

$$F(N) - \sum \delta_{S_i}F(S_i) = \beta$$

is an implication of Lemma 10, so there is a contradiction. Hence $\beta = 0$. ∎

A summary of these results is as follows.

Proposition 3: $a > 0 \Leftrightarrow \beta = 0$.

Proof: By Lemma 9, $\beta = 0 \Rightarrow a > 0$. By Lemma 11, $a > 0 \Rightarrow \beta = 0$. ∎

We now have important information about the properties of the imputations. If the core is empty, then the imputation of at least one type must equal its net marginal contribution to the grand coalition (its $a_i = 0$), and the imputations of the remaining types must be less than their marginal contributions. Another way of describing this is in terms of subsidies. Given an empty core, there are always present some types who must subsidize those who receive an imputation equal to their marginal contribution. In contrast, when the core is not empty each participant receives an imputation that is less than its marginal contribution to the grand coalition. This means each person pays some of the cost of the common goods so that no one is a free loader. Still another interpretation is in terms of pricing. Imputations in the core resemble two-part prices – one part to cover the variable and the other part to cover the fixed cost. A nonempty core requires $a > 0$ so that everyone helps pay for the fixed cost and no one pays a price equal solely to the marginal cost.

Proposition 3 has an interesting corollary. Assume the core is empty so that $\beta > 0$. Define the set S as follows:

$$S = \{a_i: a_i > 0\}$$

and the complement of S, $\overline{S} = N - S$. It is an implication of Proposition 3 that $\overline{S} \neq \varnothing$ when $\beta > 0$. Let R denote a subset of $\overline{S}$:

$$F(N) = \phi(N)a = \phi(R + S)a \leq F(R + S) + \beta$$

so that

$$\beta \geq F(N) - F(R + S)$$

is true for all R. This proves:

> **Corollary:** *If the core is empty so that* $\beta > 0$, *then*
>
> $$\beta \geq \max[F(N) - F(R + S)] \qquad (8)$$
>
> *for all* $R \subseteq \overline{S}$.

Now $F(N) - F(R + S)$ is the incremental contribution of the coalition

$$N - (S + R) = \overline{S} - R.$$

Since R is a subset of $\overline{S}$, $\overline{S} - R$ is the complement of R with respect to $\overline{S}$. The corollary asserts that β must be at least as great as the maximal incremental contribution of subsets of $\overline{S}$ to N. That is, β must exceed the maximal incremental contribution to the grand coalition of those participants who get an imputation equal to their marginal contribution to the coalition of all types. This vividly shows the necessity of subsidies when the core is empty.

Though the solution of the linear programming problem gives a unique value of β, it does not necessarily give unique a_i's. In case the solution of a is not unique, it is desirable to study particular solutions having certain attributes. Among these is one of special interest. It is the one that minimizes σ, the maximum departure from imputations equal to the marginal net benefit. This leads to the following linear programming problem.

Primal: min σ with respect to a, $\sigma \geqq 0$

subject to

$$-\phi(N)a \leq -F(N) \qquad\qquad \alpha_N, \qquad\qquad (9)$$

$$\phi(S)a \leq F(S) + \beta_0, \qquad \alpha_S, \qquad\qquad (10)$$

$$a_i \leq \sigma, \qquad\qquad\qquad \mu_i, \qquad\qquad\qquad (11)$$

where $\beta_0 = \min \beta$ determined by the solution of the linear programming problem given by (1)–(4).

Dual: $\quad \max[\alpha_N F(N) - \sum \alpha_S(F(S) + \beta_0)]$

with respect to $\alpha_N, \alpha_S \geq 0$

subject to

$$1 - \sum \mu_i \geq 0, \qquad \sigma, \qquad (12)$$

$$-\alpha_N \phi(N) + \alpha_S \phi(S) + u \geq 0, \qquad a, \qquad (13)$$

where $u = \langle \mu_1, \ldots, \mu_n \rangle$. The existence of solutions of the dual and primal constraints is guaranteed by the choice of β_0. Hence the duality theorem of linear programming gives

$$\min \sigma = \max[\alpha_N F(N) - \sum \alpha_S(F(S) + \beta_0)]. \qquad (14)$$

Since $F(N) > 0$, it is an implication of (9) that

$$\phi(N)a \geq F(N) > 0$$

so that at least one $a_i > 0$. But then (11) implies σ must be positive. It therefore follows from (14) that α_N must be positive so the constraints (9) and (12) must be satisfied as equalities. Therefore, at least one μ_i must be positive and at least one a_i, corresponding to this μ_i, actually equals σ in (11). Summarizing, there is:

Lemma 12: *$\sigma > 0$, $\alpha_N > 0$, $\phi(N)a = F(N)$, $\sum \mu_i = 1$, and for at least one i, $a_i = \sigma$.*

Corollary 1: *$\sigma \geq F(N)/n$.*

Proof: $F(N) = \phi(N)a \leq n\sigma$. ∎

A more general result along these lines is as follows.

Corollary 2: *$\sigma \geq \max_S [F(N) - F(S) - \beta_0]/(n - M_S)$, where M_S is the number of types in S so that $M_S = \phi(N)\phi(S)'$.*

Proof: This is straightforward. We have

$$\phi(N)a = F(N),$$

$$\phi(S)a \leq F(S) + \beta_0,$$

which together imply that

$$(n - M_S)\sigma \geq \phi(N - S)a \geq F(N) - F(S) - \beta_0$$

from which the desired conclusion is immediate. ∎

The preceding two corollaries show that there is a tendency to make the a_i's equal as a result of the desire to minimize the maximum departure from imputations equal to the marginal net benefit. This becomes more visible from an examination of the $n + 1$ linearly independent equations that a solution must satisfy given as follows:

$$\phi(N)a = F(N),$$

$$\phi(S_i)a = F(S_i) + \beta_0, \qquad i = 1, \ldots, k \leq n,$$

$$a_i = \sigma, \qquad\qquad i = k + 1, \ldots, n.$$

There are two extreme alternatives: 1^0, $k = n$ or 2^0, $k = 0$. In the first with $k = n$, the solution of this linear programming problem coincides with a vertex of the solution of the linear programming problem that determines β_0. In this case σ is the largest coordinate of the a that is the solution of the β_0 LP problem and the a is unique. Under the second alternative all types get the same $a_i = \sigma > 0$. Therefore, appealing to Proposition 3, the core must not be empty. That is, one can have the same a_i for all participants only if there is a nonempty core. It is in this sense that a nonempty core is conducive to equal treatment of all participants while an empty core is not.

5   Totally kind functions

The analysis in the preceding section applies to strictly convex functions whether or not they admit a nonempty core. The analysis in this section applies to a particular class of strictly convex functions that admit a nonempty core for all $t \in \Omega^n$. It is especially important to distinguish between functions having a nonempty core for all $t \geq 0$ and those that have a nonempty core for one or more $t \geq 0$. The class of functions that can admit a nonempty core for all $t \in \Omega^n$ is subject to more restrictions than the one that can do so for only some $t \in \Omega^n$. Therefore, the former is a smaller class than the latter.

Definition
(i) *A totally kind function has a nonempty core for all $t \in \Omega^n$.*
(ii) *A partly kind function has a nonempty core for at least one $t \in \Omega^n$.*

Since every totally kind function is partly kind, the latter is a bigger class of functions. An immediate consequence of this definition by Proposition 1 is that a totally kind function must be superadditive on the whole nonnegative orthant while a partly kind function must be superadditive only on $T(t)$. A more important result applies to strictly convex and totally kind function. For such functions not only is superadditivity necessary for kindness but also it is sufficient. This is to say that a strictly convex function has a nonempty core on the whole nonnegative orthant Ω^n if and only if it is superadditive on Ω^n. The same may not be said for strictly convex and partly kind functions. For these functions there are sufficient conditions for partial kindness but no necessary and sufficient conditions are known.

We begin by recalling the definition of a strictly increasing function.

> **Definition:** A function g is strictly increasing on Ω^n if for all s and for all $t \geq s$, it is true that
>
> $$g(s) < g(t). \tag{1}$$

This definition deserves careful consideration. It imposes a strong condition on the function g. By this definition (1) is true for any $t \in \Omega^n$ and for all $s \in \Omega^n$ such that $s \leq t$. It would be possible to have a function such that given an arbitrary $s \in \Omega^n$, there exists at least one $t \geq s$ such that (1) is true, but (1) would not be true for all $t \geq s$ and arbitrary $s \in \Omega^n$. That is, there are functions for which (1) would be true for *some* $t \geq s$ but not for *all* $t \geq s$. We require the latter and stronger condition.

> **Lemma 13:** Define the concave function g(s) as follows:
>
> $$g(s) = f^*(t)s - f(s), \tag{2}$$
>
> where $f(s)$ is a convex function. Assume that g(s) is strictly increasing. It follows that for arbitrary $t \in \Omega^n$ and for all $s \leq t$,
>
> $$g^*(s) > 0, \tag{3}$$
>
> where $g^*(s)$ denotes the supergradient of the concave function g.

Proof: By concavity,

$$g(t) - g(s) \leq g^*(s)(t - s). \tag{4}$$

By hypothesis, $g(\cdot)$ is a strictly increasing function so (1) is true. Hence

$$0 < g(t) - g(s) \leq g^*(s)(t - s) \tag{5}$$

is true for arbitrary $t \in \Omega^n$ and for all $s \leq t$. Therefore,

$$0 < \sum g_i^*(s)(t_i - s_i)$$

for all $t_i - s_i \geq 0$, provided the latter inequality is strict for at least one i. Take

$$t_j = s_j \quad \text{if } j \neq i$$

so that $g_i^*(s)(t_i - s_i) > 0$. Hence $g_i^*(s) > 0$. ∎

Corollary

$$g^*(s) = f^*(t) - f^*(s) > 0. \tag{6}$$

Proof: Immediate from (3). ∎

The inequality (4) is valid for any concave function that has a finite supergradient. Since we assume that the convex f has a finite subgradient, it follows that g does have a finite supergradient. Concavity alone does not of course, imply $g^*(s)$ is positive. It would follow from concavity that

$$[g^*(t) - g^*(s)](t - s) \leq 0. \tag{7}$$

On the basis of this foundation, the next result is immediate.

Lemma 14: *Let f be strictly convex and superadditive on Ω^n. It follows that $g(s)$ defined in (2) is a strictly increasing concave function so that inequality (6) is true for all $t \in \Omega^n$ and $s \leq t$.*

Proof: The argument in Lemma 6 together with Lemma 1 now applies almost word for word and yields

$$0 < f^*(t)s - f(s) < f^*(t)t - f(t).$$

Hence $g(s)$ is strictly increasing so that (3) is true by Lemma 13 and (6) is true by the corollary. ∎

Condition (6) together with the assumption $f(0) \leq 0$ is sufficient for superadditivity as the next result shows.

Lemma 15: *Let $f(0) \leq 0$. Let f be convex and satisfy (6) for all $t \in \Omega^n$ and for all $s \leq t$. It follows that*

$$f(s + r) - f(s) \le f(t + r) - f(t) \tag{8}$$

is true for all r and t $\in \Omega^n$ *and for all* $s \le t$ *so f is superadditive.*

Proof: Define the sequence $\{s_i\}$ so that

$$s_{i+1} = s_i + \alpha(t - s_0), \qquad \alpha = 1/m, s_0 = s, s_m = t.$$

By virtue of the hypothesis of convexity,

$$f(s_{i+1} + r) - f(s_i + r) \ge f^*(s_i + r)(s_{i+1} - s_i).$$

Appealing to (6), it follows that

$$f^*(s_i + r)(s_{i+1} - s_i) \ge f^*(s_i)[\alpha(t - s_0)].$$

Therefore,

$$f(s_{i+1} + r) - f(s_i + r) \ge f(s_i) - f(s_{i-1}). \tag{9}$$

It is an implication of (9) that

$$\sum_{i=0}^{m-1} [f(s_{i+1} + r) - f(s_i + r)] \ge \sum_{i=0}^{m-1} [f(s_i) - f(s_{i-1})],$$

which reduces to

$$f(s_m + r) - f(s_{m-1}) \ge f(s_0 + r) - f(s_{-1}).$$

Therefore,

$$f(s_m + r) - f(s_m) + f(s_m) - f(s_{m-1})$$
$$\ge f(s_0 + r) - f(s_0) + f(s_0) - f(s_{-1}).$$

By convexity,

$$f^*(s_m)(s_m - s_{m-1}) \ge f(s_m) - f(s_{m-1}),$$

and

$$f(s_0) - f(s_{-1}) \ge f^*(s_{-1})(s_0 - s_{-1}).$$

Therefore,

$$f(s_m + r) - f(s_m) \ge f(s_0 + r) - f(s_0)$$
$$- [f^*(s_m) - f^*(s_{-1})][\alpha(t - s_0)].$$

Define δ_m so that

$$\delta_m = [f^*(s_m) - f^*(s_{-1})][\alpha(t - s_0)] \geq 0$$

holds for all m. As $m \to \infty$, $\delta_m \to 0$ and $s_{-1} = s_0 + \alpha(t - s) \to s_0$,

$$f(t + r) - f(t) \geq f(s + r) - f(s) - \delta_m,$$

which implies the desired conclusion (8). Rearranging (8) yields

$$f(t + r) \geq f(t) + f(s + r) - f(s). \tag{10}$$

Let $s = 0$ and (10) gives the implication of superadditivity.   ∎

The crucial step in the argument linking superadditivity to total kindness of a strictly convex function is inequality (6), thanks to a fundamental result of Shapley (1971). Shapley studies the core of a convex game. The present situation where the return of each coalition is given by the strictly convex function f corresponds to what Shapley calls a convex measure game with an n-vector of measures given by the point t in the nonnegative orthant of R^n.

> **Definition:** *A convex measure game with a measure given by $t \in \Omega^n$ satisfies the condition as follows for all $r, t \in \Omega^n$ and $s \leq t$:*
>
> $$f(t + r) - f(t) \geq f(r + s) - f(s). \tag{11}$$

Shapley's principal result is that a game with a characteristic function satisfying (11) not only has a nonempty core but also that its core coincides with the Neumann–Morgenstern stable set and includes the Shapley value. On the basis of Lemmas 14, 15, and Shapley's theorem there is a stronger conclusion given as follows.

> **Proposition 4:** *Let f be strictly convex on Ω^n. The function f is totally kind if and only if it is superadditive on Ω^n.*

Proof: Necessity. This is Proposition 1.

Sufficiency. Assume f is superadditive on Ω^n. It follows from Lemma 14 that

$$f^*(s) < f^*(t) \tag{12}$$

is true for all $t \in \Omega^n$ and for all $s \leq t$. Lemma 15 applies and asserts that (8) is true. Hence Shapley's theorem gives the conclusion that f has a nonempty core for all $t \in \Omega^n$.   ∎

6   Application to semiprivate goods

Semiprivate goods are such that each member of a coalition gets the same quantity of each of the m semiprivate goods, and individuals outside the coalition neither bear the cost nor obtain the benefit of these goods. Semiprivate goods resemble private goods insofar as both the decision about how much to obtain and the cost of this decision resides within the grasp of the coalition itself and is not affected by outsiders. The relevant coalition is always an individual for a private good while for a semiprivate good it is one or more individuals. In case the coalition is one or more individuals, they must all agree on the common quantities of the semiprivate goods to have. This introduces a complication absent from the decision about private goods where each individual can decide for himself how much to have, taking into account his own cost and benefit of his own decision. Semiprivate goods also differ from public goods. The latter affect all members of the community, but semiprivate goods affect only the coalition that chooses its own quantities of these goods.

Given a coalition t contemplating how much of each of m semiprivate goods to have, it faces the problem of defection. Subcoalitions of t can decide for themselves how much q to have. Hence the coalition t is stable if and only if it can offer an imputation of the total return that is at least as good as what is available to any subcoalition. Following (1.5) the return to a coalition s is defined as follows:

$$f(s) = \max_q [\sum_i s_i B^i(q) - C(q)], \tag{1}$$

where $B^i(q)$ denotes the benefit to a participant of type i as a function of the bundle of m semiprivate goods,

$$q = \langle q_1, \ldots, q_m \rangle, \tag{2}$$

and $C(q)$ is the cost of q to the coalition s. More concisely, write

$$f(s) = sB[q(s)] - C[q(s)], \tag{3}$$

where $q(s)$ denotes the optimal choice for the coalition s so that q is an implicit function of s.

We must first verify that f is indeed a convex function of s given the hypotheses about $B^i(\cdot)$ and $C(\cdot)$. Following the discussion in Section 1, assume that each $B^i(\cdot)$ is concave and $C(\cdot)$ is convex. Let f_s denote the gradient of f with respect to s, and, more generally, subscripts denote the gradients:

$$f_s = B + sB_q \frac{dq}{ds} - C_q \frac{dq}{ds}$$

$$= B[q(s)]$$

(4)

by virtue of the fact that the first-order condition for a maximum net return to a coalition s with respect to q is that q satisfies

$$sB_q - C_q = 0$$

(5)

if the optimal $q(s) > 0$. For our purposes it is convenient and harmless to assume the latter is true. It follows from (4) that

$$f_{ss} = \left[\frac{\partial^2 f}{\partial s_i \, \partial s_k} \right] = B_q \frac{dq}{ds} .$$

(6)

Use (5) to obtain dq/ds.

$$B_q + sB_{qq} \frac{dq}{ds} - C_{qq} \frac{dq}{ds} = 0.$$

Solve this for dq/ds.

$$\frac{dq}{ds} = [sB_{qq} - C_{qq}]^{-1}(-B_q).$$

Substitute this expression for dq/ds in (6).

$$f_{ss} = -B_q[sB_{qq} - C_{qq}]^{-1}B_q.$$

(7)

The $n \times n$ matrix f_{ss} is positive definite if the $m \times m$ matrix $sB_{qq} - C_{qq}$ is negative definite. The latter is true if C_{qq} is positive definite and each B_{qq}^i is negative definite. This means that each B^i is a strongly concave function of q and C is a strongly convex function of q. Under these hypotheses the matrix

$$sB_{qq} - C_{qq}$$

is negative definite and so is its inverse. This completes the proof of:

> **Lemma 16:** *Let each $B^i(q)$ be strongly concave and let $C(q)$ be strongly convex. It follows that f is a convex function of s.*

Given that f is a convex function of s, the theory developed above is pertinent. Following the notation of the preceding sections, let x_i denote the imputation of the total return going to a type i person [cf. (3.14)], so that

$$a_i/t_i = f_i^*(t) - x_i$$

and

$$a_i = t_i \{B^i[q(t)] - x_i\} \geq 0. \tag{8}$$

This relies on (4) since

$$f_i^*(t) = B^i[q(t)]. \tag{9}$$

Thus, a_i measures the excess of the benefit to a type i individual over his imputation of the total return as established by the constraints imposed by the various coalitions. If $\sum x_i t_i = f(t)$, then

$$\sum_{i=1}^{n} a_i = C[q(t)]. \tag{10}$$

This means that just enough is collected from each member of the grand coalition to cover the total cost of $q(t)$, which is the optimal m-vector of semiprivate goods of this coalition. Moreover, if the core is empty, then on the basis of Proposition 3, at least one of the a_i's must be zero. It follows from (8) and (10) that such an individual makes no contribution to the total cost of $q(t)$. Stated differently, there must be free riders of semiprivate goods if the core is empty. Since an empty core means an unstable grand coalition, the hallmark of instability is the presence of free riders. On the other hand, everyone contributes to the cost of $q(t)$ when the core is not empty because in this case each a_i is positive.

The core can be nonempty for all possible sizes of the grand coalition if and only if f is superadditive, provided f is strictly convex. This has a simple interpretation. According to Lemmas 14 and 15 and Proposition 4, there is total kindness if and only if $f^*(t)$ is a strictly increasing function of t. In terms of our application this means that

$$B^i[q(s)] < B^i[q(t)]. \tag{11}$$

That is, there is total kindness when it is true that no matter what the size of the grand coalition, each individual derives a larger benefit from the optimal bundle for the grand coalition than he does from the optimal bundle of m semiprivate goods for any subcoalition of the grand coalition.

PART 2. STABLE COALITIONS WHOSE RETURNS ARE CONCAVE FUNCTIONS

1 Introduction

Private goods are the leading example for which the return to a coalition is a concave function of its size and composition. In contrast, this function is convex for semiprivate goods.

Assume there are m private goods. Let q_{ij} denote the quantity of commodity j going to each individual of type i. This individual obtains a bundle of m goods represented by the m-vector q^i in Ω^m, the non-negative orthant of R^m. Thus,

$$q^i = \{q_{i1}, q_{i2}, \ldots, q_{im}\}.$$

The function $B^i(q^i)$ represents the maximal amount that each type i individual would be willing to pay for the m goods q^i. We may call B^i the benefit that such an individual derives from q^i. Each person of the same type would receive the same q^i in an optimal allocation if B^i were a strictly concave function of q^i. (Strict concavity of B^i is consistent with a convex preference set – a standard assumption of the theory of demand.) Different individuals may obtain different quantities of the private goods although they all belong to the same coalition. The presence of the superscript i on B^i indicates it is usually optimal for different types to get different q^i. In contrast, for semiprivate goods all members of a coalition must obtain the same quantity of each of the semiprivate goods, and so the vector representing the semiprivate goods would have no superscript as is the case in Part 1. Private goods do not impose the restriction that all members of a coalition must get the same quantity of each good. Nevertheless individuals may gain by forming coalitions in order to produce the private goods they want at a lower total cost.

Let z denote the total quantity of the m private goods produced for the members of a coalition s. Since there are s_i individuals of type i in the coalition s and each type i person gets q^i, the total output of the m goods for the coalition s is z. By definition, therefore,

$$z = \sum_{i=1}^{n} s_i q^i. \tag{1}$$

This z is an m-vector in Ω^m. The coalition chooses the n vectors q^i to maximize its net benefit. Consequently, the return to s, the function $f(s)$, is defined as follows:

$$f(s) = \max_{\{q^i\}} [\sum_i s_i B^i(q^i) - C(z)]. \tag{2}$$

Given strict concavity of each B^i, this function $f(s)$ has a finite upper bound for each s if the total cost is an increasing convex function of the outputs z. A convex cost function is consistent with a convex set of production possibilities. The m commodities may refer to more or less aggregative categories. For instance, a commodity may refer to all beverages or to a particular beverage such as Moosehead beer. It is convenient to assume the categories are broad so that the optimal quantity of each of the m commodities is likely to be strictly positive. This would mean that each person gets a positive amount of some beverage. Assuming, therefore, that the optimal q^i is positive for each of its coordinates, a necessary condition for the maximal net benefit of a coalition s requires q^i to satisfy the following m equations:

$$s_i B^i_{q^i} - C_z \frac{\partial z}{\partial q^i} = s_i B^i_{q^i} - C_z s_i = 0.$$

This result uses the fact that $\partial z/\partial q^i = s_i$. If $s_i > 0$ so that type i individuals actually belong to s, the necessary condition becomes

$$B^i_{q^i} - C_z = 0. \tag{3}$$

This is a familiar result. The jth coordinate of C_z is the marginal cost of good j and the marginal benefit of good j to an individual of type i is the jth coordinate of $B^i_{q^i}$. According to equation (3), the marginal cost of good j equals the marginal benefit of this good to each individual i at the optimum. The optimal vectors q^i depend on the coalition. To make this clear, write $q^i(s)$ and $z(s)$ to denote the optimal vectors. Thus different coalitions will furnish their members with different amounts of the m goods.

The next step is to calculate the marginal contribution of a type i person to the coalition s. It is

$$\frac{\partial f(s)}{\partial s_i} = B^i + \sum_{k=1}^n s_k B^k_{q^k} \frac{dq^k}{ds_i} - C_z \frac{dz}{ds_i}.$$

It follows from (1) that

$$\frac{dz}{ds_i} = q^i + \sum_k s_k \frac{dq^k}{ds_i}$$

so that

$$f_{s_i} = B^i[q^i(s)] - C_z[z(s)]q^i(s) + \sum_k s_k[B^k_{q^k} - C_z]\frac{dq^k}{ds_i}$$

Here f_{s_i} denotes $\partial f/\partial s_i$. By virtue of the first-order condition (3), this expression reduces to

$$f_{s_i} = B^i[q^i(s)] - C_z[z(s)]q^i(s). \tag{4}$$

The marginal contribution of a type i individual to a coalition s has a familiar interpretation. The term $C_z q^i$ shows the marginal cost multiplied by the bundle of m goods going to the type i individual. The term $B^i[q^i(s)]$ shows the maximal amount this individual would be willing to pay for $q^i(s)$. Therefore, the marginal contribution of a type i individual to the coalition s is the excess of the total benefit over the marginal cost of supplying that individual as a member of the coalition s. If the individual must pay constant unit prices for the m private goods equal to the marginal cost of these goods, then f_{s_i} would be regarded as the consumer surplus of that individual. Since membership in a coalition is voluntary and must be beneficial to both the coalition and a potential member, the incremental contribution of each member to the coalition must be positive. Consequently, $f(s)$ must be an increasing function of s because each f_{s_i} is positive.

The next step is to verify the initial claim that f is a concave function of s. In order to simplify the notation for the present, let us assume there are only two types of participants so that $n = 2$. However, the proof is valid for arbitrary n.

From (4) for $i = 1$, it follows that

$$f_{s_1 s_1} = B^1_{q^1} \frac{dq^1}{ds_1} - C_z \frac{dq^1}{ds_1} - q^1 C_{zz} \frac{dz}{ds_1}$$

$$= -q^1 C_{zz} \frac{dz}{ds_1} .$$

More generally, by the same argument,

$$f_{s_i s_k} = -q^i C_{zz} \frac{dz}{ds_k} . \tag{5}$$

For $n = 2$, the 2×2 matrix $[f_{s_i s_k}]$ is given as follows:

$$\begin{bmatrix} f_{s_1 s_1} & f_{s_1 s_2} \\ f_{s_2 s_1} & f_{s_2 s_2} \end{bmatrix} = - \begin{bmatrix} q^1 \\ q^2 \end{bmatrix} C_{zz} \begin{bmatrix} \dfrac{dz}{ds_1} & \dfrac{dz}{ds_2} \end{bmatrix} \tag{6}$$

Use the first-order conditions (3) to calculate dz/ds_i:

$$\frac{1}{s_1} B^1_{q^1 q^1} s_1 \frac{dq^1}{ds_1} = C_{zz} \frac{dz}{ds_1}, \tag{7}$$

$$\frac{1}{s_2} B^2_{q^2 q^2} s_2 \frac{dq^2}{ds_1} = C_{zz} \frac{dz}{ds_1} . \tag{8}$$

From (1)

$$\frac{dz}{ds_1} = q^1 + s_1 \frac{dq^1}{ds_1} + s_2 \frac{dq^2}{ds_1} ,$$

use (7) and (8) to solve for the expression $(dz/ds_1 - q^1)$. In detail, from (7)

$$s_1 \frac{dq^1}{ds_1} = \left(\frac{1}{s_1} B^1_{q^1 q^1}\right)^{-1} C_{zz} \left(q^1 + s_1 \frac{dq^1}{ds_1} + s_2 \frac{dq^2}{ds_1}\right) \tag{9}$$

and from (8)

$$s_2 \frac{dq^2}{ds_1} = \left(\frac{1}{s_2} B^2_{q^2 q^2}\right)^{-1} C_{zz} \left(q^1 + s_1 \frac{dq^1}{ds_1} + s_2 \frac{dq^2}{ds_1}\right). \tag{10}$$

Sum (9) and (10) and solve for $s_1 \, dq^1/ds_1 + s_2 \, dq^2/ds_1$. For brevity, define the matrix B as follows:

$$B = [(1/s_1)B^1_{q^1 q^1}]^{-1} + [(1/s_2)B^2_{q^2 q^2}]^{-1}. \tag{11}$$

This gives

$$[I - BC_{zz}] \left(s_1 \frac{dq^1}{ds_1} + s_2 \frac{dq^2}{ds_1}\right) = BC_{zz}q^1. \tag{12}$$

By precisely the same steps, we obtain,

$$[I - BC_{zz}] \left(s_1 \frac{dq^1}{ds_2} + s_2 \frac{dq^2}{ds_2}\right) = BC_{zz}q^2. \tag{13}$$

Substituting these formulas into (6), it follows that

$$\begin{bmatrix} f_{11} & f_{12} \\ f_{21} & f_{22} \end{bmatrix} = - \begin{bmatrix} q^1 \\ q^2 \end{bmatrix} C_{zz}\{C_{zz}^{-1}$$

$$+ [I - BC_{zz}]^{-1}B\}C_{zz}[q^1 \quad q^2]. \tag{14}$$

Therefore, f is a concave function of s provided the matrix

$$C_{zz}^{-1} + [I - BC_{zz}]^{-1}B$$

is positive definite. The following lemma establishes this fact.

> **Lemma 1:** *Let C be positive definite and B negative definite. Write*
>
> $$M = C^{-1} + [I - BC]^{-1}B. \tag{15}$$
>
> *Therefore, M is a positive definite matrix.*

Proof: First, observe that

$$M = C^{-1} + [B(B^{-1} - C)]^{-1}B \qquad (16)$$
$$= C^{-1} + (B^{-1} - C)^{-1}.$$

Since C is positive definite and B is negative definite, a well-known theorem on matrices applies (Bellman 1960, p. 58). There is a nonsingular matrix P such that

$$C = P'P \quad \text{and} \quad B^{-1} = P'DP,$$

where D is a diagonal matrix whose diagonal entries are the (negative) eigenvalues of B^{-1}. Therefore,

$$M = P^{-1}P'^{-1} + (P'DP - P'P)^{-1}$$
$$= P^{-1}[I + (D - I)^{-1}]P'^{-1}.$$

Now $I + (D - I)^{-1}$ is a diagonal matrix whose jth diagonal entry is

$$1 - [1/(1 + \mu_j)] > 0,$$

where $-\mu_j$ is the jth eigenvalue of B^{-1} so that $\mu_j > 0$. Consequently, $I + (D - I)^{-1}$ is positive definite, which implies M is positive definite. ∎

This argument for $n = 2$ and m private goods readily applies to any finite number of types. As a result the following is true.

> **Proposition 1:** Given m private goods and n types of individuals such that each B^i is strictly concave and twice differentiable, C is convex, each $B^i_{q^i q^i}$ is negative definite, and C_{zz} is positive definite, then $f(s)$ as defined in (2) is a concave function of s.

Note that if C is convex and homogeneous of degree 1, then C_{zz} is a singular matrix. Therefore, in this case the hypotheses of Proposition 1 would not be satisfied for the cost function. However, a direct argument shows that with constant returns to scale the core is not empty.

> **Proposition 2:** Let each B^i be concave and let C be convex and homogeneous of degree 1. Then $f(s)$ defined in (2) has a nonempty core.

Proof: Let

$$x_i = f_i(t) \qquad (17)$$

so that as an implication of (4)

$$f_i(t) = B^i[q^i(t)] - C_z[z(t)]q^i(t).$$

We must show this imputation satisfies all of the core constraints. First,

$$\sum_i x_i t_i = f(t) \tag{18}$$

since the hypothesis that C is homogeneous of degree 1 implies that

$$C_z[z(t)]z(t) = C[z(t)],$$

which gives (18). Next, we must show that for $s \leq t$

$$\sum_i x_i s_i \geq f(s).$$

To prove this, observe that concavity of each B^i implies

$$B^i_{q^i}[q^i(t)][q^i(t) - q^i(s)] \leq B^i[q^i(t)] - B^i[q^i(s)]. \tag{19}$$

The first-order conditions are

$$B^i_{q^i}[q^i(t)] = C_z[z(t)]$$

so that it follows from (17) and (19) that

$$x_i \geq B^i[q^i(s)] - C_z[z(t)]q^i(s).$$

Multiply through by s_i and sum to obtain

$$\sum_i x_i s_i \geq \sum_i s_i B^i[q^i(s)] - C_z[z(t)] \sum_i s_i q^i(s). \tag{20}$$

Since

$$\sum_i s_i B^i[q^i(s)] - C_z[z(t)]z(s) = f(s) + C[z(s)] - C_z[z(t)]z(s),$$

the desired conclusion will follow if it is true that

$$C[z(s)] - C_z[z(t)]z(s) \geq 0.$$

However, owing to the convexity of C and the fact that it is homogeneous of degree 1,

$$C[z(s)] - C_z[z(t)]z(s) \geq C[z(t)] - C_z[z(t)]z(t) = 0,$$

which gives the desired conclusion. ∎

Unfortunately, this simple argument does not work if C is convex but not homogeneous of degree 1. The reason that x_i in (17) can satisfy all the core constraints depends crucially on C being homogeneous of degree 1 so that it is possible to cover the total cost of z by setting prices equal to the marginal costs of the elements of z.

2   Some facts about concave characteristic functions

Before proceeding to analyze the status of the core for private goods when the net benefit function is concave, we shall need some facts about such functions.

>   ***Proposition 3:*** *Let f be concave on Ω^n.*
>
>   (i) $f^*(s)s \geq f(s);$
>   (ii) $f(s + t) \geq f(s) + f(t);$
>   (iii) $f(\beta s) \geq \beta f(s)$ *for all* $\beta > 1;$
>   (iv) *for each t there is an x depending on t such that $xt = f(t)$ and $xs \geq f(s)$ for all $s \leq t$.*
>
>   *(i) $\Leftrightarrow$ (ii) $\Leftrightarrow$ (iii) $\Leftrightarrow$ (iv) (cf. Telser 1978, Lemma 4.5, p. 141).*

Proof: (i) $\Rightarrow$ (ii). Let f^* denote the supergradient of f.

$$f^*(s + t)t \leq f(s + t) - f(s),$$

$$f^*(s + t)s \leq f(s + t) - f(t).$$

Summing we obtain

$$f^*(s + t)(s + t) \leq 2f(s + t) - f(s) - f(t).$$

By hypothesis,

$$0 \leq f^*(s + t)(s + t) - f(s + t) \leq f(s + t) - f(s) - f(t).$$

(ii) $\Rightarrow$ (iii). By hypothesis for all positive integers k,

$$f(ks) \geq kf(s).$$

Let $t = \alpha ks + (1 - \alpha)s$. By concavity,

$$f(t) \geq \alpha f(ks) + (1 - \alpha)f(s) \geq [\alpha k + (1 - \alpha)]f(s).$$

Consequently,

$$f([\alpha k + (1 - \alpha)]s) \geq [\alpha k + (1 - \alpha)]f(s).$$

Let $\beta = \alpha k + (1 - \alpha)$. If $k > 1$, then $\beta > 1$. Therefore,

$$f(\beta s) \geq \beta f(s) \quad \text{for all } \beta > 1.$$

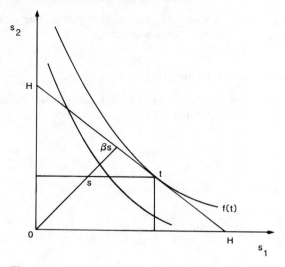

Figure 4.1

(iii) $\Rightarrow$ (i). $(\beta - 1)f(s) \le f(\beta s) - f(s) \le f^*(s)[s(\beta - 1)]$. Since $\beta - 1 > 0$, the conclusion follows.

We have (i) $\Leftrightarrow$ (ii) $\Leftrightarrow$ (iii). We shall show (iii) $\Rightarrow$ (iv) and (iv) $\Rightarrow$ (ii).

(iii) $\Rightarrow$ (iv). A glance at Figure 4.1 helps to follow the argument. Define the convex set R as follows:

$$R = \{r \mid f(r) \ge f(t)\}.$$

It has a supporting hyperplane consisting of all points s such that $xs = f(t)$. That is,

$$H = \{s \mid xs = f(t)\}.$$

For all $s \in H$, $f(s) \le xs = f(t)$. For all $s \le t$, there is a $\beta > 1$ such that $\beta s \in H$. Consequently,

$$\beta f(s) \le f(\beta s) \le f(t) = x(\beta s).$$

Therefore, $f(s) \le xs$, the desired conclusion.

(iv) $\Rightarrow$ (ii). By hypothesis f has a nonempty core. By Proposition 1, Part 1, f must be superadditive. ∎

Part 1 shows that a convex net benefit function reduces to a study of extreme coalitions, those corresponding to the verteces of $T(t)$. This reduction is not possible for concave net benefit functions. To find the status of the core when f is concave, we must study all the coalitions in T. This is the tack in the next two sections.

3   Status of the core for concave f

According to Proposition 3(i), if f is a concave function on Ω^n, it admits a nonempty core if and only if for all $t \in \Omega^n$, it is true that

$$f^*(t)t \geq f(t). \tag{1}$$

Since

$$f_i^*(t) = B^i[q^i(t)] - C_z[z(t)]q^i(t), \tag{2}$$

(1) is true if and only if

$$\sum_i t_i B^i[q^i(t)] - C_z[z(t)]z(t) \geq \sum_i t_i B^i[q^i(t)] - C[z(t)].$$

The latter inequality is equivalent to

$$C[z(t)] \geq C_z[z(t)]z(t). \tag{3}$$

This completes the proof of:

> **Proposition 4:** *Let $f(t)$ as defined in (1.2) be a concave function of t on Ω^n. It admits a nonempty core for all t in this domain if and only if (3) is true for all $z(t)$.*

This means that given a concave net benefit function and a convex total cost function, there cannot be a nonempty core unless there are nondecreasing returns to scale. Take a closer look at the properties of a cost function that satisfies (3).

> **Lemma 2:** *Let C be convex and subhomogeneous so that*
>
> $$C(\alpha z) \leq \alpha C(z) \quad \text{for all } \alpha > 1. \tag{4}$$
>
> *It follows that*
>
> $$C(z) \geq C^*(z)z. \tag{5}$$

Proof: $\alpha C(z) - C(z) \geq C(\alpha z) - C(z) \geq C^*(z)z(\alpha - 1)$ so that

$$(\alpha - 1)C(z) \geq C^*(z)z(\alpha - 1)$$

is true for all $\alpha > 1$.   ∎

Lemma 3: *Let C be convex and satisfy (5) for all* $z \in \Omega^m$. *Then C is subhomogeneous.*

Proof: The convexity of C implies that

$$(\alpha - 1)C^*(\alpha z)z \geq C(\alpha z) - C(z)$$

$$\Rightarrow C(z) \geq C(\alpha z) - (\alpha - 1)C^*(\alpha z)z$$

so that

$$C(z) \geq C(\alpha z) - C^*(\alpha z)(\alpha z) + C^*(\alpha z)z.$$

The hypothesis implies $C(\alpha z) - C^*(\alpha z)(\alpha z) \geq 0$. We may conclude that

$$C(z) \geq C^*(\alpha z)z \quad \text{for all } \alpha > 1. \tag{6}$$

Consider the function $g(\alpha)$ defined as follows:

$$g(\alpha) = \alpha C(z) - C(\alpha z).$$

It is an implication of (6) that

$$g_\alpha = C(z) - C^*(\alpha z)z \geq 0,$$

so that g is a nondecreasing function of α. Hence

$$\inf g(\alpha) = g(1) = 0,$$

and it follows that

$$\alpha C(z) - C(\alpha z) \geq \inf g(\alpha) = 0. \qquad\blacksquare$$

The third result we shall need is as follows.

Lemma 4: *Let C be convex and subhomogeneous. Then for all y and z in the convex domain of C,*

$$C(y) - C^*(z)y \geq 0.$$

Proof: By the convexity of C

$$C^*(z)(z - y) \geq C(z) - C(y). \tag{7}$$

Rearranging terms in (7) gives

$$C(y) - C^*(z)\,y \geq C(z) - C^*(z)z. \tag{8}$$

Lemma 2 asserts the expression on the right is nonnegative. $\qquad\blacksquare$

Finally, a subhomogeneous convex cost function must be subadditive.

> **Lemma 5:** *Let C be convex and subhomogeneous. Then it is subadditive.*

Proof: We must show that

$$C(y) + C(z) \geq C(y + z). \tag{9}$$

By convexity,

$$\tfrac{1}{2}[C(y) + C(z)] \geq C[\tfrac{1}{2}(y + z)]$$

so that

$$C(y) + C(z) \geq 2C[\tfrac{1}{2}(y + z)].$$

Since C is subhomogeneous

$$2C[(y + z)/2] \geq C[2(y + z)/2] = C(y + z). \qquad \blacksquare$$

All these conditions on the cost function extend to m commodities that situation for one commodity in which marginal cost is below average cost so that there are nondecreasing returns to scale. The inequality $C^*(z)z \leq C(z)$ is the m-dimensional analogue of marginal cost below average cost, or more exactly, not above average cost. Subadditivity of the total cost function means it is cheaper for a coalition to produce its own requirements than to have this done by subcoalitions. Similarly, an expansion of output of each of the m commodities that maintains its relative composition also maintains constant the unit cost of this bundle.

Owing to these interpretations of Lemmas 2–5, it is fair to describe the situation in this way. Given that each type of person has a concave benefit function and that the total cost function is convex so that the net benefit is a concave function of the size and composition of the coalition, a nonempty core exists if and only if there are nondecreasing returns to scale. The formal statement of this result is given in the following proposition.

> **Proposition 5:** *Let f be concave on Ω^n. It is totally kind if and only if C is subhomogeneous.*

Proof: Sufficiency. This is Proposition 4. Thus, by Lemma 2, a subhomogeneous function satisfies (3) for all z so it surely does so for the optimal z. Necessity. This is somewhat more subtle. Condition (3) must hold for the optimal z. However, any z can be optimal for some t so (3) must be true for an arbitrary z in Ω^n. Consequently, Lemmas 2 and 3 together require C to be subhomogeneous. ∎

Proposition 2 shows that the core is nonvoid if C is convex and homogeneous of degree 1 so that there are constant returns to scale. If C is strictly convex so that it cannot be homogeneous of degree 1, then the maximal net benefit of a coalition is a concave function of s by Proposition 1. For a nonempty core in this case, the cost function must be strictly subhomogeneous. However, in contrast to the situation with constant returns to scale, it would not be possible to obtain enough revenue to cover total cost by setting the price of each product equal to its marginal cost. In order to cover total cost, the imputations of the participants must be below their incremental contributions to the grand coalition. To be specific, write

$$x_i = f_i^*(t) - a_i, \tag{10}$$

where $a_i \geq 0$ and $f_i^*(t)$ is given in (2). Necessarily, it must be true that

$$\sum_{i=1}^{n} x_i t_i = f(t) = \sum_i t_i f_i^*(t) - \sum_i a_i t_i.$$

Hence

$$\sum_i t_i B^i[q^i(t)] - C_z[z(t)]z(t) - \sum_i a_i t_i$$

$$= \sum_i t_i B^i[q^i(t)] - C[z(t)].$$

Therefore,

$$\sum_i a_i t_i = C[z(t)] - C_z[z(t)]z(t) \geq 0. \tag{11}$$

According to this equation, $\sum_i a_i t_i$ equals the excess of the total cost above those total receipts derived from setting unit prices of each commodity equal to its marginal cost. Equation (11) is equivalent to the suggestive result as follows:

$$\sum_i \{a_i - \frac{\Theta_i}{\sum_i \Theta_i t_i} C[z(t)] + C_z[z(t)]q^i(t)\}t_i = 0. \tag{12}$$

Consider a_i defined as follows.

$$a_i = \frac{\Theta_i}{\sum_i \Theta_i t_i} C[z(t)] - C_z[z(t)]q^i(t), \tag{13}$$

with $\Theta_i \geq 0$. Since

$$C[z(t)] > C[q^i(t)] \quad \text{and} \quad C[q^i(t)] > C_z[z(t)]q^i(t)$$

where the latter inequality follows from Lemma 4, there always exists large enough Θ_i to ensure nonnegative a_i as required.

We now prove that the core constraint

$$\sum_i x_i s_i \geq f(s)$$

with x_i given by (10) would be satisfied if

$$\sum_i a_i s_i \leq C[z(s)] - C_z[z(t)]z(s). \tag{14}$$

The proof begins with the fact that since each B_i is a concave function of q^i, it is true that

$$B_{q^i}^i [q^i(t)][q^i(t) - q^i(s)] \leq B^i[q^i(t)] - B^i[q^i(s)]. \tag{15}$$

The first-order condition for the maximal net benefit of the grand coalition t requires for each i that

$$B_{q^i}^i [q^i(t)] = C_z[z(t)].$$

Substituting this in (15) and rearranging terms, we obtain

$$B^i[q^i(t)] - C_z[z(t)]q^i(t) \geq B^i[q^i(s)] - C_z[z(t)]q^i(s). \tag{16}$$

Multiply through (16) by s_i and sum over i. The result is

$$\sum_i s_i B^i[q^i(t)] - C_z[z(t)] \sum_i s_i q^i(t) \geq \sum_i s_i B^i[q^i(s)]$$

$$- C[z(s)] + C[z(s)] - C_z[z(t)] \sum_i s_i q^i(s) \tag{17}$$

$$= f(s) + C[z(s)] - C_z[z(t)]z(s)$$

Now (17) is equivalent to

$$\sum_i s_i f_i^*(t) \geq f(s) + C[z(s)] - C_z[z(t)]z(s).$$

Since $x_i = f_i^*(t) - a_i$, (14) would be true if

$$C[z(s)] - C_z[z(t)]z(s) \geq \sum_i a_i s_i \geq 0.$$

This directs us to see if a_i given by (13) can satisfy (14). Equivalently, (14) would be true if

$$\sum_i s_i \left\{ \frac{\Theta_i}{\sum \Theta_i t_i} C[z(t)] - C_z[z(t)]q^i(t) \right\}$$

$$\leq C[z(s)] - C_z[z(t)]z(s). \tag{18}$$

Since $a_i \geq 0$, the left-hand side of (18) is an increasing function of s_i. Therefore, the left-hand side of (18) satisfies

$$\sum_i s_i \left\{ \frac{\Theta_i}{\sum \Theta_i t_i} C[z(t)] - C_z[z(t)]q^i(t) \right\}$$

$$\leq C[z(t)] - C_z[z(t)]z(t). \quad (19)$$

Since it is true that

$$0 \leq C[z(t)] - C_z[z(t)]z(t) \leq C[z(s)] - C_z[z(t)]z(s), \quad (20)$$

by virtue of inequality (8), making the substitutions $y = z(s)$ and $z = z(t)$, it follows that (18) is true, which in turn implies that (14) is true as claimed. This completes the proof of the following proposition.

> **Proposition 6:** *Let C be convex and strictly increasing. Let each B^i be a concave function of its arguments so that each $B^i_{q^i q^i}$ is negative definite. Then the function $f(s)$ describing the net benefit of each coalition s is concave in s. This f is totally kind if C is subhomogeneous and $x_i = f_i^*(t) - a_i$ with a_i given by (13) for appropriate $\Theta_i \geq 0$ to ensure that each $a_i \geq 0$.*

This proposition does not assert that the a_i's are unique. This is owing to the lack of uniqueness of the Θ_i's that are chosen to ensure non-negative a_i's. Therefore the grand coalition has many ways of allocating that part of the overhead cost that is not covered by the receipts derived from prices set equal to marginal costs of the m commodities furnished to the members of the grand coalition. Although the imputation of the net benefit depends on the total benefit of each participant, the allocation of this overhead cost does not depend on the benefit. The dependence is indirect insofar as the benefits determine the optimal output rates of the m commodities for the grand coalition.

Reconsider the net benefit function $f(s)$. It determines an optimal allocation of the given total output $z(s)$ among the members of the coalition s. For a given allocation of $q^i(s)$, $f(s)$ shows the least cost of producing $z(s) = \sum s_i q^i(s)$. This means the theory implies a coalition chooses the best technology for satisfying the demands of its members as expressed by the total benefit function of the coalition, which is $\sum s_i B^i(q^i)$. The results above assert that if the total cost function is convex and each of the benefit functions is strongly concave so that the net benefit function $f(s)$ is concave, then the core is not empty if and only if the cost function is subhomogeneous. This poses the problem of the nature of convex subhomogeneous cost functions consistent with the best technology.

There is a sense in which it is unnatural to require a convex cost function to be subhomogeneous. Thus, if C is convex on Ω^m,

$$C_z(z)z \geq C(z) - C(0) \geq C_z(0)z \tag{21}$$

so that C is convex on the whole nonnegative orthant, including the origin where the output rates are zero for the m commodities. Let C represent the long-run cost so that the cost of producing nothing is zero. It would then follow from the inequalities (21) that

$$C_z(z)z \geq C(z) \quad \text{and} \quad C(z) \geq C_z(0)z. \tag{22}$$

The first inequality is consistent with a convex subhomogeneous cost function if and only if there are constant returns to scale. To prove this, observe that if the cost function were subhomogeneous then

$$C(z) \geq C_z(z)z \geq C(z)$$

so there must be equality straight through. This means constant returns to scale. The second inequality of (22) asserts that the best technology has a very large number of infinitesimally small plants so that the total cost of the output z is linear and given by the (homogeneous) linear function $C_z(0)z$. Therefore, a subhomogeneous cost function that is convex on the entire nonnegative orthant requires either constant returns to scale or, as a special case, a linear homogeneous function of the output rates. This seems to eliminate increasing returns to scale for a long-run convex total cost function. Such a conclusion would be incorrect. Make the following change. Drop the assumption that C is convex on the entire nonnegative orthant and replace it with the assumption that C is convex only for positive output rates. Indeed, it suffices to assume C is convex on the domain $\Omega^m - \{0\}$ and that

$$\lim_{z \to 0^+} C(z) = C(0^+) > 0. \tag{23}$$

To clarify this, it is helpful to define a strictly subhomogeneous convex cost function as one that is continuous and convex on $\Omega^m - \{0\}$, and that satisfies $C_z(z)z \leq C(z)$ for all $z \geq 0$. There are many examples of increasing convex functions that can meet these conditions. A simple one is as follows.

$$C(z) = \begin{cases} \alpha z + e^{-\beta z} & \text{if } z > 0, \\ 0 & \text{if } z = 0, \end{cases}$$

with z a scalar. There is no dearth of similar examples in R^m.

4   Status of the core for plants of optimal size

For a subhomogeneous cost function, either the optimal plant size is indeterminate as is the case for constant returns to scale or one plant is optimal as is true when $C_z z < C$ for all z. In the former case a coalition can choose any number of plants while in the latter case it would choose one plant. These assertions are consequences of the hypothesis that a coalition uses the technology giving it the least total cost of satisfying the demands of its members. The nature of the technology does determine the optimal number of plants if $C_z z = C$ for some but not for all rates of output. An output rate that satisfies this equation when plants make only one product is a rate that minimizes the unit cost of the plant. By extension to multiproduct plants ($m > 1$), it is reasonable, therefore, to call those plant sizes optimal for which $C_z z = C$. In contrast to the situation for $m = 1$, however, for multiproduct plants there is a set of output rates at which receipts obtained by setting prices equal to marginal costs can cover the total cost. All these output rates correspond to an optimal plant size by this definition of optimality. Let

$$Z_0 = \{z|\ C_z z = C\}. \tag{1}$$

Any $z \in Z_0$ comes from an optimal plant.

It is convenient to define the total cost function of a single plant as follows:

$$K + G(z) \quad \text{if } z \geq 0,\ K \text{ a positive scalar,}$$

$$0 \quad \text{if } z = 0,$$

where $G(z)$ is convex on the whole nonnegative orthant Ω^m and $G(0) = 0$. This definition of the plant cost function implies it is convex on $\Omega^m - \{0\}$, but it is not convex on Ω^m. The assumptions about G imply that

$$G_z z \geq G \quad \text{for all } z \in \Omega^m. \tag{2}$$

Output rates in Z_0 must satisfy the equation as follows:

$$G_z z - G = K > 0. \tag{3}$$

Although (2) is a necessary condition for (3), it is not sufficient. To see this, observe that if G were homogeneous of degree 1, it would satisfy (2) with equality for all z but would have no solution for any $K > 0$. Hence (2) is not a sufficient condition for (3). To get a sufficient condition, define the function $H(z)$ as follows:

$$H(z) = G_z z - G \tag{4}$$

so that

$$H_z = zG_{zz}.$$ (5)

If H were strictly increasing and unbounded from above, then (3) would have solutions for arbitrary $K > 0$. Formally, this hypothesis implies

$$zG_{zz} > u > 0$$ (6)

with u an m-vector of positive constants. Therefore, Z_0 is not empty.

Indeed, when (6) is true, there are many output rates in Z_0. The locus of plant output rates in Z_0 satisfies $H(z) = K$ so that

$$H_z \, dz = 0.$$ (7)

Since each coordinate of H_z is positive on this locus by hypothesis, the larger the output rates of one commodity, the lower are the output rates of the remaining commodities.

Define the set of coalitions S_0 as follows:

$$S_0 = \{s| \ f(s) = f^*(s)s\}.$$

Hence $s \in S_0$ if the optimal z for s is $z \in Z_0$. Since Z_0 is not empty, the same is true of S_0.

For these cost functions the net return to a coalition s is given by

$$f(s) = \max_{\{q^i, \mu\}} \left\{ \sum_i s_i B^i(q^i) - \mu[G(\bar{z}) + K] \right\}$$ (8)

where μ is the integer number of plants and $\bar{z}$ denotes the output rates per plant so that

$$\sum_i s_i q^i = \mu\bar{z} = z.$$ (9)

For the grand coalition t, the optimal output is $z(t)$. Let $\mu(t)$ denote the integer number of plants that can make the total output $z(t)$ at the least total cost. The minimum total cost of making $z(t)$ requires each of the μ plants to have the same output rates for each of the m commodities.

$$\mu\bar{z} = z(t) = \sum_i t_i q^i(t).$$ (10)

Let y^1 denote the optimal plant output rate for $\mu - 1$ plants and y^2 for $\mu + 1$ plants. Consequently,

$$\mu\bar{z} = (\mu - 1)y^1 = (\mu + 1)y^2.$$

Since μ is the optimal number of plants for the grand coalition t,

$$\mu[G(\bar{z}) + K] < (\mu - 1)[G(y^1) + K],$$

$$\mu[G(\bar{z}) + K] < (\mu + 1)[G(y^2) + K].$$

Necessarily, therefore,

$$\mu G(\bar{z}) - (\mu + 1)\dot{G}(y^2) < (\mu - 1)G(y^1) - \mu G(\bar{z}).$$

By convexity of G, it follows that

$$G(z^*) < [(\mu + 1)/2\mu]G(y^2) + [(\mu - 1)/2\mu]G(y^1),$$

with

$$z^* = [(\mu + 1)/2\mu]y^2 + [(\mu - 1)/2\mu]y^1.$$

Therefore, $z^* = \bar{z}$ as is required by the assumption that μ is the optimal number of plants to produce $z(t)$.

Under these cost conditions there is an empty core. This needs a proof. Define the function $g(s)$ as follows:

$$g(s) = f(s) - f^*(s^0)s \tag{11}$$

with $s^0 \in S_0$. By hypothesis for all coalitions such that it is optimal to satisfy their demands using a single plant, the cost function and the benefit functions satisfy the conditions under which the conclusions of Proposition 1 are true. Hence for these coalitions, $g(s)$ is concave because $f(s)$ is concave. For $s = s^0$,

$$g(s^0) = 0 \quad \text{and} \quad g^*(s^0) = f^*(s^0) - f^*(s^0) = 0$$

giving the conclusion that

$$g(s) < g(s^0) = 0, \tag{12}$$

for all coalitions s for which a single plant is optimal.

In fact, the same argument is valid for all coalitions for which it is optimal to use a fixed number of plants. This holds because for fixed μ, $f(s)$ is concave in s.

The members of s^0 can each obtain returns equal to their incremental contributions to s^0, an amount equal to $f^*(s^0)$. Therefore, if the grand coalition proposes an imputation of the gains given by x, then for a nonempty core, it is necessary that

$$x \geq f^*(s^0) \quad \text{and} \quad xt = f(t).$$

But since

$$g(t) = f(t) - f^*(s^0)t < 0,$$

it is impossible to satisfy these necessary conditions for a nonempty core. Hence the core is empty. This completes the proof of the following proposition.

> **Proposition 7:** *Let the cost of producing an output z using a single plant be given as follows:*
>
> $$G(z) + K \quad \text{if } z \geq 0,$$
> $$\qquad\quad 0 \quad \text{if } z = 0,$$
>
> *where K is a positive scalar and G is a convex function on Ω^m that satisfies (2) and (6) so that H as given by (4) is a strictly increasing unbounded function of z. Let each B^i be a concave function of q^i. It follows that the core is empty for almost all large enough t.*[1]

It is possible to obtain a set of imputations that can satisfy the core constraints in a certain sense by using a device equivalent to a two-part price. In this arrangement each person pays a lump-sum amount independent of the quantity bought and another amount linearly proportional to the quantities bought. In the present application this would have the effect of lowering the net return of any coalition s, which is $f(s)$, by an amount that is a strictly increasing linear function of s. The result changes the coalition's return from $f(s)$ to $f(s) - as$, where a is a nonnegative n-vector giving the lump-sum charges. Let

$$x = f^*(s^0) - a \qquad (13)$$

and choose a to satisfy $xt = f(t)$ so that

---

[1] Let the cost function of a plant be given as follows:

$$\begin{cases} 0 & \text{if } z = 0, \\ a_0 & \text{if } 0 < z \leq k_0, \\ a_0 + a_1(z - k_0) & \text{if } k_0 \leq z \leq k_1, \\ \infty & \text{if } k_1 < z. \end{cases}$$

Let $a_0 = a_1 k_0$ so that unit cost is constant for outputs in the range k_0 to k_1. Baumol, Panzar, and Willig (1982) call this a flat-bottomed unit cost curve. Now, if $k_1 \geq 2k_0$, then it is easy to verify that the industry total cost curve giving the minimal total cost of producing a prescribed total output q is as follows:

$$C(q) = \begin{cases} 0 & \text{if } q = 0, \\ a_0 & \text{if } 0 < q \leq k_0, \\ a_1 q & \text{if } k_0 \leq q. \end{cases}$$

Note that the unit cost curve for the *industry* is constant for *all* output rates above k_0 while for the *plant* it is constant only for plant output rates between k_0 and k_1. The cost curve $C(q)$ satisfies the hypotheses of Proposition 5 so there is an implication of a nonempty core for an industry with this cost curve. It is not a counterexample to Proposition 7 because it violates one of the assumptions of that proposition, namely (6).

$$at = f^*(s^0)t - f(t) = -g(t) > 0. \tag{14}$$

We must show that this x can satisfy the following constraint:

$$xs \geq f(s) - as,$$

which is in turn equivalent to

$$f^*(s^0)s > f(s). \tag{15}$$

The latter inequality is true by virtue of (12). Hence x given by (13) can satisfy the core constraints under a regime of two-part prices. Nor is this all. The receipts implied by x just suffice to cover the total cost of $z(t)$, the optimal z of the grand coalition t.

It is useful to show a specific a that can do these things. Let

$$a_i = f_i^*(s^0) - \left(B^i[q^i(t)] - \frac{C[z(t)]}{\sum_i t_i}\right). \tag{16}$$

With this a_i each person pays $C[z(t)]/\sum t_i$. The imputation of the total return thereby does cover the total cost of $z(t)$ as required. It is desirable to express these terms in a more familiar form as a two-part price. Write

$$p = C_z[z(t)]$$

as the vector whose coordinates give the constant unit prices and let δ give the fixed charge where δ is defined as follows:

$$\delta = \frac{C[z(t)]}{\sum t_i} - C_z[z(t)]q^i(t).$$

It is an implication of the definition of C that

$$G_z(\bar{z}) = C_z[z(t)].$$

Since there are many points in Z_0, it is also true there are many coalitions in S_0 that may ask for an imputation of the total return an amount equal to their incremental contribution to a coalition in S_0. As we shall see, this means there is no unique two-part pricing device associated with efficient equilibria. To see this in detail, take two distinct vectors in Z_0, say y^0 and z^0. Let $r^0 \in S_0$ have $y^0 \in Z_0$ for its optimal choice while as above $s^0 \in S_0$ has $z^0 \in Z_0$ for its optimal choice. To satisfy the optimality conditions require

$$G_z(z^0) = B_{q^i}^i[q^i(s^0)],$$

and

$$G_z(y^0) = B^i_{q^i}[q^i(r^0)].$$

Both coalitions r^0 and s^0 can cover the total cost of their optimal choices of commodity bundles by setting prices equal to the respective marginal costs of these bundles. Define the two functions g and h as follows:

$$g(s) = f(s) - f^*(s^0)s$$

and

$$h(s) = f(s) - f^*(r^0)s.$$

Hence $g(s^0) = 0$, $g^*(s^0) = 0$, $h(r^0) = 0$, and $h^*(r^0) = 0$. This means s^0 is a maximum for g and r^0 is a maximum for h. Hence there is no unique point in the core constrained to use a two-part pricing device. This is plain since either $f^*(s^0)$ or $f^*(r^0)$ can yield points in such a constrained core.

It is worth repeating that this two-part pricing device imposes a lump-sum payment on each member of the grand coalition together with constant-unit prices that are the same for everyone. The resulting receipts can cover the total cost of the bundle optimal for the grand coalition. Nevertheless, as the preceding paragraph shows, there is an indeterminacy with respect to the lump-sum payment that this theory does not resolve. Nor is this all. All members of the grand coalition must agree to impose a cost of as on each coalition so that the return of each s goes down from $f(s)$ to $f(s) - as$. Cooperation to this extent is enough for an efficient equilibrium.

PART 3. STABLE COALITIONS FOR PRIVATE AND SEMIPRIVATE GOODS

1   Introduction

This combines the situations of the two preceding parts so that each person derives benefit from both private and semiprivate goods. Thus, in Part 2 there are only private goods giving rise to a concave function representing the net return to a coalition; in Part 1 there are only semiprivate goods so that the return to a coalition is a convex function of its size and composition. In the present case with both private and semiprivate goods, it is not useful to analyze the shape of the function representing the return to a coalition since it is neither convex nor concave. Instead it is better to derive directly imputations that can satisfy the core constraints under suitable conditions on the cost and benefit functions.

Since both private and semiprivate goods enter each person's benefit function, let us adopt a notation that distinguishes between them, which will remind us of the corresponding models in Parts 1 and 2. Let $B^i(y, z^i)$ denote the benefit function for person i so that y is an m-vector of semiprivate goods and z^i is a p-vector of private goods. Assume that $B^i(y, z^i)$ is a concave increasing function of its arguments. Hence the marginal benefits of each of the private and semiprivate goods are positive. Let

$$z(s) = \sum_i s_i z^i \quad \text{(cf. 2.1.1)}. \tag{1}$$

The total cost of z and y is represented by the function $C(y, z)$. The net return to a coalition s is given as follows:

$$f(s) = \max_{\{y, z^i\}} \left[\sum_i s_i B^i(y, z^i) - C(y, z) \right] \tag{2}$$

where y, $z^i \geqq 0$ and z satisfies (1). Assume this maximum problem has an interior solution for each $s \leqq t$, where, as usual, t denotes the grand coalition. Hence the optimal choices of y and z^i by the coalition s must satisfy the following equations:

$$\sum_i s_i B^i_y(y, z^i) - C_y(y, z) = 0, \tag{3}$$

$$B^i_{z^i}(y, z^i) - C_z(y, z) = 0. \tag{4}$$

Let $y(s)$ and $z^i(s)$ denote the optimal values of these vectors for the coalition s. With this notation,

$$f(s) = \sum_i s_i B^i[y(s), z^i(s)] - C[y(s), z(s)]. \tag{5}$$

In less cumbersome notation simply write $B^i(s)$ and $C(s)$ in place of $B^i[y(s), z^i(s)]$ and $C[y(s), z(s)]$. The concise version of (5) is

$$f(s) = \sum_i s_i B^i(s) - C(s). \tag{6}$$

It is not difficult to verify that

$$\frac{\partial f(s)}{\partial s_i} = B^i(s) - C_z(s) z^i(s), \tag{7}$$

a formula of exactly the same form as when only private goods enter the benefit and cost functions [see (2.1.4)]. The stage is set for the principal result.

2   The principal result

> **Proposition 1:** Let:
>
> (i) $C(y, z)$ be an increasing convex subhomogeneous function of y and z.
> (ii) Each $B^i(y, z^i)$ be concave and strictly increasing in y and z^i. Then x_i given as follows satisfies all the core constraints:
> (iii) $x_i = B^i(t) - B_y^i(t)y(t) - B_{z^i}^i(t)z^i(t) - a_i$, where
> (iv) $a_i = \dfrac{\Theta_i}{\sum_i \Theta_i t_i}[C(t) - C_y(t)y(t)] - C_z(t)z^i(t)$
>   for $\Theta_i \geq 0$ chosen so that $a_i \geq 0$.

Proof: First, it is necessary to show that

$$\sum_i x_i t_i = f(t). \tag{1}$$

Using (iii),

$$\sum_i x_i t_i = \sum_i t_i B^i(t) - \sum_i t_i B_y^i(t)y(t) - C_z(t)z(t) - \sum_i a_i t_i,$$

making the substitution from the first-order condition (1.4) repeated as follows:

$$B_{z^i}^i(t) = C_z(t),$$

and recalling that $\sum_i t_i z^i = z(t)$. Hence

$$\sum_i x_i t_i = f(t) + C(t) - C_y(t)y(t) - C_z(t)z(t) - \sum_i a_i t_i, \tag{2}$$

using the other first-order condition (1.3) repeated as follows:

$$\sum_i t_i B_y^i(t) = C_y(t).$$

Since

$$\sum_i a_i t_i = C(t) - C_y(t)y(t) - C_z(t)z(t),$$

(1) is true as required.

Second, it is necessary to show that for all $s \le t$,

$$\sum x_i s_i \ge f(s). \tag{3}$$

By concavity of B^i,

$$B_{z^i}^i(t)[z^i(t) - z^i(s)] + B_y^i(t)[y(t) - y(s)] \le B^i(t) - B^i(s). \tag{4}$$

Rearranging terms, (4) becomes

$$B^i(s) - B_{z^i}^i(t)z^i(s) - B_y^i(t)y(s)$$

$$\le B^i(t) - B_{z^i}^i(t)z^i(t) - B_y^i(t)y(t) \tag{5}$$

The right-hand side of (5) is $x_i + a_i$. Consequently,

$$\sum x_i s_i \ge \sum s_i B^i(s) - C(s) + C(s)$$

$$- C_z(t)z(s) - \sum s_i B_y^i(t)y(s) - \sum a_i s_i.$$

This in turn is equivalent to

$$\sum x_i s_i \ge f(s) + C(s) - C_z(t)z(s) - C_y(t)y(s)$$

$$+ C_y(t)y(s) - \sum s_i B_y^i(t)y(s) - \sum a_i s_i. \tag{6}$$

The terms

$$C_y(t)y(s) = \sum s_i B_y^i(t)y(s) = \sum (t_i - s_i)B_y^i(t)y(s) \ge 0, \tag{7}$$

since $t_i - s_i \ge 0$, each $B_y(t) > 0$ because B^i is a strictly increasing function of y and z^i, and $y(s) \ge 0$. Hence (3) would be true if

$$C(s) - C_z(t)z(s) - C_y(t)y(s) \ge \sum a_i s_i. \tag{8}$$

Using the definition of a_i in (iv),

$$\sum a_i s_i = \sum s_i \left\{ \frac{\Theta_i}{\sum \Theta_i t_i} [C(t) - C_y(t)y(t)] - C_z(t)z^i(t) \right\} \tag{9}$$

and the right-hand side is an increasing function of s_i since the terms in curly brackets are nonegative as we shall verify below. Therefore,

$$\sum s_i a_i \le C(t) - C_y(t)y(t) - C_z(t)z(t). \tag{10}$$

By hypothesis, C is subhomogeneous and convex so that Lemma 4, Part 2, applies and yields the following inequality:

$$C(t) - C_y(t)y(t) - C_z(t)z(t)$$

$$\le C(s) - C_y(t)y(s) - C_z(t)z(s). \tag{11}$$

This implies (8) is true, which, in turn, implies (3) is true. The proof that x_i satisfies all of the core constraints is nearly complete save for one detail. Given that C is convex and subhomogeneous, does it follow that a_i as defined by (iv) is nonnegative? The answer is yes owing to

$$C(t) - C_y(t)y(t) \geq C_z(t)z(t) > C_z(t)z^i(t). \tag{12}$$

Hence it is always possible to choose $\Theta_i \geq 0$ and make $a_i \geq 0$. For instance, let

$$\frac{\Theta_i}{\sum \Theta_i t_i} \geq \frac{C_z(t)z^i(t)}{C_z(t)z(t)}$$

and it follows that $a_i \geq 0$. ∎

Since many choices of Θ_i can satisfy the preceding condition, there are many imputations x_i given by (iii) that can satisfy all the core constraints. This means that under the hypotheses of this proposition the core is large. However, in one important special case the core reduces to a single point. This occurs when C is homogeneous of degree 1 so there are constant returns to scale.

> *Corollary: If (i) and (ii) are true and $C(y, z)$ is homogeneous of degree 1, then x_i as given by (iii) and $a_i = 0$ can satisfy all of the core constraints.*

Proof: Routine calculations not shown here suffice. ∎

Some additional results follow from Proposition 1 and the corollary. First, since $f(\cdot)$ has a nonempty core, by virtue of Proposition 1, Part 1, it must be superadditive. Hence any two subcoalitions cannot lose by merging. Second, no subcoalition of the grand coalition can gain by seceding from it, so the grand coalition must be stable. In contrast to the results in Parts 1 and 2, which analyze the shape of f, the present conclusions follow directly by displaying imputations that satisfy all of the core constraints.

By Proposition 1, $f(s)$ as defined in (1.2) has a nonempty core if the cost function is subhomogeneous. Together with the maintained hypotheses about the shapes of the cost and benefit functions, subhomogeneity of the cost function is sufficient for a nonempty core. In a certain limited sense it is also necessary. The next two lemmas make this precise. To emphasize the general validity of these two lemmas, which are true for any function representing the return to a coalition, not just for $f(\cdot)$ as given in (1.2), let $g(\cdot)$ now denote the return to a coalition.

> **Lemma 1:** *Let $g(\cdot)$ be differentiable and admit a nonempty core. Let x denote any imputation in the core. It follows that*
>
> $$x \leq g^*(t), \tag{13}$$
>
> *where $g^*(t)$ denotes the gradient of g at t.*

Proof: Since x is in the core by hypothesis,

$$xt = g(t) \quad \text{and} \quad x(t - \Delta t) \geq g(t - \Delta t)$$

for all $\Delta t \geq 0$. Consequently,

$$-x\Delta t \geq g(t - \Delta t) - g(t) \approx -g^*(t)\Delta t$$

gives the implication that

$$x\Delta t \leq g^*(t)\Delta t \quad \text{for all } \Delta t \geq 0,$$

which implies (13) is true. ∎

> **Lemma 2:** *Under the hypotheses of Lemma 1*
>
> $$g(t) \leq g^*(t)t. \tag{14}$$

Proof: From (13)

$$g(t) = xt \leq g^*(t)t. \quad ∎$$

With the aid of these two lemmas it is possible to prove:

> **Proposition 2:** *The function defined in (1.2) admits a nonempty core only if*
>
> $$C(t) - C_z(t)z(t) \geq 0. \tag{15}$$

Proof: It follows from (1.7) that

$$\frac{\partial f(t)}{\partial t_k} = B^k(t) - C_z(t)z^k(t) \tag{16}$$

so that

$$\sum_k t_k \frac{\partial f(t)}{\partial t_k} = \sum_k t_k B^k(t) - C_z(t) \sum_k t_k z^k(t)$$

$$= f(t) + C(t) - C_z(t)z(t). \tag{17}$$

Therefore,

$$f^*(t)t - f(t) = C(t) - C_z(t)z(t). \tag{18}$$

By Lemma 2, $f(\cdot)$ admits a nonempty core only if the expression on the right of (18) is nonnegative.   ∎

If the cost function $C(y, z)$ is subhomogeneous, then

$$C(y, z) \ge C_z(y, z)z + C_y(y, z)y \tag{19}$$

is true for all outputs y and z and not only for the optimal ones, $y(t)$ and $z(t)$. Moreover, if total cost is a strictly increasing function of these outputs so that $C_y > 0$, it would follow from (19) that

$$C(y, z) - C_z(y, z)z \ge C_y(y, z)y > 0. \tag{20}$$

Consequently, if total cost is subhomogeneous and an increasing function of the outputs of both private and semiprivate goods, then (15) would be true. This does not quite say that given concave benefit functions, a nonempty core must have subhomogeneous cost functions. Nevertheless, the situation is very close to requiring this as a necessary condition. The reasons are similar to those given in the proof of Proposition 5, Part 2. Any set of outputs y and z can be optimal for some t so (15) must hold for arbitrary y and z and not just for those y and z that happen to be optimal for given t. Hence it is necessary that

$$C(y, z) - C_z(y, z)z > 0 \tag{21}$$

for all y and z. However, this condition is not equivalent to the assertion that $C(y, z)$ is a subhomogeneous function of both y and z. It is in the limited sense of (21) that subhomogeneity of the cost function with respect to private good is necessary for a nonempty core.

Turning from this formal analysis, it is useful to consider some possible institutional arrangements that might be capable of putting these results into practice. The next section describes some market mechanisms that might do so. Here suppose individuals have votes they can trade. A person joins a coalition by selling it his vote. Thus, the members of a coalition vote for its program, which is the optimal bundle of private and semiprivate goods it furnishes its members. That grand coalition will form and carry out its program that will attract the most votes. Competition among coalitions for members is equivalent to competition for votes. A nonempty core means that no subcoalition can offer a greater gain to potential members than these members would obtain by selling their votes to the grand coalition. It follows that the grand coalition is stable, that is, the core is nonvoid, if and only if it can obtain the unanimous consent of its members for the optimal bundle of private and semiprivate goods it can furnish them. Each subcoalition has an optimal bundle for its members. The point is that the gain is greater for the bundle that the grand coalition can furnish than for the bundles that any of the subcoalitions can offer its members. The imputation of the gain going to person i, which is x_i, is his return from selling his vote, his consent, to the grand coalition.

3   The invisible-hand theorem

The theory of the core as described in the preceding sections uses two primitive functions, $B^i(y, z^i)$, the benefit an individual i derives from the semiprivate goods y and the private goods z^i, and $C(y, z)$, the total cost to a coalition of producing these goods. Competition among coalitions for members occurs via the imputations they offer to individuals in return for joining the coalition. The grand coalition is stable so that no coalition can gain by seceding from it if the imputations offered to the members of the given coalition by the grand coalition can satisfy all of the core constraints. Thus the theory of the core does represent the effects of competition and the self-interest of the individuals. Nevertheless it will be illuminating to show in greater detail how this theory relates to the more familiar one that assumes each individual chooses quantities of goods to maximize utility subject to a budget constraint. This section describes the relations between the two theories. I explain below the reasons for the section title.

The return to a coalition s is given by the function $f(s)$ as defined in (1.2). The coalition s chooses y and z^i in order to solve a global maximum problem as follows:

$$\max[\sum s_i B^i(y, z^i) - C(y, z)]. \tag{1}$$

Assume this problem has a unique solution and denote it by $y(s)$, $z^i(s)$. Define the constant-unit prices at the solution as follows:

$$p_y^k = \frac{[C_y(s) - \sum_{i \neq k} s_i B_y^i(s)]}{s_k}, \tag{2}$$

where p_y^k is the price of bundle y to type k and

$$p_z = C_z(s). \tag{3}$$

Assume that each individual i can buy any quantity of both the private and the semiprivate goods that he wishes at these constant-unit prices. To assume this for private goods is a standard practice but not for semiprivate goods. For the latter it means each individual in the coalition s may choose the quantities of the semiprivate goods that are best for him at the prices defined by (2). As we shall see, it is a condition of equilibrium that there exists a set of personalized prices, p_y^k, such that each person in the coalition s motivated solely by his self-interest is led as if by an invisible hand to choose the same y, and this common y is optimal both for the coalition and himself.

The individual actually spends the amount

$$p_z z^i + p_y^i y$$

at the indicated constant-unit prices and would be willing to spend at most $B^i(y, z^i)$ so that his surplus ($=$ gain) is given by the function $S^i(y, z^i)$ defined as follows:

$$S^i(y, z^i) = B^i(y, z^i) - p_z z^i - p_y^i y. \tag{4}$$

Let I^i denote the income of individual i so that

$$I^i = p_z \bar{z}^i + p_y^i \bar{y}, \tag{5}$$

where $\bar{z}^i$ and $\bar{y}$ are the initial quantities of the private and semiprivate goods to which individual i has property rights. Note that these are valued at the prices determined by the optimal quantities given by the solutions of the global maximum problem. Let $U^i(y, z^i)$ denote the utility function of individual i. The local maximum problem is defined as follows:

$$\max U^i(y, z^i) \quad \text{with respect to } y \text{ and } z^i$$

$$\text{subject to} \quad p_y^i y + p_z z^i \leq I^i. \tag{6}$$

The Lagrangian for this problem is given by

$$L^i(y, z^i) = U^i(y, z^i) + \mu^i(I^i - p_y^i y - p_z z^i). \tag{7}$$

The first-order necessary conditions are

$$U_y^i - \mu^i p_y^i = 0, \tag{8}$$

$$U_{z^i}^i - \mu^i p_z = 0. \tag{9}$$

The solution of (8) and (9) satisfying the constraint (6) jointly determines y, z^i, and μ^i as implicit functions of the given parameters, p_y^i, p_z, and

I^i. The Lagrangian multiplier, μ^i, in this problem is called the marginal utility of income.

The solution of the local maximum problem also gives the solution of the global maximum problem if

$$B^i(y, z^i) = (1/\mu^i)U^i(y, z^i). \tag{10}$$

In view of the definition of the surplus given by (4), it is evident that

$$S^i = (1/\mu^i)L^i - I^i. \tag{11}$$

Choosing y and z^i to maximize the surplus gives the same solution as the first-order conditions (8) and (9) since μ^i is jointly determined together with y and z^i as functions of the parameters I^i, p_y, and p_z^i. Hence μ^i is most emphatically not a function of y and z^i.

The revenue generated by the expenditures from each person's solution of the local maximum problem is

$$p_z(t)z^i(t) + p_y^i(t)y(t).$$

Let us see how much of the total cost of $y(t)$ and $z(t)$ this revenue can cover. From the definitions of the prices given in (2) and (3) it follows that

$$\frac{C_y(t) - \sum\limits_{j \neq i} t_j B_y^j(t)}{t_i} = p_y^i(t), \tag{12}$$

$$C_z(t) = p_z(t) \tag{13}$$

so that these prices are determined by the optimal quantities for the grand coalition t. The total receipts of the grand coalition at these prices are

$$\sum_i t_i[p_z(t)z^i(t) + p_y^i(t)y(t)]$$

$$= C_z(t)\sum_i t_i z^i(t) + \sum_i t_i B_y^i(t)y(t) \tag{14}$$

$$= C_z(t)z(t) + C_y(t)y(t),$$

which uses the implication of (12) that $p_y^i(t) = B_y^i(t)$. This revenue covers the total cost if the cost function is homogeneous of degree 1 but not if it is strictly subhomogeneous. Therefore, the local and the global maximum problems have the same solutions if it is true both that the grand coalition chooses the prices given by (12) and (13) and the cost function is homogeneous of degree 1.

The imputations in the core do provide for covering the total cost of the optimal quantities of the private and semiprivate goods of the grand coalition. The imputation of person i as determined by the core constraints is given by

$$x_i = B^i(t) - B^i_y(t)y(t) - B^i_{z^i}(t)z^i(t) - a_i. \tag{15}$$

The term a_i gives the contribution to the overhead that suffices to cover the total cost, and this a_i is determined by the competition among the coalitions for members. Although the theory as given in Section 2 does not imply the existence of a unique set of a_i's, it does impose conditions that narrow the range of indeterminacy.

The correspondence between the benefit and utility functions given by (10) is sufficient but not necessary for the validity of the theory. It is only if you take the utility function to be the more primitive and therefore more basic relation that you try to derive the benefit function from the utility function. It is equally plausible in my view to take the benefit function as the basic concept and omit any mention of the utility function. Similarly, Cassel (1967) uses the demand function as one of the fundamental concepts in his theory.

Even the utility function is a more complex idea than the preference relation. Some economists begin with the latter as the foundation. The chief advantage of starting from as elementary assumptions as possible is their transparency, which promotes their acceptibility. It is often easier to grasp the logic underlying preference relations that imply utility or benefit functions than to accept the latter functions as basic concepts in their own right. Preference relations can reduce the more complicated properties embedded in the utility and benefit functions to combinations of simpler concepts. Thus I assume the benefit function is an increasing concave function of the private and semiprivate goods. Let us see in an informal fashion how these properties emerge from the preference relations.

A major implication of a concave benefit or utility function is that benefit or utility becomes measurable, that is, cardinal. The usual practice is to assume ordinal utility that denies that utility is measurable. Ordinal utility means that an individual can say that he prefers A to B and B to C but cannot say how much more he prefers A over B to B over C. Transitivity is a separate property. If this individual has transitive preferences then he must prefer A over C.

If an individual can say how much more he prefers A over B to B over C, then utility becomes measurable up to a linear transformation. This was shown by Alt (1936) following earlier work by Lange (1934). Moreover, Neumann and Morgenstern (1947) introduce an axiom system that shows how to measure utility. For our present purposes their procedure is as follows. Present an individual with the following two prospects:

Prospect 1	Prospect 2
A with probability p	
C with probability $1 - p$	B for sure

For $p = 1$, the individual always prefers Prospect 1 to Prospect 2. For $p = 0$, he always prefers Prospect 2 to Prospect 1. It is therefore reasonable to postulate the existence of a p between 0 and 1 such that the individual is indifferent between the two prospects. Consequently, at this value of p,

$$pU(A) + (1 - p)U(C) = U(B),$$

which gives the implication

$$p[U(A) - U(C)] = U(B) - U(C).$$

This equation implies that it is possible to measure the differences in levels of utility so that utility becomes cardinal. If one accepts this argument based on the Neumann–Morgenstern axioms, then utility is measurable up to a linear transformation without imposing any additional conditions on the shape of the utility function such as concavity. The assumption of a concave utility function also implies that utility must be cardinal. The argument to prove this is different, however. Note that cardinal utility does not mean interpersonal comparisons of utility are necessarily meaningful.

Concavity applies under the following circumstances. Assume the individual is indifferent between A and B so that either utility or benefit from A and B is the same. If the individual prefers a mixture of A and B to either A or B alone, then it follows that the utility or benefit function is quasi-concave. If in addition marginal utility or marginal benefit is a nonincreasing function of the quantity of each private and semiprivate good, then there is the further implication of concavity. The cardinality of utility makes it meaningful to measure marginal utility so that determining whether the utility function is concave becomes operational. Concavity has definite empirical implications, and the assumption of concavity places definite restrictions on the utility or benefit functions. For our purposes the most important implication of the assumption of concavity is this. In conjunction with the assumption that the total cost is an increasing strictly convex function of the quantities of private and semiprivate goods, it follows that for each coalition there exists at most one optimal choice of private and semiprivate goods. Moreover, given that the benefit is an increasing concave function of the quantities of private and semiprivate goods for each person, a unique optimal choice actually exists for each coalition that is a continuous function of the size and composition of the coalition.

Finally, it remains to explain the reasons for the title of this section, the invisible-hand theorem. Reconsider the local maximum problem. Equations (12) and (13) show the prices at which individual i may buy and sell any amount of the private and semiprivate goods. The prices of the private goods equal their marginal costs evaluated at the quantities of the private and semiprivate goods that are optimal for the grand coalition. According to (12) the prices of the semiprivate goods to type i individuals equal the marginal costs of these goods minus the weighted sum of the marginal benefits to all members of the grand coalition other than the type i members. Faced with the prices p_y^i and p_z, individual i is led by self-interest to choose those quantities of $z^i(t)$ and $y(t)$ that are compatible with the optimal choice for the grand coalition. These prices impose on the individual the monetary costs of his choices on the other members of the coalition. This creates a harmony of interest and resolves possible conflict between the solutions of the local and global maximum problems. It is this resolution of conflict and creation of harmony that underlies the invisible-hand theorem. Thus,

$$B_y^i(t) = (1/\mu^i)U_y^i = p_y^i, \tag{16}$$

$$B_{z^i}^i(t) = (1/\mu^i)U_{z^i}^i = p_z. \tag{17}$$

Nor is this all. At these prices not only is individual i led to choose these quantities out of self-interest but in addition it would defeat his self-interest to reveal false demands for either the private or the semiprivate goods. This is because it is only by revealing his true demands that he can solve his own maximum problem. Moreover, there exist sets of prices of the semiprivate goods, one for each individual i, such that the optimal y that each person i wants is the same for them all. The budget constraint as follows:

$$p_z z^i + p_y^i y \leqq I^i$$

shows that all individuals face the same prices of the private goods, p_z, and may choose possibly different quantities of these goods as is shown by the presence of the superscript i on z^i. However, they face different prices of the semiprivate goods, p_y^i, as is indicated by the superscript i on p_y^i, and in equilibrium these prices induce each person of every type to agree on the same quantities of the semiprivate goods.

When there are constant returns to scale so that $C(y, z)$ is homogeneous of degree 1, these prices convey all the information each one needs in order to choose quantities of these goods that also solve the global maximum problem. Hence the invisible-hand theorem is valid under the hypotheses of the corollary of Proposition 1. These prices alone do not convey enough information when the cost function is strictly subhomogeneous because then, as the analysis of the core demonstrates, there are additional terms in the imputation of each person that cover the difference between the revenue obtained from marginal cost pricing and the total cost of the optimal quantities of the private and semiprivate goods.

4   Relations between the neoclassical and core theories

It is now possible to describe some of the relations between the neoclassical theory and the theory of the core. This requires using the theory of noncooperative equilibria for a brief excursion into the theory of oligopoly. A more complete study of the theory of duopoly is in Chapter 7.

The analysis of the preceding section assumes that each coalition has access to the same cost conditions represented by the function $C(y, z)$ making the total cost depend on the outputs of semiprivate goods y and private goods z, both taken as nonnegative quantities. Total cost is a strictly increasing convex function of these outputs. Let any two distinct coalitions supply their members with the same quantities of semiprivate and private goods. Each coalition would then incur the same total cost. This is owing to the assumption that each coalition has access to the same technology and controls its own production facilities.

In the standard (neoclassical) theory it is different. This theory assumes there is a distinct entity, called a firm, apart from the customers it serves and for whom it performs services, makes and sells things, and so on. The theory takes firms as given and remains silent about such questions as why firms are specialized, what purposes they serve, what determines the number and sizes of the firms, and so on. In order to focus on the differences between the standard theory and the theory of the core, we may agree to omit the semiprivate goods because it is the usual practice in the standard theory, and confine our attention to the situation where there are only private goods as is the case in Part 2. Let there be m types of customers such that each type i customer has a total benefit $B^i(z^i)$ that is an increasing strongly concave function of his bundle of private goods. The total benefit of the grand coalition, including all the customers of all the types, is given as follows:

$$\sum_{i=1}^{m} t_i B^i(z^i). \tag{1}$$

It follows that this weighted sum is an increasing strongly concave function of the z^i's.

Assume along with the standard theory that there are n firms so that the total cost to firm j of its output q^j is given by $C^j(q^j)$, which is an increasing convex function of q^j for all $q^j \geq 0$. If this function represents long-term costs, then $C^j(0) = 0$ so that a firm that makes nothing incurs no costs. It incurs a positive cost only if it is active and produces positive rates of output. If $C^j(q^j) > 0$ for all $q^j \geq 0$, then the total cost function is neither continuous nor convex on the closed set $q^j \geqq 0$. These assumptions about the cost conditions closely resemble those in Part 2, Section 4, except that the present case is slightly more general since it allows firms to have different cost functions. The assumptions about cost have the virtue of implying that a firm would not be active unless its revenue can cover at least its total cost. However, the lack of continuity of the cost function complicates the nature of the equilibrium conditions, as we shall see below. Another source of complication is present for the theory of noncooperative equilibrium. Even if the benefit functions are strongly concave, firm gross receipts are generally not a concave function of the quantities it sells. The absence of concavity may result in a nondeterministic (mixed) noncooperative equilibrium.

A necessary condition for an equilibrium is that the total quantity supplied equals the total quantity demanded. That is,

$$\sum_{j=1}^{n} q^j = \sum_{i=1}^{m} t_i z^i. \tag{2}$$

Both q^j and z^i are vectors so that (2) means equality between the corresponding coordinates of these vectors.

The allocation of the total output among the n firms is efficient if and only if the following two conditions are both true.

1. It is impossible to lower the total cost of a given total output by any rearrangement of outputs among the n firms.
2. It is impossible to lower total cost of a given total output by shifting firms between the classes of active and inactive firms so that neither entry nor exit can lower the total cost of the given total output.

In a noncooperative equilibrium these conditions often do not hold so that it would be possible in such an equilibrium to reallocate a given total set of output rates among the firms and thereby achieve a reduction in their total cost. This issue arises in Chapter 8, which discusses rivalry via innovation. The standard theory of perfect competition postulates the existence of a constant-unit price vector p at which the firms can sell their outputs. In a noncooperative equilibrium, prices are not exogenous so that changes in a firm's outputs may affect them. Let π^j denote the total profit of firm j. Therefore,

$$\pi^j = pq^j - C^j(q^j) \tag{3}$$

is the profit available for distribution to the owners of firm j. (The term pq^j means the scalar product of the two vectors.)

If the grand coalition includes everyone in the economy that contains the n firms, then the owners of the firms are the same as the customers of the firms. Firms are more specialized than their customers. This does not contradict the assertion that in a closed economy every owner of a firm is a customer but not every customer is an owner. In the present actual economy where firms are corporations owned by individuals who have shares of stock in many different corporations, it is even plausible to assume that many customers are also owners. In the theory of the core as presented here, assume that the owners and the customers are the same. Therefore, the net benefit of the members of the grand coalition is given by

$$\sigma = \sum_{i=1}^{m} t_i B^i(z^i) - \sum_{j=1}^{n} C^j(q^j). \tag{4}$$

Assume, as is only reasonable, that the objective of the grand coalition is to obtain the maximal net benefit with respect to z^i and q^j subject to the constraint (2). The Lagrangian for this problem is

$$\sigma + \lambda\left(\sum_j q^j - \sum_i t_i z^i\right).$$

The optimal values of z^i and q^j, denote them by $\bar{z}^i$ and $\bar{q}^j$, must satisfy

$$\bar{\sigma}_{q^j} + \bar{\lambda} \leq 0, \tag{5}$$

and

$$\bar{\sigma}_{z^i} - \bar{\lambda} t_i \leq 0. \tag{6}$$

Since $\bar{\sigma}_{q^j} = -C^j_{q^j}(\bar{q}^j)$ and $\bar{\sigma}_{z^i} = t_i B^i_{z^i}(\bar{z}^i)$, these conditions become

$$-\overline{C}^j_{q^j} + \overline{\lambda} \leq 0, \tag{7}$$

$$\overline{B}^i_{z^i} - \overline{\lambda} \leq 0, \tag{8}$$

assuming $t_i > 0$ so it may be divided out of (6). The Lagrangian multiplier $\overline{\lambda}$ is a vector with as many coordinates as there are commodities. For goods that are actually produced and consumed, the corresponding coordinates of $\overline{\lambda}$ are both the marginal costs of the goods as shown by (7) and the marginal benefits as shown by (8). Conditions (7) and (8) must be satisfied by the optimal values of q^j and z^i.

The neoclassical theory defines a vector of constant-unit prices p and calls

$$p = B^i_{z^i}(z^i) \tag{9}$$

the (inverse) demand functions for the commodities by type i individuals. If $\overline{p} = B^i_{z^i}(\overline{z}^i)$ so that prices are set at the levels equal to the values of the Lagrangian multipliers determined by conditions (7) and (8), then some important conclusions follow. Let each firm decide how much to produce in order to maximize its profits where its profits π^j are given by

$$\pi^j = \overline{p}q^j - C^j(q^j). \tag{10}$$

Since the prices are given constants that do not vary in response to the output rates of form j, it chooses q^j to satisfy the first-order necessary conditions

$$\frac{\partial \pi^j}{\partial q^j} = \overline{p} - C^j_q(q^j) \leq 0. \tag{11}$$

Consequently, the desire for maximal profits by each firm makes it choose output rates that satisfy (11), and these output rates also satisfy (7) and (8), which are the first-order necessary conditions for the maximal net benefit of the grand coalition. Here is yet another instance of Adam Smith's invisible-hand theorem. The theorem is valid here not only because prices are given constants to the firms so that their output rates cannot affect these prices but also because the prices are set equal to the correct levels, $\overline{p} = \overline{\lambda}$.

There are complications when the firms do take into account how changes in their rates of output affect the prices of the commodities. The theory of noncooperative equilibrium tries to deal with these complications. Let

$$z^{ij} = \text{quantities sold by firm } j \text{ to a type } i \text{ person.} \tag{12}$$

Hence the total output of firm j satisfies the following equation:

$$q^j = \sum_i t_i z^{ij}. \tag{13}$$

Similarly, there is an accounting identity for the purchases by type i persons since these purchases must satisfy

$$z^i = \sum_j z^{ij}. \tag{14}$$

Keep in mind that (13) and (14) are relations among vectors and apply to each coordinate of these vectors. It is not necessary to assume that each individual buys positive quantities from each firm and that each firm makes positive quantities of each good. Some of the coordinates of z^{ij} may be zero and some of the coordinates of q^j may be zero. If so, it would change the equilibrium conditions from equalities to inequalities.

Impose the condition that every individual pays the same price for a good [cf. (9)]. As a result no firm can discriminate among its customers by selling the same commodity at different prices to different customers. The profits of firm j now satisfy

$$\pi^j = pq^j - C^j(q^j). \tag{15}$$

This expression differs from (10) owing to the fact that in (15), p does depend on q^j, whereas in (10) prices do not depend on q^j and are given constants. To have an equilibrium it is still necessary that the total quantity produced by all firms equals the total quantity demanded by all customers so that q^j and z^i must satisfy (2).

In a noncooperative equilibrium each firm chooses q^j and z^{ij} to maximize its profits without taking into account how its choices affect its rivals. Each firm acts on its own and independently of the actions of the others. However, the demand conditions given by (9) relate the prices to the quantities bought by the individuals. Hence q^j does not directly affect p, and it does so indirectly via the constraints (2), (13), and (14). Although the firms can choose independently values of some variables, these must be consistent with the accounting identities forming the constraints (2), (13), and (14). Therefore, a noncooperative equilibrium poses a constrained maximum problem for each of the n firms. The necessary conditions are the inequalities that a noncooperative equilibrium must satisfy. The constrained maximum problem is as follows:

$$\max \pi^j \quad \text{with respect to } q^j \text{ and } z^{ij}$$

$$\text{subject to} \quad \text{(2) and (13)}.$$

The Lagrangian for this maximum problem is

$$\pi^j + \mu_j(q^j - \sum_i t_i z^{ij}) + \lambda(\sum_j q^j - \sum_i t_i z^i). \tag{16}$$

The first-order conditions that a solution of this problem must satisfy, which are the same as the conditions for a noncooperative equilibrium, are as follows:

$$\frac{\partial \pi^j}{\partial q^j} + \mu_j + \lambda \leq 0, \tag{17}$$

$$\frac{\partial \pi^j}{\partial z^{ij}} - \mu_j t_i - \lambda t_i \leq 0. \tag{18}$$

Make the substitutions $\partial \pi^j / \partial q^j = p - C^j_{q^j}$ and $\partial \pi^j / \partial z^{ij} = B^i_{z^i z^i} q^j$ so that conditions (17) and (18) become more familiar as follows:

$$p - C^j_{q^j} + \mu_j + \lambda \leq 0, \tag{19}$$

$$q^j B^i_{z^i z^i} - \lambda t_i - \mu_j t_i \leq 0. \tag{20}$$

(The term $q^j B^i_{z^i z^i}$ shows the extent to which the output of firm j can affect the prices p.)

Given the assumptions that all $B^i(\cdot)$ are strongly concave and continuous for all $z^i \geq 0$ and that the total cost function is convex and positive for all $q^j \geq 0$, while $C^j(0) = 0$, questions arise concerning the number and nature of the equilibria. First, consider the receipts, pq^j. These are implicit functions of z^{ij}. Whether the receipts are concave functions of these variables depends on the third-order partials of $B^i(z^i)$. Concavity of $B^i(z^i)$ yields no implications about these partials. Before considering some consequences of this, let us turn to the cost conditions.

In order to represent the cost conditions correctly, it is assumed that $C^j(\cdot)$ is neither continuous nor convex on the closed convex set $q^j \geq 0$. This raises a difficult problem of giving sufficient conditions for the existence of a noncooperative equilibrium because the pertinent functions are not continuous on their whole domain and the most useful tool, a fixed-point theorem, does not apply. This is not to say that a noncooperative equilibrium may altogether fail to exist. However, it does mean that no deterministic noncooperative equilibrium may exist. Instead there may be a mixed noncooperative equilibrium. This alternative has even stronger credentials in light of the demand conditions. If the demand functions imply gross receipts are nonconcave functions of quantities sold, then this too can result in a mixed noncooperative equilibrium even if the cost functions were continuous on their closed domain. Taken together, the assumptions about the benefit and cost

functions combine to lend considerable plausibility to the conclusion
that there may well be a mixed noncooperative equilibrium, even perhaps more than one. (For a direct treatment of the implications of
similar cost conditions using the theory of the core, see the next
chapter.)

In the interest of avoiding these complications, for present purposes
assume that (19) and (20) have interior solutions so that they hold as
equalities. This is by no means an innocuous assumption. A more rigorous analysis would recognize the presence of the discontinuities and
the consequent absence of concavity for the firm profit functions. Assuming (19) and (20) have interior solutions, it follows that

$$-(q^j/t_i)B^i_{z^iz^i} = p - C^j_{q^j}. \qquad (21)$$

Under certain conditions (21) implies that when t_i is large relative to
q^j, the left side of (21) is small so that prices are close to marginal
costs. This would mean that the firm has little power to affect prices
by means of its output decisions. To see when this is true, observe
that $q^j = \sum_k t_k z^{kj}$ implies that

$$\frac{q^j}{t_i} = z^{ij} + \sum_{k \neq i} \frac{t_k}{t_i} z^{kj}.$$

Therefore, if t_i is large relative to all other t_k and if z^{ij} is small so that
firm j is small, then the left side of (21) is small and prices are close
to marginal cost. Under these conditions it is the case that for large
enough t_i, firms are small relative to the total size of the economy and
prices are close to marginal costs.

Equation (21), a relation among vectors, also shows that even though
the matrix $B^i_{z^iz^i}$ is negative definite owing to the strong concavity of B^i,
it does not follow that all prices exceed the corresponding marginal
costs. However, negative definiteness does imply

$$(-q^j B^i_{z^iz^i} q^j)/t_i = (p - C^j_{q^j})q^j > 0.$$

This inequality means that the difference between prices and marginal
costs, multiplied by the quantities sold by firm j, and summed over all
the goods it sells, is positive.

On the basis of these results it is possible to answer several interesting questions. First, what contract terms between the firms and the
customers would enable the customers to enlist the self-interest of the
firms to serve the best interest of the customers? The customers wish
to devise terms such that the firms seeking maximum profits will pick
output rates that will satisfy (11), which are the necessary conditions

for maximal net benefit as well as necessary for maximal firm profit. Second, the customers want procedures that can discover the quantities that will satisfy (11).

Think of the customers as the principals and the firms as their agents. The agents serve the principals' interests best by selling to the principals at prices equal to $\bar{p}$. If the principals can impose these fixed prices on the firms, then the firms will select output rates that satisfy (11) because such rates maximize their profits. This raises two problems. First, there is the problem of discovering $\bar{p}$ and second the problem of enforcing these prices.

Assuming the optimal prices are initially unknown, there are market mechanisms that can discover them under suitable conditions, conditions that admittedly rely on the assumption that the necessary conditions (19) and (20) do have a unique interior solution. Choose an arbitrary initial set of prices at which firms must sell their goods. Let the outputs they choose at these given prices then be sold for whatever prices they can fetch that clear the markets. These market clearing prices will usually differ from the arbitrarily chosen initial prices. A mechanism for revising prices is needed. Let it be as follows. For any commodity with an excess supply, the market clearing price is below the initial price. Hence on the next round let the prices of such commodities be reduced by an amount proportional to their excess supply. For any commodity with an excess demand at the initially set price, the market clearing price will exceed that price. On the next round let the prices at which the firms can sell these goods be raised. Under suitable conditions there is convergence to $\bar{p}$ from an arbitrary initial set of prices. In this fashion the standard theory explains the contract terms between firms and their customers, and it describes a mechanism capable of finding and maintaining the output rates compatible with maximum profits for the firms and maximum net benefits for the customers. These prices $\bar{p}$ equal marginal costs. There may be additional problems of generating enough revenue to cover the total cost. There is also the problem of enforcing the contract terms, which is discussed below.

As we have seen, there is a nonempty core given these assumptions about the shape of the benefit and cost functions if the aggregate cost function has nondecreasing returns to scale. When there are constant returns to scale, the number of firms is indeterminate both in the core theory and in the neoclassical theory. When there are increasing returns to scale for the aggregate total cost function, then the core theory and the neoclassical theory both imply that a single firm would be best. However, when efficiency in production requires a finite determinate number of firms as is the case, for instance, under the cost conditions described in Part 2, section 4, then the core is empty unless appropriate restrictions on the contracting terms are allowed. It is under these cost conditions that both the neoclassical and the core theories encounter similar difficulties.

These difficulties are present whether or not there is cooperation. If firms cooperate among themselves and ignore the interests of their customers, monopolistic restrictions can emerge inconsistent with the maximal net benefit of the grand coalition. The cooperation among the firms may even be self-enforcing so it can persist (see Chapter 6). Even if the monopolistic cooperation is not self-enforcing, causing a reversion to the noncooperative equilibrium as described above, the resulting rates of output will not satisfy inequalities (11), and there is an implication of inefficiency.

The issue is whether the customers can enforce the contract terms that make prices equal $\bar{p}$. Individual firms have an incentive to violate these terms if they recognize that reductions in their output rates can force prices above the prescribed level even without explicit collusion among themselves. Given prices at $\bar{p}$, firms have no reason to attempt to sell more at lower prices since this would lower their profits. Violating the contract terms takes the form of selling less than $\bar{q}^j$ at prices above $\bar{p}$. As we shall see in Chapter 6, a noncooperative equilibrium is always self-enforcing. If it is more profitable to the firms than the equilibrium with prices $\bar{p}$ and outputs $\bar{q}^j$, it follows that the efficient equilibrium cannot survive without outside intervention. Therefore, individuals who can reach an agreement with firms as their agents would impose $\bar{p}$ as the maximum prices and would need third-party enforcement.

Cheating by individual firms is different when they collude in a profit-maximizing monopolistic cartel. A cartel sets a floor on prices and a ceiling on output rates. A firm who wishes to cheat the cartel does so by offering to sell more than its assigned quota at prices below those set by the cartel. It is in sharp contrast to the preceding situation where the customers set ceiling prices and floors on the corresponding outputs.

CHAPTER 5

Equilibrium with decreasing average cost: an application of the theory of the core illustrated by production and exchange among spatially separated markets

1   Introduction

Edgeworth invented the method of analysis now known as the theory of the core in his study of exchange. This reminds us that neoclassical economic theory is the source of this approach and that the theory of the core owes its greatest achievements to refinements of the study of exchange. A coalition of traders in the current usage corresponds to a contract among them in Edgeworth's analysis. The process by which traders seek the best possible terms for themselves is called recontracting by Edgeworth. An allocation of the goods among the traders gives an equilibrium when none can get better terms. Not only does this mean that each leaves the market with a bundle of goods he does not regard as inferior to his initial one but also that he cannot obtain better terms from anyone. The theory attempts to answer the question of when there is an equilibrium and if there is one whether it is the only one. It is a major accomplishment of Edgeworth to answer these questions. Nor is this all. He found the range of possible equilibria in case there is only a finite number of traders and showed how the indeterminacy shrinks as the number of traders of each type increases. In the limit with an infinite number of traders of each type, only a single equilibrium might be compatible with the competitive process. One should keep in mind these roots of the theory of the core in considering how it applies to other economic situations.

We shall consider a situation where there is production for sale in spatially separated markets. The nature of the costs of production complicates the analysis as we shall see. If a plant has decreasing average costs and if there are plants with different costs and capacities, then there may be no equilibrium if the buyers and sellers may deal with whom they please without restriction. When this happens, the core is empty.

Many theories are available for studying what might happen when the core is empty. It is difficult to choose among them. This is because

144

manded would be larger if the price were lower. But, as we shall see, there is no loss of generality by confining our attention to the case where the maximal acceptable price is given in order to see whether an equilibrium can exist. Assume there are potential buyers at n locations so that $j = 1, \ldots, n$.

There are m plants, one at each location i. Let A_i denote the label of plant i so $i = 1, \ldots, m$. The capacity of plant A_i is c_i. If it produces any positive output, then it incurs a cost a_i independent of its actual level of output. If it produces nothing, it can avoid incurring this cost, a_i. For this reason call a_i the *avoidable cost* of A_i. It is a quasi-fixed cost because it does not depend on the actual output rate, though it may depend on the capacity of the plant. We may interpret t_{ii} as the variable cost per unit of output so that t_{ij} represents the incremental cost of producing the good for customers of type j who differ from those of type i. This is to say that each plant can produce more cheaply for sale to the customers in its home market than for those in more distant markets. There is, consequently, another application of this model to the problem of determining what variety of goods will be made for customers of different tastes as represented by their location in the product space. We shall not pursue this interpretation though it is an interesting one.

The hypothesis that there is an avoidable cost is a simple approximation to a more general cost function often used in economic theory. The total cost is a strictly increasing function of the rate of output. The marginal cost is U-shaped and has a minimum at some positive output rate. Hence the total cost function is initially concave and becomes convex for large enough rates of output. A polynomial can represent this explicitly. Write

$$A_{h,k}(q) = a_0[1 - (1 - (q/c))^h] + a_1(q/c) + a_2(q/c)^k,$$

where q denotes the rate of output of the plant and c denotes the plant capacity, which is its maximum rate of output. As h and k become large, this polynomial approaches the following limit:

$$A(q) = \begin{cases} 0 & \text{if } q = 0, \\ a_0 + a_1(q/c) & \text{if } 0 < q < c, \\ a_0 + a_1 + a_2 & \text{if } q = c. \end{cases}$$

The parameter a_0 is the avoidable cost, a_1 is the unit variable cost, and a_2 is the incremental cost of operating at capacity. In the approximation given at the outset, $a_1 = a_2 = 0$.

The demand conditions also furnish a simple approximation to one often used in economic theory. They imply that the demand at location

j is perfectly elastic at a price b_j up to the maximum quantity demanded at this location, which is d_j.

The assumptions impose certain constraints on the production decisions of each plant. Let q_{ij} denote the quantity shipped from plant A_i at location i to destination j.

$$q_{ij} \leq d_j \quad \text{and} \quad \sum_j q_{ij} \leq c_i. \tag{2}$$

The first constraint means that A_i cannot ship more to destination j than the maximum quantity that can be sold at that destination. The second constraint asserts that A_i cannot produce a total output greater than the capacity of its plant.

Let Π_i denote the net return of A_i. If A_i produces nothing, it incurs no cost and gets no revenue so its net return would be zero. If it produces some positive output, then the following equation can be satisfied:

$$\Pi_i = \sum_j p_{ij} q_{ij} - a_i. \tag{3}$$

Since shipping nothing from i to j is always feasible, it must be true that

$$\Pi_i = \max \left\langle 0, \sum_j p_{ij} q_{ij} - a_i \right\rangle. \tag{4}$$

From this result we may conclude that a necessary but not a sufficient condition for one unit of the good to go from A_i to destination j is that $p_{ij} \geq 0$. Thus, the shipments from a plant must generate enough revenue after payment of the shipping cost as will contribute to defray the avoidable cost of the plant.

> **Definition 1:** *An efficient production schedule (EPS) of A_i is a nonnegative n-vector $q_i = \langle q_{i1}, q_{i2}, \ldots, q_{in} \rangle$ such that*
>
> (i) $\sum_j p_{ij} q_{ij} - a_i \geq 0$;
>
> (ii) $\sum_j q_{ij} \leq c_i$;
>
> (iii) $q_{ij} \leq d_j$.

According to this definition, an EPS does not necessarily yield a maximum net return to A_i. However, it must not impose a loss. It also follows from this definition that a plant may have many EPSs. To distinguish an EPS from other production schedules, it is sometimes convenient to include the subscript h to denote EPS h for A_i.

Definition 2: An extreme efficient production schedule is an EPS that is not a convex combination of other EPSs.

This means there may be EPSs that are proper convex combinations of extreme EPSs. This is true when

$$q_{hi} = \sum_{h'} \delta_{h'i} q_{h'i}, \qquad \delta_{h'i} \geq 0 \quad \text{and} \quad \sum_{h'} \delta_{h'i} = 1$$

provided at least one $\delta_{h'i} \neq 1$. Since there is a finite number of destinations, the number of extreme EPSs of each A_i is also finite.

Efficient production schedules have several properties that we shall now derive. At the outset there is the question of existence. Only trivial production schedules (all q's are zero) may exist. A necessary and sufficient condition for the existence of a nontrivial EPS is the existence of a nontrivial profit-maximizing EPS. Plainly, there may not exist nonnegative q_{ij} capable of satisfying all three conditions (i)–(iii), owing to the necessity in particular of generating enough receipts to satisfy (i). Fortunately, it is very easy to determine whether or not there exists a nontrivial profit-maximizing EPS:

1. Arrange p_{ij} in order of size from the biggest to the smallest and plot the piecewise linear total revenue graph as shown in Figure 5.1.
2. Draw the line parallel to the x axis through the points $(0, a_i)$ and (c_i, a_i).
3. The most profitable EPS can be read off at a glance in Figure 5.1. If the area under the total revenue curve exceeds the avoidable cost, as is true for the point P_2, then there exists a nontrivial profit-maximizing EPS. If the total revenue is less than the avoidable cost, as is true for the point P_1, then producing nothing is optimal so the only EPS is trivial.

Assuming a nontrivial profit-maximizing EPS does exist, all EPSs are solutions of the inequalities (i)–(iii). Finding the solutions and their properties is most readily done with the aid of linear programming. To this end, rewrite the inequality constraints defining an EPS in the form of equalities as follows:

$$-\sum_{j} q_{ij} p_{ij} + u_i = -a_i, \qquad \sigma_i, \tag{5}$$

$$\sum_{j} q_{ij} + v_i = c_i, \qquad \mu_i, \tag{6}$$

$$q_{ij} + w_{ij} = d_j, \qquad \lambda_{ij}, \tag{7}$$

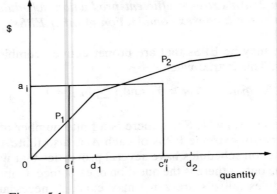

Figure 5.1

with u_i, v_i, and $w_{ij} \geq 0$. The variables to the right are the Lagrangian multipliers of the dual problem. Note that

$$u_i = \sum_j q_{ij} p_{ij} - a_i \geq 0$$

is the profit from the EPS $\langle q_{ij} \rangle$. Also observe that the three constraints (5)–(7) are in different units, u_i is in dollars while v_i and w_{ij} are in physical units of the good. Owing to this difference in units, I define the objective function as follows:

$$z = u_i / \bar{p}_i + v_i + \sum_j w_{ij} \tag{8}$$

where $\bar{p}_i$ is a deflator described more fully below. All EPSs satisfy (5)–(7), and are in turn the solutions of the following linear programming (LP) problem:

> *Primal*   min z
>
> with respect to u_i, v_i, q_{ij} and $w_{ij} \geq 0$
>
> subject to (5)–(7).

The Lagrangian for this problem is given by

$$u_i / \bar{p}_i + v_i + \sum_j w_{ij} + \sigma_i (-a_i + \sum_j q_{ij} p_{ij} - u_i)$$

$$+ \mu_i (c_i - \sum_j q_{ij} - v_i)$$

$$+ \sum_j \lambda_{ij} (d_j - q_{ij} - w_{ij}).$$

The necessary conditions that solutions of the primal problem must satisfy are as follows:

$$1/\bar{p}_i - \sigma_i \geq 0, \qquad u_i, \tag{9}$$

$$1 - \mu_i \geq 0, \qquad v_i, \tag{10}$$

$$1 - \lambda_{ij} \geq 0, \qquad w_{ij}, \tag{11}$$

$$\sigma_i p_{ij} - \mu_i - \lambda_{ij} \geq 0, \qquad q_{ij}. \tag{12}$$

The dual problem is given by

Dual $\max \mu_i c_i + \sum_j \lambda_{ij} d_j - \sigma_i a_i$

with respect to $\sigma_i, \mu_i, \lambda_{ij}$ (unrestricted signs),

subject to (9)–(12).

The Lagrangian for the dual problem is given by

$$\mu_i c_i + \sum_j \lambda_{ij} d_j - \sigma_i a_i + u_i(1/\bar{p}_i - \sigma_i) + v_i(1 - \mu_i)$$

$$+ \sum_j w_{ij}(1 - \lambda_{ij}) + \sum_j (\sigma_i p_{ij} - \mu_i - \lambda_{ij})q_{ij}.$$

It is easy to verify that the necessary conditions for solving the dual problem derived from this Lagrangian coincide with (5)–(7).

While (9)–(11) establish upper bounds on the multipliers, σ_i, μ_i, and λ_{ij}, the lower bounds are not immediately apparent. In fact, these multipliers must be nonnegative. To prove this, use complementary slackness, which implies that

$$u_i(1/\bar{p}_i - \sigma_i) = 0 \Rightarrow u_i/\bar{p}_i = u_i \sigma_i \geq 0,$$

$$v_i(1 - \mu_i) = 0 \Rightarrow v_i = v_i \mu_i \geq 0,$$

$$w_{ij}(1 - \lambda_{ij}) = 0 \Rightarrow w_{ij} = w_{ij} \lambda_{ij} \geq 0.$$

Since u_i, v_i, and $w_{ij} \geq 0$, it follows from these inequalities that

$$\sigma_i, \mu_i, \lambda_{ij} \geq 0. \tag{13}$$

These results lend special interest to (12), which shows relations among the shadow prices in the various destinations.

It is also true that the EPSs that are the solutions of the LP problem must be extreme EPSs. This follows from the fact that no solution of the primal problem can have u_i, v_i, and w_{ij} all positive. The proof is by contradiction. Suppose u_i, v_i, and w_{ij} were all positive. This would enable at least one q_{ij} to be larger so that at least one of the values among the positive u_i, v_i, and w_{ij} could be reduced in violation of the maintained hypothesis that there is a minimum of z. As a corollary of this result, it follows that if $u_i > 0$, so that an EPS gives a positive profit, then either $v_i = 0$ or at least one $w_{ij} = 0$. Hence either the capacity constraint must be binding ($v_i = 0$) or at least one demand constraint must be binding ($w_{ij} = 0$).

It is an implication of the duality theorem of linear programming that

$$\mu_i c_i + \sum_j \lambda_{ij} d_j - \sigma_i a_i = u_i/\overline{p}_i + v_i + \sum_j w_{ij} \geq 0. \tag{14}$$

Useful definitions of the deflator, $\overline{p}_i$, emerge from consideration of (14). It is helpful to introduce a break-even factor θ_i defined as follows:

$$a_i = \theta_i \overline{p}_i c_i \tag{15}$$

so that θ_i is the fraction of total receipts generated by unit revenue $\overline{p}_i$ that just suffices to cover the avoidable cost, a_i. Rewrite the dual objective as follows:

$$(\mu_i c_i - a_i/\overline{p}_i) + (1/\overline{p}_i - \sigma_i)a_i + \sum_j \lambda_{ij} d_j \geq 0. \tag{16}$$

Consequently,

$$(1/\overline{p}_i - \sigma_i)a_i + \sum_j \lambda_{ij} d_j \geq (a_i/\overline{p}_i - \mu_i c_i). \tag{17}$$

But

$$a_i/\overline{p}_i - \mu_i c_i = (\theta_i - 1)c_i + (1 - \mu_i)c_i.$$

Therefore, (17) becomes

$$(1/\overline{p}_i - \sigma_i)a_i + \sum_j \lambda_{ij} d_j \geq (1 - \mu_i)c_i + (\theta_i - 1)c_i. \tag{18}$$

The left-hand side always has a nonnegative lower bound. The larger is θ_i, the break-even fraction, the higher is this lower bound. There is the smallest lower bound if $\overline{p}_i$ is chosen such that

$$\overline{p}_i = a_i/c_i \quad \text{and} \quad \theta_i = 1. \tag{19}$$

For this choice, $\overline{p}_i$ is the unit avoidable cost when the plant operates at its installed capacity and it breaks even with $\theta_i = 1$.

All solutions of the LP problem must give the same value of the objective function

$$z = u_i/\overline{p}_i + v_i + \sum_j w_{ij}.$$

The most profitable EPS is one of the solutions, namely, the one for which u_i is the largest. For this solution either $v_i = 0$ or at least one $w_{ij} = 0$. But the most profitable EPS is not always the only solution of the LP problem. In working through examples, we shall encounter many cases where a plant has several extreme EPSs that yield profits below the maximum and that appear in an equilibrium.

In concluding this discussion of the properties of the EPS, there remains one final and important point. Every solution of the LP problem is an extreme EPS by virtue of the fact that in each solution at least one of the variables u_i, v_i, and w_{ij} must actually be zero.

Each plant A_i calculates its EPS without regard to the actions of the other plants. To make this clear there is:

Definition 3: S_{hi} *is a simple coalition if it includes A_i together with the buyers implied by an EPS q_{hi}.*

The members of a simple coalition can make mutually advantageous bargains among themselves without interference from any of the other individuals. To show this formally, we shall write a certain inequality that describes the feasibility of the bargain. Let r_i denote the gain (or revenue) of A_i and let s_j denote the gain per customer at destination j. Acting on their own, the members of the coalition S_{hi} obtain a net return given as follows:

$$V(S_{hi}) = \sum_j q_{hij}p_{ij} - a_i \geq 0. \qquad (20)$$

The result of an equilibrium for all of the plants and the customers must be a set of returns, $r_1, r_2, \ldots, r_m$ to the A_i's and gains to the buyers at the n destinations, $s_1, s_2, \ldots, s_n$ such that

$$r_i + q_{hi}s \geq V(S_{hi}). \qquad (21)$$

(The term $q_{hi}s$ represents the scalar product $\sum_j q_{hij}s_j$.) Inequality (21) is one of the constraints that r and s must satisfy in order to have a nonempty core.

There may be nonextreme EPSs. Plainly, however, if there are r and s that can satisfy (21) for all extreme efficient production schedules, then the same is true for all convex combinations of these extreme EPSs. Hence without loss of generality we may confine our attention to the extreme EPS in order to see if there are distributions capable of satisfying (21).

Our first task is to see whether an equilibrium exists. To solve this problem it is necessary to see if the sum of the gains to the A_i's and the buyers at the n destinations capable of satisfying the constraints imposed by the simple coalitions is feasible. This poses two problems. First, we must determine the feasibility of a proposed imputation of the gains. Second, we must compute the minimal gains acceptable to all of the participants in the market. The solution of the first problem is an exercise in integer programming. The solution of the second is one in linear programming. The next section treats the linear programming problem and the following section the integer programming problem. As we shall see, the two are closely related and we shall exploit their close relation in order to study the existence of an equilibrium.

3   The linear programming problem

The preceding section defines a linear programming (LP) problem for which the solutions are efficient production schedules and shadow prices for each A_i. These shadow prices are specific for each plant A_i. They do not correspond in an immediately apparent way to equilibrium outputs and prices for all the plants and customers in all of the locations. The purpose of the present section is to describe another LP problem that gives the first approach to a determination of a global equilibrium. The solutions of this problem give the distributions of the minimally acceptable gains to the buyers and sellers. The equilibrium prices and output rates are the result of an implementation of this distribution of the gains as determined by the solutions of the linear and integer programming problems.

The primal problem is defined as follows:

$$\min \sum_{i=1}^{m} r_i + \sum_{j=1}^{n} d_j s_j \tag{1}$$

with respect to r_i and s_j subject to

$$r_i + \sum_{j} q_{hij} s_j \geq V(S_{hi}), \qquad \delta_{hi}, \tag{2}$$

$$r_i \geq 0, \qquad \alpha_i, \tag{3}$$

$$s_j \geq 0, \qquad \beta_j. \tag{4}$$

$V(S_{hi})$ denotes the gain of a simple coalition S_{hi} as defined in (2.20) so that q_{hi} is an efficient production schedule. Every EPS is included in (2). The dual variables for these constraints are shown on the right of the corresponding inequalities, and they are all nonnegative.

The dual problem is as follows:

$$\max \sum_{h,i} \delta_{hi} V(S_{hi}) \tag{5}$$

with respect to δ_{hi}, α_i, and β_j nonnegative and subject to

$$\sum_h \delta_{hi} + \alpha_i \leq 1, \qquad r_i, \tag{6}$$

$$\sum_{i,h} \delta_{hi}q_{hij} + \beta_j \leq d_j, \qquad s_j. \tag{7}$$

With the aid of the following relations of complementary slackness,

$$\delta_{hi}\left[V(S_{hi}) - r_i - \sum_j q_{hij}s_j \right] = 0, \tag{8}$$

$$\alpha_i[0 - r_i] = 0, \tag{9}$$

$$\beta_j[0 - s_j] = 0, \tag{10}$$

$$r_i\left[1 - \sum_h \delta_{hi} - \alpha_i \right] = 0, \tag{11}$$

$$s_j\left[d_j - \sum_{h,i} \delta_{hi}q_{hij} - \beta_j \right] = 0, \tag{12}$$

we can simplify the primal and dual problems by eliminating the dual variables α_i and β_j. Thus, it follows from (9) that (11) reduces to

$$r_i\left[1 - \sum_h \delta_{hi} \right] = 0, \tag{13}$$

and from (10) that (12) becomes

$$s_j\left[d_j - \sum_{h,i} \delta_{hi}q_{hij} \right] = 0. \tag{14}$$

Therefore,

$$r_i > 0 \Rightarrow 1 - \sum_h \delta_{hi} = 0; \tag{15}$$

$$1 - \sum_h \delta_{hi} > 0 \Rightarrow r_i = 0. \tag{16}$$

Also, the gains of the customers in market j must satisfy the following relations:

$$s_j > 0 \Rightarrow d_j - \sum_{h,i} \delta_{hi}q_{hij} = 0; \tag{17}$$

$$d_j - \sum_{h,i} \delta_{hi}q_{hij} > 0 \Rightarrow s_j = 0. \tag{18}$$

Relations (15) and (16) refer to the sellers. According to (15), if A_i has a positive gain, then it fully uses its capacity. According to (16), if A_i uses only part of its capacity, then its gain is zero. Relations (17) and (18) refer to the buyers. If the buyers at destination j have a positive gain, which means they pay a price per unit below the maximum they would be willing to pay, then the weighted sum of the shipments to this destination j must equal the total quantity demanded. According to (18), if the total quantity demanded in market j exceeds the weighted sum of the shipments, then the gain of each buyer in market j must be zero. The gain of the buyers may be zero for two different reasons. First, though there are positive shipments to destination j, these are too small to satisfy the whole demand. Consequently, the buyers must pay their maximal acceptable price. Second, there may be no shipments to market j so that the potential customers in this market obtain none of the good and therefore have a zero gain.

A solution of the primal LP problem entails the solution of $m + n$ linearly independent equations. These come from the constraints for the simple coalitions of which there are at least m, and from the $m + n$ constraints imposing nonnegativity on the gains of the buyers and sellers.

Owing to complementary slackness, (9) and (10), it is unnecessary to take explicit account of α_i and β_j, the dual variables for r_i and s_j. This means the LP problem reduces to the following:

$$\textit{Primal} \qquad \min \sum_{i=1}^{m} r_i + \sum_{j=1}^{n} d_j s_j \tag{19}$$

with respect to r_i, $s_j \geq 0$ subject to

$$r_i + \sum_{j=1}^{m} q_{hij} s_j \geq V(S_{hi}), \qquad \delta_{hi} \geq 0. \tag{20}$$

$$\textit{Dual} \qquad \max \sum_{h,i} \delta_{hi} V(S_{hi}) \tag{21}$$

with respect to $\delta_{hi} \geq 0$ subject to

$$\sum_{h} \delta_{hi} \leq 1, \qquad r_i \geq 0, \tag{22}$$

$$\sum_{h,i} \delta_{hi} q_{hij} \leq d_j, \qquad s_j \geq 0. \tag{23}$$

There is the legitimate question of how to relate the solutions of this LP problem to the one described in Section 2 that gives the efficient production schedules. A solution of the LP problem gives an equilibrium distribution of the gains

$$r_1, \ldots, r_m, s_1, \ldots, s_n.$$

Since a buyer in market j is willing to pay up to b_j per unit and his gain is s_j per unit, the price he does pay must satisfy

$$p_j = b_j - s_j. \tag{24}$$

Let

$$p'_{ij} = p_j - t_{ij} \tag{25}$$

so that p'_{ij} denotes the net revenue per unit after payment of unit shipping costs that A_i obtains from a sale of one unit in market j. The total profit of A_i is

$$r_i = \sum_j p'_{ij} q_{ij} - a_i. \tag{26}$$

Substitute p_j from (24) into (25) and obtain

$$p'_{ij} = b_j - t_{ij} - s_j = p_{ij} - s_j \qquad [\text{cf. } (2.1)].$$

Therefore, (26) can be rewritten as follows:

$$r_i = \sum_j p_{ij} q_{ij} - \sum_j s_j q_{ij} - a_i,$$

where $\langle q_{ij} \rangle$ is an EPS, and

$$r_i + \sum_j s_j q_{ij} = \sum_j p_{ij} q_{ij} - a_i = V(S_i) \tag{27}$$

for a simple coalition S_i and its corresponding EPS. Now A_i can use p'_{ij} in order to compute its internal shadow prices as the solution of the LP problem for finding its EPS as described in Section 2. It follows that since each A_i has its own avoidable cost and capacity, it will have its own shadow prices that are related to the common market prices. Everything now depends on whether the s_j's and r_i's do give an efficient market equilibrium.

4   The optimal assignment

Given the nature of the cost and the demand conditions, there is a corresponding optimal assignment of the customers in the spatially separated markets to the plants as their sources of supply. This optimal assignment gives the maximal total gain to all of the members of the group. Finding this optimal assignment requires the solution of a certain integer programming problem. However, owing to its special structure, its solution is closely related to the solution of the LP problem as described in the preceding section.

Without loss of generality we may take $b_j = b$ for all j. The optimal assignment is given by the solution of the following problem:

$$\max \sum_{i,j} q_{ij}(b - t_{ij}) - \sum_i \sigma_i a_i \tag{1}$$

with respect to $q_{ij} \geq 0$ and σ_i subject to

$$\sum_{i=1}^{m} q_{ij} \leq d_j, \tag{2}$$

$$\sum_{j=1}^{n} q_{ij} \leq \sigma_i c_i, \tag{3}$$

$$\sigma_i = 0 \text{ or } 1. \tag{4}$$

Denote the value of the objective function in (1) by $V(N)$. The first term of $V(N)$ shows the return to the members of the group net of the shipping cost. The second term shows the avoidable costs. Since the control variables σ_i are restricted to 0 or 1, it follows that $\sigma_i = 0$ means A_i is an inactive plant. Hence it does not incur the avoidable cost a_i as is apparent from (3), and it makes no shipments. The constraints (2) represent the demand conditions. The total quantity sent to destination j from all sources must not exceed the total demand in that destination, which is d_j. In contrast to the LP problem of the preceding section, there is now an explicit constraint on the shipments from the various plants to ensure the consistency of their choices. This point requires additional explanation.

In the LP problem as described in the preceding section the individual sources of supply, the A_i's, may compete independently for customers. This competition is represented by the inequality constraints for the simple coalitions. The corresponding dual constraints for the demand conditions in each of the n destinations is given by (3.23). However, this constraint does not prevent the individual plants from attempting to ship a larger quantity to a given destination than can be sold there. We may put it this way. If the shipments from all sources of supply satisfy the constraint (2), then surely they satisfy (3.23). However, if the total shipments satisfy (3.23), then they do not necessarily satisfy (2). Therefore, consistency in the form of (2) is more restrictive than the demand constraints imposed by (3.23).

The supply constraint (3) also deserves a few remarks. It does not follow from this constraint that a plant must operate up to its installed capacity c_i. The solution may require A_i to be active so that $\sigma_i = 1$ and yet (3) allows $\sum_{j=1}^n q_{ij} < c_i$ so that A_i may have some unused capacity. In the LP problem of the preceding section it is also possible to have some plant operating below its installed capacity. But this can happen only as a result of the nature of the demand conditions. Perhaps A_i cannot obtain enough customers in any of the destinations where it can sell at a price not below its unit shipping cost that will enable operation of its plant at its installed capacity. However, the globally optimal assignment may require a plant to operate below its installed capacity when its myopic self-interest inclines it to operate at a higher rate and there is enough demand in its available markets to permit this.

There is an illuminating way to represent $V(N)$. Let R_i denote a subset of some simple coalition S_{hi}. Formally, $R_i \subseteq S_{hi}$. The claim is that

$$V(N) = \sum_{i=1}^m V(R_i) \tag{5}$$

and

$$R_i \cap R_i', \ = \varnothing \quad \text{for all } i \text{ and } i' \neq i. \tag{6}$$

The coalition R_i can be a singleton containing A_i or it can be a subset of customers who would be served under some efficient production schedule, q_{hi}. In case R_i contains A_i alone, this would mean that A_i is inactive.

The validity of the representation given by (5) may be verified by noting that the contribution to $V(N)$ from any active A_i satisfies

$$\sum_j q_{ij}(b - t_{ij}) - a_i \geq 0.$$

The corresponding production schedule is either efficient or is dominated by an EPS of A_i. Therefore, $R_i \subseteq S_{hi}$. Owing to the demand constraint given by (2), no customer belongs to more than one R_i. Similarly, no A_i is a member of more than one R_i. This shows that each R_i is a subset of at most one simple coalition and that each A_i belongs to at least one R_i. Therefore, the R_i's do not overlap so (6) is true. Owing to the linearity of $V(R_i)$ as shown by

$$V(R_i) = \sum_j q_{ij}(b - t_{ij}) - a_i,$$

we may conclude that

$$V(R_i \cup R_{i'}) = V(R_i) + V(R_{i'}). \tag{7}$$

Let $\Pi(N)$ denote the value of the objective function giving the solution of the LP problem defined in the preceding section. We shall now prove the following:

> **Proposition 1:** *If the values of all the dual variables that solve the LP problem are 1's or 0's, then*

$$\Pi(N) = V(N). \tag{8}$$

Proof: We note first of all that always

$$\Pi(N) \geq V(N) \tag{9}$$

because as the discussion of the demand constraints (2) shows, the demand constraints (3.23) properly include (2) and similarly for the capacity constraints (3.22), which properly include (3). Therefore, since the hypothesis asserts the δ's giving the dual variables that solve the LP problem are 1's or 0's, it follows that the q's of the LP problem also satisfy the constraints (2) and (3). This gives an implication of equality in (9). ∎

> **Corollary:** *If $\sum_h \delta_{hi} = 0$ or 1 for each i, then $\Pi(N) = V(N)$.*

Proof: Let $q_i = \sum_h \delta_{hi} q_{hi}$ so that q_i is a convex combination of extreme EPSs with weights given by the values of the dual variables. The hypothesis asserts that for each i, the sum of these weights is 1. We may therefore replace the set of extreme EPSs for A_i by the convex combination q_i. This does not change the value of the objective function $\Pi(N)$. With these replacements the solution of the dual problem gives dual variables for each A_i that are either 1 or 0. Proposition 1 then gives the desired conclusion. ∎

The remaining alternative is the subject of:

> **Proposition 2:** *If for some A_i, $\sum_h \delta_{hi}$ is a positive fraction in the solution of the dual LP problem, then $\Pi(N) > V(N)$.*

Proof: The hypothesis that $\sum_h \delta_{hi} < 1$ and positive together with (3.16) implies that $r_i = 0$. Also by hypothesis at least one $\delta_{hi} > 0$ so there is equality in the constraint for the simple coalition S_{hi} giving

$$\sum_j q_{hij} s_j = \sum_j q_{hij}(b - t_{ij}) - a_i = V(S_{hi}), \tag{10}$$

where the value of the right-hand side must be nonnegative. We may assume without loss of generality it is actually positive since otherwise it could not contribute to the value of the objective function in the dual problem. Hence at least one of the terms on the left-hand side of (10) must be positive. Say it is the first so that

$$q_{hi1}s_1 > 0. \tag{11}$$

Consequently, both q_{hi1} and s_1 must be positive. This implies there must be equality in the dual constraint (3.23) at $j = 1$. Therefore,

$$\sum_{i'} \sum_h \delta_{hi'} q_{hi'1} = d_1 - \sum_h \delta_{hi} q_{hi1}, \qquad i' \neq i. \tag{12}$$

As in the proof of the corollary of Proposition 1, replace the efficient production schedules on the left-hand side by $q_{i'}$. Since the hypothesis asserts that $\sum_h \delta_{hi}$ is a positive fraction, it follows that

$$d_1 - \sum_h \delta_{hi} q_{hi1} > d_1 - \sum_h \delta_{hi} q_{hi1} / \sum_h \delta_{hi} \tag{13}$$

giving the implication in conjunction with (12) that

$$\sum_{i'} q_{i'1} + \sum_h \delta_{hi} q_{hi1} / \sum_h \delta_{hi} > d_1. \tag{14}$$

This says that in the solution of the LP problem the quantity shipped to destination 1 exceeds the quantity demanded. Since there is strict inequality, the solution of the dual LP problem must violate the demand constraint (2) of the $V(N)$ problem. It follows that $\Pi(N) > V(N)$. ∎

Incidentally, as a theoretical curiosum, if $\Pi(N) = 0$, then obviously, it must equal $V(N)$, and in this case it would be possible to have equality although $\sum_h \delta_{hi}$ is a positive fraction. But then it would be true that choosing all q's equal to 0 gives a solution.

5   Status of the core

The LP problem of Section 3 uses constraints for the simple coalitions and nonnegativity of r_i and s_j. The former includes all extreme EPSs. Let us now consider dominated production schedules and unions of simple coalitions. This is for several reasons. First, although A_i can obtain a larger net return from an efficient production schedule than from one it dominates, the latter can still yield a positive gain. Second, an optimal equilibrium may require some plant to use a dominated production schedule. Third, the core allows formation of coalitions among sellers and their customers so the analysis must take this into account.

Lemma 1: *Let q denote an n-vector and let* $\Delta q \geq 0$. *Assume that*

$$r_i + qs = q(b - t) - a_i. \tag{1}$$

(i) *It follows that*

$$r_i + (q - \Delta q)s \geq (q - \Delta q)(b - t) - a_i. \tag{2}$$

(ii) *The following inequality is true:*

$$r_i + (q + \Delta q)s \geq (q + \Delta q)(b - t) - a_i \tag{3}$$

if and only if

$$\Delta q_{ij}[s_j - (b - t_{ij})] = 0. \tag{4}$$

Proof: To show that (1) implies (2), it suffices to have

$$-s(\Delta q) \geq -(b - t)\,\Delta q,$$

which is equivalent to

$$(b - t - s)\,\Delta q \geq 0. \tag{5}$$

Because each coordinate of $b - t - s$ is nonnegative, (5) is true so (4) is true.

Turning to (ii), sufficiency is obvious. To prove necessity, observe that if (3) is true and because (1) is true by hypothesis, it follows that

$$s(\Delta q) \geq (b - t)\,\Delta q,$$

which is equivalent to

$$[s - (b - t)]\,\Delta q \geq 0. \tag{6}$$

Because each coordinate of $s - (b - t) \leq 0$ so that

$$[s - (b - t)]\,\Delta q \leq 0, \tag{7}$$

(6) and (7) imply

$$[s - (b - t)]\,\Delta q = 0. \tag{8}$$

Therefore, $\Delta q_{ij} > 0$ implies $s_j - (b - t_{ij}) = 0$. This proves (4). ■

The second part of the lemma has an interesting interpretation. If both (1) and (3) are true, there is an efficient production schedule, $q + \Delta q$, dominating the production schedule q that satisfies (1). Hence q is not an extreme EPS. Nevertheless, the constraint imposed by the simple coalition in the shape of (3) is true because for any destination

j for which source i gives $\Delta q_{ij} > 0$, the gain to the customers at this destination, namely s_j, just equals the maximum price they are willing to pay less the unit shipping cost, $b - t_{ij}$.

Using these results we can prove:

> **Proposition 3:** *For any simple coalition for which there is equality in the primal constraint of the LP problem, the core constraints are satisfied for all production schedules that they dominate.*

Proof: If q_{hi} is an extreme EPS and S_{hi} the corresponding simple coalition, the hypothesis asserts that

$$r_i + q_{hi}s = q_{hi}(b - t) - a_i. \tag{9}$$

If q_{hi} dominates q, then $q \le q_{hi}$. The core constraints for such dominated q are given as follows:

$$r_i + qs \ge q(b - t) - a_i.$$

Inequality (2) of Lemma 1 applies and gives the desired conclusion. ∎

Proposition 3 applies to those simple coalitions for which the corresponding primal constraints hold as equalities. There are also primal constraints holding as strict inequalities, and we must show that the core constraints are satisfied for the production schedule dominated by these simple coalitions. The next proposition covers this case.

> **Proposition 4:** *Let r and s denote solutions of the LP problem defined in Section 3. For any simple coalition such that*
>
> $$r_i + qs > q(b - t) - a_i, \tag{10}$$
>
> *and for all $\Delta q \ge 0$, there is the implication*
>
> $$r_i + (q - \Delta q)s > (q - \Delta q)(b - t) - a_i. \tag{11}$$

Proof: It suffices to show that

$$-(\Delta q)s > -(\Delta q)(b - t). \tag{12}$$

Because $s \le (b - t)$, (12) is true. By hypothesis, (10) is true. Together with (12) it follows that (11) is true. ∎

It remains to study the core constraints for unions of simple coalitions. It suffices to consider pairs of simple coalitions. Let S_i and $S_{i'}$ denote such a pair for distinct A_i and $A_{i'}$. Define C so that

$$C = S_i \cap S_{i'}. \tag{13}$$

Hence there is a coalition S such that

$$S = (S_i \cup S_{i'}). \tag{14}$$

Proposition 5: *The solution of the LP problem of Section 3 satisfies the core constraint for S.*

Proof: In case $C = \varnothing$, the conclusion is obvious. Assume $C \neq \varnothing$. Define B_i and $B_{i'}$, so that $B_i \cap B_{i'} = \varnothing$ and

$$S_i = B_i \cup C, \qquad S_{i'} = B_{i'} \cup C. \tag{15}$$

Using the same kind of argument that establishes (4.5) gives the result that there is a partition of C given by C_i and $C_{i'}$, such that

$$V(S) = V(B_i \cup C_i) + V(B_{i'} \cup C_{i'}), \tag{16}$$

where $(B_i \cup C_i) \subseteq S_i$ and $(B_{i'} \cup C_{i'}) \subseteq S_{i'}$. Possibly C_i or $C_{i'}$, but not both, is empty. Also, the inclusion is proper for at least one of the two coalitions, S_i, $S_{i'}$. The desired conclusion will follow if the solution of the LP problem satisfies the core constraints for each of the two disjoint dominated production schedules for $B_i \cup C_i$ and $B_{i'} \cup C_{i'}$. Propositions 3 and 4 assert this. ∎

Therefore, the solution of the LP problem does satisfy all of the proper core constraints. If the solution is also globally feasible, then the core is not empty. It is empty if and only if $\Pi(N) > V(N)$. This is true only if the constraints for the simple coalitions giving the solution of the LP problem that hold as equalities do not constitute a partition of N. This means there must be at least one pair of simple coalitions, S_i, $S_{i'}$ that overlaps so that $C \neq \varnothing$, and for these coalitions the solution of the LP problem gives

$$r_i + \sum_j q_{ij}s_j = V(S_i) \quad \text{and} \quad r_{i'} + \sum_j q_{i'j}s_j = V(S_{i'}). \tag{17}$$

It follows from (4.5) that

$$V(N) = \sum_i V(R_i) \tag{18}$$

with each $R_i \subseteq S_i$. The LP problem would give a solution consistent with a nonempty core only if the constraints for R_i were satisfied as equalities. But for any R_i such that $R_i \subset S_i$, the solution of the LP problem gives strict inequality for the core constraints corresponding to R_i. That is, if $R_i \subset S_i$ and r_i^0, s_j^0 are a solution of the LP problem, then

$$r_i^0 + \sum_j q_{ij}^0 s_j^0 > V(R_i). \tag{19}$$

Because $R_i \subset S_i$, it is also true that the EPS for S_i is given by $q_{ij}^0 + \Delta q_{ij}$ with at least one $\Delta q_{ij} > 0$. One can allow competition among the A_i's and have a nonempty core by imposing additional constraints on the simple coalitions so that

$$(b - t_{ij} - s_j)\Delta q_{ij} = 0 \tag{20}$$

for all efficient production schedules that dominate the ones determined by the R_i. Permitting competition among the A_i's is equivalent to solving an LP problem subject to the appropriate additional constraints, the topic of the next section. In this event it is always true that

$$b - t_{ij} - s_j \geq 0. \tag{21}$$

Therefore, it is necessary to impose production quotas on any A_i for which (21) is true as a strict inequality.

Observe that (21) does not imply that price differentials in different markets are bounded by the cost of shipping goods between them. This is to say that although (21) is always true for the solutions of the LP problem, it does not follow that

$$|p_j - p_{j'}| \leq t_{jj'}, \tag{22}$$

where p_j, $p_{j'}$ denote the prices at destinations j and j' and are defined as follows:

$$p_j = b - s_j, \qquad p_{j'} = b - s_{j'}. \tag{23}$$

Summarizing, given some destination j with several sources of supply and different shipping costs from them, there may be a source with a nonbinding capacity constraint. From this source $b - t_{ij} > 0$, and it is the source for which the marginal shipping cost is a maximum. There can be a nonempty core compatible with maximum competition among the sellers by setting an upper bound on the total output from this source of supply that is below its installed capacity. In this way it becomes possible to satisfy all of the constraints consistent with this upper bound that would furnish a nonempty core as if the installed capacity of this source were equal to the upper bound imposed on its total output.

6   An algorithm for finding the optimal assignment

This section describes an algorithm to find the optimal equilibrium in a number of steps proportional to the number of destinations and origins. It does so by placing upper bounds on total shipments from certain origins. The algorithm finds both the sources that will be subject to these bounds as well as the size of the bounds. Consequently, for given cost and demand conditions, there always exists a set of bounds on the total output from each source that can give the optimal assignment of customers to the sources. Given these bounds on total shipments, the core becomes nonempty. As a result competition among sellers for customers establishes an equilibrium that is optimal.

The algorithm is as follows. First, solve the primal and dual LP problem as described by (3.19)–(3.23). If $\sum_h \delta_{hi} = 1$ or 0 for each A_i, then the core is not empty by Proposition 1. In this case the algorithm terminates since the solution of the LP problem gives the correct answer. If $\sum_h \delta_{hi}$ is a positive fraction for at least one A_i, then the core is empty by Proposition 2 so that $V(N) < \Pi(N)$. Let x_i denote the excess supply. Rounding down to the nearest integer, if necessary, the excess supply is

$$x_i = (1 - \sum_h \delta_{hi})c_i. \tag{1}$$

This x_i shows how much to lower the total output of at least one of the plants serving the same destination as does A_i. This reduction may apply to A_i itself. Proceed as follows:

1. Take all destinations served by that A_i for which $\sum_h \delta_{hi}$ is a positive fraction. Find all other sources for these destinations. Choose from among these that source for which $b - t_{ij}$ is least. This chosen source has the highest shipping cost. Place an upper bound on total production from this source so that its permissible output goes down by x_i. To be specific, say source $A_{i'}$ has the lowest $b - t_{ij}$. Lower the permissible output of $A_{i'}$ so that, if k denotes the iteration number,

    $$c_{i',k} = c_{i',k-1} - x_{i,k}, \tag{2}$$

    where $c_{i',k}$ gives the permissible capacity of $A_{i'}$ on iteration k. Recalculate the extreme EPSs for $A_{i'}$ for the new values of the permissible capacity given by (2) but with no change in the avoidable cost, $a_{i'}$. The avoidable cost stays the same for each A_i for every iteration of the algorithm.
2. Calculate the solution of the primal and dual LP problem using

the new values of $V(S_{hi'})$ for $A_{i'}$, for which there is a lower permissible output and the old values of $V(\cdot)$ for all simple coalitions for which the c_i's are unchanged. If $\sum_h \delta_{hi} = 1$ or 0 for each source, then Proposition 1 asserts the core is not empty, and the value of the objective function of the solution on this step is $V(N)$. The iteration terminates and we have the solution. If $\sum_h \delta_{hi}$ is a positive fraction, go to step 1 and repeat that procedure.

The iterations continue until there is a solution of the LP problems for which $\sum_h \delta_{hi} = 1$ or 0 for each A_i. Because the permissible capacity of some source goes down on each iteration, because the avoidable costs remain the same throughout, and because the demands at each destination stay the same, the algorithm reduces shipments to those destinations where there would be excess supply. It does this by placing upper bounds on the sources with the highest unit shipping cost.

This algorithm results in a binding constraint on the total output of each active plant so that either the available demand or the upper bound on its total shipments prevent an increase in its shipments. Consequently, each active plant has an EPS on the final iteration. This is true although the requirement of an optimal assignment may prevent the plant from producing at a rate equal to its installed capacity.

It is easy to verify that when the demand at each market is not less than the installed capacity of that plant for which the unit cost of shipping to that market is least, then the core is not empty. Hence a necessary condition for an empty core is that there is some market for which the installed capacity of the plant with the lowest cost of shipping to that market is greater than the demand. An empty core results either because some plant must produce at a rate below its installed capacity or because it must produce nothing at all, although it has an EPS that would permit a positive net return. In the latter case the plant and its customers could make agreements on mutually satisfactory terms so that both could gain. However, these agreements would be incompatible with the optimal assignment for the whole group of plants at all sources and customers at all destinations.

As we shall see, the prices implied by a nonempty core depart from marginal cost differentials. It is possible to have lower prices at destinations than at their sources of supply, a phenomenon known as *dumping* in international trade. It is also possible to have shipments going from a source to some destination, although the price at the destination minus the price at the source is below the unit cost of the shipment. The numerical examples in the next section illustrate this.

It is now convenient to consider some objections to the procedure that converts an initial empty core to a final nonempty core by the imposition of upper bounds on total shipments from certain sources of supply. A plausible alternative works on prices instead. It would seem possible to have a nonempty core by lowering prices in order to increase demand by enough to remove the excess capacity that is the cause of the empty core. There are several reasons why this will not work.

First, changes in the demands at the destinations in response to changes in b would also change the value of the optimal assignment, $V(N)$. It is not necessarily true that a nonempty core would result. The cause of the empty core lies in the nature of the cost conditions. These assume decreasing average cost at each plant up to its installed capacity. Different plants have different installed capacities. These create indivisibilities explaining why the supply response comes in discrete packages depending on which of the plants are active. More precisely, changes in the identities of the active plants cause discrete changes in the output rate while changes in the individual output rates of the active plants may permit a continuous response to new demand conditions. A nonempty core corresponds to an equilibrium for a given set of plants corresponding to the given demand conditions. The presence of the indivisibilities complicates the calculation of determining whether an equilibrium exists but does not alter its basic logic. Nor is this all. For any given b, there is a set of quantities demanded at each destination, the d_j's. As long as it is true that each d_j is finite. there is the legitimate question of whether an optimal equilibrium exists that can satisfy these demands.

Second, the theory does include the forces of competition. Buyers may bargain independently among competing sellers. Indeed, it is owing to this very competition that there may be an empty core. This competition may drive prices so low that some core constraints cannot be satisfied simultaneously with a globally feasible outcome.

Third, upper bounds on the total output rates of some plants still permit as much competition as is compatible with an optimal equilibrium. These bounds restrict none of the prices. Plants may still compete with each other so the beneficial effect on individual incentive is a maximum. Moreover, for any given set of demands corresponding to the given b, there is a set of upper bounds on total plant output rates with two virtues as follows:

1. The process of finding these bounds by iterations of the LP problem results in the discovery of the value of $V(N)$.

2. An optimal assignment can always be obtained by choosing appropriate upper bounds on the plants' total output rates.

Note that restrictions on prices cannot accomplish these goals.

The solution has two other important features. First, the optimal equilibrium may not be unique. The next section gives an example of this. Second, neither the distribution of the returns to the plants nor the distribution of the gains to the buyers is necessarily unique. When this is so, one must rely on other theories to predict the actual distribution of the gains.

7 Some numerical examples for illustrating the theoretical results

Figure 5.2 shows the locations of the plants and the customers for the numerical examples. There are five points with a plant and customers at each one. The only feasible routes are shown by the line segments linking the nodes. Figure 5.2 also shows the capacities, avoidable costs, and the quantities demanded at each of the nodes together with the costs of shipping one unit of the good between adjacent nodes. It is assumed that the maximal price a customer at any location is willing to pay is 4 so that $b = 4$ in each location. To see how to calculate efficient production schedules, consider A_1. It has five EPSs shown in Table 5.1. For convenience these are given as follows:

$$q_{11} = \langle 40, 60, 0, 0, 0 \rangle, \quad V(S_{11}) = 140,$$
$$q_{21} = \langle 40, 10, 0, 0, 50 \rangle, \quad V(S_{21}) = 140,$$
$$q_{31} = \langle 10, 90, 0, 0, 0 \rangle, \quad V(S_{31}) = 110,$$
$$q_{41} = \langle 10, 0, 0, 0, 90 \rangle, \quad V(S_{41}) = 110,$$
$$q_{51} = \langle 40, 0, 35, 25, 0 \rangle, \quad V(S_{51}) = 20.$$

The sum of the quantities shipped is 100, which is the capacity of A_1. In each EPS, demand in some market is a binding constraint. In the first two EPSs, A_1 produces 40 units for sale in its home market and can get up to $4 each. In q_{11} it ships 60 units to destination 2 and since the shipping cost is $1, its net proceeds from these shipments is $3 per unit. Hence

$$V(S_{11}) = (4 \times 40) + (3 \times 60) - 200 = 140.$$

All the EPSs for all five plants are given in Table 5.1. The constraints

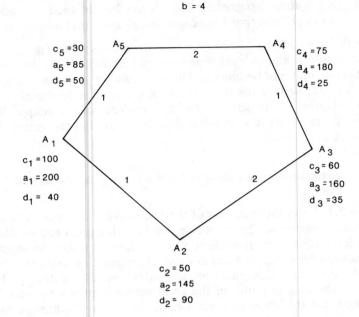

Figure 5.2

for the primal problem are

$$r_i + \sum_j q_{hij}s_j \geq V(S_{hi}). \tag{1}$$

Each column in Table 5.1 represents such a constraint. Thus, for S_{11} there is

$$r_1 + 40s_1 + 60s_2 \geq 140. \tag{2}$$

Table 5.1 shows the δ_{hi}'s giving the solutions and these happen to be unique. However, there are no unique solutions giving the distributions of the gains. Three solutions are given as follows:

	r_1	r_2	r_3	r_4	r_5	s_1	s_2	s_3	s_4	s_5
Solution 1	0	0	16.5	0	2	0.1	1.1	1.1	0	1.1
Solution 2	0	5	0	0	5	2.0	1.0	1/7	2.0	1.0
Solution 3	140	55	0	0	35	0	0	1.0	0.8	0

(There are other solutions as well.) The value of the objective function,

Table 5.1. *Example 1 with a nonempty core and several solutions*

r_1	1	1	1	1	1												1
r_2						1	1	1									1
r_3									1								1
r_4										1	1	1	1	1	1		1
r_5															1	1	1
s_1	40	40	10	10	40	40								15		30	40
s_2	60	10	90		10	50			25			15					90
s_3				35			35	35				35	35	35	35	15	35
s_4				25			25			25			25	25	25	25	25
s_5		50		90							50	40	15		35	30	50
$V(S)$	140	140	110	110	20	15	55	55	30	20	5	55	40	40	35	35	5
δ_{hi}	0.6	0.4	0	0	0	0	1.0	1.0	0	0	0	0	0	0	0	1.0	0

$\Pi(N)$ is 285, and this is also the value of $V(N)$. There is an implication of a nonempty core. The plant at site 4 is idle. The whole demand at each location is filled. The dual variables δ_{hi} satisfy the conditions for each i that $\sum_h \delta_{hi} = 0$ or 1. The EPSs that implement the solutions of this LP problem are given as follows:

$$
\begin{array}{llllll}
A_1 & 40 & 40 & 0 & 0 & 20 \\
A_2 & 0 & 50 & 0 & 0 & 0 \\
A_3 & 0 & 0 & 35 & 25 & 0 \\
A_4 & 0 & 0 & 0 & 0 & 0 \\
A_5 & 0 & 0 & 0 & 0 & 30 \\
d_j & 40 & 90 & 35 & 25 & 50
\end{array}
$$

The last row shows the demand in each of the markets. These are all satisfied by the EPSs. The first production schedule for A_1 is a convex combination of its two EPSs given by columns 1 and 2 in Table 5.1 with weights as determined by $\delta_{11} = 0.6$ and $\delta_{22} = 0.4$. Implicit in the gains of the customers is the unit price they pay.

	p_1	p_2	p_3	p_4	p_5
Solution 1	3.9	2.9	2.9	4.0	2.9
Solution 2	2.0	3.0	3.857	2.0	3.0
Solution 3	4.0	4.0	3.0	3.2	4.0

Though the EPS calls for shipments from market 1 to market 2, note that the price in market 2 does not necessarily exceed the price in market 1 by the marginal shipping cost, which is 1.

In the second example all of the data are the same as in the first save that the demand in location 4 is lower by 1 unit. Thus, d_4 becomes 24 instead of 25 as in the initial example. Table 5.2 shows the efficient production schedules. Note that as a result of the lower demand in location 4, there are now EPSs such that one unit is offered in markets in which this did not occur before. In effect competition has become keener. The result is an empty core. Some of the solutions are given as follows:

	r_1	r_2	r_3	r_4	r_5	s_1	s_2	s_3	s_4	s_5
Solution 1	0	0	17.5	0	2	1.85	1.1	0	1.475	1.1
Solution 2	0	0	0	0	2	1.85	1.1	1/14	2.1	1.1

The value of the objective function giving the solution of the LP problem, $\Pi(N)$, is 282.9 but $V(N)$ is 282.0 so there is an implication of an empty core. Table 5.2 shows the values of the dual variables, δ_{hi}, which are uniquely determinate. For this example, in agreement with Proposition 2, for one plant, namely A_2, the value of its dual variable is a positive fraction, 0.98, and its $r_2 = 0$.

In order to get a nonempty core, the algorithm requires an upper bound on the output rates of those plants serving the markets supplied by A_2. Three plants include market 2 in their EPS, A_1, A_2, and A_3. The one with the highest marginal shipping cost is A_3. The algorithm requires an upper bound on the total output of A_3. Since $\delta_2 = 0.98$, $x_2 = (1 - 0.98)50$ and

$$c_{3,1} = c_{3,0} - x_2 = 60 - 1 = 59.$$

This requires recalculation of $V(S_{h3})$ for A_3 using $c_{3,1} = 59$. The new constraints for A_3 are as follows:

$$r_3 + 35s_3 + 24s_4 \geq 52 = V(S_{13}), \qquad \delta_{13},$$

$$r_3 + 24s_2 + 35s_3 \geq 28 = V(S_{23}), \qquad \delta_{23},$$

as replacements for the original constraints of the simple coalitions of A_3. A solution of this LP problem is given by

r_1	r_2	r_3	r_4	r_5	s_1	s_2	s_3	s_4	s_5
0	5	0	0	5	2	1	8/7	2	1

Table 5.2. *Example 2 with an empty core and several solutions*

r_1	1	1	1	1	1	1													1
r_2							1	1											1
r_3									1	1									1
r_4											1	1	1	1	1	1			1
r_5																	1	1	1
s_1	40	40	10	10	40	40	40									16	30		40
s_2	60	10	90	1		10	50	1	25					16					90
s_3				35	35			35	35	1	35	35	35	35	15				35
s_4				24	24			24		24		24	24	24	24				24
s_5		50		90			1			50	40	16				36	30		50
$V(S)$	140	140	110	110	22	22	15	55	54	30	19	5	53	37	37	33	35	5	
δ_{hi}	0.6	0.4	0	0	0	0	0	0.98	1.0	0	0	0	0	0	0	0	1.0	0	

The values of the dual variables giving the solution are the same as those in the bottom row of Table 5.2 with the exception of δ_{12}, which is now equal to 1.0 instead of 0.98. The value of the objective function is now $\Pi(N) = 282$ and this is also $V(N)$. Proposition 1 gives the conclusion there is a nonempty core, and Proposition 2 verifies that $\sum_h \delta_{hi} = 1$ or 0 as required. The efficient production schedules are the same as in Example 1 (Table 5.1) save for A_3 for which it is

$$A_3 \quad 0 \quad 0 \quad 35 \quad 24 \quad 0.$$

No demand is unsatisfied. The prices implied by the solution are

p_1	p_2	p_3	p_4	p_5
2	3	2.857	2	3

Although A_3 ships 24 units to market 4 where the price is 2, this is below the price in the home market of A_3 where it is $2\frac{6}{7}$. The same is true for one of the solutions in Example 1 (Table 5.1), for which there is a nonempty core without the necessity of imposing upper bounds on the outputs of any plant. The imposition of an upper bound on the output of A_3 required by the need to have an efficient equilibrium does not necessarily have the effect of raising prices. Indeed under Solution 2, which corresponds most closely to the solution where the core is not empty, the price in market 3 is actually lower.

One should not come away from these examples with the belief that

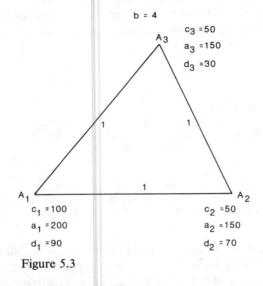

Figure 5.3

one iteration always suffices to get a nonempty core. A finite number does suffice, but it can be a large number. These two examples have another trait that is not generally true. A_3 remains active at a lower output rate. In general it is possible for a plant to become active on the last iteration although it was inactive on the first and for a plant inactive on the last iteration to have been active initially. Moreover, in such a case it is true that the plant shut down on the last iteration could have made bargains acceptable to its customers that would have yielded a positive net gain to all. Nevertheless, allowing these mutually acceptable bargains would give an empty core and would destroy the global optimum. Finally, in these examples all the demand is satisfied on the last iteration. This need not be true in general. One can have a nonempty core with some demand unsatisfied although the total capacity exceeds the total demand. This can happen because the unsatisfied customers would not be willing to pay enough to cover the total cost of furnishing them with the goods. It is also possible to have some demand unsatisfied in a given destination. In such a case, if the core is not empty, it must be true that none of these demanders get a positive gain. This requires a high enough price in that destination so that a potential customer is indifferent between getting the good at this high price or not getting it at all.

Figure 5.3 shows the third example that has two optimal assignments. The optimal equilibrium is as a result not unique. Table 5.3 shows the primal and dual LP problems and their solutions for iteration 1. Because

Table 5.3. *Primal and dual linear programming problem for Example 3 with an empty core and two optimal equilibria*

Primal $\quad \min \sum\limits_{i=1}^{3} r_i + 90s_1 + 70s_2 + 30s_3$

with respect to r_i and s_j subject to

$$r_1 + 90s_1 + 10s_2 \geq 190, \qquad \delta_{11}$$

$$r_1' + 90s_1 + 10s_3 \geq 190, \qquad \delta_{21}$$

$$r_2 + 50s_2 \geq 50, \qquad \delta_2$$

$$r_3 + 20s_1 + 30s_3 \geq 30, \qquad \delta_{13}$$

$$r_3 + 20s_2 + 30s_3 \geq 30, \qquad \delta_{23}$$

Dual $\quad \max 190(\delta_{11} + \delta_{21}) + 50\delta_2 + 30(\delta_{13} + \delta_{23})$

with respect to $\delta_{hi} \geq 0$ subject to

$$\delta_{11} + \delta_{21} \leq 1$$

$$\delta_2 \leq 1$$

$$\delta_{13} + \delta_{23} \leq 1$$

$$90(\delta_{11} + \delta_{21}) + 20\delta_{13} \leq 90$$

$$10\delta_{11} + 50\delta_2 + 20\delta_{23} \leq 70$$

$$10\delta_{21} + 30\delta_{13} + 30\delta_{23} \leq 30.$$

Solution: $r_1 = 130, \quad r_2 = 20, \quad r_3 = 0, \quad s_1 = s_2 = s_3 = 0.6;$
$\quad \Pi(N) = 264, \quad \delta_{11} = 0.4, \quad \delta_{21} = 0.6, \quad \delta_2 = 1, \quad \delta_{13} = 0,$
$\quad \delta_{23} = 0.8$

If $c_3' = 40$ the optimal equilibrium satisfies

$$r_3 = s_2 = s_3 = 0, \quad r_1 + 90s_1 = 190, \quad \Pi(N) = V(N) = 240$$

If $c_1' = 90$ the optimal equilibrium satisfies $\Pi(N) = V(N) = 240$ and

$$r_1 + 90s_1 = 160; \quad r_2 + 50s_2 = 50; \quad r_3 + 20s_2 + 30s_3 = 30$$

$$s_1 \geq s_2 \geq 0$$

the sum of the dual variables for A_3 is the positive fraction 0.8, the core is empty. More directly, $\Pi(N) = 264$ while $V(N) = 240$ so the core is empty. The excess supply according to (6.1) is $10 = 0.2 \times 50$. A_3 has all three markets in its efficient production schedules. It competes with A_1 in market 1, with A_2 in market 2, and with A_1 in market 3. A_3 is the higher cost supplier for destinations 1 and 2 while A_1 is the higher cost supplier in destination 3. However, in all three destinations the difference between the marginal shipping cost of the higher cost and next lower cost supplier is the same, namely 1. As a result, the value of the objective function is the same whether the output of A_1 is lowered by 10 units, the output of A_3 is lowered by 10 units, or any combination of reductions adding up to 10 units is allocated to A_1 and A_3. The two extreme solutions for the optimal assignments are given in Table 5.3. Note there is no unique imputation of the gains for each of these, a phenomenon visible in the first two examples as well. However, there would be a unique optimal assignment in Example 3 (Table 5.3) with a slight perturbation of the unit shipping cost that would eliminate the indifference between imposition of the upper bound on A_1 or A_3. For example, an arbitrarily small increase in the unit shipping cost between source 1 and destination 3 removes the indeterminacy.

8   Prices paid and prices received

The algorithm described in Section 6 and illustrated with numerical examples in Section 7 shows how to find upper bounds on the plant output rates that can give an efficient equilibrium compatible with competition among the plants for customers. In the absence of these upper bounds the core would be empty and no equilibrium could exist. Another avenue of approaching this problem would seem to be via price floors instead of output ceilings. One would think that price floors could work just as well as output ceilings. The purpose of this section is to show precisely how prices can have a role. The principal conclusions are as follows. First, in order to have an efficient equilibrium, it is necessary to allocate outputs among the plants. This must be done explicitly because prices alone cannot convey the correct signals to the plants. Second, for prices to have a role, it is sufficient to introduce a set of taxes such that there is a gap between the price a customer pays and the price a seller receives. The purpose of these taxes is to redistribute the gains from production and trade among the market participants in order to satisfy the core constraints.

We begin with a description of an LP problem that can generate the tax rates capable of solving the problem. It is closely related to the one defined in Section 3.

$$Primal \quad \min \sum_{j=1}^{n} d_j\sigma_j$$

with respect to σ_j, s_j, and r_i nonnegative and subject to

$$\sum_j d_j s_j + \sum_i r_i \quad \leq V(N), \quad \Delta_N, \tag{1}$$

$$\sum_j q_{hij}(s_j + \sigma_j) + r_i \geq V(S_{hi}), \qquad \Delta_{hi}. \tag{2}$$

$$Dual \qquad \max [\sum_{hi} \Delta_{hi}V(S_{hi}) - \Delta_N V(N)]$$

with respect to Δ_N, Δ_{hi} nonnegative and subject to

$$d_j - \sum_{hi} \Delta_{hi}q_{hij} \geq 0, \qquad \sigma_j, \tag{3}$$

$$\Delta_N d_j - \sum_{hi} \Delta_{hi}q_{hij} \geq 0, \qquad s_j, \tag{4}$$

$$\Delta_N - \sum_h \Delta_{hi} \geq 0, \qquad r_i. \tag{5}$$

Before explaining the relevance of this problem for the taxation scheme, it is necessary to establish some properties of the solution.

Proposition 6: *The core is nonempty if and only if the solution of this problem gives $\sigma_j = 0$ for all j.*

Proof: Sufficiency is trivial. Necessity is true by virtue of the duality theorem of linear programming. ∎

Corollary 1: *If the core is empty, then $\sigma_j > 0$ for at least one j, and $\Delta_N \geq 1$.*

Proof: Proposition 6 shows that at least one σ_j must be positive. Since $\sigma_j > 0$, it is an implication of (3) and (4) that

$$d_j = \sum_{hi} \Delta_{hi}q_{hij} \leq \Delta_N d_j \Rightarrow d_j(1 - \Delta_N) \leq 0. \qquad ∎$$

Corollary 2: *The core is not empty if the LP problem has a solution such that $s_j = 0$ for all j.*

Proof: It suffices to observe that the hypothesis implies that all σ_j are zero so Proposition 6 gives the desired conclusion. ∎

Corollary 3: *If the core is empty, then $\Delta_N \leq 1$.*

Proof: By Corollary 2, at least one s_j must be positive if the core is empty. Say $s_j > 0$ and it follows from (3) and (4) that

$$\Delta_N d_j = \sum_{hi} \Delta_{hi}q_{hij} \leq d_j \Rightarrow d_j(1 - \Delta_N) \geq 0. \qquad ∎$$

Proposition 7: If the core is empty, then $\Delta_N = 1$.

Proof: Immediate from Corollaries 1 and 3.   ∎

It is now possible to show how this relates to a taxation scheme. Suppressing the information about the shipping costs, t_{ij}, of sending a unit of the good from source i to destination j, we may assume that a customer in market j is willing to pay at most b_j per unit. The gain to a customer in destination j is the excess of the maximum price he is willing to pay over the price he does pay, call the latter $P_{j,pd}$. Thus,

$$s_j = b_j - P_{j,pd}. \tag{6}$$

The higher is s_j, the lower is the price he pays. Now define the price received by a seller as follows:

$$P_{j,rcd} = b_j - (s_j + \sigma_j). \tag{7}$$

The difference between the price a seller receives and the price a buyer pays is σ_j, which resembles a tax. The purpose of the tax is to redistribute the net gains from production and trade; it is not to drain revenue from the system to the outside. This is evident from the constraint (1). Also note that all proper core constraints include the sum $s_j + \sigma_j$. By making $\sum_j d_j \sigma_j$ as small as possible compatible with satisfying the constraint (1), two goals are met. First, the gains of the buyers are as large as possible, and second, the discrepancy between the price paid and the price received is as small as possible. Note that by Proposition 7, if the core is empty, then $\Delta_N = 1$. It then follows there must be equality in (1). Therefore, the gains of the customers and the returns of the plants add up exactly to the maximal net benefit, which is $V(N)$. Hence the taxes do not drain revenue from the system.

The solution of the LP problem (1)–(5), call it the σ–LP problem, has several interesting features. It is first of all essentially the same as the solution of the LP problem described in Section 3. Let r_i^0, s_j^0, and σ_{hi}^0 denote a solution of the Section 3 LP problem.

$$s_j + \sigma_j = s_j^0, \quad r_i = r_i^0, \quad \text{and} \quad \Delta_{hi} = \sigma_{hi}^0 \tag{8}$$

furnish a solution of the σ–LP problem. This has two implications. First, in general there is no unique set of s_j's giving a solution of the σ–LP problem although, of course, the value of the objective is unique. Second, and more important, in order to generate enough surplus to satisfy the constraint (1) with equality, it is necessary to use the optimal assignment of active plants that is determined by the solution of the

Table 5.4. *An example to illustrate the algorithms for five plants in one market*

Plant	c_i	a_i	$V(S_i)$	a_i/c_i	$V(S_i)/c_i$
A_0	1	5	0	5	0
A_1	2	8	2	4	1
A_2	4	15	5	3.75	1.25
A_3	8	28	12	3.5	1.5
A_4	16	52	28	3.25	1.75

integer programming problem. Neither the solution of the σ–LP problem nor the solution of the Section 3 LP problem gives the optimal assignment. Indeed, the assignment of active plants and output rates of these two LP problems cannot generate a large enough gain to satisfy (1). It is, therefore, necessary to find the optimal assignment by using the iterative algorithm given in Section 6. Consequently, it is generally necessary to use the proceeds of the taxes to cover deficits incurred by some of the active plants that do not receive enough revenue from the customers to cover their total cost.

Numerical examples are helpful for illustrating these conclusions. Table 5.4 contains the relevant data about cost and capacity for five plants all in the same market. Assume all buyers are alike and that each is willing to pay up to 5 and is willing to buy at most one unit of the product. Table 5.5 shows the solutions for the optimal assignment and the σ–LP problems for rates of demand between 19 and 24 units. The optimal supply response is given by the solution of the integer programming problem that imposes optimal upper bounds on plant output rates according to the algorithm described in Section 6. Note that the optimal supply output rate rises as the quantity demanded rises, but the equilibrium price is not a monotonically increasing function of the optimal supply response. Table 5.5 also shows the prices received by sellers and σ for these rates of demand. Table 5.6 shows in detail the constraints for the primal and dual problems of the σ–LP problem if the quantity demanded is 19. For this case,

$$s + \sigma = \tfrac{3}{2}, \quad r_4 = 4, \quad \Delta_N = \Delta_4 = 1, \quad \Delta_3 = \tfrac{3}{8}, \quad s = \tfrac{26}{19}, \quad \sigma = \tfrac{5}{38}$$

and all other primal and dual variables are 0. The price received by sellers is never above the optimal price consistent with maximal competition and optimal output constraints as determined by the solution of the integer programming problem. For $Q = 19$, if plants A_3 and A_4 were active, because it is for these two plants that the primal constraints

Table 5.5. *Summary of results for preceding example*

Quantity		Price	$V(N)$	P_{rcd}	σ	Optimal plant assignment
Demanded	Supplied					
19	18	5.00	30	3.5	5/38	A_1, A_4
20	20	3.75	33	3.5	1/20	A_2, A_4
21	20	5.00	33	3.75	5/42	A_2, A_4
22	22	4.00	35	3.5	2/11	A_1, A_2, A_4
23	22	5.00	35	3.5	11/46	A_1, A_2, A_4
24	24	3.75	40	3.75	0	A_3, A_4

Table 5.6. *Example to illustrate σ–LP problem for quantity demanded = 19*

Primal	min 19σ

$$r_0 + (s + \sigma) \geq 0, \quad \Delta_0$$

$$r_1 + 2(s + \sigma) \geq 2, \quad \Delta_1$$

$$r_2 + 4(s + \sigma) \geq 5, \quad \Delta_2$$

$$r_3 + 8(s + \sigma) \geq 12, \quad \Delta_3$$

$$r_4 + 16(s + \sigma) \geq 28, \quad \Delta_4$$

$$r_0 + r_1 + r_2 + r_3 + r_4 + 19s \leq 30, \quad \Delta_N$$

Dual   max $0\Delta_0 + 2\Delta_1 + 5\Delta_2 + 12\Delta_3 + 28\Delta_4 - 30\Delta_N$

$$\Delta_0 + 2\Delta_1 + 4\Delta_2 + 8\Delta_3 + 16\Delta_4 - 19\Delta_N \leq 0, \quad s$$

$$\Delta_0 + 2\Delta_1 + 4\Delta_2 + 8\Delta_3 + 16\Delta_4 \leq 19, \quad \sigma$$

$$\Delta_0 - \Delta_N \leq 0, \quad r_0$$

$$\Delta_1 - \Delta_N \leq 0, \quad r_1$$

$$\Delta_2 - \Delta_N \leq 0, \quad r_2$$

$$\Delta_3 - \Delta_N \leq 0, \quad r_3$$

$$\Delta_4 - \Delta_N \leq 0, \quad r_4$$

are valid as equalities, then the gain would only be 15 because the benefit would be 19×5 and the total cost would be $52 + 28$. With a net surplus of 15 it would not be possible to satisfy (1) with equality as is required by the solution of the σ–LP problem. Therefore it would be necessary to direct which plants to operate and which to keep idle without using prices as a signal for this purpose. In contrast, by imposing upper bounds on output rates, no additional constraints are necessary. Competition among the plants for customers can be relied upon to generate enough revenue to satisfy all of the appropriate core constraints. With the taxation scheme there are two additional complications that this example illustrates. First, plant A_1 ought to be active under the optimal assignment. The price it receives is $\frac{7}{2} = 5 - \frac{3}{2}$, since $s + \sigma = \frac{3}{2}$. Since it sells 2 units, its revenue is 7, but its avoidable cost is 8 so it would incur a loss of 1. In order to satisfy the core constraint of the σ–LP problem, it must therefore receive a subsidy of 1. The second complication arises from the fact that under the optimal assignment one unit of demand is not satisfied. However, each potential customer must receive the same gain given by $s = \frac{26}{19}$ so a customer unable to buy the product must get a compensation under this scheme of taxation.

9   Conclusions

The assumptions about cost and demand conditions herein are approximations to the ones in the standard model of price theory. The cost curves approximate U-shaped average cost with nondecreasing marginal cost. The demand curves approximate a perfectly elastic demand with an upper bound on the total quantity demanded. These cost and demand conditions are present in Viner industries (Telser 1978, Chapter 3). Viner industries have empty cores. This holds true in the present case as well. An empty core means there is no equilibrium compatible with independent actions of the buyers and sellers that can be Pareto optimal. Therefore, the buyers and sellers have compelling reasons to seek arrangements capable of giving a Pareto optimal equilibrium. Such arrangements exist. They come in the form of upper bounds on plant output rates that do not exceed the installed capacity of the plants. Given these upper bounds, maximal competition among the plants for customers is consistent with Pareto optimality determined by the optimal assignment of customers to plants. Because the optimal assignment is a solution of an integer programming problem, it is a difficult problem to solve. Trial-and-error procedures would be prohibitively costly for problems of even moderate size. The analysis given here furnishes an iterative procedure for finding the solution in a finite number of iterations by solving a sequence of LP problems. The algorithm is a systematic process for finding which plants should be active, the maximum output they should produce, to which markets they should ship their output, and which plants should be idle. Finding the optimal set of active plants is a combinatorial problem that has a straightforward solution thanks to this algorithm.

There is an optimal amount of competition compatible with an optimal assignment. Too much competition can cause an empty core. Too little imposes a loss of efficiency. The participants in the market have the most to gain under those arrangements that result in an optimal assignment between customers and plants. This equilibrium has several interesting properties. No active plant operates at a loss. The equilibrium gives the maximum net gain to consumers. There generally is not marginal cost pricing. Prices do not serve an allocative function.

This theory has some interesting implications about the effects of fluctuations of aggregate demand. Given the array of plants with their installed capacities and the associated costs, a drop in demand results in excess capacity in some markets. Consequently, an empty core may result. This has the symptom of driving prices down to levels at which sellers cannot operate save at a loss. To obtain an equilibrium requires constraints on total output rates of the individual plants. The upper bounds depend on the circumstances in the individual markets. An empty core is much less likely to arise when demand is high so there is little or no idle capacity. One may argue against this that during prosperous periods plant capacity might increase above the optimal level, and this can result in an empty core. Still one must admit that while individual firms can control their capacities, they cannot control aggregate demand. Hence they are more vulnerable to the effects of a decline in demand than to the effects of a rise in demand.

10   Appendix: multiproduct plants

This section extends the results to multiproduct plants. The extension reveals some interesting relations between the integer programming problem and a certain maximum problem that sheds more light on the economic implications of the analysis.

Product i is described by n characteristics represented by an n-vector $F_i = \{f_{i1}, f_{i2}, \ldots, f_{in}\}$, $i = 1, \ldots, m$, where f_{ij} denotes the amount of characteristic j in one unit of product i. For example, suppose product i is some type of cargo to be carried on a ship. If cargo has two characteristics, volume and weight, $n = 2$. Plant h has n kinds of capacities installed to make products with these n characteristics. These various capacities are given by the n-vector $C^h = \{c_{h1}, c_{h2}, \ldots, c_{hn}\}$, where c_{hj} denotes the capacity of plant h with respect to characteristic j. As in Section 4 define the control variable σ_h so that

$$\sigma_h = \begin{cases} 1 & \text{if plant } h \text{ is active,} \\ 0 & \text{if plant } h \text{ is inactive.} \end{cases}$$

q_{hi} = output of product i from plant h.

The first constraint shows how much of the various products plant h can make given its available capacity of characteristic j.

$$\sum_i q_{hi} f_{ij} \leq \sigma_h c_{hj}, \qquad \lambda_{jh}. \tag{1}$$

Let d_i denote the maximal demand for product i.

$$\sum_h q_{hi} \leq d_i, \qquad \Theta_i, \tag{2}$$

shows the demand constraint. Relax the constraint on σ_h so that instead of being restricted to 0 and 1, it may be any nonnegative real number not above 1. Thus,

$$\sigma_h \leq 1, \qquad \rho_h. \tag{3}$$
$$\pi_h = \sum_i q_{hi} b_i - \sigma_h a_h, \tag{4}$$

defines the net benefit from plant h where a_h is the avoidable cost of plant h and b_i is the unit benefit from product i. The maximum problem is defined as follows:

$$\max \sum_h \pi_h \text{ with respect to } q_{hi}, \sigma_h \geq 0$$

subject to (1)–(3). The Lagrangian for this maximum problem is

$$\sum_h \pi_h + \sum_h \sum_j \lambda_{jh}(\sigma_h c_{hj} - \sum_i q_{hi} f_{ij}) + \sum_h \rho_h(1 - \sigma_h) \tag{5}$$
$$+ \sum_i \Theta_i(d_i - \sum_h q_{hi}).$$

The first-order necessary conditions for a maximum satisfy

$$-a_h + \sum_j c_{hj}\lambda_{jh} - \rho_h \leq 0, \qquad \sigma_h, \tag{6}$$
$$b_i - \sum_j f_{ij}\lambda_{jh} - \Theta_i \leq 0, \qquad q_{hi}. \tag{7}$$

For future reference note that

$$\rho_h > 0 \Rightarrow \sigma_h = 1 \Rightarrow \sum_j c_{hj}\lambda_{jh} = a_h + \rho_h > a_h,$$
$$q_{hi} > 0 \Rightarrow b_i - \Theta_i = \sum_j f_{ij}\lambda_{jh}.$$

If the solution of this maximum problem gives $\sigma_h = 0$ or 1 for all h, then it is also a solution of the integer programming problem. However, if the solution of this maximum problem gives a positive fraction for some σ_h, then there is a procedure that will lead to a solution of the integer programming problem that generalizes the one described in Section 6. Say $\sigma_{h'}$ is a positive fraction. Impose an upper bound on the operating capacity of plant h' such that

$$\sigma_{h'}c_{h'j} = c'_{h'j} \quad \text{for all } j. \tag{8}$$

Thus plant h' is required to lower its operating capacity by $1 - \sigma_{h'}$. With the new capacities $c'_{h'j}$ rewrite the output constraints (1), which become

$$\sum_i q_{h'i}f_{ij} \leq \sigma_{h'}c'_{h'j}. \tag{9}$$

Owing to this revision plant h' cannot produce as much as before. Consequently, it may be unable to recover its avoidable cost so that it may be forced to cease production altogether. Solve the maximum problem for the new constraints. Note that the avoidable costs of the plants remain the same throughout the iterations. Eventually there will arrive a stage such that all of the σ_h are 0 or 1. At this stage there is an implication of a nonempty core.

The economic implications readily follow from these results. Call p_i the price of product i. Now Θ_i is the gain per unit to buyers of product i while b_i is the most they are willing to pay for it. Consequently, from (7)

$$p_i = b_i - \Theta_i \leq \sum_j f_{ij}\lambda_{jh}. \tag{10}$$

The Lagrangian multiplier λ_{jh} is the shadow cost of characteristic j for plant h. It follows from (6) that

$$\sum_j c_{hj}\lambda_{jh} \leq a_h + \rho_h. \tag{11}$$

The term ρ_h is the excess of the receipts of plant h over its avoidable cost. Thus, in the notation of Section 3, ρ_h corresponds to the return to the owner of plant h. Similarly, Θ_i corresponds to the consumer surplus of the buyers of product i.

Before continuing the economic interpretation of these results, let us note a few interesting aspects of this solution. First, it is always necessary to recalculate the solution of the maximum problem whenever there is a positive fraction for some σ_h. It is incorrect simply to reduce the permitted capacity utilizations for that plant where σ_h is a positive fraction and claim that the remainder of the solution is unaffected. Upper bounds on the capacity utilization rates of a plant usually require a different optimal production schedule for all of the plants and not just for the one directly affected. Second, there is the same proportional reduction of capacity with respect to all of the product characteristics for any plant for which it turns out that σ_h is a positive fraction. Third, although (10) seems to put an upper bound on the prices, it is not a meaningful one because it is ancillary to the upper bounds on the operating rates needed for a nonempty core. Without the latter, no equilibrium prices would exist.

It is now convenient to use a more concise notation for the remainder of this analysis. Let

$$F = [f_{ij}] \quad \text{and} \quad p = b - \Theta, \tag{12}$$

so that F is an $m \times n$ matrix and p is an $m \times 1$ vector. Corresponding to (7), there is

$$F\lambda^h \geqq p, \tag{13}$$

and to (6),

$$C^h\lambda^h \leqq a_h + \rho_h. \tag{14}$$

Similarly, for the constraints (1) and (2) we have

$$q^hF \leqq C^h\sigma_h, \tag{15}$$

and

$$\sum_h q^h \leqq d. \tag{16}$$

Keeping in mind the nonnegativity of the various controls, from (13) it follows that

$$q^hF\lambda^h \geqq q^hp,$$

and from (15)

$$q^hF\lambda^h \leqq C^h\lambda^h\sigma_h.$$

Therefore,

$$q^hp \leqq q^hF\lambda^h \leqq C^h\lambda^h\sigma_h \leqq (a_h + \rho_h)\sigma_h. \tag{17}$$

At the solution there is equality straight through (17). If some plant h is inactive, $\sigma_h = 0$, which implies $q^h = 0$. If some plant h is active, then $\sigma_h = 1$. The imputed shadow cost equals the receipts at the prices p, and these receipts can exceed the avoidable cost. If there are more commodities than basic characteristics, $m > n$, and the rank of $F \leq n$. The number of commodities it is optimal for any plant h to make is at most equal to the rank of F. In the shipping application where a product is a cargo with at most two characteristics, volume and weight, it means a ship would carry at most two different kinds of cargo, and these would differ with respect to density and, say, volume.

Since both F and p are the same for each plant, q^h and λ^h will differ from one plant to another only if

   (i) a_h differs among the plants,
   (ii) C^h differs among the plants.

> **Proposition 8:** *Imputed shadow costs are the same for any two plants that produce the same products.*

Proof: Immediate from (14). ∎

> **Proposition 9:** *Two plants will produce the same products if they have the same avoidable costs and the same capacities of basic characteristics.*

Proof: It follows from (1) that if two plants are active and have the same c_{hj}, then they must also have the same q^h if their avoidable costs are also the same. ∎

However, different plants may produce the same quantities even if they have different capacities and avoidable costs because of offsetting differences among the coordinates of C^h.

CHAPTER 6

A Theory of self-enforcing agreements

A prudent ruler ought not to keep faith when by so doing it would be against his interest, and when the reasons which made him bind himself no longer exist. If men were all good, this precept would not be a good one; but as they are bad, and would not observe their faith with you, so you are not bound to keep faith with them. Nor have legitimate grounds ever failed a prince who wished to show colourable excuse for the nonfulfillment of his promise.
Niccolo Machiavelli, *The Prince*

1 Introduction

A self-enforcing agreement between two parties remains in force only as long as each one believes himself to be better off by continuing the agreement than he would be by ending it. It is left to the judgment of the parties themselves to decide whether or not there has been a violation. If one party violates the terms, then the other party has as his only recourse termination of the agreement after he discovers the violation. No third party intervenes to determine whether a violation has taken place or to estimate the damages that may be attributed to such a violation. No third party decides whether a violation has been "willful" or "accidental." A party to a self-enforcing agreement calculates whether the gain from violating the agreement is greater or less than the loss of future net benefits from detection of the violation and the consequent termination of the agreement by the other party. If the violator believes he gains more than he loses from a violation, then he will violate the agreement. Hence both parties continue to adhere to an agreement if and only if each gains more from adherence to than from violation of the terms.

Many economic transactions are self-enforcing agreements. Since it is costly to rely on the intervention of third parties such as the courts to enforce agreements and to assess damages of violations, the parties to an agreement devise the terms to make it self-enforcing, if this can be done cheaply enough. Thus, one of the strongest incentives for honesty of a seller is the desire to obtain the continued patronage of the buyer. In situations where a similar transaction between the two

187

parties is unlikely to be repeated in the future so that the loss of future business is an ineffectual penalty, substitutes for self-enforcing agreements will appear. As an illustration consider a transaction between a traveler and an airline and suppose it is unlikely that the traveler will have another occasion to use that airline. The traveler is vulnerable to being cheated by that airline. However, if the traveler has a travel agent with whom he does business frequently and the travel agent in turn does business frequently with the airline, then the circumstances for a self-enforcing agreement between the traveler and the agent on one side and the agent and the airline on the other are present. Employment agencies furnish another example.

A prudent person avoids dealing with someone he suspects will be unreliable. People seek information about the reliability of those with whom they will deal. But reliability is not an inherent personality trait. A person is reliable only if it is more advantageous to him than being unreliable. It is information about someone's return from reliability that is pertinent in judging the likelihood of his reliability. For example, an itinerant is less likely to be reliable if it is more costly to impose penalties on him.

A basic premise of this approach is that someone is honest only if honesty or the appearance of honesty pays more than dishonesty. Someone who thinks he can gain from dishonesty with impunity will be dishonest. Several important results follow. If two parties are in a sequence of transactions such that both know for sure which transaction will be the last, then each also knows that violating the agreement on the last transaction cannot evoke a sacrifice of the net gains thereafter. Consequently, each party would be under no compulsion to abide by the terms of the agreement on the last transaction. Since the same argument applies to the next to the last and so on to the first, we seem driven to the conclusion that no finite sequence of transactions can be self-enforcing if both parties are certain about which transaction will be the last. Assuming that every sequence of transactions in the real world is finite, a sequence of self-enforcing transactions must have no last one. How can this be? A sequence has no last term if there is always a positive probability of continuing. As long as this is true, anyone who violates the terms at one time incurs the risk of future loss. Therefore, there is no certainty of gain from a present violation because there is always a chance of continuing to another transaction. Owing to this, there is a positive probability that current violations are punished later.

A theological argument helps illustrate the importance of a finite uncertain horizon. Suppose that after a sinful life on earth, the punishment after death is the torment of the soul in hell. Assume a sinner can obtain forgiveness by doing various things before death: good works, confession to a priest, and so on. If the time of death is uncertain, then a would-be sinner faces the risk of being unable before he dies to do the good works or the other appropriate things that can avoid punishment in hell. If he were certain of the date of his death, then he could allow some time before his death for those actions that would remove the consequences of sinning that would follow his demise. Even a nonbeliever in the existence of hell and punishment after death can accept this argument provided he is willing to concede there is a small positive probability that hell exists and that the disutility of the torments of hell is unboundedly large. Given the uncertainty of the date of death, although the short-term gain of sinning exceeds that from a good life, one should be good all the time because the expected long-term penalty of sinning is so large.

Consider now some formal aspects of this theory. Assume two parties are contemplating whether or not to begin a sequence of transactions that would be equivalent to a self-enforcing agreement. We must calculate the expected gain to each party of such a sequence.

Let u_j denote the net gain to a party during time period j if there is a transaction at time j. The sequence terminates either because one party stops it or because an event occurs that stops the sequence and neither party has any control over this event. Thus there is a distinction between stopping that is the result of an action taken by one of the parties, which he induces, and stopping that is fortuitous. The latter is autonomous stopping equivalent to the outcome of a random event. We confine our attention at the outset to fortuitous stopping.

Let T denote the time of stopping, a random variable for that stopping that is autonomous. Let p_t denote the probability that T equals t so that p_t is the probability of a horizon of finite duration t. Since the stopping time is autonomous, p_t does not depend on current or past gains. Assume the parties know the sequence of stopping probabilities. It is certain that the process comes to a halt eventually so that

$$\sum_{t=0}^{\infty} p_t = 1. \tag{1}$$

Let q_t denote the probability of a horizon lasting for more than t periods. Hence

$$q_t = \sum_{t+1}^{\infty} p_j. \tag{2}$$

The expected duration of the horizon, denote it $E(T)$, satisfies

$$E(T) = \sum_0^\infty tp_t = \sum_0^\infty q_t. \tag{3}$$

Notwithstanding (1) so that a finite horizon is certain, the *expected* duration of the horizon can be infinite.

Given the possibility of stopping at time t, there is the question of whether the gain at time $j < t$, namely u_j, ought to depend on t. It should not. Since the horizon is a random variable, the return at an earlier time cannot depend on the value of a random variable at a later time.

Other possible complications deserve mention. One is whether fortuitous events that cause the process to stop for one or both of the parties are independent of each other. Another is whether the probability of stopping depends on the age of the agreement. The present formulation is commodious enough to embrace these factors.

Putting these complications aside for the moment, let us calculate the expected return to one of the parties. Define s_t as follows:

$$s_t = \sum_{j=0}^t u_j, \tag{4}$$

so that s_t is the sum of the returns to a party for a sequence of $t + 1$ periods. This formulation permits discounting since u_j has a time subscript j and the present value of the returns can decrease as j increases. The probability of s_t is p_{t+1} so that $p_{t+1}s_t$ is the contribution to the expected value of the return for a horizon of length t. Summing over horizons of all possible durations gives the expected value of the return, denote it $E(U)$, as follows:

$$E(U) = \sum_0^\infty p_{t+1}s_t. \tag{5}$$

Alternatively, from (2) and (4) there is

$$E(U) = \sum_0^\infty q_t u_t. \tag{6}$$

It is now convenient to consider some possible complications. A self-enforcing agreement refers to a sequence of transactions between at least two parties. Fortuitous events can affect at least one of them, bringing their relation to a halt. The relation can continue if and only if no chance event stops the process for either one. Hence the length of the horizon, t, satisfies

$$t = \min\langle t_1, t_2 \rangle, \tag{7}$$

where t_i is the time when some event would occur that would prevent the continued participation of the ith party. Therefore, p_t is the probability of $T = t$ with t as defined by (7). Consequently, it does not matter in this formulation whether the fortuitous events stopping the participation of one or both of the parties to the transaction are independent or dependent.

The age of the relation between the two parties does not affect the probability of ending their agreement if and only if the conditional probability of stopping is the same through time. This requires in particular that the conditional probability of stopping at time t must be the same as the probability of never starting, which is p_0. This is true if and only if

$$p_t = p_0(1 - p_0)^t \tag{8}$$

(Feller 1957, vol. I, chap. XIII, sec. 9). For future reference note that in this case

$$q_t = (1 - p_0)^{t+1}. \tag{9}$$

From (3) and (9) it follows that the expected horizon is

$$E(T) = (1 - p_0)/p_0 \tag{10}$$

The sequence of transactions may stop because one party believes this would be profitable for him. Let Δu_t denote the increment on the return to a party who stops the sequence at time t. This refers to induced not autonomous stopping. Write the sequence ΔU^t so that

$$\Delta U^t = \langle 0, \ldots, 0, \Delta u_t, -u_{t+1}, -u_{t+2}, \ldots \rangle.$$

With this notation, the sequence of gains to a party who takes an action that stops the transactions starting in period $t + 1$ is given by $U + \Delta U^t$ (the superscript shows when the relation stops). Therefore,

$$E(U + \Delta U^t) = E(U) + q_t \Delta u_t - \sum_{t+1}^{\infty} q_j u_j. \tag{11}$$

It is an implication of (11) that the return from continuing exceeds the gain from stopping at time t if and only if for all t it is true that

$$E(U + \Delta U^t) - E(U) = q_t \Delta u_t - \sum_{t+1}^{\infty} q_j u_j \le 0. \tag{12}$$

In applications of this theory, the return u_t depends on the terms of the transaction at time t, and Δu_t depends on how much the party can gain from violating them at time t. Therefore, the problem of finding terms that can give a self-enforcing agreement reduces to that of finding a sequence $\{u_t\}$ that can satisfy (12) for all Δu_t. If so, $E(U)$ gives a maximum with respect to all sequences $U + \Delta U^t$.

At this point we should consider whether this theory captures the main factors of the problem. If one party takes an action giving him a net gain of Δu_t at time t that is an unfavorable surprise to the other party and violates their agreement, then the theory assumes the victim responds by terminating the agreement. This is the maximal penalty the victim can impose on the violator of a self-enforcing agreement. He cannot levy a fine because he cannot collect it without intervention by a third party, which is ruled out by hypothesis. It is only with a feasible action within his grasp that the victim can impose a penalty on a violator of a self-enforcing agreement. If the maximal penalty cannot deter a violation because $E(U + \Delta U^t) - E(U) > 0$, then no smaller one will suffice. Hence inequality (12) is both a necessary and a sufficient condition for a self-enforcing agreement.

The victim may not immediately discover the violation. If he finds out after k periods, then the violator gains $\Delta u_t, \Delta u_{t+1}, \ldots, \Delta u_{t+k-1}$. Slowness in the detection of violations raises the profit to the violator. For the sake of keeping the algebra simple, the preceding formulation assumes detection of a violation with a minimal delay so that $k = 1$. This does not affect the validity of the analysis in any important respect.

Third, the reader may object that the theory fails to allow for deviations from the expected return and seems to require rigid and continuously perfect obedience to the terms of the agreement. Here, too, nothing essential is lost with this approach. To see why, consider how to take deviations into account. Assume there is a band around the expected return so that actual returns falling inside the band are consistent with the terms of the agreement. Actual returns outside the band indicate violations. The deviation between the actual and the expected return should behave like a sequence of independent and identically distributed random variables if the parties are in compliance with the agreement. There is a violation either when the actual returns go outside the limits or stay too close to the boundaries for too long a time. The parties to the agreement would therefore pay careful attention to those returns that are close to the boundaries. Consequently, the boundary lines themselves have a role in the analysis allowing for deviations just like u_t.

In this theory each party compares the current gain from cheating the other party to the expected return from continuing the relation honestly. The probability of continuing does not depend on the past history of their transactions with each other. Some may wish to argue that previous favorable experience raises whereas previous unfavorable experience lowers the probability of continuing. To examine the validity of this argument we may proceed as follows. Assume a party to an agreement accumulates a stock of goodwill toward the other depending on the nature of past experience. Favorable past experience raises and unfavorable past experience lowers this stock of goodwill. The party terminates the relation when the stock of goodwill diminishes to zero.

The argument claiming there is a stock of goodwill based on past experience faces a fatal objection because it is inconsistent with rational behavior. To see why, suppose that a buyer, for instance, accumulates goodwill toward a seller based on the excess of his favorable over his unfavorable experiences with that seller. Each past favorable experience raises and each past unfavorable experience lowers the buyer's goodwill. A seller aware of this has many tempting ways of cheating the buyer. With a new customer the seller would deliberately act honestly at first to obtain the buyer's confidence so as to cheat the buyer more profitably later on. Moreover, the seller need only maintain the stock of goodwill of old customers at a level just high enough to obtain their continued patronage. In so doing, he can cheat them, but not too often. The accumulation of a fund of goodwill of a buyer toward a seller that depends on past experience stands as a temptation to the seller to cheat the buyers and turn their goodwill into ready cash. It is the prospect of the loss of future gain that deters and the existence of past goodwill that invites cheating. Therefore, rational behavior by the buyers to an agreement with a seller demands that the probability of continuing their relation does not depend on their past experience with each other. This condition is simply another version for an efficient market of rational traders.

2   Long-term versus short-term contracts

The leading example that raises most of the pertinent issues in a self-enforcing agreement is the choice between a long-term or forward contract and a short-term or spot contract. The parties to a forward contract agree in advance on the quantities and prices at which their trades will occur over a stipulated length of time. A long-term contract also includes numerous other provisions that are important but are not of present concern. Each party to a forward contract has the alternative of buying or selling in the spot market at the spot price that can and does vary from one trade to the next. Should the current spot price exceed the forward price, it is the forward seller who faces the temptation to breach; should the spot price fall below the forward price, then the temptation to breach rests on the forward buyer. Consider the case where the spot price lies above the forward price. The forward seller can get a temporary gain by selling at the spot price, not at the agreed-upon forward price. This gain is at the expense of breaching the long-term arrangement with his customer. Suppose the forward price equals the expected spot price, which is the mean of all spot prices. It is nearly certain that any spot price will differ from the forward price so that at each instant of time either the buyer or the seller has a temporary gain by trading at the spot price instead of at the agreed-upon forward price. Here is the problem. Is it possible to find a forward price mutually agreeable to the buyer and the seller such that it is in the interest of each to adhere to the forward price and never succumb to the temptation of the temporary gain offered by a trade at the spot price instead?

Implicit in this question is the assumption that the parties to a long-term agreement have no recourse to a third party who can enforce the terms of their contract. It means the terms must be self-enforcing. For this to be true, both parties must believe it in the interest of each to adhere to the forward contract and not to breach it. Begin with the situation from the seller's point of view.

Assume the forward contract specifies the same quantity sold at each transaction at a forward price denoted p^*. Alternatively, the seller can sell this quantity at the prevailing spot prices, and the expected receipts per unit would be the mean of the spot prices. The forward contract is said to be breached when the seller refuses to sell at the forward price agreed upon and instead sells at the current spot price. If the seller trades at the spot price p_2 thereby breaching the forward contract, he can expect the return

$$U(p_2) + \overline{U} \tag{1}$$

whereas if he remains faithful to the forward contract and always sells at the forward price p^*, then his return is

$$U(p^*) + U(p^*). \tag{2}$$

The term $\overline{U}$ denotes the expected return from a strategy of selling at the prevailing spot price. Thus, assume the price is a random variable

P, and for the sake of simplicity, it can have only two values, p_1 and p_2 with $p_1 < p_2$ so that

$$P = \begin{cases} p_1 & \text{with probability } \alpha \\ p_2 & \text{with probability } 1 - \alpha. \end{cases}$$

Consequently, the expected return from sales on the spot market is

$$\overline{U} = \alpha U(p_1) + (1 - \alpha)U(p_2). \tag{3}$$

Evidently, the seller has an incentive to breach and sell at the spot price only if it happens to be high and equal to p_2. Having breached, the expected return to the seller would be $\overline{U}$ thereafter. On the other hand, should the seller remain faithful to the forward contract, then he would get $U(p^*)$ now and thereafter, so his return is given by (2). Neither (1) nor (2) has a discount factor to apply to the future. Below we shall see how the presence of a discount factor changes the analysis. Assume that U is a concave function of P. If it is strictly concave, it represents risk aversion, whereas if it is linear, the seller has risk neutrality. In both cases,

$$\overline{U} \le U(\overline{P}), \tag{4}$$

where

$$\overline{P} = \alpha p_1 + (1 - \alpha)p_2, \tag{5}$$

is the expected price. I also assume the buyer and the seller both know α so they agree on the nature of the probability distribution that generates the price as a random variable. Assume as well that given the spot price is observed to be either p_1 or p_2, then the buyer or the seller can trade at this price. A highly liquid market is a close approximation to this assumption.

The seller gets a higher return from faithfulness to the forward contract if and only if

$$U(p^*) > [U(p_2) + \overline{U}]/2. \tag{6}$$

There is a critical forward price, call it p_a^*, defined so that

$$U(p_a^*) = [U(p_2) + \overline{U}]/2. \tag{7}$$

At this critical price the seller is indifferent between breaching and faithfulness to the forward contract. A major concern of this analysis is the relation between the critical forward price of the seller and the expected spot price. The easiest and perhaps most important case is a linear function that represents risk neutrality.

Proposition 1: *For a linear U given by*

$$U(P) = b_0 + b_1 P, \qquad b_1 > 0, \tag{8}$$

it follows that $p_a^* > \overline{P}$ so that the critical forward price of the seller exceeds the expected spot price.

Proof: Linearity implies that $\overline{U} = U(\overline{P})$. Therefore,

$$U(p_a^*) = \tfrac{1}{2}[U(p_2) + \overline{U}] = \tfrac{1}{2}[U(p_2) + U(\overline{P})] = U[\tfrac{1}{2}(p_2 + \overline{P})]$$

so that

$$p_a^* = \tfrac{1}{2}(p_2 + \overline{P}) \quad \text{since } p_2 > \overline{P}. \qquad \blacksquare$$

The analysis for strictly concave U is not much more complicated though it is more difficult to describe the results. Consider Figure 6.1. It has a graph of the strictly concave $U(P)$ passing through the points A_3 and A_4. The claim is that for any strictly concave U there is some expected spot price $\overline{P}$ that equals the seller's critical forward price p_a^*. It is easy to find the $\overline{P}$ possessing this property. It is given by the P coordinate of that point A_5 that lies on the midpoint of the segment $A_1 A_2$. The U coordinate of the point A_1 is $\overline{U}$. According to (7), p_a^* is that price for which the utility equals the midpoint of $U(p_2)$ and $\overline{U}$, namely A_5. Whenever the price coordinate of this midpoint is the same as the expected spot price, it follows that $p_a^* = \overline{P}$, which is the result desired. The fact that there exists an expected spot price that equals the seller's critical forward price is important in the subsequent analysis concerning the existence of a self-enforcing long-term contract.

It is also desirable to see whether there are simple relations between the critical forward price and the expected spot price. Unfortunately, this does not seem to be the case. In order to appreciate the source of the complexity, start from the point A_1 in Figure 6.1 and consider a small increase in $\overline{P}$ to $\overline{P} + \Delta \overline{P}$. This raises $\overline{U}$ to $\overline{U} + \Delta \overline{U}$ so that the distance from $U(p_2)$ to $\overline{U}$ decreases by an amount equal to the slope of the line segment $A_3 A_4 \times \Delta \overline{P}$.

$$\text{Slope of } A_3 A_4 = [U(p_2) - U(p_1)]/(p_2 - p_1).$$

$$\Delta \overline{U} = \text{slope of } A_3 A_4 \times \Delta \overline{P}.$$

$$\Delta U(p_a^* + \Delta p^*) \approx \frac{dU(p_a^*)}{dp} \Delta p^* = \tfrac{1}{2} \Delta \overline{U}.$$

It follows that

$$\frac{\Delta p^*}{\Delta \overline{P}} = \frac{(\tfrac{1}{2})[U(p_2) - U(p_1)]/(p_2 - p_1)}{dU(p_a^*)/dp}. \tag{9}$$

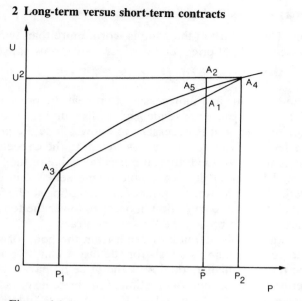

Figure 6.1

Formula (9) shows it is not possible to draw general conclusions about the relation between Δp^* and $\Delta \overline{P}$ even when starting from a point where $p_a^* = \overline{P}$. The new $p^* = p_a^* + \Delta p^*$ can be higher, lower, or the same as the new $\overline{P}$ depending on the size of the ratio given on the right side of (9). It is even possible for the new p^* to be the same as the new $\overline{P}$ so that there can be intervals where the two are equal. By drawing U of different shapes we can see a variety of alternatives. For instance, if U is very sharply curved so that the seller has extreme risk aversion, then there will be a wide range where the acceptable forward price is below the expected spot price.

Before going on to the analysis from the buyer's point of view, it remains to consider the effect of discounting. Let $\beta = 1/(1 + \rho)$, where ρ is the discount rate so that β, the discount factor, is a positive number less than one.

If the seller stops the forward contract, he expects to get $U(p_2) + \beta \overline{U}$.

If the seller sticks to the forward contract, he gets $U(p^*) + \beta U(p^*)$. He is better off by adhering to the forward contract if and only if

$$U(p^*) > [U(p_2) + \beta \overline{U}]/(1 + \beta). \tag{10}$$

It is instructive to compare this inequality to (6). In (6) the current return and the expected return get equal weight whereas in (10), as one would expect, the current gain gets relatively more weight than the expected gain. Thus, a bird in the hand is worth more than two in the bush. The critical forward price, call it p_a^* as above, now satisfies

$$U(p_a^*) = [U(p_2) + \beta \overline{U}]/(1 + \beta). \tag{11}$$

It would be both tedious and unnecessary to repeat the preceding analysis in order to derive the consequences of discounting. A diagram like Figure 6.1 reveals all it is necessary to know. Since the presence of β has the effect of giving relatively less weight to the expected spot price because it applies to the future, it raises the value of the forward price that would be minimally acceptable to the seller. Discounting makes a violation of the forward contract more tempting so the forward price must be higher in compensation in order to lower the temptation for the forward seller to breach the forward contract.

Having considered the situation in detail from the point of view of the seller, the corresponding analysis for the buyer can be brief. For the buyer the return is higher, the lower the price he pays. Let $V(P)$ denote the return to the buyer as a function of the price he pays. Hence V varies inversely with P. Assume that V is a concave function of P so that $\overline{V} \leq V(\overline{P})$ is true as it is in (4). To keep the analysis simple, assume the discount rate is zero so that $\beta = 1$. Faithfulness of the buyer to the forward contract is the more profitable strategy if and only if

$$V(p^*) > \tfrac{1}{2}[V(p_1) + \overline{V}], \tag{12}$$

where the term in brackets shows that the buyer would breach when the spot price is low, p_1, so that he could buy the good more cheaply than at the forward price, p^*. There is a critical forward price for the buyer, denote it by p_b^*, such that

$$V(p_b^*) = \tfrac{1}{2}[V(p_1) + \overline{V}]. \tag{13}$$

Proposition 2: *For linear V so that*

$$V(P) = c_0 - c_1 P, \qquad c_1 > 0, \tag{14}$$

it follows that $\overline{P} > p_b^*$.

Proof: It is the same as for Proposition 1.   ∎

The buyer and the seller can have a self-enforcing long-term contract only if the highest acceptable forward price that the buyer is willing to pay exceeds the lowest acceptable forward price that the seller is willing to take. Therefore, the following is true.

Proposition 3: *To have a self-enforcing forward contract it is necessary that*

$$p_b^* > p_a^*. \tag{15}$$

From this result there follows an important conclusion:

> **Corollary 1:** *No self-enforcing forward contract exists if both U and V are linear so that both the buyer and the seller are risk neutral.*

Proof: The hypothesis together with Propositions 1 and 2 give the result

$$p_b^* < \overline{P} < p_a^* \tag{16}$$

so by Proposition 3 there is a violation of the necessary condition for the existence of a self-enforcing forward contract. ■

It follows from this corollary that nonlinearity of U or V is a necessary condition for a self-enforcing forward contract. Such nonlinearity is compatible with risk neutrality if the return is a strictly concave function of the price owing to the nature of the costs of the traders. A good illustration is in the copper industry where for many years copper mining companies in the United States sold copper at stable prices on forward contracts sometimes below the spot copper price. It may be that the producers of copper could lower their cost of production by having the steady demand attracted by stable forward prices. Hence the sellers may be regarded as having a strictly concave function of the price such that the return rose with the price but less rapidly.

There is a simple sufficient condition for the existence of a self-enforcing forward contract that is an immediate implication of (15).

> **Corollary 2:** $p_b^* > \overline{P}$ and $\overline{P} > p_a^*$ are sufficient for the existence of a self-enforcing forward contract.

According to this corollary, a self-enforcing forward contract is possible if the mean spot price is below the buyer's critical forward price and above the seller's critical forward price. This gives them both room for a mutually satisfactory bargain.

3   A principal-agent problem: Prizzi's honor

The theory of self-enforcing agreements may also apply to the principal-agent problem. Having a concrete instance in mind is helpful. Say that the agent operates a gambling casino owned by the principal. The agent may cheat the principal by skimming some of the casino receipts for himself and not pay the principal the total amount due him. In order to deter cheating, the principal may inspect his agent continuously or intermittently. If the principal discovers that he has been cheated by the agent, then he has several penalties available that he can impose on the agent. The principal may simply terminate the relation with the agent. The principal may attempt to recover what the agent has taken from him plus an additional amount. The agent may be required to post a bond so that in case of malfeasance he forfeits the bond. Still more severe penalties are available – the agent may be severely injured or iced. The roles of agent and principal are asymmetrical. The agent is subject to a risk of false accusation. Presumably, the compensation of the agent must be higher to the extent that the principal may falsely accuse the agent of malfeasance solely in order to collect the penalty. I assume there are no false accusations and that inspection is completely reliable so that it can flawlessly discover whether or not cheating has occurred. Under these assumptions the principal-agent problem is readily analyzed in terms of a two-person non-zero-sum noncooperative game.

Let us summarize the relevant data. If the agent does not cheat and the principal does not inspect, then the return of each is zero. Thus, without loss of generality zero is the base amount. If the agent does not cheat and the principal does inspect, then the return to the agent is zero, but since the principal incurs the cost of inspection, his return falls to $-\delta_1$. The agent can cheat the principal successfully if the principal fails to inspect. If so, the gain to the agent, which is δ_2, is the same as the loss to the principal. In the remaining alternative the agent cheats and is caught. Assume that the agent must repay what he has stolen and pay a penalty in addition. Hence the agent pays δ_3, the penalty, and the principal's return is δ_3 minus the cost of inspection, δ_1.

Table 6.1 shows the payoff matrix of the agent and the principal. An agent's strategy is a choice of row and a principal's strategy is a choice of column. For a sensible problem one must assume that

$$\delta_3 - \delta_1 > -\delta_2 \Leftrightarrow \delta_2 + \delta_3 > \delta_1. \tag{1}$$

If (1) were false, then, evidently, it would never pay for the principal to inspect and it would always pay for the agent to cheat. No reasonable person would become a principal under these circumstances. Stated differently, if (1) were false, then operators of gambling casinos must

Table 6.1. *Principal-agent problem*

| | Principal | |
Agent	Don't inspect	Inspect
Don't cheat	0, 0	$0, -\delta_1$
Cheat	$\delta_2, -\delta_2$	$-\delta_3, \delta_3 - \delta_1$

also own them. Hence assume (1) is true so there is a sensible principal-agent problem.

Let α_i denote the probability the agent chooses row i and β_j the probability the principal chooses column j. Let λ be the expected return of the agent and μ be the expected return of the principal. A non-cooperative equilibrium is a set $\{\alpha, \beta, \lambda, \mu\}$ that satisfies the inequalities as follows:

$$E(r_1) = 0\beta_1 + 0\beta_2 \leqq \lambda, \qquad \alpha_1, \tag{2}$$

$$E(r_2) = \delta_2\beta_1 - \delta_3\beta_2 \leqq \lambda, \qquad \alpha_2, \tag{3}$$

$$\beta_1 + \beta_2 = 1, \qquad \beta_j \geqq 0. \tag{4}$$

$$E(c_1) = 0\alpha_1 - \delta_2\alpha_2 \leqq \mu, \qquad \beta_1, \tag{5}$$

$$E(c_2) = -\delta_1\alpha_1 + (\delta_3 - \delta_1)\alpha_2 \leqq \mu, \qquad \beta_2, \tag{6}$$

$$\alpha_1 + \alpha_2 = 1, \qquad \alpha_i \geqq 0. \tag{7}$$

$E(r_i)$ denotes the expected return to the agent from his choice of row i and $E(c_j)$ the expected return to the principal from his choice of column j. Hence

$$\lambda = \alpha_1 E(r_1) + \alpha_2 E(r_2), \tag{8}$$

$$\mu = \beta_1 E(c_1) + \beta_2 E(c_2). \tag{9}$$

In a noncooperative equilibrium, the agent chooses α, giving him the maximal expected return for the best choice of β by the principal. Likewise, the best β for the principal yields him the maximal expected return given the optimal α's chosen by the agent. The α's and β's satisfying (2)–(7) furnish both the solution of these maximum problems and the noncooperative equilibrium. By examining the properties of the solution of (2)–(7), we learn those of the noncooperative equilibrium.

The first important result is that there is no pure, that is, deterministic noncooperative equilibrium. The only noncooperative equilibrium is mixed, that is, nondeterministic. In the equilibrium it is always true that the agent cheats with some positive probability, and he will get away with it with some positive probability. Certain inspection by the principal is never optimal. The probabilities of cheating and of being caught are equilibrium values determined by the model, not numbers arbitrarily imposed from outside. The lower is the cost of inspection, δ_1, the lower the agent's equilibrium cheat probability. The higher is the sum $\delta_2 + \delta_3$, the lower the probability of the agent cheating. The equilibrium probability of principal inspection does not depend on its cost; it depends only on the size of the loss, δ_2, and the size of the penalty, δ_3. To verify these assertions requires examination of the equilibrium conditions.

It follows from (2) that the expected return of the agent, which is given by λ, must be nonnegative. It also follows that β_1 must be positive. The proof is by contradiction. Suppose β_1 were zero, which would require β_2 equal to one, meaning that the principal always inspects. It would follow from (2) and (3) that

$$\lambda \geq \max \{0, -\delta_3\} = 0.$$

Equality in (3) would not be possible as a consequence so that α_2 would be zero and $\lambda = 0$. It would then follow from (5) and (6) that

$$\mu \geq \max \{0, -\delta_1\} = 0.$$

But $\beta_2 = 1$ would imply equality in (6) and with $\alpha_2 = 0$, μ would have to equal $-\delta_1 < 0$, thereby giving a contradiction. Therefore, as we set out to show, β_1 must be positive. Next suppose β_1 were equal to one. We shall prove this is impossible. If β_1 were equal to one so that β_2 were necessarily equal to 0, then it would follow from (2) and (3) that

$$\lambda = \delta_2 \quad \text{and} \quad \alpha_1 = 0.$$

But $\alpha_1 = 0$ would require $\alpha_2 = 1$. According to (1),

$$\mu = (\delta_3 - \delta_1) > -\delta_2$$

so that $\beta_1 = 0$ giving a contradiction as claimed. We may conclude that β_1 is positive and between zero and one. This means inspection by the principal is not certain; it is a random event by design.

Since both β's are positive, there is an implication of equality in both (5) and (6) and

$$\mu = -\delta_2\alpha_2. \tag{10}$$

Solving (5)–(7) for α_2 gives

$$\alpha_2 = \delta_1/(\delta_2 + \delta_3), \tag{11}$$

which is between zero and one by virtue of (1). Hence there must also be equality in (2) and (3). Therefore,

$$\lambda = 0 \tag{12}$$

and

$$\beta_2 = \delta_2/(\delta_2 + \delta_3). \tag{13}$$

Substitute the value of α_2 from (11) into (10) and obtain

$$\mu = -\delta_1\beta_2. \tag{14}$$

This says that the expected return of the principal is the probability of inspection multiplied by the cost of inspection. As (14) shows, it is always negative, and according to (12) the expected return of the agent is zero. Hence the expected return of the principal (the owner of the gambling casino) is always below the expected return of the agent, who operates it.

According to (13), the equilibrium probability of inspection does not depend on its cost, whereas the probability of cheating does depend on the cost of inspection. In fact, the probability of cheating is lower, the lower the cost of inspection. It is also lower, the greater the penalty for cheating, δ_3. If δ_3 can become unboundedly large, say that the penalty for cheating is that the agent is iced, then the equilibrium probability of cheating approaches zero. Moreover, the probability of cheating decreases as the sum $\delta_2 + \delta_3$ increases. Consequently, in equilibrium the larger is the amount that can be stolen and the larger the penalty for stealing, the smaller is the probability of theft. The probability of inspection actually depends on the ratio δ_3/δ_2. The larger is the penalty relative to the principal's loss, the lower is the equilibrium inspection probability.

This model can also answer the interesting question as to which is more effective as a deterrent against cheating, an increase in the penalty, δ_3, or a reduction in the inspection cost, δ_1. We seek a combination of δ_1 and δ_3 capable of maintaining a constant value for the equilibrium cheating probability. From (11) it follows that

$$\Delta\alpha_2 = (\delta_3 + \delta_2)\,\Delta\delta_1 - \delta_1(\Delta\delta_3 + \Delta\delta_2) = 0$$

if and only if

$$\frac{\Delta\delta_1}{\delta_1} = \frac{\Delta\delta_2 + \Delta\delta_3}{\delta_2 + \delta_3}. \tag{15}$$

Assume the principal cannot control the size of his loss, which is δ_2 so it is a given that implies that $\Delta\delta_2 = 0$. It follows from (15) that in this case

$$\Delta\delta_1 = \alpha_2 \Delta\delta_3. \tag{16}$$

It is clear from (16) that a change in the cost of inspection is a more effective deterrent than a change in the size of the penalty. For example, suppose that $\alpha_2 = 0.05$ so that in equilibrium there is only a 5 percent chance that the agent would cheat the principal. A \$1 increase in the cost of inspection could offset the effect of a \$20 increase in the size of the penalty.

Reconsider the payoff matrix in Table 6.1. The sum of the entries in each cell shows the joint return to the principal and agent. In the column labeled "Don't Inspect" the joint return is zero while in the column "Inspect" it is $-\delta_1$, the cost of inspection. The highest joint return is when the agent does not cheat and the principal does not inspect. However, under the noncooperative equilibrium the agent's expected return is zero and the principal's is $-\delta_1\beta_2$. This seems to give room for a mutually advantageous bargain between the two such that the agent does not cheat and the principal does not inspect. A cautious principal calculates that his best result in the worst case is $-\delta_1$ while the agent's best return in the worst case is zero. So a pessimistic and conservative principal, a minimaxer, would always inspect and a minimaxing agent would never cheat. But this is not an equilibrium.

What are the prospects for a self-enforcing agreement? The agent would get zero if he abides by the agreement or under the mixed noncooperative equilibrium. If he cheats and the principal fails to inspect, he gets δ_2. The principal gets zero under the cooperative agreement, $-\delta_2$ if the agent violates the agreement (because the principal does not inspect if there is a cooperative agreement), and under the noncooperative equilibrium the principal can expect to receive $-\delta_1\beta_2$. These facts make plain the conclusion that there is no chance of a self-enforcing agreement. The principal can hope to keep the agent in line only if he inspects at least some of the time, and he must also have the capability of punishing the agent whenever he detects cheating.

The same conclusion applies to a general situation where an employee occupies a position of trust for the employer. A self-enforcing agreement between the two is not possible. The employer, who is the principal, must have the capability of imposing and collecting a penalty whenever he detects cheating by his employee.

4 Research and development: a free-loader problem

Begin with the assumption that two firms produce and sell a product that their customers regard as equivalent so that each firm's product is a perfect substitute for the other's. In the initial equilibrium each firm has the same cost conditions, produces and sells the same quantity at the same price, and gets the same profit. By assuming the profit is zero, it becomes the benchmark for measuring the gains of the alternatives available to the firms. Each firm can lower its cost of production as a result of successful research. Assume that by allocating resources to research and development a firm can successfully learn how to lower its cost of production. However, it is unable to prevent other firms from copying its discovery and cannot stop them from using the results of its own research. Hence a firm doing none of the research itself can nevertheless reap the result of the research done by the other firm. Assume it costs less to copy the results of others than to discover new knowledge yourself. That firm not doing its own research but copying its rival's results is a free-loader. Therefore, a firm that does its own research and incurs the cost of finding new knowledge gets a lower return than its rival that does no research and copies its results. The situation is symmetric because by hypothesis either firm can do the research while the other free-loads.

Table 6.2 shows the payoff matrix. If neither firm does research, then the return of each is zero. If one firm does research and the other copies, then the return to the research firm is δ_1 and is $\delta_1 + \delta_2$ to the free-loader. If both firms do the research, the return of each is δ_1. Though a firm doing its own research is better off than by not doing it, it is still better off if it can copy the research results of its competitor. Several interesting conclusions follow from the model shown in Table 6.2.

The efficient arrangement is plain; only one firm should do the research. There is wasteful duplication if both firms do research. However, a cautious firm would do its own research and not rely on the chance that the other would. Formally, this is the minimax solution where both firms do research. To verify this, note that firm 1 has the worst outcome in row 1 if firm 2 does no research, and firm 1's worst outcome in row 2 is where it does its own research. Hence for firm 1 the best of these worst cases is always to do its own research. Since the same is true for firm 2, in the minimax solution both firms pay for and do their own research.

As we shall see, there are three noncooperative equilibria. Let $E(r_i)$

Table 6.2. *Research and development: the free-loader problem*

| | Firm 2: R&D outlay | |
Firm 1: R&D outlay	Zero	Positive
Zero	0, 0	$\delta_1 + \delta_2, \delta_1$
Positive	$\delta_1, \delta_1 + \delta_2$	δ_1, δ_1

denote the expected return to firm 1 (the row player) and $E(c_j)$ the expected return to firm 2 (the column player). A noncooperative equilibrium must satisfy the following conditions:

$$E(r_1) = 0\beta_1 + (\delta_1 + \delta_2)\beta_2 \leq \lambda, \qquad \alpha_1, \tag{1}$$

$$E(r_2) = \delta_1\beta_1 + \delta_1\beta_2 \leq \lambda, \qquad \alpha_2, \tag{2}$$

$$\beta_1 + \beta_2 = 1, \qquad \beta_j \geq 0. \tag{3}$$

$$E(c_1) = 0\alpha_1 + (\delta_1 + \delta_2)\alpha_2 \leq \mu, \qquad \beta_1, \tag{4}$$

$$E(c_2) = \delta_1\alpha_1 + \delta_1\alpha_2 \leq \mu, \qquad \beta_2, \tag{5}$$

$$\alpha_1 + \alpha_2 = 1, \qquad \alpha_i \geq 0. \tag{6}$$

The probability that the row player chooses row i is α_i and that the column player chooses column j is β_j. Although the situation is symmetric and there is a symmetric mixed equilibrium, there are also two asymmetric pure equilibria. Thus a symmetric situation can have asymmetric equilibria. In one of these, firm 1 does the research so that $\alpha_2 = 1$, and firm 2 does none, $\beta_1 = 0$. In the other the roles are reversed so that $\alpha_1 = 1$ and $\beta_2 = 1$.

If $\alpha_2 = 1$ and $\beta_1 = 1$, then $\lambda = \delta_1$ and $\mu = \delta_1 + \delta_2$.

If $\alpha_1 = 1$ and $\beta_2 = 1$, then $\lambda = \delta_1 + \delta_2$ and $\mu = \delta_1$.

Plainly, these give two distinct solutions of (1)–(6) so that each one is a pure noncooperative equilibrium. The theory of noncooperative equilibria is silent on the choice between these two distinct solutions. Moreover, it is important to recognize that each of these pure noncooperative equilibria is efficient whereas, as we shall see, the symmetric mixed noncooperative equilibrium is inefficient.

The third noncooperative equilibrium, nondeterministic and symmetric, is as follows:

$$\alpha_2 = \beta_2 = \delta_1/(\delta_1 + \delta_2), \tag{7}$$

and

$$\lambda = \mu = \delta_1. \tag{8}$$

In this equilibrium all four outcomes have a positive probability of occurring, including the two that are inefficient. The outcomes are inefficient a proportion of the time given as follows:

$$\alpha_1\beta_1 + \alpha_2\beta_2 = (\delta_1^2 + \delta_2^2)/(\delta_1 + \delta_2)^2. \tag{9}$$

In the absence of a unique noncooperative equilibrium, firms do not know what to expect. Theorists have no basis for predicting the outcome. It is an unsatisfactory situation.

Since the knowledge resulting from the research of one firm is valuable to both, and it would be wasteful for them both to do the research, they would seem to have an incentive for an agreement. The nature and terms of an agreement would depend on whether the situation will occur only once or is likely to recur.

First, assume the situation will occur once. In one type of agreement one firm does the research and the other pays half the total cost. One way of arranging this is for the potential free-loader to pay half the cost in advance to the other firm who will do the actual research. The paying firm bears the risk that the other will take the payment but fail to do the research as agreed. Alternatively, the paying firm may promise to pay the researching firm but only after the research is done. In this case the researching firm incurs the risk of not being paid its share of the research cost.

A description of the agreement in its extensive form enables a full step-by-step analysis. The size of the research outlay must be related to the gain to the free-loader since it is the expense the free-loader avoids by copying the rival's results. Therefore, the research outlay must equal δ_2, the gain of free-loading. Figure 6.2 shows the alternatives. The top panel assumes firm 2 pays half the research cost in advance to firm 1 who agrees to do the actual research. P means firm 2 pays and $\bar{P}$ means it reneges on its promise to pay. R means firm 1 does the research and $\bar{R}$ that it reneges. We wish to see whether this agreement can be self-enforcing so that it is in the self-interest of each to live up to its promise. It is clear from Figure 6.2 that firm 2 has no reason to abide by its promise since no matter what it does, firm 1 will do the research not out of altruism but out of self-interest. The

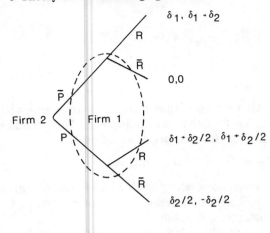

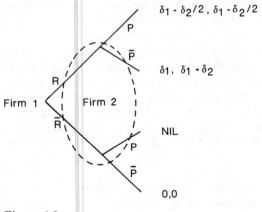

Figure 6.2

case where firm 2 puts up all the funds for research in advance and gets half of it back from firm 1 after the research is done is an open invitation from firm 2 to firm 1 to keep all the money. Rational parties would never consent to this arrangement so it needs no further consideration.

The bottom panel of Figure 6.2 shows another possible agreement. This time it is firm 1 that does the research and expects payment from firm 2 for half the cost. It is again plain that firm 2 would have no incentive to fulfill its part of the bargain while it is always in the self-interest of firm 1 to do the research.

Because the situation is completely symmetric, any firm that agrees to do the research in a once-and-for-all setting like this could not expect the other firm to fulfill its part of the agreement. Yet it is always in the selfish interest of the firm promising to do the research actually to do it. Hence no self-enforcing agreement exists in this case. Any agreement between the two firms would seem to require enforcement by a third party.

Next assume the situation is recurrent. In each period there is a research project that created new knowledge on how to lower costs. The projects are independent over time so that the results of the later periods do not depend on the results of the preceding ones. It is the purpose of these assumptions to ensure that each firm can in fact do one of the research projects on its own in each period independently of what came before or will come after. Finally, assume this situation is equivalent to an infinite horizon because the stopping date is uncertain, though it will occur eventually. Under these hypotheses it is plausible that the firms would agree to alternate their research so that one firm does the research in one period and the other in the next. In this fashion each firm would expect to be the researcher half the time and the beneficiary of the other firm's research half the time. Ignoring discounting, consider the sequence of returns to a firm under two alternatives, faithfulness to the cooperative agreement and cheating. Recall that in the once-and-for-all situation, a firm that has promised to do the research is always better off by adhering to its promise. Is this also true in the recurrent case?

Period	1	2	3	4 ...
Cooperate	δ_1	$\delta_1 + \delta_2$	δ_1	$\delta_1 + \delta_2$
Cheat	0	$\delta_1 + \delta_2$	0	$\delta_1 + \delta_2$

Assume the firm has agreed to do the research in the odd-numbered periods and obtain the results of the other firm's research in the even-numbered periods. Therefore, under the cooperative agreement, it would get the same return as a free-loader in the even-numbered periods, $\delta_1 + \delta_2$, whereas in the odd-numbered periods it would receive δ_1, the same as a firm doing and paying for its own research. It would have no incentive to cheat in those periods when it obtains the research results from the other firm. If it fails to do the research during the odd-numbered periods as it had promised, then, evidently, it is worse off because its return is zero in these periods. Consequently, the sequence of returns under the cooperative agreement is never less than the sequence from cheating. It follows that recurrence with an uncertain stopping time implies the existence of a self-enforcing agreement.

This model of a free-loader problem assumes that the optimal research outlay does not depend on the number of firms. Thus, one firm can have the optimal program and the second firm would not contribute to it. Hence the scale of the total research effort does not rise with the number of firms. In practice this is unlikely. Cooperation between the two firms would result in a larger total research program than for one. The theory of the core is a more useful tool for studying this situation. The allocation of resources designed to expand the stock of knowledge creates a semiprivate or public good depending on whether the cooperating firms can or cannot prevent the noncontributors from getting the research results. If free-loading cannot be stopped, knowledge becomes a public good. If free-loading can be stopped, then knowledge is a semiprivate good. Analyzing the creation of new knowledge as a noncooperative equilibrium reveals little about the substantive issues raised by the creation of that knowledge, which is semiprivate or public. Chapter 8 continues the analysis of these problems.

5   The Prisoners' Dilemma

No simple two-person game is better known than the Prisoners' Dilemma. As applied in economic theory it goes as follows. Two firms are considering whether or not to collude. They each make the same product under the same cost conditions and sell it at the same unit price. If the two firms collude, say each one gets a profit of δ_1. Table 6.3 shows the returns for the various alternatives. If the firms collude, the returns are in the cell labeled "honest" to indicate that the firms are faithful to their agreement. If one of the firms, the column player, produces and sells the output assigned him by the terms of the cartel agreement while the other firm, the row player, cheats, then the cheater gets the net return $\delta_1 + \delta_3$ while the victim loses δ_2 (all δ's in Table 6.3 are positive). If both firms cheat, then the net return of each is zero.

Several facts about this situation are important. First, a victim of cheating is worse off than he would have been in the absence of a collusive agreement. Collusion exposes the parties to the risk of getting less than they would receive without collusion under the noncooperative equilibrium. In the noncooperative equilibrium for this case, both firms cheat simultaneously and each would then obtain a net return of zero. However, the honest victim of cheating by the other firm would get a return of $-\delta_2 < 0$. Therefore, cooperation exposes each firm to the prospect of being made worse off. Moreover, the sum of the returns

Table 6.3. *Payoff matrix for the Prisoners'
Dilemma*

	Column player	
Row player	Honest	Cheats
Honest	δ_1, δ_1	$-\delta_2, \delta_1 + \delta_3$
Cheats	$\delta_1 + \delta_3, -\delta_2$	$0, 0$

under a collusive agreement is larger than the sum if one firm cheats
and the other honestly abides by the terms of the agreement. Formally,

$$2\delta_1 > \delta_1 + \delta_3 - \delta_2$$

so that

$$\delta_1 > \delta_3 - \delta_2.$$

It is the latter condition that poses the dilemma. There is a conflict
between the collective interest of the two firms and the self-interest of
each one. Suppose the row player is honest. Then the column player
maximizes his net return by cheating the row player. But then if he
does cheat, the row player too maximizes his return if he cheats. Given
cheating by the row player, the best response of the column player is
to cheat. Hence cheating or, equivalently, noncooperation becomes
the equilibrium strategy for both. The larger joint return, which is the
fruit of cooperation, lies tantalizingly beyond the reach of each selfish
firm. All this is familiar. Less familiar are several other properties of
the Prisoners' Dilemma.

In this case the noncooperative equilibrium is also a saddle point.
Let a_{ij} be the return to the row player for row i, column j, and b_{ij} be
the return to the column player from row i, column j. A necessary and
sufficient condition for a pure (deterministic) saddle value is that

$$\max_j \min_i [a_{ij}] = \min_i \max_j [a_{ij}] \tag{3}$$

and

$$\max_i \min_j [b_{ij}] = \min_j \max_i [b_{ij}]. \tag{4}$$

Now

$$\min_j [a_{ij}] = \min\{-\delta_2, 0\} = 0 \quad \text{and} \quad \max_i \{-\delta_2, 0\} = 0.$$

$$\max_i [a_{ij}] = \max\{\delta_1 + \delta_3, 0\} = 0 \quad \text{and} \quad \min_j\{\delta_1 + \delta_3, 0\} = 0.$$

Therefore, (3) is true for the row player and row 2, column 2, is his saddle value. By symmetry exactly the same argument is valid for the column player and his matrix $[b_{ij}]$ so we may conclude that (4) is true for the column player. Consequently, the noncooperative equilibrium is also the deterministic saddle value in the Prisoners' Dilemma. This means that noncooperation is the best conservative strategy.

In a malevolent equilibrium each player chooses the strategy that minimizes the net return of his adversary. This resembles the noncooperative equilibrium turned on its head. In a noncooperative equilibrium each player attempts to maximize his return given the strategy of the other player. In a malevolent equilibrium each player tries to minimize the return of the other by a suitable choice of his strategy given the strategy of his adversary. It is not difficult to verify that row 2, column 2, is the unique malevolent equilibrium in the Prisoners' Dilemma. Hence the noncooperative equilibrium is also the best punishing strategy as well as the safest. The conjunction of these three strategies distinguishes the Prisoners' Dilemma from all other finite two-person non-constant-sum games.

> **Proposition 4.** In a symmetric Prisoners' Dilemma, the deter-
> ministic saddle value, the noncooperative equilibrium, and the
> malevolent equilibrium are unique and coincide.

If both players know they are in the situation described by the Prisoners' Dilemma for precisely one occasion, then although cooperation is efficient because it maximizes the sum of their returns, it is not individually rational. The selfish interest defeats the common interest.

It may seem that the equilibrium should depend on whether the situation described by the Prisoners' Dilemma recurs or is known to happen only once. In fact, recurrence for a known finite number of times does not change the equilibrium, which remains noncooperation every time. To show this, it suffices to take the case where the game will be played exactly twice for sure. One way to prove this, discussed more fully below, is by backward induction using the argument given by Luce and Raiffa (1957, pp. 94–102). Another way proceeds as follows. Table 6.4 shows the payoff matrix. The matrix has 16 entries, one for each of the 16 possible outcomes. An outcome requires a choice of two elements, each from two alternatives by the two players. The row player chooses which row to pick in the first and second period from the matrix given in Table 6.3. The column player similarly chooses columns for each period. In each period the players choose simultaneously so neither player knows the choice of the other in advance

Table 6.4. *Payoff matrix for two times repeated Prisoners' Dilemma*

Row player	Column player			
	1, 1	1, 2	2, 1	2, 2
1, 1	$2\delta_1, 2\delta_1$	$\delta_1 - \delta_2, 2\delta_1 + \delta_3$	$\delta_1 - \delta_2, 2\delta_1 + \delta_3$	$-2\delta_2, 2(\delta_1 + \delta_3)$
1, 2	$2\delta_1 + \delta_3, \delta_1 - \delta_2$	δ_1, δ_1	$\delta_1 + \delta_3 - \delta_2, \delta_1 + \delta_3 - \delta_2$	$-\delta_2, \delta_1 + \delta_3$
2, 1	$2\delta_1 + \delta_3, \delta_1 - \delta_2$	$\delta_1 + \delta_3 - \delta_2, \delta_1 + \delta_3 - \delta_2$	δ_1, δ_1	$-\delta_2, \delta_1 + \delta_3$
2, 2	$2(\delta_1 + \delta_3), -2\delta_2$	$\delta_1 + \delta_3, -\delta_2$	$\delta_1 + \delta_3, -\delta_2$	$0, 0$

of his own. For instance, in Table 6.4 take row (1,2) and column (1,1). This means that in period one the row player picks row 1 and the column player picks column 1 from the payoff matrix of Table 6.3. In the second period, the row player takes row 2 and the column player column 1. In the first period the row player gets δ_1 and in the second period he gets $\delta_1 + \delta_3$, summing to $2\delta_1 + \delta_3$ for both periods as shown in Table 6.4. For the column player, the first period return is δ_1 and owing to his being cheated in the second period his loss is then δ_2. Hence Table 6.4 shows the return of the column player is $\delta_1 - \delta_2$.

The unique noncooperative equilibrium for the payoff matrix in Table 6.4 is row 4, column 4. To check this, note that when the game is repeated exactly twice, a strategy for the row player is a choice of one of the four rows of Table 6.4, and for the column player it is one of the four columns of Table 6.4. Therefore, the unique equilibrium giving each player the maximum return for a given strategy of the other is to cheat in each period, the cheating strategy of Table 6.3. This result is remarkable. One would think that the magnitudes of the parameters should enter the picture but they do not.

Consider, for instance, choosing row 3 in Table 6.4 so that the row player cheats in the first period but not in the second. He may suppose that the column player uses a tit-for-tat strategy such that the column player is not the first to defect and punishes cheating by the row player in a period by his own defection in the next period (Axelrod 1984). The row player would come out ahead if $\delta_1 + \delta_3 - \delta_2$ were positive. However, if the row player chooses row 3, then the best choice for the column player would not be column 2, the tit-for-tat strategy, but would be column 4. Given that column 4 is the best response to the row player's choice of row 3, now the row player's best reply is row 4. Hence row 4 is the best reply to column 4 and column 4 is the best reply to row 4. We may conclude that row 4, column 4, is the noncooperative equilibrium. The conclusion does not depend on the size of $\delta_1 + \delta_3 - \delta_2$.

The conclusion remains valid no matter how many times the players repeat the situation described by the Prisoners' Dilemma if the number of times is known for sure in advance by both players. In case this number is n, the payoff matrix has an unwieldy number of rows, 2^n. In the noncooperative equilibrium each player cheats in each of the n repetitions.

Something seems missing from this analysis. The missing element is found by looking at the repeated Prisoners' Dilemma in another way following a proposal of Luce and Raiffa (1957). To pave the way, let us now consider the argument using backward induction. Assume both players know their situation will recur n times for sure. Also assume there exists an optimal strategy. It determines the choices for each of the n periods. In the last period, having made the best choices for each of the preceding $n - 1$ periods, the row player can argue that his best choice for the last, that is the nth period, cannot depend on anything that happens in the future since by hypothesis he is certain this is the last occasion for play. Therefore, he can determine the best strategy for the nth period with precisely the same reasoning as if he were in the Prisoners' Dilemma for exactly one period. In this case he knows the answer given by the analysis above. Namely, it is to cheat. Having determined this optimal choice for the nth period, move back one period to period $n - 1$ and again the optimal choice is to cheat in period $n - 1$. Continuing the backward induction to the first period gives the same conclusion as above, which is to cheat in each period. However, the analysis brings to light the important point that the backward induction relies on the certainty that the game is repeated for precisely n periods for sure so that there is a last period for sure. This assumption gives the result that the optimal strategy for the nth period is the same as for a one-period Prisoners' Dilemma. What if there were no last period? This means there is a positive probability that the situation can continue. Since each player must reckon with the possibility that he can become subject to punishment later on for a current defection, the preceding argument based on backward induction does not apply. The cost of the punishment weighs against the gain from defection and may be heavy enough to deter him from dishonesty.

It is not difficult to modify the analysis to cover the probability of continuing. Let p denote the probability that the game is played on trial i and let $1 - p = q$ denote the probability that play stops forever on trial i. The probability of playing and stopping in a given period does not depend on the previous history. Once the game has stopped, it cannot resume. Continuing and stopping are autonomous events beyond the control of the players. We may interpret continuing to mean that the present circumstances will continue. Let r_i denote the return to a player in period i. The probability that play continues for exactly n periods is $p^n q$. The expected return from play for n periods is $(r_1 + r_2 + \cdots + r_n)p^n q$ so that the expected return for all n-period horizons is

$$\sum_{n=1}^{\infty} \sum_{i=1}^{n} r_i p^n q = \sum_{i=1}^{\infty} r_i p^i. \tag{5}$$

Thus, in this formula the probability of continuing plays the role of a discount factor.

We may use formula (5) to calculate the expected return to a player who is loyal to the agreement for the first t periods, cheats in period $t + 1$, and is punished relentlessly thereafter. The point is that if relentless punishment cannot deter cheating, then a fortiori lighter punishment cannot do so either. Hence to see if loyalty promises the highest expected return, there is no loss of generality from confining the investigation to the deterrent effect of relentless punishment. The difference between the expected return from this strategy and that from continuous loyalty is as follows:

$$(\delta_1 + \delta_3)p^{t+1} - \delta_1 p^{t+1} - \delta_1 \sum_{t+2}^{\infty} p^i = \delta_3 p^{t+1} - \delta_1 p^{t+2}/(1 - p).$$

Dishonesty is more lucrative than honesty if this expression is positive. Dividing out the term p^{t+1}, it follows that dishonesty is more profitable if

$$\delta_3 - \delta_1 p/(1 - p) > 0. \tag{6}$$

Given the values of δ_3 and δ_1, there is an upper bound on p, the probability of continuing such that for all values of p below this upper bound, (6) is true so that dishonesty is the more profitable strategy. This says that the less likely is continuing, the greater the expected return from cheating. Under these conditions the noncooperative equilibrium implies the absence of collusion. Plainly, (6) is also necessary for dishonesty to yield a higher return than loyalty to an agreement, assuming a victim allows himself to be cheated only once. The punishment for cheating is refusal to cooperate thereafter.

This analysis has direct application to a cartel. It asserts that no cartel beset by repeated violations of its rules can survive. The firms loyal to the cartel are made worse off as victims of the disloyal firms than they would be without a cartel. Therefore, if there is a cartel, inequality (6) must be false so that loyalty to the cartel gives a higher expected profit to each of its members than disloyalty, and cheating does not occur.

This argument must answer the objection that cheating may still allow the victim a higher expected return than he would get in the absence of a cartel provided the cheating is not too frequent. Thus, suppose the row player's cheating occurs as a random event with the frequency $1 - a$. Assume that the column player is always loyal to the cartel so that his expected return is given as follows:

$$E(c) = a\delta_1 - (1 - a)\delta_2.$$

This exceeds his return under the noncooperative equilibrium if $E(c)$ > 0, which sets a lower bound on the frequency of loyalty of the row player given as follows:

$$a > \delta_2/(\delta_1 + \delta_2).$$

It would seem, therefore, that the column player is better off in the cartel even if he is cheated by the row player provided the row player does not cheat him too often. However, this argument suffers from some obvious flaws. First, it begs the question of who is the cheater and who is the victim. This is owing to the fact that the cheater always gains more than the victim. Thus, the row player, by hypothesis the cheating member of the cartel, has the expected return as follows:

$$E(r) = a\delta_1 + (1-a)(\delta_1 + \delta_3)$$

and $E(r) > E(c)$ as we may readily verify. Second, if the same person is always the victim, why does he accept the less profitable situation. It is a symmetric game. A dishonest player can expect a greater return than an honest one. Consequently, each player faces the tempting prospect of occasional cheating. Once this is admitted, then it becomes a problem of how to exploit the situation. We are led back to the theory of the noncooperative equilibrium, which is a consistent explanation of how to pursue self-interest. The excursion into an objection to the theory of cartels given here strengthens the conclusion that either the cartel persists and there is no cheating or there is no cartel. In the latter case there is a noncooperative equilibrium. Occasional cheating as a theory cannot withstand critical scrutiny.

This argument implies that each player finds continuous cooperation best serves his selfish profit-maximizing goal if and only if

$$\delta_3/\delta_1 \leq p/(1 - p). \tag{7}$$

Several conclusions follow from this. First, given p, (7) is true when the gain from cheating, δ_3, is small enough relative to the return from cooperation, δ_1. Second, given the δ's, (7) is true when the uncertainty of continuing, measured by p, is high enough so that p is close enough to one. This is a satisfying result. It means that when the two players expect their current circumstances to last long enough and do not know for sure when these will change, they are more likely to cooperate because it is the most profitable policy for each one.

This argument implies the members of a cartel do not cheat because the loss it would invoke as the punishment for cheating is a sufficient incentive to assure loyalty to the cartel. It follows there would be no secret price cutting. Now if the threat to impose penalties deters and the occasion to carry out the threat never occurs, what makes the threat credible? The answer begins by observing that price cutting as retaliation is feasible. If the present value of the loss imposed by a relentless penalty, which means stopping the collusion forever, cannot deter cheating, plainly there can be no cartel at the outset. This is owing to the greater loss loyal members would sustain as victims of the cheating members than they would obtain in the absence of a cartel. If relentless punishment suffices to make loyalty the more profitable alternative for each cartel member, then there is the question of what is the lightest punishment that suffices. The smaller the loss incurred by the one who punishes, the more credible is the threat of punishment. Hence the deterrent effect is greater, the smaller is the cost of the punishment because a potential violator can compute his expected return and conclude that he will not gain from a violation. He also knows that the potential victim loses more by punishing than by not doing so. Therefore, either there is a cartel and there is no cheating or, if we observe "cheating," it means there is no cartel.

6   Summary

This chapter studies four different situations using the theory of self-enforcing agreements. This theory seeks conditions such that two or more persons who can obtain a mutual benefit from cooperation will actually do so, taking into account the possible gains each may obtain from violations of their cooperative agreement. The theory predicts the emergence of a self-enforcing cooperative agreement if and only if it is in the selfish interest of each party who calculates not only the returns from faithful adherence to the agreement but also the returns from violations of it, taking into account the losses and penalties such violations can provoke. Only the parties to a self-enforcing agreement can themselves impose penalties whenever they please, and they do not rely on outsiders for its enforcement. A violator of a self-enforcing agreement, knowing there will be retaliatory responses, chooses his subsequent strategies accordingly. The penalty for violation of a self-enforcing agreement may be a noncooperative equilibrium. It is, therefore, the breakdown of the cooperative agreement.

In Section 2 the theory of self-enforcing agreements applies to the choice between a forward and a spot contract. The parties to a forward contract agree on the terms, notably the forward price, and know that each may breach the contract by trading in the spot market in order to take advantage of a temporary opportunity present there. Necessary for a self-enforcing agreement in this application is that either the return to the seller or to the buyer is a concave, nonlinear function of the spot price, taken as a random variable. One may interpret this necessary condition to mean that one or both parties to the agreement is risk averse. For a self-enforcing agreement it is sufficient that the actuarial expectation of the spot price satisfies a particular inequality. Consequently, in this situation a self-enforcing agreement does not always exist.

The second application of the theory is to a principal-agent problem, Prizzi's honor. The principal owns a gambling casino that the agent manages. This application focuses on violations of the agreement – when the agent will cheat and how the principal can deter this. It is shown that a unique mixed noncooperative equilibrium exists that determines the probability of cheating by the agent and discovery by the principal. Thus, neither cheating nor discovery is certain. There is no self-enforcing agreement in this situation. More prosaic applications are the relations between an employer and employee. Given that the employee can cheat the employer who has various ways of detecting and deterring violations of the terms of employment, it follows that since a self-enforcing agreement does not exist, third-party enforcement in some form becomes necessary.

In the third application two firms contemplate whether they can cooperate on research and development that will lower their cost of production. It is cheaper to copy the research results than to discover them for yourself so there is a free-loader problem. The situation is symmetric for the two firms, but there are three distinct noncooperative equilibria: the symmetric one is mixed and gives an inefficient outcome while the two asymmetric equilibria are both efficient and deterministic. Incidentally, this illustrates the point that a noncooperative equilibrium can be efficient. Cooperation between the two firms would also be efficient by saving the cost of duplicated research. However, cooperation is not self-enforcing. Therefore, in this application, like the principal-agent problem, there is no self-enforcing agreement.

The fourth application, best known as the Prisoners' Dilemma, treats collusion between two firms as a possible self-enforcing agreement. Here the unique noncooperative equilibrium was found by Cournot in 1838. The next chapter analyzes in detail the Cournot problem. However, contrary to Cournot, cooperation is a possible outcome in this case, even though each firm seeks to maximize only its own profit. A self-enforcing agreement can exist if the horizon is finite, uncertain, and expected to last long enough.

CHAPTER 7

Some new results on duopoly applied to theories of Cournot, Bertrand, and Edgeworth

1 Introduction

With the aid of clear and explicit assumptions about the nature of the cost and demand conditions, one can expose the inner structure of the mechanism underlying the theories of duopoly proposed by Cournot in 1838, Bertrand (1883), and Edgeworth (1925). These theories have been the subject of continuous analysis by many economists over a long period of time and remain the starting point of all contributions to this subject. Despite this, their theories are ambiguous because they lack clear descriptions of the economic reality they purport to explain. The standard these theories ought to satisfy is this. It should be possible to state the rules for the situations they describe with enough clarity so that treated as a game, in the sense that poker is a game, the participants would know precisely what they can do under the various circumstances that can occur. The models I shall describe intend to meet this criterion.

The difference between Cournot's theory and the Bertrand–Edgeworth theories are the topic of the next section. Briefly, the Cournot model assumes the duopolists choose output and allow the demand conditions to determine the price at which the total output can be sold. The Bertrand–Edgeworth models allow the duopolists to choose their prices. Consequently, there is the question of what happens if a firm is unable to fill the demand forthcoming at this price or if the demand is below the firm's expectation. All of these theories assume the buyers regard the products of the firms as perfect substitutes, and this raises some problems. Section 2 considers some of these.

Some interesting new results in my model correspond to the Bertrand–Edgeworth setup. An immense number of mixed noncooperative equilibria share the property that for every one of these the expected net return of each firm is zero. Each mixed noncooperative equilibrium has a probability distribution of prices and output rates across the firms. The Cournot model also has many equilibria both mixed and pure, but the firms do not have the same expected net return nor are the expected net returns equal to zero. One of the noncooperative equilibria in the Cournot model I believe deserves special consideration as the most plausible outcome under assumptions appropriate to the model.

The Bertrand–Edgeworth model allows the firms to post different prices. The Cournot model rules this out by hypothesis. It is, therefore, necessary to describe fully the conditions of sale and production consistent with the assumptions of these models, the task of the next section.

2   Assumptions of the model

Start with the demand conditions. All buyers are alike in the sense that each is willing to pay at most b per unit of the good and is willing to buy at most one unit. The number of customers coming to the market who plan to buy the good depends on the price they expect to pay. Assume m potential customers come to the market. This number m depends on b. Assume the good is prohibitively expensive to store so that neither producers nor consumers hold inventories. There are no forward transactions. This means no customer arranges terms of sale in advance with a seller that will result in actual delivery of the good later on. There are no order backlogs. If a buyer cannot obtain the good now, then he cannot arrange with the seller to fill his order later on. The buyers regard all units of the good as perfect substitutes. Assume it is costless for them to obtain a price quotation from a seller. Because the assumption that buyers consider the identity of the sellers as irrelevant implies that price is the decisive consideration for them, a buyer will purchase the good from the seller who asks the lower price. In case the sellers all ask the same price, the situation is a bit more complicated and needs the more detailed explanation given below.

Next consider the supply side. There are two sellers. Each has the same cost of production and can make the good at the same constant unit cost c. There are no avoidable or setup costs. There are no fixed costs. Assume the sellers know the demand conditions, namely b and m and also know each other's unit costs, c. No firm can sell more than its current output. The sellers make no transactions with each other. They act independently and simultaneously so that neither knows in advance what the other will do. Let q_i be the quantity sold by firm i, and x_i be the quantity produced by firm i. Firm i can control its output, but if it quotes a price at which it is ready to sell, then it cannot control how much buyers will take at this price. These assumptions imply that

$$0 \leq q_i \leq x_i \quad \text{and} \quad q_1 + q_2 \leq m. \tag{1}$$

The production decision determines the maximum quantity the firm can sell during the period, and it cannot change its output until the beginning of the next period. Price as a strategic variable poses some difficult issues. There are two useful alternative assumptions about prices. First, assume a seller posts a price that remains in force during the whole period. This makes the choice of a price like that of an output rate. Even if the seller has some unsold output, he does not lower the price. There is also the question of whether the sellers post the same price. If they do, then each is equally likely to attract a potential buyer. If the sellers do not post the same price, the buyers know this because by hypothesis it is costless for the buyers to get price quotations from the sellers. In this case the seller asking the lower price can sell an amount equal to the smaller of the two numbers, m and his output, x. If his output is below m, then the other seller who has posted the higher price can sell only to the remaining customers. Second, we may assume the sellers put their output on the market for whatever price it can fetch. Both sellers must then get the same price. Since the output is the only strategic variable, the second case corresponds to the Cournot model. The latter is formally described as follows.

> *Assumption 1 (Cournot): The two sellers place their output for sale in a single store where it is sold under a common label at the same price.*

This assumption ensures that buyers cannot distinguish between the two sellers' outputs. Provided the price does not exceed the maximal price that the buyers are willing to pay, each seller must get the same revenue per unit sold.

> *Proposition 1: Under Assumption 1,*
>
> if $x_1 + x_2 \geq m$ then $q_i = mw_i$ where $w_i = x_i/(x_1 + x_2)$;
>
> if $x_1 + x_2 < m$ then $q_i = x_i$.

Proof: In the first case w_i gives the probability a buyer chooses the product made by firm i. This probability is the same as firm i's share of the total stock in the store. In the second case there is excess demand so each seller is sure of selling his entire output. ■

The purpose of Assumption 2 is to describe a situation allowing the two firms to quote different prices.

Assumption 2 (Bertrand–Edgeworth): Buyers can distinguish between the products of the two firms and at equal prices regard the two products as perfect substitutes. At different prices buyers prefer the lower priced product. Say that the products of the two sellers are sold in adjacent shops and not in the same shop.

1. *If the posted prices of the two products are the same, then each buyer is equally likely to enter either store provided the posted prices do not exceed the buyer's maximally acceptable price. If the good is available in the store, the buyer will purchase it.*
2. *If the sellers post different prices, then all buyers first enter the store displaying the lower price, and this store can sell all that it has in stock up to a maximuum of m, which is the total number of buyers in the market. The store quoting the higher price can make sales only if its competitor is out of stock and there is unsatisfied demand.*

Proposition 2: *Under Assumption 2.1 where the sellers post the same price,*

if $x_1 + x_2 < m$ then $q_i = x_i$;

if $x_1 + x_2 \geq m$ then;

if $x_1 \leq x_2$ then $q_1 = \min\{m/2, x_1\}$ and $q_2 = m - q_1$;

if $x_1 \geq x_2$ then $q_2 = \min\{m/2, x_2\}$ and $q_1 = m - q_2$.

Proof: The proof of the first assertion is obvious. To prove the second assertion, observe that the expected number of customers entering a store for the first time is $m/2$. If, say, firm 1 produces $x_1 \leq m/2$, then it can expect to sell its entire output. On the other hand, if it produces $x_1 > m/2$, then, because on average half of all customers will have made their initial visit to its rival, it can expect to sell $m/2$ units. ∎

What happens to quantity sold of each firm if they post different prices is clear. Less obvious is the nature of the equilibrium in this case, the topic of the next section.

Both propositions ignore the random variability of firm sales implicit in the description of the models. Under Assumption 1 (Cournot), the value of q_i when $x_1 + x_2 \geq m$ is the expected, but not the actual, sales. The latter are a random variable from a hypergeometric distribution. This distribution arises in random sampling without replacement from a finite population. Let Q_i denote actual sales by firm i, which is a random variable, and let q_i denote the realization of Q_i. The probability that $Q_1 = q_1$ and $Q_2 = q_2$ is given as follows:

$$\binom{x_1}{q_1}\binom{x_2}{q_2} \bigg/ \sum_{q_1=0}^{x_1} \binom{x_1}{q_1}\binom{x_2}{q_2}$$

assuming that $x_1 < x_2$ so that $q_2 = m - q_1$. Feller (1957, p. 218) shows that

$$E(q_1) = [x_1/(x_1 + x_2)]m,$$

which is the same as it would be for a binomial distribution for random sampling with replacement. The higher-order moments are different, however.

Under Assumption 2 (Bertrand–Edgeworth) both firms posting the same price and $x_1 + x_2 \geq m$, q_i is interpreted as the expected, not the actual, sales. Here actual sales have a binomial distribution but in contrast to the situation in the Cournot model (Assumption 1); under Assumption 2 the probability a buyer chooses product 1 is $\frac{1}{2}$. For large enough m, the error from substituting expected for actual sales is small. From now on, I shall make this substitution and ignore the random variability resulting from the sampling process.

3   Noncooperative equilibria under Assumption 2, Bertrand–Edgeworth

In this case a pure strategy for each seller is a pair consisting of a price and an output rate. The price component is defined as follows:

$$p = c + s. \tag{1}$$

A firm seeking to maximize its net return would never choose a price below its marginal cost. This implies s is nonnegative. The output rate of the firm's strategy pair is

$$x = m/2 + t. \tag{2}$$

This formulation distinguishes $m/2$ since a firm can expect to sell this much if it posts the same price as its competitor. However, both firms must post their prices simultaneously so neither has advance information about the other's choice. A pure strategy for firm i is a pair

(p_i, x_i) or the equivalent pair (s_i, t_i), $s_i \geq 0$ and $-m/2 \leq t_i \leq m/2$. The lower bound on t_i follows from the nonnegativity of the sales rate; the upper bound is a consequence of the fact that because each firm knows the total quantity demanded is m, neither would wish to produce more than this amount. The definition of the net revenue of firm i is

$$r_i = p_i q_i - c x_i, \tag{3}$$

where $p_i q_i$ is the revenue from selling q_i units at a price p_i and $c x_i$ is the total cost of producing the output x_i. The principal result under Assumption 2 is the absence of a unique deterministic noncooperative equilibrium and the presence of many mixed noncooperative equilibria.

The situation under Assumption 2 resembles the one Bertrand uses in his criticism of Cournot, and it is in turn like Edgeworth's model in his criticism of Bertrand. However, unlike Edgeworth's setup, Assumption 2 allows each firm to satisfy the entire demand, if it wishes, so that the firm asking the higher price cannot rely on selling to the customers left unsatisfied by the firm charging the lower price. For this situation Bertrand asserts there is only one equilibrium given by $p = c$ and $x = m/2$. Provided one admits mixed noncooperative equilibria, this assertion is false. Out of fairness to Bertrand, however, recall that it was much later, in 1928, that the concept of a mixed equilibrium was invented by Neumann in the first article he published on game theory.

Turning to the analysis of the implications of Assumption 2, plainly no firm would produce more than the maximum quantity it can expect to sell, which is m:

$$0 \leq x \leq m. \tag{4}$$

Because each firm seeks the largest possible net return for itself, neither would choose a price below c. By hypothesis, no buyer would pay more than b. Hence

$$c \leq p \leq b. \tag{5}$$

Because the firms are alike in every respect and each acts on its own, whatever strategy pair one chooses is also a feasible choice for the other. Both firms have access to precisely the same pairs. There is no reason why one firm would have a different set of strategies than the other. Indeed, one firm would possibly have an advantage if it had different strategies than the other and this would contradict the assumptions about these firms. Neither firm can have an advantage if their strategy sets are the same. Although the sets are the same, the outcomes from a mixed noncooperative equilibrium may differ. There is ex ante symmetry but ex post asymmetry.

In order to find the equilibria, start with the special case where each seller chooses among three pure strategies. This is the smallest number that allows a mixed noncooperative equilibrium because one of the pure strategies must always be the pair $(c, m/2)$.

> *Lemma 1: Each set of mixed noncooperative equilibria contains the pair $(c, m/2)$. At $p = c$, $x = m/2$ is the largest output consistent with the demand conditions and a symmetric strategy set.*

Proof: By contradiction. Suppose the set of pure strategies composing a mixed noncooperative equilibrium had a lowest price for one of the firms, say firm 1, above the marginal cost c. Knowing this, firm 2 could choose a slightly lower price for sure, produce enough to satisfy the whole demand, m, and the first firm would incur a loss for sure equal to c times its output rate. Therefore, the supposed price choice of the first firm could not be an equilibrium contrary to the hypothesis.

The set of pure strategies in the mixed equilibrium must contain one pair with $p = c$ as its price component. A firm choosing a price equal to c can be sure of selling the smaller of the two quantities, $m/2$ and its rate of output. By producing more than $m/2$, it runs the risk of a loss whenever the other firm happens to set its price equal to c, and this event has a positive probability as shown above. The given firm can expect to sell more than $m/2$ only when the rival firm happens to set a price above c. Even so, the given firm would gain no advantage because at a price of c, its net return per unit sold is zero. For $p = c$ the largest output consistent with symmetric strategy pairs is $x = m/2$. ∎

The three elements in the set of pure strategies are as follows:

$(c, m/2)$

$(c + s_1, m/2 + t_1)$ 	$s_1, t_1 > 0$

$(c + s_1 + s_2, m/2 + t_1 + t_2)$ 	$s_2, t_2 > 0$.

(Although $t_j < 0$ is possible, it is convenient to defer consideration of this case in order to simplify the present analysis.) The entries in Table 7.1 show the return of firm 1 for the nine possible combinations of strategy pairs of the two firms. For instance, consider the entry in row 2, column 1. Firm 1 chooses $p_1 = c + s_1$ and $x_1 = m/2 + t_1$ while

Table 7.1. *Net returns of firm 1 under Assumption 2 (Bertrand–Edgeworth) with three pairs of pure strategies*

Firm 1 \ Firm 2	$c, m/2$	$c + s_1, m/2 + t_1$	$c + s_1 + s_2,$ $m/2 + t_1 + t_2$
$c, m/2$	0	0	0
$c + s_1,$ $m/2 + t_1$	$s_1(m/2) - ct_1$	$s_1(m/2) - ct_1$	$s_1[(m/2) + t_1]$
$c + s_1 + s_2,$ $m/2 + t_1 + t_2$	$s_1(m/2) - ct_1$ $+ [s_2(m/2) - ct_2]$	$[s_1(m/2) - ct_1]$ $+ [s_2(m/2) - ct_2]$ $- (s_1 + s_2 + c)t_1$	$(s_1 + s_2)(m/2)$ $- c(t_1 + t_2)$

firm 2 chooses $p_2 = c$ and $x_2 = m/2$. Because firm 2 has a lower price than firm 1, firm 2 can sell its entire output of $m/2$ while firm 1 has unsold output equal to t_1. The net revenue of firm 1 according to equation (3) is

$$r_1 = (c + s_1)m/2 - c[(m/2) + t_1]$$
$$= s_1(m/2) - ct_1$$

as shown in row 2, column 1, of Table 7.1.

Table 7.1 shows that firm 1 can be certain of a net return equal to zero, no matter what firm 2 does, by setting $p_1 = c$ and $x_1 = m/2$ so that firm 1 chooses row 1. It follows that firm 1 cannot have a negative expected return in any mixed noncooperative equilibrium. By symmetry the same is true for firm 2. This completes the proof of the following lemma.

> **Lemma 2:** *Under Assumption 2, the Bertrand–Edgeworth model, $Er(\cdot) \geq 0$, where $Er(\cdot)$ denotes the expected return of a firm.*

By Lemma 1 $(c, m/2)$ always appears in the set of active strategies of any mixed noncooperative equilibrium. The net return of a firm choosing this pure strategy is zero no matter what its rival does. Therefore, the expected net return of every active strategy must be zero because each active strategy yields the same expected net return in a mixed noncooperative equilibrium. This result is summarized in the following corollary.

> **Corollary:** *Under Assumption 2, $Er(\cdot) = 0$.*

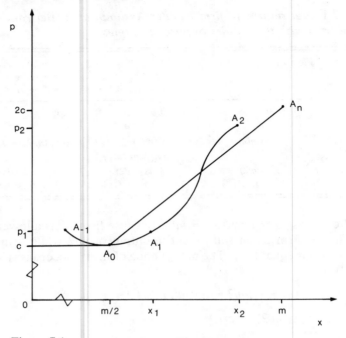

Figure 7.1

Consider Figure 7.1. The line segment A_0A_n shows the locus of pairs (p, x) such that $r = 0$.

$$A_0A_n = \{(p, x) \mid r = p(m/2) - cx, p \le b \text{ and } r = 0\}. \qquad (6)$$

Thus, the point A_0 with coordinates $(c, m/2)$ belongs to the set. At $p = 2c$, $x = m$, and this pair belongs to the line segment only if $b \ge 2c$.

A necessary condition for a mixed noncooperative equilibrium is that the rows of Table 7.1 do not dominate each other. Because each entry in row 1 is zero, there must be at least one positive and one negative entry in each row. The case where all the entries in row 2 or 3 are zero cannot occur owing to the presence of a strictly positive entry in row 2, column 3, which results when firm 1 has a price below firm 2 and thereby obtains a positive profit. This positive entry implies that the other two (equal) entries in row 2 must be negative because the weighted sum of the three entries must be zero. In row 3 the entries in columns 1 and 3 are equal and exceed the entry in column 2. If the entries in columns 1 and 3 of row 3 were negative then all the entries in this row would be negative, and row 1 would dominate row 3 contrary to the hypothesis. Therefore, the entries in columns 1 and 3 of row 3 must be positive. It also follows that the entry in column 2, row 3, must be negative in order to satisfy the requirement that the weighted sum of the three entries be zero. In column 3 both entries in rows 2 and 3 must be positive. In addition, the entry in row 2 must exceed the entry in row 3 so that

$$s_1[(m/2) + t_1] > [s_1(m/2) - ct_1] + [s_2(m/2) - ct_2]. \tag{7}$$

The proof is by contradiction. If (7) were false, then it would follow that row 3, column 3, would furnish a pure strategy equilibrium as is easily verified. But then each firm would get a positive profit giving a contradiction. Hence (7) must hold.

It is also interesting to observe that it is impossible to have row 1, column 1, as a pure equilibrium Suppose not. Then if firm 1 chooses the strategy given by row 1, firm 2 would obtain a higher net return by choosing column 3. But row 1 is not firm 1's best response to firm 2's choice of column 3. Consequently, row 1, column 1, cannot be a pure strategy equilibrium. Indeed, in this version of the Bertrand–Edgeworth model, there is no pure strategy equilibrium.

This type of analysis shows why a mixed noncooperative equilibrium must have at least three pure strategies because one of these must be row 1. In Figure 7.1, points below A_0A_n give firm 1 a negative net return, and points above this line segment yield a positive net return. Thus, the net return for the pair (p_1, x_1) must lie below A_0A_n, and the net return for the pair (p_2, x_2) must lie above the line segment.

Before describing the general situation, it is well to furnish a numerical example showing there does exist a set of numbers consistent with the theory that can realize a mixed noncooperative equilibrium. For the following triplet of pure strategies, $m = 100$, and $b > 13$:

$$p_1 = 10, \quad x_1 = 50;$$
$$p_2 = 11, \quad x_2 = 60;$$
$$p_3 = 13, \quad x_3 = 64.$$

Table 7.2 shows the net returns of the two firms for the nine possible combinations of pure strategy pairs. The mixed noncooperative equilibrium is as follows:

$$\alpha_1 = \beta_1 = \tfrac{67}{143}, \quad \alpha_2 = \beta_2 = \tfrac{1}{13}, \quad \alpha_3 = \beta_3 = \tfrac{5}{11}.$$

Each firm chooses its first pure strategy 47 percent of the time, its second 8 percent of the time, and its third 45 percent of the time.

Table 7.2. *Example showing a realization of Table 7.1*

Firm 1 \ Firm 2	10, 50	11, 60	13, 64
10, 50	0, 0	0, −50	0, 10
11, 60	−50, 0	−50, −50	60, −120
13, 64	10, 0	−120, 60	10, 10

$$p_1 = c = 10, \; x_1 = m/2 = 50$$

$$p_2 = c + s_1 = 11, \; x_2 = m/2 + t_1 = 60 \text{ so } s_1 = 1 \text{ and } t_1 = 10$$

$$p_3 = c + s_1 + s_2 = 13, \; x_3 = m/2 + t_1 + t_2 = 64 \text{ so } s_2 = 2 \text{ and } t_2 = 4$$

Figure 7.1 shows the nature of the general solution. Take any continuous curve passing through the three points A_0, A_1, and A_2 whose coordinates are the pure strategies as given in Table 7.1. Because A_1 lies below the line segment A_0A_n, the net return of the firm is negative at this point. Because A_2 lies above A_0A_n, the net return is positive at this point. Any curve starting from A_0 and winding above and below the line segment A_0A_n has points whose coordinates are pure strategy pairs in a mixed noncooperative equilibrium. Each noncooperative equilibrium must give a positive probability to the pair $(c, m/2)$, the point A_0, and the expected net return of each firm is zero for each mixed noncooperative equilibrium. Since there are many continuous curves with the required property, and there is a large number of points on each curve that can give the coordinates of pure strategy pairs for a mixed noncooperative equilibrium, it follows that the number of mixed noncooperative equilibria is truly immense. As Figure 7.1 shows, it is even possible to have curves that go to the left of the point A_0 provided the price coordinate does not dip below c. The extension $A_{-1}A_0$ illustrates this possibility. Points on this arc would give the firm a positive net return so they must be offset by points below A_0A_n. For points on this arc, the output rate would be less than $m/2$, and this is compatible with a mixed noncooperative equilibrium.

For each mixed noncooperative equilibrium, there is a positive probability that both firms post different prices as well as a positive probability they both post the same price. In contrast to Edgeworth's model, in no mixed noncooperative equilibrium is there a regular oscillation between the highest and the lowest prices among the pairs of elements of pure strategies. The observed sequence of pairs constitutes independent random events with probabilities as determined by the noncooperative equilibrium. Thus, the theory shows how to calculate these probabilities. The following proposition is a summary of these results.

Proposition 3: Under Assumption 2 (Bertrand–Edgeworth), a noncooperative equilibrium is given by a mixture of a suitably chosen finite number of strategy pairs (p_i, x_i) on any curve winding around the line segment A_0A_n such that A_0 is a member of each noncooperative equilibrium and occurs with a positive probability. The expected net return of each firm is zero in every noncooperative equilibrium. There is no pure noncooperative equilibrium in this model.

Given so many noncooperative equilibria under Assumption 2, it is fair to ask whether any empirical evidence can refute the theory, assuming the validity of the assumptions about the cost and the demand conditions. First, the theory asserts that each firm gets the same average net return, zero. Second, it asserts that the observed price-output pairs forming the pure strategies that enter a mixed noncooperative equilibrium are a sequence of independent random events with probabilities as determined by the theory itself. Third, from the observed pairs one can discover whether there is agreement between the theoretical and the observed frequencies. Fourth, the theory predicts a distribution of prices among the firms even though it is costless to obtain price quotations. That is, although information about prices is free, there is an equilibrium price distribution that can persist. This price distribution is the hallmark of a mixed noncooperative equilibrium. According to this theory, therefore, it is not necessary to assume there is a positive cost of search in order to explain why a price distribution among competing firms can persist. Fifth, because the expected return of each firm is zero, there is no incentive for entry or exit. The firms can remain indefinitely in their present situation.

4   Noncooperative equilibria under Assumption 1, Cournot

In this case the two sellers place their output for sale under a common label in one place at the same price. The buyers regard their products as perfect substitutes and cannot distinguish between them by hypothesis so this arrangement makes the hypothesis operational. The two sellers must accept whatever price their combined output can fetch under the given demand conditions. Because the total sales cannot exceed m and no buyer is willing to pay more than b per unit, the following conclusions hold:

1. When the total quantity offered is below m, the equilibrium price is b.
2. When the total quantity offered is above m, the equilibrium price is 0.
3. When the quantity offered is m, the price p satisfies $0 \leq p \leq b$.

Assumption 1 corresponds to the situation as described by Cournot. Each seller independently chooses his own output rate. Given the sum of the output rates of the two sellers, the demand conditions determine the market clearing price. Cournot's assumptions about the demand differ slightly from mine. In my model the number of buyers who appear in the market is given and known to both sellers. Each buyer is willing to buy at most one unit provided the price asked does not exceed b. A lower price does not attract more buyers nor does it stimulate any buyer who is present in the market to purchase more. The quantity demanded, m, and the maximal acceptable price, b, can be interpreted as the coordinates of a point on a more general demand curve. Cournot allows the quantity demanded to vary inversely with the price.

This model has two principal results. First, there are many pure noncooperative equilibria. Second, there are many mixtures of noncooperative equilibria and each of these is also a noncooperative equilibrium. Despite the indeterminacy, one particular pure noncooperative equilibrium seems the best candidate.

Begin with a description of the net revenue of firm i.

$$
r_i = \begin{cases} (b - c)q_i & \text{if } x_1 + x_2 < m, \\ (p - c)q_i & \text{if } x_1 + x_2 = m, \\ -cx_i & \text{if } x_1 + x_2 > m. \end{cases} \tag{1}
$$

Because each firm can sell its entire output if $x_1 + x_2 < m$, we may substitute x_i for q_i in (1). Given $b - c > 0$, net revenue is an increasing function of the firm's rate of output if $x_1 + x_2 < m$. It is a decreasing function of output if $x_1 + x_2 > m$. The claim is that $x_1 = x_2 = m/2$ is a noncooperative equilibrium. To prove this, it suffices to show that $x_1 = m/2$ gives the maximum of r_1 if $x_2 = m/2$ and that $x_2 = m/2$ maximizes r_2 if $x_1 = m/2$. Checking this for r_1 will suffice. Let $x_2 = m/2$. Hence r_1 is an increasing function of x_1 for $x_1 < m/2$ and a decreasing function of x_1 for $x_1 > m/2$. There is the complication, however, that r_1 is continuous from the left if $p = b$ while r_1 is discontinuous at $x_1 = m/2$ if $p < b$. Figure 7.2 shows this. For $x_1 < m/2$, points on the ray OA contain r_1 while for $x_1 > m/2$, line BC contains r_1. At x_1

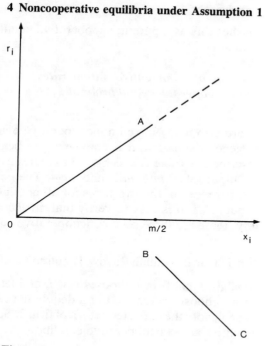

Figure 7.2

$= m/2$, r_1 equals the coordinate of point A if and only if $p = b$. This means that if $p < b$, then r_1 has a least upper bound (supremum) given by $(b - c)(m/2)$ but has no maximum. For a maximum it is necessary and sufficient that $p = b$ when $x_1 + x_2 = m$. This completes the proof of the following.

> **Proposition 4:** *Under Assumption 1 (Cournot), there is a pure noncooperative equilibrium given by* $x_1 = x_2 = m/2$ *and* $p = b$.

Our next task is to derive the other noncooperative equilibria. By examining these, we can convince ourselves that the noncooperative equilibrium as described in this proposition has the most satisfactory properties.

Considering the proof of Proposition 4, it is evident that any pair of output rates such that $x_1 + x_2 = m$ together with $p = b$ furnishes a pure noncooperative equilibrium. There is nothing special about the pair $(m/2, m/2)$. Take any $x_1 < m$ and $x_2 = m - x_1$ and exactly the same argument establishes this as a pure noncooperative equilibrium. Record this result as follows.

> **Corollary:** *Any pair of nonnegative output rates* (x_1, x_2) *furnishes a pure noncooperative equilibrium if* $x_1 + x_2 = m$ *and* $p = b$.

Nor is this all. There are also many mixed noncooperative equilibria. In order to study the general situation, it is convenient to begin with the special case as described in Table 7.3. Table 7.3 assumes each firm chooses one of three output rates: $m/4$, $m/2$, and $3m/4$. The entries in Table 7.3 show the net revenues of the two firms for all possible combinations of these output rates. It is easy to verify that, in accord with the preceding corollary, there are three pure noncooperative equilibria as follows:

row 3, column 1; row 2, column 2; row 1, column 3.

Let α_i denote the probability that firm 1 chooses row i, and let β_j give the probability that firm 2 chooses column j. Let μ denote the expected return of firm 1, and let λ denote the expected return of firm 2. Solutions of the following inequalities are noncooperative equilibria.

$$(b - c)m/4 \leq \mu \quad \beta_1,$$

$$(b - c)(m/2)\alpha_1 + (b - c)(m/2)\alpha_2 - c(m/2)\alpha_3 \leq \mu \quad \beta_2, \qquad (2)$$

$$(b - c)(3m/4)\alpha_1 - c(3m/4)\alpha_2 - c(3m/4)\alpha_3 \leq \mu \quad \beta_3,$$

$$(b - c)m/4 \leq \lambda \quad \alpha_1,$$

$$(b - c)(m/2)\beta_1 + (b - c)(m/2)\beta_2 - c(m/2)\beta_3 \leq \lambda \quad \alpha_2, \qquad (3)$$

$$(b - c)(3m/4)\beta_1 - c(3m/4)\beta_2 - c(3m/4)\beta_3 \leq \lambda \quad \alpha_3.$$

> **Proposition 5:** *There is a noncooperative equilibrium given by a mixture of all three pure strategies.*

Proof: Such an equilibrium must satisfy (2) and (3) as equalities and give nonnegative values of α_i and β_j such that $\sum_i \alpha_i = 1$ and $\sum_j \beta_j = 1$. It is easy to verify that the following meet these requirements.

$$\alpha_1 = \beta_1 = \tfrac{1}{3} + (2c/3b),$$

$$\alpha_2 = \beta_2 = \tfrac{1}{6}[(b - c)/b],$$

$$\alpha_3 = \beta_3 = \tfrac{1}{2}[(b - c)/b],$$

$$\lambda = \mu = (b - c)(m/4). \qquad \blacksquare$$

Table 7.3. *Net returns of the firms under Assumption 1 (Cournot) for three pure strategies*

Firm 2		Output rates	
Firm 1	$m/4$	$m/2$	$3m/4$
$m/4$	$(b - c)m/4,$ $(b - c)m/4$	$(b - c)m/4,$ $(b - c)m/2$	$(b - c)m/4,$ $(b - c)3m/4$
$m/2$	$(b - c)m/2,$ $(b - c)m/4$	$(b - c)m/2,$ $(b - c)m/2$	$-cm/2, -c\ 3m/4$
$3m/4$	$(b - c)3m/4,$ $(b - c)m/4$	$-c\ 3m/4, -c\ m/2$	$-c\ 3m/4, -c\ 3m/4$

Even for as simple a situation as the one in Table 7.3, there are still other mixed noncooperative equilibria composed of appropriate pairs of pure strategies. The next proposition describes them all.

> *Proposition 6: There are noncooperative equilibria given by mixtures of*
>
> (i) *rows 1 and 3, columns 1 and 3, so that*
> $$\lambda = \mu = (b - c)(m/4);$$
> (ii) *rows 2 and 3, columns 1 and 2, so that*
> $$\lambda = (b - c)(m/2), \mu = (b - c)(m/4);$$
> (iii) *rows 1 and 2, columns 2 and 3, so that*
> $$\lambda = (b - c)(m/4), \mu = (b - c)(m/2).$$

Proof: (i) This requires a nonnegative solution of

$$\alpha_1 + \alpha_3 = 1,$$

$$(b - c)(3m/4)\alpha_1 - c(3m/4)\alpha_3 = (b - c)(m/4) = \mu,$$

The solution is given by

$$\alpha_3 = \tfrac{2}{3}[1 - (c/b)], \qquad \alpha_1 = \tfrac{1}{3} + \tfrac{2}{3}(c/b).$$

By symmetry, $\beta_1 = \alpha_1$ and $\beta_3 = \alpha_3$.

(ii) This requires a nonnegative solution of

$$\alpha_2 + \alpha_3 = 1,$$

$$(b - c)(m/2)\alpha_2 - c(m/2)\alpha_3 = (b - c)(m/4) = \mu,$$

$$\beta_1 + \beta_2 = 1,$$

$$(b - c)(m/2)\beta_1 + (b - c)(m/2)\beta_2 = \lambda,$$

$$(b - c)(3m/4)\beta_1 - c(3m/4)\beta_2 = \lambda.$$

The solutions are as follows:

$$\alpha_3 = \tfrac{1}{2}[1 - (c/b)], \qquad \alpha_2 = \tfrac{1}{2}[1 + (c/b)],$$

$$\beta_2 = \tfrac{1}{3}[1 - (c/b)], \qquad \beta_1 = \tfrac{2}{3} + \tfrac{1}{3}(c/b),$$

$$\lambda = (b - c)(m/2).$$

(iii) Exchange α's for β's, and μ for λ and this is the same as case (ii).

It is easy to verify that these solutions also satisfy the inequalities as required by (2) and (3). ∎

There are a plethora of noncooperative equilibria both mixed and pure. Even so, I believe the symmetric one with pure strategies given by the pair $(m/2, m/2)$ deserves special consideration. To see why, consider an asymmetric alternative, the pure noncooperative equilibrium given by the pair $(m/4, 3m/4)$. Let the first firm choose the output rate $m/4 + \delta$ with δ small and positive. It incurs a loss of $-c[(m/4) + \delta]$ and forces its rival to lose $-c(3m/4)$, an amount nearly three times its own loss. In general the firm with the larger net return in any of the asymmetric pure noncooperative equilibria is quite vulnerable to such consequences should its rival depart ever so slightly from its non-cooperative strategy by a small increase of its output. The symmetric noncooperative equilibrium has the property that each firm loses more itself than does its rival by any departure from the symmetric equilibrium. As the last point in favor of the symmetric equilibrium, observe that each firm gets the same net positive return $(b - c)(m/2)$. This fact is important in judging arguments for the mixed noncooperative equilibria.

In any of the mixed noncooperative equilibria for the Cournot model, a firm can expect *at most* a net return equal to $(b - c)(m/2)$ on average. But if each firm chooses the output $m/2$, then each can get a net return equal to $(b - c)(m/2)$ *every time*. It seems to me this is a decisive argument against all the mixed noncooperative equilibria in the Cournot model. The situation in the Bertrand–Edgeworth model is different. There all of the noncooperative equilibria have the same expected return, zero. No sure-thing principle discriminates among them as is true in the Cournot model.

Another point should be mentioned. In contrast to the predictions of the Bertrand–Edgeworth model, where each firm can expect a zero net return no matter how many competitors it may have, the non-cooperative equilibrium singled out in Proposition 4 implies each firm can expect a positive net return. Also, as is well known, depending on the shape of the demand function, the Cournot model predicts an inverse relation between profits per firm and the number of firms, a prediction that seems in closer agreement with some empirical evidence than that of the Bertrand–Edgeworth model. However, in the Cournot model all the firms always charge the same price so there is no price distribution across firms while in the Bertrand–Edgeworth model as is shown in the preceding section, there is a price distribution across firms even if the cost of search is zero. With respect to these predictions about the price distributions, the evidence favors the Bertrand–Edgeworth model over the Cournot model. Moreover, the Cournot model faces the problem of explaining why there is no entry despite the fact that in all the equilibria the firms get positive profits. In contrast, expected profits are zero in the Bertrand–Edgeworth model so there is no incentive for entry or exit, and two firms can remain indefinitely in their present situation.

This is an appropriate place for a few remarks on the generality of these results. Many of the results remain valid for more general demand conditions where the quantity demanded varies inversely with the price. It can be shown that the mixed noncooperative equilibrium under the Bertrand–Edgeworth model as given in Table 7.1 is essentially the same for more general demand functions. However, under the Cournot assumption there may be a unique pure noncooperative equilibrium depending on the precise shape of the demand function. The preceding conclusions are quite sensitive to the assumptions about the cost of holding inventories. The models in this chapter assume no inventories are held because it is prohibitively expensive to store the good. If on the contrary the firms do hold inventories, then not only are the alternative strategies more complicated but in addition an element of uncertainty is introduced by virtue of the fact that a firm may not be able to calculate how much its rival has sold even if both firms know the demand function. This complicates the analysis under both assumptions, Cournot as well as Bertrand–Edgeworth.

5   Additional tests of the rival theories

Some interesting tests of the rival theories of Bertrand–Edgeworth versus Cournot are suggested by some conceptual experiments under alternative assumptions about the cost conditions. Recall the assumptions about cost have two elements. First, both firms have the same unit costs and, second, each firm knows this. Hence each firm knows both its own and its rival's cost of production. We can drop the first and retain the second assumption, and we can drop both assumptions. Though this may be a surprise, it is definitely worthwhile to derive the implications of the case where the two firms have different costs and know each other's costs. Start with this case.

According to the version of the Bertrand–Edgeworth model as given here, a pure strategy is a pair (p_i, x_i) for each firm, and the firms can choose different prices. Say that firm 1 has the lower cost, $c - \Delta c$. Because it also knows that the unit cost of its rival, firm 2, is c, it can set a price equal to $c - \delta$, $\delta > 0$ and arbitrarily small. The second firm can meet this price only by accepting a loss. Hence the first firm can have the field to itself with the strategy $(c - \delta, m)$ and its profit is $(\Delta c - \delta)m$ for sure. Compare this situation to the Cournot model that requires each firm to choose its output and sell it for whatever price competition among the buyers can fetch. Though the two firms have different costs and know this, it remains true there are many pure noncooperative equilibria just as described by the corollary of Proposition 4. Still this case does present a new feature owing to the difference in cost. The noncooperative equilibrium given by the pair $(m/2, m/2)$ is vulnerable. Let firm 1 choose an output larger than $m/2$ while firm 2 adheres to $m/2$. As a result, firm 2 suffers a larger loss than firm 1, which has the lower unit cost. That is, the pair $(m/2, m/2)$ permits firm 1 to impose a bigger loss on its rival than on itself by a slight increase in its rate of output. This suggests an argument for a particular noncooperative equilibrium pair in the Cournot model when the firms have different unit costs and each knows the other's cost. Take the pair (x_1, x_2) such that

$$x_1 + x_2 = m, \qquad x_i \geq 0, \tag{1}$$

and

$$(c - \Delta c)x_1 = cx_2. \tag{2}$$

A departure from this equilibrium by firm 1 that raises its output by a small positive amount δ would inflict a greater loss on itself than on its rival. Under the equilibrium (1) and (2), it is also true that the firm with the lower cost gets a proportionately larger share of the market.

Summarizing, if the firms have different unit costs and know each other's costs, then under the Bertrand–Edgeworth model, there will be a pure noncooperative equilibrium with the price equal to $c - \delta$, $\delta > 0$ and arbitrarily small. The firm with the lower unit cost supplies the whole demand m and gets a positive profit equal to $(\Delta c - \delta)m$. Under Assumption 1, which is the Cournot model,

$$r_1 = (b - c + \Delta c)x_1, \qquad r_2 = (b - c)x_2, \tag{3}$$

and x_1, x_2 satisfy (1) and (2). Both firms are active in the Cournot model though this is socially wasteful, while only the firm able to produce at the lower unit cost is active in the Bertrand–Edgeworth model. Hence the equilibrium in the latter model is socially optimal.

Next consider the different implications of these two models if the firms are ignorant of each other's costs. Because the strategy pair under the Bertrand–Edgeworth model includes the choice of a price and an output rate, the price conveys information to both firms. Because neither firm knows which has the lower cost, neither can be sure of selling its entire output initially even at a price equal to its unit cost. There are three questions. What can a firm deduce about its rival's cost from its rival's posted price? Would a profit-maximizing firm post a price below its unit cost? What is the nature of the equilibrium?

As argued above, the firm that discovers it is the one with the lower cost has a superb strategy, namely, set $p = c - \delta, x = m$, with δ small and positive. Its rival cannot survive in the industry unless it will accept perpetual losses. However, by hypothesis, neither firm knows its rival's cost so it does not know if it is the one with the lower cost. In particular, firm 1 does not know it is the lower cost firm. Each firm gets some clues by observing its rival's prices. Suppose each firm uses the following strategy. It will match the lowest price it has observed up to now if this price is not above its unit cost and it will post a slightly lower price if this least price is above its unit cost. Thus, a firm with losses at the current price is not the one to cut the price. This strategy is close to that proposed by Bertrand himself. Eventually, the lower cost firm must prevail and have the field to itself. There is also the question of finding the initial prices. In particular, would either firm commence by setting a price below its unit cost? Plainly, the answer is no for any but a suicidal firm. Therefore, we may conclude that given cost differences between the firms, this policy must inevitably lead to the same pure equilibrium as would occur if the firms did know each other's cost in the Bertrand–Edgeworth model. Nor is this all. In case the firms had the same cost, they would ultimately discover this fact, and the noncooperative equilibria would be the same as given in Section 3.

It may seem that another outcome is more plausible. Suppose the firms do choose initial prices above their unit costs. It is most likely that these are different prices. Say that the firms do embrace the strategy of meeting the lowest price that has previously been observed. Knowing this, both firms will also know that in the next period the price will equal the lower of the two current prices. If this lower price exceeds the unit cost of the firm with the higher cost, then both firms get a positive profit, and this situation can persist. By hypothesis, neither firm knows the other's cost. It must balance the hope of greater profit should it be the lower cost firm against the fear of loss should it be the higher cost firm. This may suffice to deter both firms from price cutting. Hence it would seem that in the Bertrand–Edgeworth model, where firms do not know each other's cost, the equilibrium may be at some common price above c with equal market shares.

A slightly more formal analysis sheds more light on this case. Not knowing each other's cost resembles a situation where a firm does not know which firm it is, whether it is firm 1 or firm 2. In order to explore the consequences of this, consider the payoff matrix given in Table 7.4. The entries in Table 7.4 show the expected profits of each firm. Thus, if both firms had the same cost equal to c, then the expected profit of each would be zero as is shown by the entry in row 1, column 1. The term $-K$ shows the loss to the firm with the higher cost that is eventually forced out of the industry. My profits in row 2 dominate those in row 1, and similarly your profits in column 2 dominate those in column 1. This means that in a noncooperative equilibrium the firms would pursue the aggressive strategies as described at the outset and would eventually discover which is the lower cost firm that would remain as the sole survivor in the industry.

In the Cournot model, where the firms do not know each other's unit costs, a new feature enters the scene. Let each firm choose the output rate $m/2$. If the firms do know each other's cost, the Cournot model implies market shares do depend on costs while the equilibrium price does not. For the reasons given above, knowing each other's cost implies equilibrium outputs that satisfy (2). In case there is ignorance of costs, the lower cost firm lacks a convincing way of forcing its higher cost rival to accept a lower market share according to formula (2). Given mutual ignorance about costs, neither firm may be willing to run the risk of discovering it is the higher cost firm. Each may be content with a market share of $m/2$ since both firms would get a positive profit and the lower cost firm would obtain more profit than its rival by an amount equal to $(\Delta c)(m/2)$.

Accepting this reasoning leads to the conclusion that under the Cournot model, where the firms have different unit costs and do not know each other's unit costs, there would be no relation between market share and profit. This is in contrast to the situation where they do know each other's cost. In that situation the firm with the lower cost gets the larger market share and the greater profit. Unlike the Bertrand–Edgeworth model, lower unit cost does not result in a lower price in the Cournot model whether or not the firms do know each other's unit

Table 7.4. *Payoff matrix*

If my cost is	If your cost is	
	c	$c - \Delta c$
c	$0, 0$	$-K, (\Delta c)m$
$c - \Delta c$	$(\Delta c)m, -K$	$0, 0$

cost. In the Cournot model the main difference between knowing and not knowing each other's unit cost is an implication with respect to the relation between profits and market share. If the firms do know each other's unit cost, then there is a positive association between profits and market share; but if they do not know these costs, then there is no relation between profits and market share.

CHAPTER 8

Rivalry by means of innovation

PART 1. SOME EMPIRICAL RESULTS

1   Introduction

Innovation is the term coined and disseminated by Schumpeter to describe the application by entrepreneurs of that new knowledge that raises real per capita income. This happens in two ways. First, firms introduce new products or improve existing ones. These directly benefit their customers. Second, firms learn how to lower their costs of making and distributing existing products. The economy benefits from these changes as well. However, this distinction, better or new products and better or new ways of making them, is more useful as a theoretical device than as an exact description of reality. The fuzzy boundary is illustrated by the use of new products in order to lower production costs.

Actual innovations fall between two extremes. At one extreme, the knowledge of the innovator is secret. No one can learn what he knows or imitate what he does without his consent. It is prohibitively costly for anyone to obtain or copy the new knowledge of the innovator. At the other extreme, anyone who desires can obtain at little or no expense the newly found knowledge of the innovator. The first extreme implies the innovation is a private good and the second that it is a public good. It is hardly novel to remark that valuable new knowledge, costly to discover but costless to copy, poses a free-rider problem. It is perhaps slightly less banal to remark that innovators may still have incentives to incur the expense of the quest for new knowledge even if others can use the result without contributing to the cost of searching for it.

Analysis of innovation by private firms who cannot keep their findings exclusively for themselves gives some interesting results described in Chapter 6, Section 4. Assume the firms are alike, do not cooperate, and pursue their own independent policies. These assumptions imply there exist several possible noncooperative equilibria ranging from a symmetric nondeterministic one, which is inefficient, to asymmetric

deterministic noncooperative equilibria where only one firm undertakes the expense of the research and its rivals copy its results. Although the latter equilibria are all efficient, the theory does not discriminate among them and predict which will occur. Also, none of these
equilibria are self-enforcing. This situation raises two questions. First,
under what conditions is it likely that the quest for knowledge gives
results in the form of a public good? When there is a free-rider problem, private firms have an incentive to devise collective solutions so
that noncooperation is an implausible assumption. This leads to the
second question, namely, what arrangements would the firms make to
encourage innovation when free-loading is a problem? The analysis
seeks solutions by private firms. There are other kinds of solutions
under circumstances giving rise to difficult free-rider problems. In these
the government intervenes either directly by organizing, financing, and
arranging the research itself or by financing research that is undertaken
by certain private organizations such as research institutes, universi-
ties, and so on. The list of research activities that governments have
sponsored is impressive. For the United States, it includes, for example, several important developments in computing, starting with the
work leading to the invention of punch cards and tabulating equipment
for the 1890 census by Hollerith following a suggestion by Billings and
going on to the work sponsored by the Bureau of Ordnance in both
world wars, which in World War II led directly to electronic digital
computers (Goldstine 1972). It is outside the scope of my present analysis to study the nature of the factors that might determine the allocation of research areas between the private and the public sectors.

A model of innovations faces another central question at the outset.
Let all firms initially have the same cost conditions and the same access
to the same prospects. What mechanisms lead to differences among
them so that in the final equilibrium they will not have the same costs?
The model referred to in the preceding paragraph can explain differences among the firms with respect to their rates of return because
those who bear the cost of the innovation get a lower return than the
free-loaders, but it predicts that aside from this, the firms would have
the same costs of production. A model capable of explaining how firms
can emerge with different costs of production in equilibrium, though
starting from the same costs and from the same opportunities, assumes
that research results can be kept private. Outlays on research yield the
firm new knowledge so that it learns how to lower its costs of production. The firms do not know in advance what they will discover
and research has unpredictable consequences that may be treated as
random variables. Some firms become more successful than their ri-

vals. In this way innovation can create differences among firms who are initially alike. These differences should not persist, however, owing to the gains to the firms from eliminating them. In a noncooperative equilibrium where firms have different costs, the allocation of output among the firms is not efficient. This is true because each firm chooses its output rate where its marginal cost equals its marginal revenue. Even if the buyers regard the firms' products as being perfect substitutes so that all firms get the same unit price for their output, in a noncooperative equilibrium the marginal revenue of each firm is below the price by an amount that varies inversely with its market share. Therefore, the marginal costs at the equilibrium output rates of the firms are different. It follows that in a noncooperative equilibrium where the firms have different costs owing to the private knowledge they acquire from their research the allocation of output among them is not efficient.

Firms can remove this inefficiency by selling each other information about their methods of production, say in the form of licensing the use of their patents. Even if they do not do this, they could produce the total industry output at a lower cost by reaching an agreement on outputs such that the smaller firms produce more and the larger ones less. To obtain even bigger cost reductions, the firms would have to share their knowledge about methods of production. One way of judging the importance of the sale of technical information among firms is from the figures on royalties. These figures show how much revenue firms obtain in return for allowing others to use their patents. In fact, royalty receipts are a very small fraction both of total revenue and total outlays on research even in those industries that have large outlays on research and development such as the chemical, scientific instrument, and machinery industries.[1]

Firms have another avenue of cooperation to secure the gains from innovation by combining the knowledge discovered by each of the firms that otherwise would be kept secret from each other. This avenue is merger. Mergers inspired by the desire to obtain new knowledge have several advantages over transactions confined to the purchase of the information alone. It is first necessary to admit that the information may be enormously detailed so that it is very costly to transmit it all from one firm to another. Often the cheapest way is for one firm to buy the whole firm that is the source and creator of the new information. The acquiring firm can then learn from all those who were

---

[1] Machlup (1962) has an elaborate discussion of inventing, patenting, and the quest for knowledge. Yet nowhere in the book does he mention royalties. The relatively small size of royalties is a major empirical finding.

responsible for the discovery and development of the new technology. Consequently, the employees of the acquiring firm, like apprentices, can learn the new technology from those who have created it in the acquired firm. It is interesting to see a new way being developed intended to reduce the cost of transmitting new knowledge. It is the "expert systems" developed by pioneers in artificial intelligence (AI). This is a formal scheme of eliciting information from experts by asking them an elaborate set of questions and of organizing their responses so that their knowledge can become available to others who are less expert. For these purposes it is a more effective technique than deriving the information from textbooks written by the experts even if the experts were assumed capable of writing good enough texts. The knowledge extracted from the experts is stored in a computer memory so as to be easily accessible to users who ask and answer a series of questions interactively with the computer. As yet expert systems are very costly and require elaborate preparation. Their future is bright for the purpose of communicating specific and specialized new technology from its creators to others.

The theory that assumes research results are private predicts there is a positive association between merger activity and measures of technical change. Empirical evidence for the period from 1879 to 1930 supports this prediction. The correlation between a measure of merger activity and industry growth is nearly 0.69 for 18 two-digit SIC manufacturing industries. Additional support for this theory comes from some findings in an important article by Gort (1969).

2   Innovation when research results are private

Research results are private when it is prohibitively costly for one firm to obtain the results of the research of another firm without its consent. Consequently, no firm can get a free ride at the expense of the originator of the new knowledge. Each firm can learn how to lower its own cost only by its own efforts.

There are two ways of making research results into a private good. First, the state can allow property rights for that knowledge it defines to be a private good. It does this when it decides what kinds of discoveries can obtain a patent. Second, the individual firm can keep its knowledge secret. This, too, requires legal protection in the form of defining what can be regarded as proprietary knowledge. The first way makes the knowledge public and enlists the powers of the state to stop others from using it, while the second way keeps the knowledge secret and thus prevents its use by others. There are good reasons for believing that the second way deserves considerable attention as a working hypothesis for understanding and explaining innovation.

Secrecy as a way of making knowledge into a private good is a plausible hypothesis owing to the distinction between basic and applied research. This distinction is useful not because of an invidious comparison between the two but instead because of the difference in the costs of disseminating these two types of knowledge. Basic research refers to general principles with wide application and these are more easily communicated than is applied research.[2] Perhaps "specific" is a better adjective than "applied." The former refers to specific problems that require solutions of many detailed subproblems. A useful analogy to see the distinction between basic and specific research comes from computer languages and computer programs. A computer language such as FORTRAN or Pascal corresponds to basic research. These languages may be described concisely and are easy to learn just as it is easy to learn the rules of chess. There are many good books for teaching the reader these languages. A specific computer program written in one of these languages does a specific task such as calculating a regression equation to fit a given body of data. Such a program is very elaborate and has many steps. These include reading in the data, storing it in an appropriate form, allowing the user to correct or change the data, manipulating and transforming the data, calculating the results, storing them, and writing them on a console or printing them as hard copy. The particular computer program has many features specific to the hardware on which it runs, the nature of the input devices – disks or tapes – the output devices, the operating system of the computer, and so on. An actual program is far more detailed and specific than the manual describing the language in which the program is written. A program in an assembly language is still more detailed and specific than one in a higher level language. A program often has a narrow range of applications, whereas the computer language has an enormously wide range. Sometimes even if one has the actual program and is a skillful programmer in the language in which it is written, it is still very costly to determine how the specific program actually works. Having read and understood a manual describing a high-level computer language is necessary but not sufficient for becoming a competent programmer in that language. One must learn many tricks as well. There are many other examples of this phenomenon. An automobile engine is a good one. The basic principles of an automobile engine are much

---

[2] For an interesting discussion of the relation between science and technology, see Sahal (1981) and especially Chapter 2.

more easily described than is the sequence of engineering problems that must be solved in order to manufacture an engine. All of these considerations make it plausible to assume a firm can keep secret at least some of the results of the research it undertakes in order to lower its costs of production.

Granting this, we can deduce some implications. Assume that all of the firms in an industry begin with the same knowledge so that all have the same costs. We can regard the outcome of research efforts as analogous to a random event like a horse race. Some firms are more successful than others just as some horses run faster than others. At the outset one may assume that each horse has the same chance of winning just as one may assume that initially all firms have the same chance of lowering their production cost if each spends the same amount on this task. Eventually differences emerge among the firms. The more successful firms discover how to make the product at a lower cost than the less successful ones. Under these conditions there is a noncooperative equilibrium such that each firm produces at that output rate where its net revenue is a maximum. It is not the output rate where its marginal cost equals the price owing to the nature of a noncooperative equilibrium. At the noncooperative equilibrium output rates, marginal cost equals marginal revenue, which is below the price. This noncooperative equilibrium marginal revenue is closer to the price than is the marginal revenue of a profit-maximizing monopoly. The excess of the price over marginal revenue is bigger for the firms with the bigger market shares. This is true although by hypothesis all buyers regard the products of the firms as perfect substitutes for each other. Therefore, in this noncooperative equilibrium the allocation of the output rates among the firms is inefficient if their cost curves are not the same. It follows that the total cost of all firms would be lower for a given total output rate if they would cooperate to the extent of an appropriate reallocation of output among themselves. Doing so would require the firms with the higher cost curves to produce more and those with the lower cost curves to produce less than they would under the noncooperative equilibrium (the details are in Part 2). To obtain these cost reductions, the firms need not exchange information about their methods of production. However, even bigger cost savings are available to the firms if they could adopt the method of production of that firm with the most successful research program. With such more complete cooperation, all firms would have the same technology and would produce the same equilibrium output rate at the same cost. With less complete cooperation extending only to an agreement on rates of output without an exchange of information about methods of production, there is a smaller cost saving and a partial approach to equality of market shares.

Firms can cooperate in order to lower their costs in at least three different ways. First, they can agree on rates of output and refuse to reveal to each other their private knowledge about methods of production. Second, they can sell each other some or all of this private knowledge. Third, they can merge. The first is an inferior alternative. Without knowledge about production costs, there is no basis for a reallocation of output rates. The firms would lack the information needed to determine an optimal assignment of output rates.

The second approach assumes the firms sell knowledge to each other. The figures in the Statistics of Income for Corporation Tax Returns shed some light on the actual importance of this. The receipts of corporations from the sale of licenses under their patents is an item that they must report separately on their tax returns as royalties. Some corporations also report these figures in the annual reports to shareholders. As a rule income received as royalties is less than 1 percent of total revenue. In 1981, royalties were 0.35 percent of the total revenue of all manufacturing corporations whereas it was 0.07 percent in 1946. From a very low level in 1946, royalties as a percentage of total corporate receipts have risen steadily over the past 35 years but nevertheless are still exceedingly small. In 1946, royalties were 0.14 percent of total revenue for corporations manufacturing chemicals, and this figure had risen to 0.56 percent by 1981. For corporations manufacturing electrical machinery, the figures are 0.12 percent and 0.40 percent in these two years. In the scientific instruments category the 1948 figure (the earliest available) is 0.10 percent, and it had risen to 0.45 percent by 1981. The industry showing the most dramatic change is nonelectrical machinery. In 1963 royalty income was only 0.24 percent of total revenue; it had risen to 1.35 percent of total revenue by 1980, second only to the category with the highest figure, amusement and entertainment, for which it was 1.68 percent in 1980. There are some corporations for which royalties are relatively substantial. These tend to be young corporations in the early stages of innovation that are not producing or selling actual commodities. Instead they derive much income in the form of royalty fees from others who are developing applications of the new technology. As a general rule, it is safe to conclude that royalty income is below 10 percent of research outlays even for firms with very big research programs such as Dow Chemical and DuPont.

Finding that royalty income is so small surprises me. It does not follow that patents are unimportant. Nor does it follow that the number of licensing agreements is small. Nevertheless, it does seem that the value of the marginal product of a patent license agreement is relatively small according to these figures. Why is this?

One possible explanation begins with the preceding analysis. The information that can be conveyed under the terms of a license agreement often must necessarily lack the details needed to use it successfully. In many cases the licensee must discover for himself a large portion of the knowledge that will create a profitable application of the patent. The knowledge in the patent itself is complementary with that discovered by the patent user who is licensed by the patent owner. Nevertheless, the patent owner has a monopoly over the knowledge in the patent so it would seem possible for him to collect all of the rent from the patent user. Yet the rent he does collect is relatively small. Because the licensee must make a substantial investment of his own in order to use the patent successfully in his own application, and because the outcome is uncertain, a prudent potential licensee would agree only to those terms in advance that would prevent the patent owner from holding him hostage in case his use of the patent turns out to be highly profitable. The situation resembles one between the owner of property where there may be oil, who corresponds to the patent owner, and the firm who will attempt to produce oil from the property, who corresponds to the licensee. Is it not plausible that the return on average to each is commensurate to each of their respective investments? Hence those who make the lion's share of the capital outlay obtain a return in proportion.

Still one may ask why the patent owner does not convey more of the needed knowledge to a potential patent user and collect a larger royalty income. An inventor who wishes to obtain a patent must reveal enough information in the patent application to persuade the government agency that a patent is warranted. Sometimes this information is sufficiently complete so that anyone who reads the patent gets enough information to duplicate the knowledge of the patent owner. In this case the patent is particularly valuable both to the owner and to a potential licensee. Pharmaceuticals may be like this. In other cases the description of the patent itself, while sufficient to convince the authorities they should grant a patent, does not reveal enough to enable another firm to use it successfully even with additional information from the patent owner. Moreover, the person applying for a patent has no incentive to conceal information relevant for using it. It is only by revealing all the pertinent general information that he can establish well-defined property rights to his invention and thereby protect himself against infringement. Whatever information is lacking from the patent description and is needed for using it must be knowledge that would be specific to a potential user of the patent. Otherwise, the patent owner would surely include it in the patent description out of self-interest. Therefore, it is the existence of this knowledge specific to the patent user and its cost relative to the total cost of exploiting the patent that explains why royalty income is a relatively small source of income to patent owners on average.

3   **Some empirical results relating merger intensities to growth rates, 1895–1930, and merger rates to measures of innovation, 1951–9**

There are incentives for cooperation when the research results can be kept secret so that the knowledge is a private good. The argument in the preceding section directs attention to the relation between research programs and mergers.

Since some mergers arise from a desire to pay less taxes, it is desirable to confine the empirical analysis to a time when these motives are weak. For this reason in the first set of empirical results the sample period ends in 1930. A sample unit is a two-digit SIC manufacturing industry as described in the notes of Table 8.1. Figures on mergers by two-digit industry for selected time periods are available thanks to Ralph Nelson (1959) and his student, C. Eis (1969), who uses the same method.

A word about the nature of the merger figures is necessary. There are two kinds of mergers, consolidations and acquisitions. A consolidation combines firms into a single new firm, and the original firms all disappear as separate entities. Consolidations were common from 1895 to 1904. An acquisition is a purchase of one firm by another. The acquired firm disappears as a separate entity, and the acquiring firm remains. The figures giving the total merger capital measures the book value of the firms that disappear either by consolidation or by acquisition. It does not measure the new capital of the firms that result from merger. There is another complication. Since the measure of merger activity spans several years, there is both the possibility and the reality of double counting. Two firms, for instance, may consolidate to form a new firm. This new firm may subsequently join with another firm. Each consolidation counts as a disappearance of capital by merger and thereby increases the measured amount of capital disappearing through merger. The variable, merger intensity, in Table 8.1 shows the importance of this. Merger intensity is the ratio of the capital disappearing by merger over the time period to the book value of the capital in the

Table 8.1. *Merger intensity and the annual rate of growth of book value of capital, 18 two-digit SIC manufacturing industries*

Industry	Merger intensity[a]					Growth rate[b]	
	1895–1904	1905–14	1915–20	1919–29	Mean	Current dollars	1929 dollars
Food	0.9376	0.1450	0.0527	0.2683	0.3509	0.05815	0.04695
Tobacco	3.2042	0.2353	0.0957	0.1273	0.9156	0.06406	0.05309
Textiles	0.2325	0.0780	0.0439	0.0665	0.1052	0.05114	0.04127
Apparel	0.0036	0.0261	0.0032	0.0140	0.0117	0.05291	0.04399
Lumber	0.0519	0.0350	0.0027	0.0439	0.0334	0.04662	0.03034
Furniture	0.0521	0.01037	0.0071	0.1042	0.0434	0.04191	0.02472
Paper	1.3527	0.0251	0.0403	0.2037	0.4054	0.07323	0.06622
Printing	0.0512	0.03384	0.0144	0.0756	0.0438	0.06447	0.05379
Chemicals	1.0172	0.1265	0.5151	0.4146	0.5183	0.06819	0.06010
Petroleum refining	0.9480	0.4842	2.7605	1.8904	1.5208	0.09856	0.09096
Rubber	2.1669	0.5610	0.1000	0.1248	0.7382	0.09747	0.09427
Leather	0.1442	0.0689	0.0140	0.0507	0.0695	0.04470	0.02768
Stone, clay, glass	0.6231	0.0223	0.0636	0.2953	0.2511	0.06547	0.05602
Iron, steel	6.2751	0.3441	0.2351	0.5833	1.8594	0.06183	0.05486
Metal products	1.6169	0.1723	0.1993	0.3674	0.5890	0.06953	0.06260
Machinery (nonelectric)	0.6896	0.1505	0.05070	0.1477	0.2596	0.05924	0.04842
Electric machinery	4.1242	0.1574	0.0878	0.2895	1.1647	0.13131	0.12226
Transportation	5.1520	0.8820	0.6067	0.3468	1.7469	0.11559	0.10067

[a] Merger disappearances in the four periods are divided by book value on the dates as follows: 1889, 1905, 1914, 1919. This approximates book value of capital in the year preceding the period of merger disappearances.

[b] Book value of capital comes from *Historical Statistics of the United States*, Series P30-133 for the years 1879, 1889, 1899, 1904, 1909, 1919, and 1929.

The estimated annual rate of growth of the book value of capital is the regression coefficient of t in the regression as follows:

$$\log BV_{it} = a_{0i} + a_{li}t + \text{residual},$$

where BV_{it} is the book value of the capital in industry i, year t. Thus, a_{li}, is a least-squares estimate of the annual growth rate of capital in industry i. The R^2 of the 18 regressions are all very high. The figures giving the book value of capital are available at either 5- or 10-year intervals. Since t is the actual year at one-year intervals starting in 1879, the varying intervals for the available sample have the proper effect on the estimate in the regression.

The last column of the table gives estimates of the growth rates in 1929 dollars. Although such growth rates are lower than for those using current prices, the two sets of growth rates are highly correlated.

industry at the beginning of the period. A ratio above 1 shows the likely occurrence of multiple counts of mergers. The iron and steel industry from 1895 to 1904 is the best example. The fleeting appearance of new firms during a period of merger activity surely overstates the pertinent aspects of mergers. In the regression below the R^2 would have been bigger had the merger figures excluded multiple counts. It would also have been desirable to measure how much the book value of the firms after merger exceeds their book value before the merger. This would supply an estimate of the increment of the book value owing to the merger. The last complication refers to the classification of mergers by industry. If both the acquiring and acquired firms are in the same industry or all the firms being consolidated are in the same industry, then the industry class of the merger is unambiguous. At the two-digit level this is usually true. If, however, the two firms are in different industries, there is the question of which to take as governing. The general rule in the data sources is to take the industry of the surviving firm. However, Gort (1969) classifies the merger according to the industry of the acquired firm.

The proxy for technical progress in an industry is an estimate of its annual growth rate. Unfortunately, no figures are available giving output growth rates by two-digit manufacturing industries for the sample period. (However, see the pertinent results from Gort's study described below.) There is instead the book value of the capital in these industries for selected years (see the notes of Table 8.1). This measures one industry input, the book value of tangible capital. Merger could raise the book value if after consolidation it exceeds the sum of the book values of the firms being consolidated. Acquisition could also raise the book value of the acquiring firm by more than the initial book value of the acquired firm if the buyer pays more than the book value of the firm it acquires. Mergers are not the only reason for an increase in book value. In a growing industry another reason is that gross investment exceeds depreciation allowances.

There is a more cogent point about the relation between mergers and book value. According to the theoretical model, cost reduction is an incentive for merger. The lower cost owing to merger has two sources. First, there is the closer approach to an efficient allocation of output among the firms that merge. Second, the merging firms exchange information about production methods that enable them all to lower their costs to the level of the most efficient producer. For both of these reasons the value of the surviving enterprise may be bigger than the sum of the values of the original firms. Hence the theory predicts that mergers have a positive effect on the book value of the new or surviving firm.

This argument ignores the possible effect merger may have as an avenue toward monopoly. It is doubtful on theoretical grounds that merger alone without barriers to entry can create a monopoly except temporarily. Aside from this theoretical objection, there are also empirical difficulties. A common measure of monopoly is the relative sizes of the firms in an industry, usually the concentration ratio. The present empirical study does not consider this aspect. Partly it is because relative firm size is inappropriate and partly it is because there is no theoretical relation between merger intensity and concentration. It would be consistent with the theory to find that concentration is higher or lower as a result of merger. For example, mergers among the smallest firms in an industry is consistent with the theory; such mergers would lower the concentration ratio. Acquisitions of the smallest by the largest firms in the industry are also consistent with the theory; such mergers would raise concentration. Obviously, as a matter of simple arithmetic, the Herfindahl index always increases as a result of merger, but this fact has no clear economic significance. Because any relation between concentration and merger intensity is consistent with the theory and would not test it, it is pointless to relate merger intensity to concentration.

For the 18 two-digit SIC manufacturing industries in the sample, the regression relating merger intensity, y, to the annual rate of growth of the book value of capital, x, is as follows:

$$y = -0.6015 + 16.9685x$$
$$(-1.815) \qquad (3.801) \qquad\qquad (1)$$
$$R^2 = 0.4746$$

where the numbers in parentheses are t-ratios.

This empirical relation may help explain an old puzzle. Nelson finds a positive correlation of nearly 0.47 (R not R^2) between the cyclical component of merger disappearances and the cyclical component of industrial stock prices using quarterly time series for the period from 1895 to 1920 (Nelson 1959, Table 60). He gives no theoretical explanation of his finding. The theoretical model I describe above together with regression 1 suggests a possible reason for Nelson's empirical finding. The positive relation may reflect the presence of a common factor moving both series. This common factor is the effect of technological change, which waxes and wanes procyclically.

Gort's results (1969) gives additional empirical support for my theory. Using FTC data for manufacturing companies aggregated to 46 three-digit SIC industries, the most pertinent of his regressions for my purposes is as follows:

$$X_1 = -4.8314 + 0.0481X_2 + 0.1780X_3 + 0.0271X_4,$$
$$(-0.41) \qquad (4.45) \qquad (1.64) \qquad (0.84)$$

$$R^2 = 0.590; \tag{2}$$

where X_1 = merger rate from January, 1951, to June, 1959, as measured by the ratio of the number of companies acquired to the total number of companies in the industry in 1954; X_2 = technical personnel ratio, 1950 with respect to total number of employees; X_3 = productivity change, 1947–54, per employee; X_4 = growth of output from 1947 to 1954; X_5 = concentration ratio, 1954. The most important fact in this regression for my theory is the highly significant positive association between merger intensity and the technical personnel ratio. Nor is this all. The highest simple correlation between merger intensity and the four explanatory variables is for the technical personnel ratio. This is also the outstanding variable in a regression that has the concentration ratio as an explanatory variable of the merger rate. The regression is as follows:

$$X_1 = 4.0795 + 0.0505X_2 + 0.4134X_5,$$
$$(1.05) \qquad (6.47) \qquad (4.05)$$

$$R^2 = 0.669. \tag{3}$$

The collinearity among the explanatory variables in regression 2 may explain the lower t-ratio of X_2 in regression 2 as compared to regression 3. The causal status of the concentration ratio X_5 in regression 3 is doubtful since it is measured around the middle of the sample period so it may reflect the effect of mergers.

4   Empirical evidence from cross sections of manufacturing industries over time, 1947–72

Rivalry among firms resulting in lower costs and better products leaves its traces in the figures collected and compiled by the Census of Manufactures. By comparing changes in the values of pertinent and available variables from one census to the next, we can obtain valuable quantitative clues about the effects of innovations.

The census has made major revisions of its industry definitions twice since 1947: in 1957 when half of all industries were affected and again in 1972. In the latter census year, 130 four-digit industries, 29 percent, have no comparable historical data. The census revises industries when old products disappear, new products appear, and production methods change. The principal hypothesis is that most of the effects of research and development occur in the industries that are revised and much less in the others. The four-digit SIC manufacturing industries in the 1967 census present in the same form in the 1947, 1972, and 1963 censuses are the unrevised industries. The sample contains 111 such industries. There are 207 industries present in the 1963 and 1967 censuses that are absent from either 1947 or 1972. These are called the revised industries in my analysis. Some industries that satisfy these criteria nevertheless do not appear in my sample owing to the fact that some data are missing for them. In many instances the data are missing because the Census Bureau refuses to publish these figures on the ground they could reveal information about individual companies. In other cases the Census Bureau does not publish certain data for some industries because it doubts the accuracy of these figures. In the remaining cases the industries had to be omitted simply because the data for them are missing for reasons unknown to me.

Before continuing, it is necessary to describe briefly some facts about manufacturing and about the census definitions of industries. A plant may manufacture more than one four-digit product. The total shipments of a plant are divided into two categories, called primary and secondary products. It is the former that determines to which four-digit industry the Census Bureau assigns the plant. This means the bureau places each manufacturing plant into one four-digit industry although plants sometimes make some products in different four-digit categories. The total shipments of the plants assigned to a given four-digit class therefore include shipments of secondary as well as of primary products. The ratio of the shipments of the primary product to total shipments is called the *primary specialization ratio* (specialization ratio, for brevity). This ratio measures the degree to which the plants assigned to a given four-digit industry specialize in making that four-digit product. Consequently, some shipments of a given product come from plants that are outside that given product class. Total shipments of a given product come from two places, plants in the industry and plants outside the industry. The *coverage ratio* is the ratio of product shipments from plants inside the industry to the total shipments of the product. It measures how much of the total product shipments are covered by the plants in that product class.

Table 8.2 provides evidence to support the view there is more innovation among the revised than among the unrevised industries. Two variables distinguish the sample of the 207 revised from the 111 unrevised industries; the increase in the value of shipments and the rise of coverage. During the period 1963–7, shipments grew at a significantly more rapid pace for the revised than for the unrevised industries. The difference between the rates of increase of coverage between the two samples is even more remarkable. This greater rise of coverage for the sample of revised industries means that a larger fraction of total shipments of the products comes from plants in the revised industries than is true of the unrevised industries. The explanation is not that the census revised the industry categories to bring this about: recall that the major revisions did not occur in these years but in 1957 and 1972. The bigger rise of coverage for the revised industries is consistent with there having been more entry of firms into the revised than into the unrevised industries. Note that over the longer time period, 1947–72, both the coverage and the specialization ratios actually declined for the 111 unrevised industries. Plants in these industries were reducing shipments of their primary products relative to shipments of their secondary products. This means they were becoming less specialized producers of their primary products. Simultaneously, coverage was going down. Hence a larger share of total shipments of the products primary to the unrevised industries was coming from plants outside the industry. Therefore, products made in the unrevised industries were becoming increasingly the secondary products of other industries. Continuation of these trends would lead to the eventual disappearance of the 111 unrevised industries who would eventually join the buggy whip industry.

According to the model, a firm that successfully lowers the level of its cost as a result of its research program obtains a larger equilibrium output rate. Rival firms with unsuccessful research results will have smaller equilibrium output rates and thus their total costs of producing at these rates will be lower. Because total industry output is larger in equilibrium, those firms with successful research obtain higher equilibrium market shares. Therefore, the theory predicts a positive association between the change in the value of shipments and the change in the four-firm concentration ratio. If there were more innovation among the revised than among the unrevised industries, then there would be a larger positive association between Dlog VS (the change in the log of the value of shipments) and Dlog V-4 (the change in the log of the four-firm concentration ratio) for the sample of revised than for the sample of unrevised industries.

Table 8.2. Comparisons among the differences between the means of selected variables for four-digit manufacturing industries

| | 1963–7 | | | | | | 1947–72 | | Mean rates of change per year | | |
| | 207 revised industries | | 111 unrevised industries | | Differences | | 111 unrevised industries | | "207" 1963–7 | "111" 1963–7 | "111" 1947–72 |
Variable	μ_1	σ_1	μ_2	σ_2	σ	t-ratio	μ_3	σ_3			
Dlog V-4	0.03145	0.18820	0.02076	0.12014	0.01735	0.616	0.04710	0.39909	0.00786	0.00519	0.00188
Dlog VS	0.29715	0.18510	0.25798	0.18064	0.02144	1.827	1.24065	0.70435	0.07429	0.06450	0.04963
Dlog NO	-0.01522	0.17260	-0.00503	0.19104	0.02174	-0.469	0.03310	0.62812	-0.00381	-0.00126	0.00132
Dlog Covg	0.02430	0.10362	0.00541	0.05000	0.00863	2.189	-0.01170	0.09574	0.00608	0.00135	-0.00047
Dlog Spec	0.00392	0.04134	0.00206	0.03354	0.00429	0.434	-0.00145	0.06867	0.00098	0.00052	-0.00006

Dlog means the first differences of the logarithms between the two years; V-4, share of four-digit industry sales by the four leading companies; four-firm concentration ratio; VS, value of shipments by four-digit industry; NO, number of companies in the 4-digit industry; Covg, coverage: fraction of total product shipments coming from plants assigned to four-digit industry; Spec, primary product specialization: proportion of total plant shipments in a four-digit industry in that four-digit industry.

Table 8.3 contains the results. The partial correlation between Dlog V-4 and Dlog VS is 0.2055 for the revised industries, and it is only 0.0576 for the unrevised industries over the period 1963–7. Even for the longer time period, 1947–72, the partial correlation between Dlog V-4 and Dlog VS is only 0.1025 for the sample of 111 unrevised industries. For the sample of revised industries, a one percent increase in the four-firm concentration ratio accompanies a 0.2 percent rise in the growth rate of the value of shipments, the t-ratio is nearly 3, while for the unrevised industries the corresponding number is only 0.08 percent with a t-ratio of 0.6. This is consistent with larger cost reductions for the revised than for the unrevised industries. For 1947–72, the slope of Dlog V-4 is only 0.15 and the t-ratio is 1.1 in the regression for which Dlog VS is the dependent variable. The sample of unrevised industry thus shows evidence of fewer cost reductions over the longer period as well as over the shorter one.

Consider an alternative explanation of these results. Suppose they were due to shifts in demand instead of supply. To explain lower unit costs would then require assuming that firms have economies of scale. This alternative hypothesis encounters at least two difficulties in explaining the empirical results. First, why is there such a weak relation between sales and concentration for the sample of unrevised industries and a much stronger one for the sample of revised industries To reconcile these findings, one must assume there are larger economies of scale for the revised than for the unrevised industries. This would merely beg the question of why the two are different. Second, there is a more direct objection to the hypothesis of increasing returns. It is finding a positive association between Dlog VS and Dlog NO (the percentage change in the number of firms in the industry). The t-ratio for the regression coefficients of these variables is 6.14 for the sample of revised and is 3.57 for the sample of unrevised industries. This means there is a positive relation between the percentage change in sales and the percentage change in the number of firms for both sets of industries, revised as well as unrevised. But if there were economies of scale at the firm level, then one ought not observe a rise in the percentage change of the number of companies accompanied by a rise in the percentage change of total industry sales. It is therefore plausible to conclude that the pattern for Dlog VS, Dlog V-4, and Dlog NO is explained better by supply shifts coming from innovations than by the combination of the two hypotheses, demand shifts, and firm economies of scale.

The second set of interesting results refers to changes in the coverage and specialization ratios. For the sample of revised industries, coverage

Table 8.3. *Selected statistics for regression equations relating Dlog V-4, Dlog VS, Dlog NO, Dlog Covg, and Dlog Spec*

207 revised industries, 1963–7

Dlog V-4 = $-0.04123 + 0.2116$ Dlog VS -0.4352 Dlog NO $+0.2193$ Dlog Covg -0.5545 Dlog Spec
  (-1.71) (2.98) (-5.88) (1.84) (-1.91)
  $F = 11.69$, $R^2 = 0.1880$, S.E. $= 0.1713$

Dlog VS = $0.2885 + 0.1996$ Dlog V-4 $+0.4385$ Dlog NO $+0.3630$ Dlog Covg $+0.05021$ Dlog Spec
  (23.91) (2.98) (6.14) (3.18) (0.18)
  $F = 13.30$, $R^2 = 0.2085$, S.E. $= 0.1663$

Dlog NO = $-0.1083 - 0.3360$ Dlog V-4 $+0.3590$ Dlog VS -0.06756 Dlog Covg -0.3607 Dlog Spec
  (-5.42) (-5.88) (6.14) (-0.64) (-1.41)
  $F = 17.27$, $R^2 = 0.2548$, S.E. $= 0.1505$

Dlog Covg = $-0.01683 + 0.07475$ Dlog V-4 $+0.1312$ Dlog VS -0.02983 Dlog NO -0.1667 Dlog Spec
  (-1.19) (1.84) (3.18) (-0.64) (-0.98)
  $F = 4.82$, $R^2 = 0.08715$, S.E. $= 0.09998$

Dlog Spec = $0.004291 - 0.03196$ Dlog V-4 $+0.003069$ Dlog VS -0.02693 Dlog NO -0.02836 Dlog Covg
  (0.74) (-1.91) (0.18) (-1.41) (-0.98)
  $F = 1.58$, $R^2 = 0.0325$, S.E. $= 0.04111$

Table 8.3. (cont.)

111 unrevised industries, 1963–7

Dlog V-4 = 0.01095 + 0.04297 Dlog VS − 0.09131 Dlog NO − 0.2437 Dlog Covg − 0.2020 Dlog Spec
             (0.51)   (0.59)   (−1.41)   (−0.95)   (−0.57)

$$F = 0.97, \quad R^2 = 0.03543, \quad \text{S.E.} = 0.1202$$

Dlog VS = 0.2514 + 0.07719 Dlog V-4 + 0.2955 Dlog NO + 1.109 Dlog Covg + 0.2141 Dlog Spec
            (16.05)   (0.59)   (3.57)   (3.40)   (0.45)

$$F = 8.07, \quad R^2 = 0.2334, \quad \text{S.E.} = 0.1611$$

Dlog NO = −0.09541 − 0.2014 Dlog V-4 + 0.3628 Dlog VS + 0.2779 Dlog Covg − 0.2586 Dlog Spec
            (−3.10)   (−1.41)   (3.57)   (0.73)   (−0.49)

$$F = 4.99, \quad R^2 = 0.1585, \quad \text{S.E.} = 0.1785$$

Dlog Covg = −0.01728 − 0.03498 Dlog V-4 + 0.08855 Dlog VS + 0.01808 Dlog NO + 0.3177 Dlog Spec
             (−2.15)   (−0.95)   (3.40)   (0.73)   (2.43)

$$F = 6.63, \quad R^2 = 0.2001, \quad \text{S.E.} = 0.04553$$

Dlog Spec = −0.00086 − 0.01513 Dlog V-4 + 0.008926 Dlog VS − 0.008777 Dlog NO + 0.1658 Dlog Covg
             (−0.15)   (−0.57)   (0.45)   (−0.49)   (2.43)

$$F = 2.10, \quad R^2 = 0.07347, \quad \text{S.E.} = 0.03289$$

111 unrevised industries, 1947–72

Dlog V-4 = −0.02920 + 0.07154 Dlog VS − 0.2804 Dlog NO + 0.4124 Dlog Covg − 1.144 Dlog Spec
             (−0.32)   (1.06)   (−3.98)   (0.96)   (−2.09)

$$F = 5.80, \quad R^2 = 0.1796, \quad \text{S.E.} = 0.3682$$

111 unrevised industries, 1947–72

$$\text{Dlog VS} = \underset{(24.13)}{1.238} + \underset{(1.06)}{0.1468}\ \text{Dlog V-4} + \underset{(6.89)}{0.6194}\ \text{Dlog NO} + \underset{(3.62)}{2.119}\ \text{Dlog Covg} + \underset{(0.36)}{0.2883}\ \text{Dlog Spec}$$

$$F = 22.54, \quad R^2 = 0.4596, \quad \text{S.E.} = 0.5275$$

$$\text{Dlog NO} = \underset{(-5.42)}{-0.5631} \ \underset{(-3.98)}{-0.4641}\ \text{Dlog V-4} + \underset{(6.89)}{0.4997}\ \text{Dlog VS} + \underset{(0.37)}{0.2044}\ \text{Dlog Covg} - \underset{(-0.45)}{0.3196}\ \text{Dlog Spec}$$

$$F = 21.84, \quad R^2 = 0.4518, \quad \text{S.E.} = 0.4738$$

$$\text{Dlog Covg} = \underset{(-4.03)}{-0.07687} + \underset{(0.96)}{0.02078}\ \text{Dlog V-4} + \underset{(3.62)}{0.05204}\ \text{Dlog VS} + \underset{(0.37)}{0.006222}\ \text{Dlog NO} + \underset{(3.38)}{0.4019}\ \text{Dlog Spec}$$

$$F = 10.39, \quad R^2 = 0.2817, \quad \text{S.E.} = 0.08266$$

$$\text{Dlog Spec} = \underset{(-0.13)}{-0.002083} - \underset{(-2.09)}{0.03471}\ \text{Dlog V-4} + \underset{(0.36)}{0.004264}\ \text{Dlog VS} - \underset{(-0.45)}{0.005859}\ \text{Dlog NO} + \underset{(3.38)}{0.2420}\ \text{Dlog Covg}$$

$$F = 5.02, \quad R^2 = 0.1592, \quad \text{S.E.} = 0.06415$$

Numbers in parentheses are the t-ratios.

is an increasing function of the growth rate of shipments and of the growth rate of the four-firm concentration ratio but is almost unrelated to changes of the specialization ratio. Interpreting a rise in concentration as correlated with a fall in costs, it follows that for the sample of revised industries, lower costs result in a larger share of total shipments coming from the industries where costs have gone down. But the firms with the lower costs do not become more specialized in their primary industries. For the sample of unrevised industries there is a different picture. Here changes in coverage are negatively related to changes in concentration, albeit not significantly so, while coverage and specialization move together. Although coverage rises with rising growth rates as in the sample of revised industries, in contrast to that sample, among the unrevised industries changes in coverage are not positively related to changes in concentration (save to a slight degree from 1947 to 1972).

PART 2. A THEORY OF INNOVATION AND ITS EFFECTS

1   Introduction

Competition in a modern economy is not the impersonal kind popular in many textbooks. There is instead keen rivalry among firms to find better products and cheaper ways of making them. The winners of these contests may obtain large profits, and this stimulates their research. Theories that take technology as a given are useful only as a first approximation toward a theory of innovation and its effects if our goal is better understanding of an actual economy.

We shall consider a theory of innovation similar to that of the economics of information. In particular, the theory of optimal sequential search by traders in a market inspires this theory of innovation and its consequences. A firm must incur the expense of research in order to obtain new knowledge that may enable it to lower its costs. Although research outlays are necessary to obtain new knowledge, there is no certainty that this new knowledge will reduce costs. The firm uses its new knowledge only if this does lower its costs.

A theory of innovation can be constructed more easily using two simpler components. The next section studies one of these. Sequential research and the nature of production costs permit only one firm at a time to be an active producer of the commodity. Section 3 studies the second major component of the theory. Here n firms seek knowledge to enable them to produce a given product at the least cost. This search occurs simultaneously, like a horse race where the fastest horse is the only one to win a prize. Section 4 is a synthesis of these two models that assumes there is sequential research by n firms in each period. Each of the firms has research outlays to discover how to lower its costs. All make the identical product and must sell it at the same price. However, unlike the theory of the two preceding sections, in Section 4 the cost conditions permit the survival of more than one active producer in the industry. The active firms have different cost functions and obtain different profits. During the research era of the industry, firms have research outlays, prices tend to fall, and industry output rises at a decreasing rate. Eventually, given a constant demand function, it no longer pays for anyone to continue research, and the industry is mature. Entry and exit occur during the research but not during the mature era. Section 5 describes a number of testable predictions of the theory. An appendix contains more technical propositions and related material.

All of these models assume each firm can keep secret the knowledge that results from its research outlays. Equivalently, it is cheaper for a firm to learn by its own efforts than by copying others. Whether this is true is a factual not a theoretical question. In practice firms can and do keep secret their knowledge about their operations. It is somewhat naive to believe there is a single fact that is crucial to a product or process innovation. I assume the firm can keep its secrets and shall study the consequences of this assumption. It is equivalent to the assumption that firms obtain property rights in their knowledge, which, therefore, they can protect and defend.

This theory also assumes the output of a firm is a large enough part of the industry output so that it has a perceptible effect on the price. The rivalry among the firms to seek ways of lowering their costs yield benefits to their customers even though no firm takes the price as given.

Among the more interesting results are these. In an industry where cost conditions permit the survival of more than one firm, sequential research results in a level of cost at the end of the research era and the beginning of the mature era that is lower the smaller is the number of firms then in the industry. There will be a positive association between a firm's market share and its rate of return. The larger is a firm's market share, the more stable over time it is likely to be.

The theory of innovation given here owes much to Schumpeter.[3] By

---

[3] Innovation as the main form of rivalry in a capitalist system is most forcefully argued in *Capitalism, Socialism and Democracy* (1954). Nelson and Winter (1982) follows this theme in their work. Still lacking is more development of the theory to the point where we can obtain detailed empirical verification. Whether a capitalist system furnishes the socially optimal amount of research outlays is a theme of Dasgupta and Stiglitz (1980). Kamien and Schwartz (1975) give an excellent survey of this and related topics.

presenting a formal theory using his ideas, we may open promising avenues of research in industrial organization.

2   Optimal sequential research from a known distribution

The simplest model that contains the main features of the situation is as follows. A single firm can make and sell the given product at a constant unit cost c. All customers may buy this product at the same unit price p. They are willing to buy more, the lower the price. Their demand is represented by the continuous function as follows:

$$p = b(q). \tag{1}$$

At a high enough price, p_M, they are unwilling to buy anything and even at a zero price they are unwilling to take more than a finite maximum quantity q_M. Hence the pairs $(p_M, 0)$ and $(0, q_M)$ both satisfy (1). The net revenue of the firm, call it r, is a function of q and c defined as follows:

$$r = R(q, c) = [b(q) - c]q. \tag{2}$$

By virtue of these assumptions, r is a continuous bounded function of q for all q such that $0 \le q \le q_M$. Therefore, for each c there is a q giving the maximum net return.

The firm need not remain content with the unit cost c. By spending x dollars on research, it hopes to discover how to reduce c. The outcome of its research is uncertain, so we represent it by a random variable Y that we regard as a drawing from a cumulative density function (cdf) $F(y, x)$ where y denotes the realization of Y.

$$\text{Prob } (Y \le y) = F(y, x) = \int_0^y f(z, x)\, dz, \tag{3}$$

and $f(\cdot)$ denotes the probability density function (pdf). It is convenient to define $y = 1/c$ so that the unit cost is lower, the higher the y. By spending x_t at the beginning of period t, the firm can draw a value of the random variable Y from the cdf $F(y_{t-1}, x_t)$ where y_{t-1} denotes the value of y at the beginning of period t. If the realization of Y in period t, denoted by y_t, satisfies $y_t \le y_{t-1}$, then the firm continues to use its present method of production represented by y_{t-1}. If $y_t > y_{t-1}$, then it can have a lower cost by using the technology represented by the higher level of y, namely y_t. Thus $F(y_{t-1}, x_t)$ is the probability of the failure to obtain a realization of Y greater than the one in hand. Assume that the drawings of Y are independent over time. Therefore, the probability of a failure to surpass the y in hand is an increasing function of

y. Consequently, decreasing returns with respect to the research outlays take hold eventually. This is because large values of y are in the right-hand tail of the distribution, and the bigger is y, the less probable that it can be surpassed. These are consequences of the independence assumption. One could assume instead that the y in hand enters the pdf $f(\cdot)$ as a parameter directly so that $f(\cdot)$ would depend on y_{t-1} and x_t. It would then follow that the probability of surpassing y_{t-1}, which is the y in hand at the beginning of period t would become

$$\int_{y_{t-1}}^{\infty} f(z, y_{t-1}, x_t) \, dz.$$

The presence of y_{t-1} as a parameter in the pdf implies a less restrictive representation of the effects of the accumulation of knowledge than does the assumption of independence.

The independence assumption has several advantages. First, it does allow for the accumulation of knowledge via the effect of x_t on the pdf and by this route to the realizations of increasing y. Now decreasing returns with respect to y must be present to ensure the existence of an equilibrium. The independence assumption does this easily. Finally, the alternative that puts y_{t-1} as a parameter in $f(\cdot)$ is more complicated because it would require suitable restrictions on how y_{t-1} affects $f(\cdot)$ in order to have decreasing returns as required for an equilibrium.

The larger is the research outlay, x, the lower the probability of failure.

$$F_x(y, x) = \int_0^y f_x(z, x) \, dz < 0. \tag{4}$$

It follows that the probability of success is an increasing function of x given

$$\int_y^{\infty} f_x(z, x) \, dz = -F_x(y, x) > 0. \tag{5}$$

Only the current, not past research outlays, enters $F(\cdot)$. The effect of past research outlays appears via y_{t-1} because y_{t-1} is likely to be larger, the greater were the past research outlays. The current research outlay, x_t, determines the cdf from which Y is drawn, but it does not determine the actual realization of the random variable, which is y.

The assumption that the average cost of the firm is independent of its output rate, an assumption that applies to this and the next section only, has some important consequences. Under these cost conditions, the firm with the least average cost can profitably satisfy the whole market demand and offer its customers more favorable terms than anyone else can. No firm with an average cost above the least-cost producer can survive in the industry without its sufferance. Possibly, several firms can have an average cost equal to the minimum, but this is highly improbable by virtue of the assumption that the level of the average cost is determined by independent random draws from a *continuous* cdf. The presence of higher cost competitors can set upper bounds on the terms the most efficient firm can get from its customers, but, plainly, it can always offer them terms more favorable than any rival save one willing to absorb losses. Therefore, we may conclude that only one firm at a time can be an active producer if average cost is constant. However, the incumbent firm, the one currently active in the industry, can be replaced by any other able to produce at a lower average cost.

Write the profit function as follows:

$$r_t = R(q_t, y_t). \tag{6}$$

Having obtained a realization of Y, the firm chooses its output rate to maximize its profit. This makes the optimal q_t depend on y_t because it is the solution of

$$\max R(q_t, y_t) \quad \text{with respect to } q_t.$$

Substituting the optimal q as a function of y allows the suppression of q in the function $R(\cdot)$, and we may write

$$r = R(y) = \max_q R(q, y). \tag{7}$$

Assume this function is a bounded, continuous increasing and asymptotically concave function of y.

Let the firm choose its research outlays during a sequence of time periods in order to obtain the maximum expected present value of its net return. At the start of each period it has in hand the largest realization of Y resulting from its research during all the preceding periods. It can either accept this outcome and stop further research or it can continue its research hoping to obtain a still larger realization of Y. It does whichever it expects will be most profitable. It proceeds sequentially until it gets a y so big it does not believe profitable an attempt to surpass it.

To represent this formally, we may proceed as follows. Define the function

$$v = V(y, x), \tag{8}$$

which is the expected present value of the returns if the initial value of $Y = y$ and x is the research outlay at the beginning of the period. Define $V^*(y)$ so that

$$V^*(y) = \max_x V(y, x). \tag{9}$$

Let β denote the discount factor so that $\beta = 1/(1 + \alpha)$ where α is the discount rate and β the present value of one dollar. We wish to write the basic sequential relation. If there is a positive research outlay, which is necessary for an opportunity to draw a realization of Y from the cdf $F(y, x)$, then there are two mutually exclusive alternatives. Either the realization of Y, call it z, does not exceed the current value of y or it does.

> $z \leq y$ implies $r = R(y)$ and $v = V^*(y)$ with probability $F(y, x)$;
>
> $z \geq y$ implies $r = R(z)$ and $v = V^*(z)$ with probability $1 - F(y, x)$.

Therefore, the expected present value satisfies the fundamental sequential relation given as follows[4]:

$$V(y, x) = \beta \left\{ [R(y) + V^*(y)]F(y, x) \right.$$

$$\left. + \int_y^\infty [R(z) + V^*(z)]f(z, x)\, dz \right\} - x. \tag{10}$$

The optimal x gives the maximum of $V(y, x)$ with respect to x. This relation (10) applies at the beginning of each period t with the substitutions $y = y_{t-1}$ and $x = x_t$.

The expected return in a period depends on the y in hand at the beginning of the period and on the research outlay, x, during that period. Define the expected return $E(r)$, as follows:

$$E(r) = R(y)F(y, x) + \int_y^\infty R(z)f(z, x)\, dz. \tag{11}$$

Propositions A.1 and A.2 in the appendix assert that the research era stops as soon as there is a realization of Y such that

$$\max_x [E(r) - \alpha x] \leq R(y). \tag{12}$$

---

[4] The analysis would remain essentially the same with the substitution of a concave utility function in place of the monetary return. This is owing to the assumption that the monetary return is a strongly concave function of the controls. For a discussion of strong convexity (equivalent to strong concavity), see Telser and Graves (1972). A strongly convex function has a unique minimum on any closed convex set, not necessarily bounded. A strictly convex function is not necessarily strongly convex.

This has an appealing interpretation. The left side of (12) gives the maximum expected return for the period if x is spent on research at an interest cost given by αx. The right side gives the return if the firm accepts y as final and stops further research. The first time that (12) is true is a random variable marking the end of the research era and the beginning of the mature era for the given product.

Depending on the properties of the revenue function $R(y)$ and the cdf $F(y, x)$, there is a minimally acceptable level of y, call it y^*, such that (12) holds as an equality. (Proposition A.3 gives the details.) The following happens. The smaller is y, the larger is the left side of (12) and the smaller is the right side. It then pays to spend money on research. The optimal amount maximizes the expected present value, $V(y, x)$. As research continues, the left side of (12) goes down and the right side goes up. The critical value of y at which the two sides are equal is y^*. It marks the lower bound of acceptable levels of y. The research era is when the research results are as yet unacceptable because its pays to continue. The mature era starts as soon as a research result falls in the acceptance region.

The sequential decision-making procedure has an upper bound for the expected duration of the research era. According to the optimal sequential decision rule, the firm stops research the first time a realization of Y exceeds y^*. Each period t of the research era has an optimal research outlay, x_t^*, depending on the previous period's research result, y_{t-1}. This x_t^* is found from the solution of the necessary condition for maximizing the expected present value of the net return. The probability of stopping at the end of period T is the same as the probability of the event that each realization of Y, namely y_t, is below y^* for the first $T - 1$ periods and $y_t \geq y^*$ occurs for the first time on trial T when $t = T$. Keeping in mind that the drawings of y_t are mutually independent over time, the probability of stopping at the end of period T is given as follows:

$$F(y^*, x_1^*)F(y^*, x_2^*) \cdots F(y^*, x_{T-1}^*)[1 - F(y^*, x_T^*)].$$

Proposition 1: $E(T) \leq 1/[1 - F(y^*, x^*)]$, where x^* is the maximizing value from the left side of (12).

Proof: We use the following two facts. First, because the firm never uses a realization of Y below the one in hand, we may say that $\{y_t\}$ is a nondecreasing sequence. Second, x_t^* varies inversely with y_{t-1}. (See the remarks after the proof of Proposition A.3.) Therefore, the x_t^*'s form a nonincreasing sequence and by virtue of (4),

$$F(y^*, x_t^*) \leq F(y^*, x_T^*). \tag{13}$$

Given that $x^* = x_T^*$ because T is the last period of the research era by hypothesis, the upper bound for the probability of stopping on trial T is given by

$$F(y^*, x^*)^{T-1}[1 - F(y^*, x^*)].$$

With this bound and a standard result in probability theory (Feller 1957, Vol. I, Chapter XI, Section 1), we obtain the desired conclusion. ∎

This result furnishes another interesting interpretation of the necessary and sufficient condition for stopping the research in a finite time. The condition that determines the critical y^* is as follows:

$$R(y^*) = R(y^*)F(y^*, x^*) + \int_{y^*}^{\infty} R(z)f(z, x^*)\, dz - \alpha x^*. \quad (14)$$

The expected return per period conditional on realizing $Y \geq y^*$ is

$$E(r: Y \geq y^*) = \int_{y^*}^{\infty} R(z)f(z, x)\, dz \Big/ \int_{y^*}^{\infty} f(z, x)\, dz. \quad (15)$$

Define $E(T^*)$ as follows[5]:

$$E(T^*) = 1/[1 - F(y^*, x^*)] \quad (16)$$

so that it is the upper bound on the expected duration of the research era. With this definition and (15), (14) reduces to

$$R(y^*) = E(r: Y \geq y^*) - \alpha x^* E(T^*). \quad (17)$$

Let a firm start with $y = 0$ and spend x^* on research in every period until it obtains a $y \geq y^*$. Its total expected outlay would be $x^* E(T^*)$ and an interest cost of $\alpha x^* E(T^*)$ per period. The expected net return to such an entrant starting from scratch would be given by the right side of (17), while the return to a firm that had attained its goal and is now active in the industry, the incumbent firm, would be given by the left side of (17).

[5] Let $p = F(y^*)$ and $q = 1 - F(y^*)$ so that q is the probability of stopping. Define the generating function $\phi(s)$ as follows:

$$\phi(s) = qs + pqs^2 + p^2qs^3 + \cdots$$
$$= qs(1 + ps + p^2s^2 + \cdots)$$
$$= qs/(1 - ps).$$

It follows from this generating function that

$$E(T^*) = \frac{d\phi(s)}{ds}\bigg|_{s=1} = \phi'(1) = \frac{1}{q}$$

which is (2.16).

These results suggest a few comments. One may say that because the incumbent firm has the knowledge represented by the current value of y_t, entry by a new firm would be wasteful because it would have to spend enough to learn what the incumbent already knows, this cost is $x^*E(T^*)$,[6] and more besides in order to displace it. The latter contributes to total knowledge while the former does not. Yet without the protection of secrecy, the incumbent firm might not have spent the funds to acquire the knowledge enabling it to produce at the cost corresponding to y_t. Though secrecy may cause duplication, it also furnishes an incentive to innovate.

Also of some interest are the effects of α, an exogenous variable in this theory, on $E(T^*)$, the upper bound for the expected duration of the research era. Because $E(T^*)$ depends on y^* and x^*, we must first consider how these depend on α. First, y^* varies inversely with α. This means the firm sets a lower goal on the minimally acceptable research result, the higher is the discount rate. Second, if there are decreasing returns to success as measured by how x^* affects the cdf $F(\cdot)$, then x^* varies inversely with α. Therefore, a change in α gives rise to opposing effects on $E(T^*)$. Specifically, let the discount rate be higher. The firm sets its sights lower on y^* and this lowers $E(T^*)$ because it does not take as long on average to attain a less demanding goal. However, at a higher discount rate, less is spent on research, and this delays attaining an acceptable outcome. Hence the net effect on $E(T^*)$ of a change in α is indeterminate. (See the appendix for additional details.)

3   *N* Simultaneous independent research programs

A useful analogy for this analysis is a horse race.[7] An optimal sequential research program corresponds to a race in which the owners enter their horses one at a time after having observed how long it took the preceding horses to run the course. One horse at a time runs against the clock. The time it takes a horse to run the course behaves like a random

---

[6] An upper bound on the expected cost of entering the industry is $x^*E(T^*)$, and Bain (1956) might call this a barrier to new competition. Equation (2.17) is an equilibrium condition.

[7] The analogy between research and a horse race is an old idea (Hirshleifer 1971). Hirshleifer argues that more is spent on a horse race than is socially optimal, assuming we wish to know which is the fastest horse. This makes an implicit judgment about the utility that individuals may derive from entering their horses in a race and that others may derive from betting on the horses and observing the outcome. Such judgments are outside the ordinary province of economics. McGee (1971) uses the analogy of a sporting contest in his study of competition in a manner congenial to the theory herein.

drawing from a given distribution (cdf). It is as if each owner draws a random number from the same distribution when he pays the fee in order to enter his horse in the race. He does so only if he believes it can run faster than all of its predecessors. As soon as a horse's speed exceeds a prescribed number corresponding to y^* in Section 2, it no longer pays for an owner to enter his horse because his cost would exceed his expected return. Although a sequential horse race can attain the objective of finding the winning horse with fewer horses than the more familiar horse race in which all horses start simultaneously, in contrast to the common horse race, a sequential horse race takes longer to determine the winner. We now study the situation analogous to the ordinary horse race where n horses start running simultaneously, and there is only one prize going to the fastest horse. If time is of the essence, the ordinary horse race is better than a sequential horse race.

For research, perhaps unlike a horse race, the cdf of the outcome depends on the research outlay, and there may be no prescribed cost of entry. It is useful to consider two different situations. In the first a single firm chooses the number of its n independent research laboratories and their research outlays. In the second situation each of n independent firms has a research laboratory. The n depends on how much profit each expects. The expected profit is a decreasing function of the number of firms doing the research. The equilibrium number is such that the expected profit is zero. The winning firm, the one which finds the cheapest way of making the good, becomes the sole producer and chooses the output rate for which its net return is a maximum.

We now proceed to the formal analysis starting with the first situation where one firm decides the number and level of support for its independent research laboratories. The prize is the function

$$R(y) = \max_{q} R(q, y) < \max_{q} R(q, \infty) = R(\infty), \tag{1}$$

an inequality valid for all finite y. The probability that the largest number in a simple random sample of size n does not exceed y is $F(y, x)^n$ so that the probability density function (pdf) is given by

$$dF(y, x)^n = nF(y, x)^{n-1}f(y, x)\,dy \tag{2}$$

(Cramèr 1946, Section 28.6). Therefore the winner can expect the prize to be

$$E(R) = K(x, n) = \int_0^\infty R(y)\,dF(y, x)^n. \tag{3}$$

Integrating by parts

$$K(x, n) = R(\infty) - \int_0^\infty R_y(y)F(y, x)^n \, dy. \tag{4}$$

Treating n as a continuous variable, there are[8]

$$K_n(x, n) = -\int_0^\infty R_y F^n \log F \, dy > 0, \tag{5}$$

$$K_{nn}(x, n) = -\int_0^\infty R_y F^n (\log F)^2 \, dy < 0. \tag{6}$$

This completes the proof of:

> **Lemma 1:** *For each research outlay x, the expected prize, K(x, n) is an increasing, bounded, concave function of n.*

The optimal n and x furnish the solution of the following maximum problem:

$$\max \, [K(x, n) - nx] \quad \text{with respect to } n \text{ and } x.$$

The first-order necessary conditions are

$$K_n - x = 0 \quad \text{and} \quad K_x - n = 0. \tag{7}$$

These two equations can have a solution only if both expected marginal returns, K_n and K_x, are positive. The former is positive by (5). To verify that the expected marginal return with respect to the research outlay, K_x, is positive, we have

$$K_x = -\int_0^\infty R_y n F^{n-1} F_x \, dy > 0$$

because $F_x(\cdot) < 0$ [see (2.4)].

In the second situation there are n independent contestants who all enter the race at the same time. The winner can expect a prize of $E(R)$ shown in (3). Since all firms are equally able ex ante because each draws his y from the same cdf, each has the same chance of winning, $1/n$, if each spends the same amount on research. Assume each contestant is willing to enter only if he expects a positive return. Therefore, the equilibrium number satisfies the condition that the expected net return is zero. This is true when

$$(1/n)E(R) - x = 0 \Leftrightarrow E(R) - nx = 0. \tag{8}$$

---

[8] Although n is an integer, taking derivatives with respect to n in order to approximate the first and second differences is a standard device in analysis and has a rigorous justification.

Given the number of contestants who enter the race simultaneously, each chooses x to maximize $E(R)/n - x$ so x must satisfy

$$K_x(x, n) - n = 0. \tag{9}$$

Therefore, the equilibrium x and n satisfy (8) and (9) when entry is unrestricted, and the equilibrium x and n satisfy (7) when a single firm controls them in order to maximize $E(R) - nx$. To ensure the existence of a maximum, let the expected net return be a strongly concave function of both x and n. Hence the matrix

$$\begin{bmatrix} K_{nn} & K_{nx} - 1 \\ K_{xn} - 1 & K_{xx} \end{bmatrix}$$

is negative definite.

With these results in hand, we now compare the two equilibria. Let (x_0, n_0) denote the equilibrium pair when a single firm controls entry, and (x_1, n_1) the equilibrium pair when entry is unrestricted. Thus, (x_0, n_0) satisfies (7) while (x_1, n_1) satisfies (8) and (9). In either case one firm emerges as the sole producer of the commodity – the one that obtains the largest y, which means it has the lowest unit cost. The principal result is that for large enough n, the unit cost and the price of the commodity are lowest when a single firm controls entry than when there is unrestricted entry, if the equilibrium n_0 is large enough because there is an inverse relation between n and the research outlay per firm. First, we prove:

> **Lemma 2:** *The equilibrium number of research laboratories is smaller when a single firm controls this number and the research outlay per laboratory than when there is unrestricted entry and independence among the laboratories. Thus, $n_0 < n_1$.*

Proof: Call the expected net return $H(x, n) = K(x, n) - xn$. It is a strongly concave function of x and n by hypothesis. Let H_x^1 denote $\partial H/\partial x$ at (x_1, n_1) and H_n^1 denote $\partial H/\partial n$ at (x_1, n_1). Concavity implies that

$$H_x^1(x_1 - x_0) + H_n^1(n_1 - n_0) \le H(x_1, n_1) - H(x_0, n_0) < 0. \tag{10}$$

From (9), $H_x^1 = 0$ and from (8), $H(x_1, n_1) = 0$ so (10) implies

$$H_n^1(n_1 - n_0) \le -H(x_0, n_0) < 0. \tag{11}$$

Appealing again to concavity, write

$$H_x^1(x_1 - 0) + H_n^1(n_1 - 0) \le H(x_1, n_1) - H(0, 0). \tag{12}$$

Given $H(x_1, n_1) = 0$ from (8) and $H_x^1 = 0$ from (9), (12) implies that

$$H_n^1 n_1 \leq -H(0, 0) = 0.$$

Since $n_1 > 0$, $H_n^1 < 0$ and (11) gives the desired conclusion. ∎

This result asserts that more firms compete for first prize when entry is unrestricted than when n and x give the maximum expected net return. We now proceed with the analysis of which equilibrium gives the lower production cost. We start with Figure 8.1, which shows the cdf $F(y, x)$. The intersection of the horizontal line $1 - (1/n)$ with the cdf shows the characteristic extreme, which is the largest observation in a simple random sample of size n (Gumbel 1958, Section 3.1.4). The characteristic extreme is an increasing function of n. Let y^e denote this characteristic extreme.[9] It satisfies

$$1 - (1/n) = F(y^e, x) = \int_0^{y^e} f(y, x)\, dy. \tag{13}$$

It follows from (13) that

$$F_y(y^e, x)\, dy^e = (1/n^2)\, dn - F_x(y^e, x)\, dx. \tag{14}$$

Consequently, the slope of the characteristic extreme with respect to n is

$$\frac{dy^e}{dn} = \frac{[(1/n^2) - F_x(y^e, x)(dx/dn)]}{F_y(y^e, x)}. \tag{15}$$

For n large enough, the first term in the brackets is small and the sign of dy^e/dn depends on the sign of dx/dn. Given $F_x < 0$, dy^e/dn is negative if the research outlay per firm varies inversely with n so that dx/dn is negative $[F_y(y^e, x) = f(y^e, x) > 0]$. The pair (x, n) is endogenous and depends on which is the equilibrium, control of x and n to maximize the expected net return or unrestricted entry. In either case the research outlay per firm satisfies $H_x(x, n) = 0$ so that the expected net marginal return with respect to the research outlay per firm is zero. Therefore, we may use this result to find the relation between dx and dn from $dH_x = 0$. We obtain

$$dH_x = K_{xx}\, dx + (K_{xn} - 1)\, dn = 0 \tag{16}$$

[9] Gumbel calls these "the characteristic extremes." In addition to their intuitive appeal, they are far more tractable than the expected value of the extremes, which often do not exist, or other statistics of the distribution of extreme values.

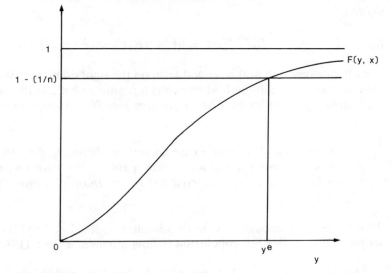

Figure 8.1

giving the implication

$$\frac{dx}{dn} = -\frac{K_{xn} - 1}{K_{xx}}.\tag{17}$$

Recalling that $K_{xx} < 0$ because the expected net return is strongly concave, the sign of dx/dn is negative if and only if $K_{xn} - 1 < 0$. Therefore, to see how research outlays per firm vary with the number of firms, we must see how the expected marginal return to research varies with n.

> **Lemma 3:** *For all large enough n, $K_{xn} - 1 < 0$ so that the larger is n, the lower is the expected marginal return to research outlays.*

Proof: It is an implication of (2) that

$$1 = \int_0^\infty dF^n = \int_0^\infty nF^{n-1}f \, dy.$$

Together with the following expression for K_{xn},

$$K_{xn} = -\int_0^\infty R_y F^{n-1} F_x (n \log F + 1) \, dy,$$

we obtain

$$K_{xn} - 1 = - \int_0^\infty [R_y F^{n-1} F_x + n F^{n-1}(R_y F_x \log F + f)] \, dy. \qquad (18)$$

For all large enough n, the second term on the right dominates the first term so that although the first term has a negative sign and the second a positive sign, the integral has a positive sign for all large enough n. ∎

> **Proposition 2:** *For all large enough n, $dy^e/dn < 0$ so that the cost of production is lower with a single firm choosing n and x to maximize its expected net return than with unrestricted entry.*

Proof: For large enough n, Lemma 3 implies $K_{xn} - 1 < 0$ so (17) gives $dx/dn < 0$. The desired conclusion is now immediate from (15). ∎

This result is important. It means that when the equilibrium number of firms, n_0, is large enough, the level of the cost of production is higher and the price of the commodity is higher if n firms can decide independently how much to spend on research in order to lower their production costs than if a single firm can choose the optimal combination of x and n giving it the maximum expected profit. In the latter case it is still true that each of the n research laboratories pursues an independent research program. The single firm chooses the number of laboratories and the research budget of each in order to maximize its expected profit from all.

To emphasize the role of n, we have the following:

> **Corollary:** *The sign of dy^e/dn is indeterminate if n is not large.*

Proof: Plainly, (18) implies that $K_{xn} - 1$ can be positive if n is not large, and then the ratio $(K_{xn} - 1)/K_{xx}$ would be negative, which would imply that dx/dn would be positive, and so dy^e/dn would be positive. But even with a small n, $K_{xn} - 1$ could be negative, and then we would have both dx/dn and dy^e/dn negative. ∎

This theory also illuminates the nature of the returns to scale with respect to research outlays. Call the total research outlay $X = nx$. Assume the size of a research activity has no positive lower bound so that a trial corresponds to a dollar's worth of resources allocated to research. This is equivalent to the hypothesis of constant returns to scale such that

$$\text{Prob } [\max (y_i) \le y; X] = F(y)^X. \tag{19}$$

$$E(R) = K(X) = \int_0^\infty R(y) \, dF(y)^X \quad \text{and} \quad H(X) = K(X) - X.$$

A contestant expects a net return given by $K(X)/n - x$. For given n he chooses x to maximize this expression. Therefore, x must satisfy

$$K_x/n - 1 = 0 \Rightarrow K_X - 1 = 0 \tag{20}$$

because $K_x = K_X(\partial X/\partial x) = nK_X$. The first-order condition for x is the same as the first-order condition for X that maximizes $H(X)$. These have a unique solution if K_{XX} is negative. But

$$K_{XX} = - \int_0^\infty R_y \, (\log F)^2 F^X \, dy < 0,$$

so the necessary conditions do have a unique solution. However, not surprisingly, n is indeterminate whether there is free entry or a single firm controls entry. Only the total X is determinate and not how it is divided among n if there are constant returns to scale with respect to research outlays. Also, if $K(X) - X$ happens to be positive, then no finite n can attain an equilibrium if there is free entry.

4   The unified theory

This section contains a unified theory of sequential search by n competing firms using the components described in the two preceding sections. Above, the hypothesis of innovation to find the optimal cost curve among the class of constant-unit-cost curves implies that only one firm at a time is an active producer of the good. This section assumes more general cost conditions that imply more than one firm at a time can profitably make and sell the good. Let

$$c = C(q) \tag{1}$$

denote the basic cost function of a firm. Assume that $C(0) = 0$ and for all positive rates of output $C_q(q) > 0$ and $C_{qq}(q) > 0$. Hence marginal cost exceeds average cost, which is a monotonically increasing function of the output rate. Average cost is a minimum at the zero output rate. Consequently, there is no positive minimal optimal size of a firm.

A fruitful hypothesis about innovation is this. By spending x_i dollars on research, firm i can draw a random variable Y from the cdf $F(y, x_i)$. As a result, it can obtain the cost function given by

$$c = C(q)/y. \tag{2}$$

The larger is the realization of the random variable Y, that is, the larger is y, the lower is the total cost function for all output rates. Although each firm has access to the same cdf, $F(y, x)$, as we shall see, it does not follow that each spends the same amount on research. This is because the outlay also depends on the value of y in hand.

The net revenue of firm i, call it r_i, is defined as follows:

$$r_i = R(q_i, y_i, Q) = b(Q)q_i - C(q_i)/y_i, \tag{3}$$

where Q denotes the output rate of all the active firms so that

$$Q = \sum_{i=1}^{n} q_i. \tag{4}$$

Customers regard the firms' outputs as perfect substitutes so there is a common price, p, and a demand function $p = b(Q)$. It is important to observe that the form of the net revenue function is the same for all firms, and differences among the firms are represented by the values of the variable y_i. Also, $F(y, x_i)$ depends only on the research outlays of firm i and not on the outlays of the other firms. This is owing to the hypothesis that firms keep secret knowledge about their methods of production. Nor is this all. The uncertainty surrounding the outcome of the research of each firm implies that a self-enforcing collusive agreement with respect to output rates would promise each firm a lower expected return than would independent actions designed to maximize its own net return. For this reason we shall use the Cournot–Nash theory of the noncooperative equilibrium as the appropriate one in this setting (cf. Chapter 6, Section 4).[10]

In period t the firms having seen the results of their research, choose their output rates to maximize their net returns, r_{it}. Hence, conditional on y_{it} the ex post equilibrium is given by the solution of

$$\frac{\partial R}{\partial q_{it}} = b(Q_t) + q_{it}b_Q - \frac{C_q}{y_{it}} = 0. \tag{5}$$

[10] Briefly, a noncooperative equilibrium, despite its inefficiency, is plausible during the research era because efficiency would require cooperation among the firms. Such cooperation is vulnerable to cheating by one of them. The penalty for cheating is a suspension of the agreement and the consequent loss of the future gains of cooperation. But the research era has a finite expected life that may be short so the deterrence of the penalty may be insufficient to outweigh the gain from cheating. The flux of events during the research era works against attempts to reach agreement.

The marginal revenue facing each firm, which is $b(Q_t) + q_{it}b_Q$, depends on the industry output rate. The existence of a deterministic Cournot–Nash equilibrium can be assured for all realizations y_{it} if the marginal revenue facing each firm is a decreasing function of the industry output rate. Because this condition is both plausible and useful, assume that

$$\frac{\partial}{\partial Q} (b + q_i b_Q) = b_Q + q_i b_{QQ} < 0. \tag{6}$$

It is apparent from (5) that there is no implication of efficiency because the firms have different marginal costs at their equilibrium output rates. The n firms could produce the total output implied by the Cournot–Nash equilibrium at a lower total cost if they did not act independently. Even so, the firms with the lower costs do produce the larger outputs. To prove this, sum (5) across the n active firms and obtain

$$b(Q) = -\frac{Q}{n} b_Q + \frac{\sum_j C_q(q_j)/y_j}{n}.$$

In conjunction with (5), it follows that

$$\left(q_i - \frac{Q}{n} \right) b_Q = \frac{C_q(q_i)}{y_i} - \frac{\sum_j C_q(q_j)/y_j}{n}. \tag{7}$$

Since $b_Q < 0$, it is an implication of (7) that firms with below-average marginal cost produce at above-average output rates, and firms with above-average marginal cost produce at below-average output rates.

According to (5), the term $-q_i b_Q(Q)$ gives the gap between the equilibrium price $b(Q)$ and the marginal cost at the equilibrium output rate of firm i, which is $C_q(q_i)/y_i$. Therefore, the excess of the price over firm i's marginal cost is an increasing function of its equilibrium output rate. In contrast to the collusive equilibrium, the Cournot–Nash equilibrium implies that the firms with the largest output rates also have the largest excess of the price over marginal cost evaluated at equilibrium output rates.

The present case, an industry with several competing firms, is more complicated than the predecessors. We begin by studying the ex post equilibrium after the firms know the results of their research activities. We wish to see how changes in the y's, the research results, affect the ex post equilibrium. To be specific, let y_1 change while all other y's stay the same. We expect q_1 and Q to change in the same direction as y_1, and the other q's to change in the opposite direction. Put differently, lower cost of firm 1 owing to an increase of y_1 causes a larger equilibrium output rate for the industry but by a smaller amount than the increase in firm 1's output because the competing firms will lower their equilibrium output rates. Hence firm 1's market share goes up if its costs go down. For a proof, differentiate the equilibrium conditions (5) with respect to y_1 and obtain

$$(b_Q + q_1 b_{QQ}) \frac{dQ}{dy_1} + \left(b_Q - \frac{C_{qq}}{y_1} \right) \frac{dq_1}{dy_1} = - \frac{C_q(q_1)}{y_1^2}, \qquad (8)$$

$$(b_Q + q_i b_{QQ}) \frac{dQ}{dy_1} + \left(b_Q - \frac{C_{qq}}{y_i} \right) \frac{dq_i}{dy_1} = 0, \qquad i \geq 2. \qquad (9)$$

Define

$$\sigma_i = b_Q + q_i b_{QQ}, \quad \mu_i = b_Q - C_{qq}/y_i, \quad \delta_1 = -C_q(q_1)/y_1^2.$$

Now, $\mu_i < 0$ and (6) asserts $\sigma_i < 0$. It readily follows from (8) and (9) that

$$\frac{dQ}{dy_1} = \frac{\delta_1/\mu_1}{1 + \sum (\sigma_i/\mu_i)} > 0, \qquad (10)$$

so that the industry equilibrium output changes in the same direction as y_1;

$$\frac{dq_i}{dy_1} = - \frac{\sigma_i}{\mu_i} \frac{dQ}{dy_1} < 0 \quad \text{if } i \geq 2, \qquad (11)$$

so that output rates of the competitors of firm 1 change in the opposite direction as y_1;

$$\frac{dq_1}{dy_1} = \frac{dQ}{dy_1} - \sum_2^n \frac{dq_i}{dy_1} > 0, \qquad (12)$$

so firm i's output rate changes in the same direction as y_1.

These results for the ex post equilibrium are essential for deriving the properties of the ex ante equilibrium, the result of the research outlays of the firms. A firm planning its research program calculates the possible outcomes by taking into account not only the effect of its own research but also the effects of competitors' researches. Since n firms are in the industry, it may seem the given firm has the complicated problem of determining how the research results of each of its $n - 1$ competitors will affect it. However, the hypothesis that the products of the firms are perfect substitutes enables all of the competitive forces impinging on one of them to be collapsed into one variable, the equilibrium industry output rate. Consequently, the given firm can sum-

marize the factors relevant for its ex ante decision on research in period
t in two variables that describe the initial conditions, $y_{i,t-1}$ and Q_{t-1}.
It can summarize the factors entering the t-period cdf by calculating
the joint distribution of the two random variables y_t and Q_t. To see
why this is so, consider the effect on the t-period net revenue of firm
i, r_{it}, of various possible research outcomes in period t.

First, assume that $y_{it} \le y_{i,t-1}$ so that the firm's research would not
enable a lower production cost in period t. One might think that it could
still have the same net revenue in period t as in period $t - 1$ because
it could use the same methods of production in both periods. Though
this is true, it does not follow that its net revenue would be the same
in both periods. This depends on what happened to its competitors.
There is only one circumstance under which $y_{it} \le y_{i,t-1}$ implies that
firm i can have the same net return in both periods t and $t - 1$ so that
$r_{it} = r_{i,t-1}$. This is when *every* firm in the industry obtains $y_{i,t-1} \ge$
$y_{i,t}$. Let v_{it} denote the present value of the net return of firm i. We
have the following result:

$$y_{it} \le y_{i,t-1} \quad \text{for all } i \text{ implies } r_{it} = r_{i,t-1}$$

$$\text{and} \quad v_{it} = v_{i,t-1} \quad \text{for all } i.$$

Second, assume that for at least one firm i, $y_{it} > y_{i,t-1}$. The analysis
of the ex post equilibrium summarized by (10)–(12) implies the net
returns and present values differ in periods t and $t - 1$. From (5),
giving the marginal revenue and marginal cost of firm i, we see that
only Q_t and y_{it} determine q_{it}. Although the effects of changes of y_i on
q_j are complicated, dQ/dy_{it} is unambiguously positive (and incidentally
dp_t/dy_{it} is unambiguously negative). Because the ex post industry equilibrium output rate depends on the realizations of the random variables
y_{it} that represent the research results, Q_t is itself a random variable,
which has a cdf depending on the research outlays of the firms, x_{it},
which are their control variables. Call this cdf $G(Q, x_{1t}, \ldots, x_{nt})$.
According to this argument,

(i) $y_{it} \le y_{i,t-1}$ for all i implies $Q_t = Q_{t-1}$;
(ii) $y_{it} > y_{i,t-1}$ for at least one i implies $Q_t > Q_{t-1}$.

We may now conclude that

$$\text{Prob}(Q_t > Q_{t-1}) = 1 - \text{Prob}(y_{it} \le y_{i,t-1} \text{ for all } i).$$

For the sake of brevity, define the vector of research outlays as follows:

$$X_t = \langle x_{1t}, x_{2t}, \ldots, x_{nt} \rangle.$$

The cdf relevant for firm i is

$$G(Q_t, y_{it}, X_t) = \int_0^{y_{it}} \int_0^{Q_t} g(Q, y_i, X_t) \, dQ \, dy_i. \tag{13}$$

Also, define the function $R(Q_t, y_{it})$ as in (2.7) so that

$$\max_{q_{it}} R(q_{it}, Q_t, y_{it}) = R(Q_t, y_{it}), \tag{14}$$

and q_{it} becomes an implicit function of Q_t and y_{it}. Both Q_t and y_{it} are random variables drawn from the cdf $G(\cdot)$. The equilibrium X_t depends on Q_{t-1} as a state variable and on the equations implied by the Cournot–Nash equilibrium. Firm i expects a return in period t defined as follows:

$$E(r_{it}) = R(Q_{t-1}, y_{i,t-1})G(Q_{t-1}, y_{i,t-1}, X_t)$$

$$+ \int_{Q_{t-1}}^{\infty} \int_0^{y_{i,t-1}} R(Q, y_{i,t-1})g(Q, z_i, X_t) \, dz_i \, dQ \tag{15}$$

$$+ \int_{Q_{t-1}}^{\infty} \int_{y_{i,t-1}}^{\infty} R(Q, z_i)g(Q, z_i, X_t) \, dz_i \, dQ.$$

The first term represents the event $y_{it} \le y_{i,t-1}$ for all i, which is equivalent to $Q_t = Q_{t-1}$. The second term represents the event $y_{i,t} \le y_{i,t-1}$ and $y_{jt} > y_{j,t-1}$ for at least one firm $j \ne i$ so that $Q_t > Q_{t-1}$. In the latter event the net revenue of firm i is $r_{it} = R(Q_t, y_{i,t-1})$ because it can still use the methods of production given by $y_{i,t-1} \ge y_{i,t}$. The third term represents the event $y_{i,t} > y_{i,t-1}$, which in itself implies $Q_t > Q_{t-1}$ by virtue of (10). There is a similar expression for the expected value of v_{it}, the present value of the net return, which may be obtained by replacing r_{it} by v_{it} in (15).

Despite the greater complexity of this case as compared with the one in Section 2, it has important features in common with the model that assumes a constant marginal cost of production and only one firm active in the industry in each period. In particular, although now more than one firm at a time can be active in the industry, there is still a research era and a mature era. The research era ends when continuing outlays on research are no longer expected to be profitable. The condition corresponding to the stopping rule (2.11) is as follows:

$$\max_{x_{it}} [E(r_{it}) - \alpha x_{it}] \le R(Q_{t-1}, y_{i,t-1}). \tag{16}$$

Firm i stops its research as soon as (16) is true. The time when this happens, call it T as above, is a random variable. Because $E(r_{it})$ depends on Q_{t-1} and $y_{i,t-1}$, this makes the x_{it}, the solution of the maximum problem posed by the left side of (16), an implicit function of Q_{t-1} and $y_{i,t-1}$. It is important to realize that Q_{t-1} appears not because firm i expects the same industry output in period t as in period $t - 1$ but because Q_{t-1} is the pertinent state variable for optimal decision making at the beginning of period t. Once having decided to stop research in period T, it will not be profitable for the firm to resume research at some later period. This is for two reasons. First, by hypothesis, the total demand function is constant over time. Were the demand to rise over time, continuing research outlays might be profitable indefinitely. Second, the firm's net revenue after it decides to stop its research cannot increase subsequently owing to competitive pressures from other firms for whom continuing research may be profitable for a while because their current costs of production are high. As the dynamic process unfolds, not all firms will find it optimal to stop their research at the same time because of differences among their production costs, although, of course, all face the same Q_{t-1}.

Study of the implications of (16) as an equality yields some important results. Write

$$\max_{x_i} [E(r_i) - \alpha x_i] = R(Q, y_i). \tag{17}$$

To convince ourselves that it is possible to satisfy the necessary conditions for the maximum called for by the left side of (17), there is:

> **Lemma 4:** *If the probability of success is an increasing function of the research outlays in the sense of (A.30) and (A.31), then the marginal expected return with respect to research outlays is positive so that $\partial E(r_i)/\partial x_i > 0$.*

(See the appendix for a proof.) Together with the hypothesis that the marginal expected return is a decreasing function of x_i, it follows that the necessary condition $\partial E(r_i)/\partial x_i - \alpha = 0$ has a solution.

Reconsider (17). The x_i that maximizes the left side of (17) is an implicit function of y_i and Q. Call this function $\phi(\cdot)$ and write

$$x_i = \phi(y_i, Q).$$

Substitute this function in place of x_i in (17) and solve the resulting expression for y_i as a function of Q. Call the solution y_i^*. Because it depends on Q, it must be the same for all i, recalling that all firms have functions of the same form and that differences among firms are represented by the values of certain parameters. This common y^* is the stopping value for y, and it depends on Q^*, the industry equilibrium output. The latter in turn depends on how many firms are in the industry. To close the theory requires a statement about the equilibrium number of firms in the industry given that the Cournot–Nash theory is silent on this point.

> *Assumption: The characteristic equilibrium number of firms in the industry is such that it is almost certain that $y \geq y^*$ for the least efficient firm able to remain active in the industry.*[11]

The results we shall obtain from the following analysis have a simple explanation. In this model the demand function remains constant by hypothesis, and changes in the equilibrium come from successful research that lowers the cost and generates a sequence of points along the given demand curve. Because the research results behave like random drawings, it is as if they are exogenous variables to which price and quantity respond.

Each y_i is a random drawing from the same cdf $F(y_i, x_i)$, independent of the drawings of competing firms. Moreover, in terms of the theory of the equilibrium given above, x_i^* is also the same for each firm. Following Gumbel (1958, Section 3.1.4), the characteristic smallest number satisfies

$$1/n = F(y^*, x^*) \tag{18}$$

so that

$$dn = (-n^2)[F_y \, dy^* + F_x \, dx^*]. \tag{19}$$

Since x^* satisfies the necessary condition, $\partial E(r_i)/\partial x_i - \alpha = 0$, taking the differential of this expression we obtain

$$E(r_i)_{xx} \, dx^* + E(r_i)_{Qx} \, dQ^* + E(r_i)_{xy} \, dy^* = 0. \tag{20}$$

Solve (20) for dx^* and substitute the result in (19) thereby obtaining

$$dn = (-n^2)[F_y - F_x E(r)_{xy}/E(r)_{xx}] \, dy^*$$
$$- [F_x E(r)_{Qx}/E(r)_{xx}] \, dQ^*. \tag{21}$$

We know that $F_x < 0$ because the probability of failure is a decreasing function of the research outlay; $E(r)_{xx} < 0$ because there is decreasing marginal expected returns to research outlays, $E(r)_{xy} < 0$ because the higher is y, the lower the marginal expected return to research outlays;

---

[11] The term *almost certain* refers to convergence in probability. Think of many repetitions of the dynamic stochastic process. It must always be true that the firm with the highest cost just able to survive in the industry has a level of $y \geq y^*$. The assumption refers to the number of firms for which the probability of this event is nearly certain.

and $E(r)_{Qx} < 0$ because the larger is the equilibrium industry output, the lower the marginal expected return to research outlays. We may now prove:

> *Proposition 3:* $\partial n/\partial y^* < 0$ and $\partial n/\partial Q^* < 0$ so that the characteristic equilibrium number of firms varies inversely with the minimally acceptable level of cost and the industry equilibrium output.

Proof: $\partial n/\partial y^*$ is the coefficient of dy^* in (21) and $\partial n/\partial Q^*$ is the coefficient of dQ^*. For the reasons given just before Proposition 3, these coefficients are negative. ∎

On the basis of this result we may say that the smaller is the characteristic equilibrium number of firms in the industry at the end of its research era, the lower is the level of costs in that industry and the larger is the equilibrium industry output, Q^*. Recall that there are no economies of scale. Nevertheless, the theory predicts that industries with a smaller number of firms at the start of their mature era are more likely to have lower costs and prices than are those that then have a larger number of firms.

5   Predictions

Choose the firm indexes so that $y_i > y_{i+1}$. Consequently, firm 1 has the lowest cost, firm 2 the second lowest cost, and so on. Call r_i the net return of firm i and s_i its market share. The theory predicts a positive association between r_i and s_i. Empirical studies showing a positive correlation between the four-firm concentration ratios and industry net returns support this prediction. Also, according to the Cournot–Nash noncooperative equilibrium, price relative to marginal cost evaluated at the firm's equilibrium output rate should be an increasing function of its market share. During the research era there is a tendency for the market shares of the leading firms in the industry to fall. This tendency is weaker, the larger is the firm's market share. Consequently, the leading firm should have the most stable market share over time, the second firm the next most stable share, and so on. This is because a firm's market share depends on the level of its cost function, which in turn depends on y. The leading firm has the biggest y that may be regarded as the largest number in a random sample of size n from the cdf $F(y, x)$. The bigger is y_1, the less likely that another firm can surpass it. This theory also implies that $s_{i+1} - s_i < s_i - s_{i-1}$ so that differences between adjacent market shares increase with firm rank in the industry.

The theory also has interesting implications about the pattern of innovations over time. Following Schumpeter (1954), assume that invention is an unpredictable random event. Innovation is the adaptation of invention in order to lower cost, and it occurs during the research era. It continues for a finite and unpredictable time and is followed by the mature era. Invention marks the end of a mature era and the beginning of a research era and may also occur during a research era. This theory predicts alternating eras of research and maturity of random durations.

The industry price tends to fall as long as there are positive research outlays. The price declines occur at a decreasing rate during the research era, and prices are constant during the mature era. Industry output moves inversely to prices along the demand function. During the research era industry output grows at a decreasing rate. There is no growth in the mature era. In the Cournot–Nash equilibrium, the allocation of the industry equilibrium output among the active firms in the industry is inefficient. Mergers among firms can increase efficiency so that the same output can be produced at a lower total cost. Such mergers are most likely to occur during the mature eras. During mature eras, self-enforcing agreements on the allocation of outputs among the firms are more likely to be profitable and furnish an alternative to merger as a means of obtaining an efficient allocation of output among the firms. The random outcomes of the research outlays during the research era increase the expected return to those who would cheat on an agreement with respect to the assignment of outputs and makes it more difficult to agree on merger terms.

Once a firm stops its research it will not resume later unless there is invention. This is because the sequence of its expected returns, while it was out of the race, cannot have been increasing. Therefore, if it did not pay to stay in the race at an earlier time, then surely it would not pay at a later time. A potential entrant calculates whether he can surpass the least efficient active firms in the industry. Once the latter firm stops its research, the theory predicts entry will not occur. Nor is this all. Once the marginal firm terminates its research program, the other firms in the industry whose costs are even lower will have terminated their research programs as well. During the mature era all active firms in the industry obtain a positive return, that is, positive profits, even the highest cost firm still active in the industry. The number of active firms during the mature era is a random variable. Proposition 3 describes the relation between this number and the level of costs in the industry. It predicts an inverse relation between the two.

A growth in demand can stimulate resumption of research during the mature era. More generally, research eras are likely to last longer for products with growing demand.[12]

Although the theory makes research outlays necessary for cost reductions, the relation between the two is not deterministic. Empirical analysis of the relation between research outlays ought to take this explicitly into account. The *expected* cost reduction is an increasing function of the research outlay and not the *actual* cost reduction, which is a random variable. Econometric analysis of innovation and its effects on costs is more likely to give useful results if it relies on an explicit theory of the process.

Some open questions arise. What is the relation between the distribution of output rates among the firms and the distribution of the y's that determine the levels of their cost functions? The active firms in an industry represent those with the lowest costs and therefore come from the right hand tail of the cdf $F(y, x)$. How does the distribution of survivors depend on their number? Is it true, for example, that an industry with a smaller number of firms in equilibrium will display greater differences among their cost functions and returns? This seems likely and requires a theoretical analysis. The theory focuses on cost reductions. What sort of theory would give insight into product innovation? A promising way of approaching this problem would retain the emphasis on cost and would assume a general demand curve for basic goods. These basic goods are analogous to chemical elements, and commodities are analogous to chemical compounds. Product innovation occurs when there is new knowledge that lowers the cost of making certain elements. Much would depend on a clever choice of elements in order for this approach to be useful.

6   Technical appendix

This section begins with proofs of the following four propositions:

Proposition A1: *A necessary condition for stopping in a finite*

---

[12] For an example of a study finding a positive relation between the industry return and the four-firm concentration ratio that takes into account several other pertinent variables see Telser (1972, Chapter 8). Gort (1963) gives evidence showing that the stability of market share increases with the four-firm concentration ratio. Demsetz (1973) and McGee (1971) were among the first to explain the positive association between rates of return and four-firm concentration as the result of relatively lower costs of the firms with larger market shares. For elaborate tests of these ideas, see Peltzman (1977). Arthur F. Burns (1934) has evidence supporting the prediction of my theory that growth rates of a given set of industries tend to decline and prices to fall at a decreasing rate.

time T is the existence of a finite y^* such that for all $y \geq y^*$,

$$\max_x [E(r) - \alpha x] \leq R(y). \tag{1}$$

Proposition A2: *Inequality (1) is also sufficient for a finite stopping time.*

Propostion A3: *Assume that the following three conditions are true:*

(i) $\partial^2 E(r)/\partial y \partial x < 0$;
(ii) $\partial^2 E(r)/\partial x^2 < 0$;
(iii) *There is a finite $\bar{y}$ such that for all $y \geq \bar{y}$, $\partial E(r)/\partial x \,|_{x=0}$ has a finite upper bound and has no positive lower bound. Then there is a finite $\bar{y}^*$ such that for all $y \geq \bar{y}^*$*

$$\partial E(r)/\partial x \,|_{x=0} \leq \alpha. \tag{2}$$

Remark: The $\bar{y}^*$ referred to in Proposition A3 satisfies $\bar{y}^* > y^*$ because it is generally optimal to stop research before y is so large that the expected marginal return to research is less than α.

Proposition A4: *The uniform continuity of*

$$\int_y^\infty \frac{\partial^m f(y, z)}{\partial x^m} \, dz$$

implies the uniform continuity of all partial derivatives of lower orders.

Proof of Proposition A1: If $x_t > 0$ then $y \leq y_{t-1}$ implies $r_t = R(y_{t-1})$ with probability $F(y_{t-1}, x_t)$, and $y > y_{t-1}$ implies $r_t = R(y)$ with probability $1 - F(y, x_{t-1})$.

$$E(r_t) = R(y_{t-1})F(y_{t-1}, x_t) + \int_{y_{t-1}}^\infty R(z)f(z, x_t) \, dz. \tag{3}$$

The sequence of expected returns if research stops at the end of period T is

$$E(r_1), E(r_2), \ldots, E(r_T), E(r_T), \ldots. \tag{I}$$

If research stops at the end of period $T - 1$, the sequence of expected returns would be

$$E(r_1), E(r_2), \ldots, R(y_{T-1}), R(y_{T-1}), \ldots. \tag{II}$$

Call the present value of the first sequence V_{I} and the second sequence V_{II}. Research outlays are made at the beginning of each period so the present value of x_T is $\beta^{T-1}x_T$ and revenue is received at the end of each period. The present value of the difference between the two policies is as follows:

$$V_{\mathrm{I}} - V_{\mathrm{II}} - \beta^{T-1}x_T = \beta^T[E(r_T) - x_T/\beta - R(y_{T-1})]$$
$$+ \beta^{T+1}[E(r_T) - R(y_{T-1})] + \cdots$$
$$= [\beta^T/(1 - \beta)][E(r_T) - \alpha x_T - R(y_{T-1})],$$

recalling that $\beta = 1/(1 + \alpha)$ so that $\alpha = (1 - \beta)/\beta$.

$$\max_{x_T} [V_{\mathrm{I}} - V_{\mathrm{II}} - \beta^{T-1}x_T]$$

$$= \beta^T/(1 - \beta) \{\max_{x_T} [E(r_T) - \alpha x_T] - R(y_{T-1})\} \quad (4)$$

because y_{T-1} does not depend on x_T (although the optimal x_T does depend on y_{T-1}). If the expression in (4) were positive, it would not be optimal to stop in period $T - 1$. That is,

$$\max_{x_T} [E(r_T) - \alpha x_T] > R(y_{T-1}) \quad (5)$$

for each pair T, $T - 1$ implies it is not optimal to stop in period $T - 1$. Therefore, as claimed, a necessary condition for stopping in some finite period $T - 1$ is that (5) is false for some y^*. Given $\{y_T\}$ is a nondecreasing sequence, this is to say that (1) is true for all $y \geq y^*$. ∎

Proof of Proposition A2: The present value of the sequence of revenue $\{r_t\}$ at the beginning of the initial period, call it $V_0 = \sum_1^\infty \beta^t r_t$ because the t-period revenue is received at the end of the period. Hence $V_0 = \beta(V_1 + r_1)$. This explains the form of (2.10) that we now rewrite slightly differently as follows

$$V(y, x) = \beta\{[R(y) + V^*(y)]F(y, x) - \alpha x$$
$$+ \int_y^\infty [R(z) + V^*(z)]f(z, x)\, dz - x\} \quad (6)$$

where $V^*(y) = \max_x V(y, x)$. It is an implication of (1), which is true by hypothesis, and the relation between stocks and flows that

$$\max_x [V^*(y)F(y, x) + \int_y^\infty V^*(z)f(z, x)\, dz - x] \leq R(y)/\alpha. \quad (7)$$

It follows from (6) that

$$V^*(y) \le \beta \{\max_x [E(r) - \alpha x] + \max_x [E(v) - x]\}, \tag{8}$$

where

$$E(v) = V^*(y)F(y, x) + \int_y^\infty V^*(z)f(z, x) \, dz.$$

Since stopping is always a feasible strategy, necessarily,

$$V^*(y) \ge R(y)/\alpha. \tag{9}$$

From (8) and (9) we may conclude that

$$[(1 + \alpha)/\alpha]R(y) \le \max_x [E(r) - \alpha x] + \max_x [E(v) - x]. \tag{10}$$

From (1) and (7),

$$\max_x [E(r) - \alpha x] + \max_x [E(v) - x] \le [1 + (1/\alpha)]R(y). \tag{11}$$

Together (10) and (11) give equality straight through, and we have

$$V^*(y) \le R(y)/\alpha \tag{12}$$

so (9) and (12) imply there is equality. This means that for $y \ge y^*$, stopping is the optimal strategy.   ∎

Proof of Proposition A3: This proposition establishes sufficient conditions for the existence of a unique solution of the necessary condition for a maximum of $E(r) - \alpha x$ with respect to x. Because α is positive, we begin by showing that if $R(y)$ is an increasing function of y, then $\partial E(r)/\partial x > 0$.

$$\frac{\partial E(r)}{\partial x} = R(y)F_x(y, x) + \int_y^\infty R(z)f_x(z, x) \, dz. \tag{13}$$

Because $F(y, x) + \int_y^\infty f(z, x) \, dz = 1$ is an identity, it follows that

$$F_x(y, x) = -\int_y^\infty f_x(z, x) \, dz.$$

Substituting this in (13) gives

$$\frac{\partial E(r)}{\partial x} = \int_y^\infty [R(z) - R(y)]f_x(z, x) \, dz > 0 \tag{14}$$

because $R(z) - R(y) > 0$ if $z > y$ and $\int_y^\infty f_x(\cdot) \, dz > 0$.

Continuing with the proof, (i) asserts that $\partial E(r)/\partial x$ is a decreasing function of y and (ii) that $\partial E(r)/\partial x$ is a decreasing function of x. Therefore, for each y the necessary condition has at most one solution. Condition (iii) studies the behavior of $\partial E(r)/\partial x$ evaluated at $x = 0$ as a function of y. It implies that for all large enough y, $\partial E(r)/\partial x$ eventually becomes less than any prescribed positive value of α. Therefore, eventually y becomes large enough so that the optimal x that would satisfy the necessary condition is zero. ∎

Remarks: By differentiating $\partial E(r)/\partial x - \alpha = 0$ with respect to y, we find

$$\frac{dx}{dy} = -\frac{\partial^2 E(r)/\partial x^2}{\partial^2 E(r)/\partial x\, \partial y} < 0$$

so that x varies inversely with y. Second, at time T when it is optimal to stop research, the x giving the maximum of $E(r_T) - \alpha x_T$ will usually be positive. However, the optimal x given by the solution of the dynamic programming problem will then be zero.

Proof of Proposition A4: This is an application of a standard result in the theory of functions of a real variable. It follows from a result given by Graves (1946, Chapter VII, Section 2, Theorem 8). Uniform continuity of a higher-order partial derivative implies uniform continuity of all lower-order partials. ∎

In order to apply Proposition A3 in empirical work, the cdf $F(y, x)$ must satisfy certain conditions. A generally useful one is as follows:

$F(y, x)$ is uniformly lower semicontinuous for all y.

This means there is a cdf $H(y)$ that does not depend on x, which gives a lower bound on the probability of failure. Because $H(y)$ is itself a cdf, it is almost certain that failure will occur if y is large enough no matter how much is spent on research. Formally, for any $\epsilon > 0$,

$$F(y, x) - H(y) \geq \epsilon \tag{15}$$

for all $y \geq y_0$ for some finite y_0 and for all $x \geq 0$.

Next we study how α affects $E(T^*)$, the upper bound on the expected duration of the research era, defined by (2.16).

Rewrite (2.14) in the following shape:

$$\int_{y^*}^{\infty} [R(z) - R(y^*)] f(z, x)\, dz - \alpha x^* = 0. \tag{16}$$

Since x^* gives the maximum of $E(r) - \alpha x$ for $y = y^*$, x^* must satisfy the first-order necessary condition, $\partial E(r)/\partial x - \alpha = 0$. The latter is equivalent to

$$\int_{y^*}^{\infty} [R(z) - R(y^*)] f_x(z, x)\, dz - \alpha = 0. \tag{17}$$

For brevity, call the integral in (16), $J(x, y)$, and replace (16) and (17) with the following more concise expressions:

$$J(x^*, y^*) - \alpha x^* = 0, \tag{18}$$

$$J_x(x^*, y^*) - \alpha = 0. \tag{19}$$

Because x^* gives the maximum of $E(r) - \alpha x$ for $y = y^*$, it follows that x^* is an implicit function of y^* and α. Equation (18) defines y^* as an implicit function of α.

$$\frac{dE(T^*)}{d\alpha} = \frac{\partial E(T^*)}{\partial y^*}\frac{dy^*}{d\alpha} + \frac{\partial E(T^*)}{\partial x^*}\frac{dx^*}{d\alpha}. \tag{20}$$

We must evaluate the terms on the right side of (20).

$$\frac{\partial E(T^*)}{\partial y} = \frac{F_y(y^*, x^*)}{[1 - F(y^*, x^*)]^2} > 0. \tag{21}$$

$$\frac{\partial E(T^*)}{\partial x} = \frac{F_x(y^*, x^*)}{1 - F(y^*, x^*)} < 0 \tag{22}$$

by virtue of (2.4). To find $dy^*/d\alpha$ and $dx^*/d\alpha$, use (18) and (19).

$$J_y(x^*, y^*)\frac{dy^*}{d\alpha} = x^*. \tag{23}$$

$$J_{xx}(x^*, y^*)\frac{dx^*}{d\alpha} + J_{xy}(x^*, y^*)\frac{dy^*}{d\alpha} = 1. \tag{24}$$

Take $J_{xx} < 0$ because this is a sufficient condition for the existence of a maximum of $E(r) - \alpha x$ with respect to x.

$$J_y = -R_y(y^*)\int_{y^*}^{\infty} f(z, x)\, dz < 0. \tag{25}$$

Consequently, we may conclude that

$$\frac{dy^*}{d\alpha} = \frac{x^*}{J_y} < 0. \tag{26}$$

This result means that the higher the discount rate α, the lower is the minimally acceptable level of y, an intuitively plausible result. Solving (24) for $dx^*/d\alpha$, we obtain

$$\frac{dx^*}{d\alpha} = \frac{1 - J_{xy}(dy^*/d\alpha)}{J_{xx}}, \tag{27}$$

and we wish to analyze the numerator of the right side.

$$J_{xy} = -R_y(y^*) \int_{y^*}^{\infty} f_x(z, x) \, dz. \tag{28}$$

After some reductions we obtain

$$1 - J_{xy} \frac{dy^*}{d\alpha} = \frac{\int_{y^*}^{\infty} [f(z, x) - x f_x(z, x)] \, dz}{\int_{y^*}^{\infty} f(z, x) \, dz}. \tag{29}$$

The term $f(z, x) - x f_x(z, x)$ is positive if f/x is a decreasing function of x. Because $f(\cdot)$ is a pdf, f/x is a decreasing function of x when the probability of success gives decreasing returns with respect to the research outlay. This concludes the proof of:

Lemma A.1: $dx^*/d\alpha < 0$ if and only if $\int_{y^*}^{\infty} (f - x f_x) \, dz > 0$.

Now we can see why α has an indeterminate effect on $E(T^*)$. The first term on the right side of (20) is negative because of (21) and (26). The second term on the right side is positive if there are decreasing returns for the probability of success because of (22) and Lemma A.1. Hence the sign of the net effect is indeterminate. Summarizing, we have:

Proposition A5: *The sign of $dE(T^*)/d\alpha$ is indeterminate if $dx^*/d\alpha < 0$.*
The sign is positive if $dx^*/d\alpha > 0$.

The last topic we consider in this appendix is a proof of Lemma 4 restated as follows.

Lemma 4: *If the probability of success is an increasing function of the research outlays in the sense of (30) and (31), then the marginal expected return with respect to research outlays is positive, so that $\partial E(r_i)/\partial x_i > 0$.*

Proof: We assume that research outlays affect the probability of success as follows:

$$\int_{Q^*}^{\infty} \int_{y_i^*}^{\infty} g_{x_i}(Q, z_i, X) \, dz_i \, dQ > 0 \tag{30}$$

so that the probability of getting a larger y_i and larger Q is an increasing function of the research outlay [see (4.13)]. Second, assume that

$$\int_0^{\infty} g_{x_i}(z_i, Q, X) \, dz_i < 0. \tag{31}$$

Now the marginal distribution of Q obtained by integrating out z_i is defined by

$$\Gamma(Q, X) = \int_0^{\infty} g(z_i, Q, X) \, dz_i. \tag{32}$$

It is, therefore, an implication of (31) that the probability of $Q \leq Q^*$ is a decreasing function of the research outlay by firm i. To show the implications of these two assumptions, start by writing $\partial E(r_i)/\partial x_i$ as follows:

$$\begin{aligned}
\frac{\partial E(r_i)}{\partial x_i} &= R(y_i^*, Q^*)G_{x_i}(Q^*, y_i^*, X) \\
&+ \int_{Q^*}^{\infty} \int_0^{y_i^*} R(y_i^*, Q)g_{x_i}(\cdot) \, dz_i \, dQ \\
&+ \int_{Q^*}^{\infty} \int_{y_i^*}^{\infty} R(z_i, Q)g_{x_i}(\cdot) \, dz_i \, dQ.
\end{aligned} \tag{33}$$

(Q^* and y_i^* are nonrandom variables given by the stopping values of Q and y_i.) Since

$$G(Q^*, y_i^*, X) + \int_{Q^*}^{\infty} \int_0^{y_i^*} g(\cdot) \, dz_i \, dQ$$

$$+ \int_{Q^*}^{\infty} \int_{y_i^*}^{\infty} g(\cdot) \, dz_i \, dQ \equiv 1,$$

the partial derivative of this expression with respect to x_i is zero and

$$G_{x_i}(Q^*, y_i^*, X) = - \int_{Q^*}^{\infty} \int_0^{y_i^*} g_{x_i}(\cdot) \, dz_i \, dQ$$

$$- \int_{Q^*}^{\infty} \int_{y_i^*}^{\infty} g_{x_i}(\cdot) \, dz_i \, dQ.$$

Substitute this expression for $G_{x_i}(\cdot)$ in (33) and obtain

$$
\frac{\partial E(r_i)}{\partial x_i} = \int_{Q^*}^{\infty} \int_0^{y_i^*} [R(y_i^*, Q) - R(y_i^*, Q^*)] g_{x_i}(\cdot)\, dz_i\, dQ
$$
$$
+ \int_{Q^*}^{\infty} \int_{y_i^*}^{\infty} [R(z_i, Q) - R(y_i^*, Q^*)] g_{x_i}(\cdot)\, dz_i\, dQ. \tag{34}
$$

Write

$$
R(z_i, Q) - R(y_i^*, Q^*)
$$
$$
= R(z_i, Q) - R(y_i^*, Q) + R(y_i^*, Q) - R(y_i^*, Q^*)
$$

and substitute this into the second integral on the right of (34). This gives a simpler expression for (34) as follows:

$$
\frac{\partial E(r_i)}{\partial x_i} = \int_{Q^*}^{\infty} \int_{y_i^*}^{\infty} [R(z_i, Q) - R(y_i^*, Q)] g_{x_i}(\cdot)\, dz_i\, dQ
$$
$$
+ \int_{Q^*}^{\infty} [R(y_i^*, Q) - R(y_i^*, Q^*)] \int_0^{\infty} g_{x_i}(\cdot)\, dz_i\, dQ. \tag{35}
$$

First, for given Q, $R(y_i, Q)$ is an increasing function of y_i. Therefore, $[R(z_i, Q) - R(y_i^*, Q)] > 0$ in the first integral on the right of (35). By virtue of (30), it follows that this first integral is positive. Second, for given y_i^*, $R(y_i^*, Q)$ is a decreasing function of Q. Therefore, in the second integral on the right side of (35), $[R(y_i^*, Q) - R(y_i^*, Q^*)] < 0$. Together with (31), we may conclude that the sign of the second integral is also positive. Therefore, $\partial E(r_i)/\partial x_i$ is positive. ∎

References

Alt, F. 1936. Uber die Messbarkeit des Nutzens. *Zeitschrift fur National-okonomie* **7**(2): 161–9. Trans. by Siegfried Sachs. Chipman, J.S., Hurwicz, L., Richter, M.K., and Sonneschein, H.F., eds. 1971. On the measurability of utility, in *Preference, utility and demands*. New York: Harcourt Brace Jovanovich.

Axelrod, R. 1984. *The evolution of cooperation*. New York: Basic Books.

Bain, J.S. 1956. *Barriers to new competition*. Cambridge, Mass.: Harvard University Press.

Baumol, W.J., Panzar, J.C., and Willig, R.D. 1982. *Contestable markets and the theory of industrial structure*. New York: Harcourt Brace Jovanovich.

Bellman, R. 1960. *Introduction to matrix analysis*. New York: McGraw-Hill.

Bertrand, J. 1883. Review of Cournot, "Recherches." *Journal des Savants,* (Sept.) p. 503.

Bittlingmayer, G. 1981. Competition and the nature of costs: the cast iron pipe industry, 1890–1910, and the case of Addyston Pipe. PhD Dissertation, University of Chicago.

Bittlingmayer, G. 1982. Decreasing average cost: a new look at the Addyston Pipe case. *Journal of Law and Economics* **25**(Oct.): 201–29.

Bittlingmayer, G. 1985. Did antitrust policy cause the great merger wave? *Journal of Law and Economics* **28**(Apr.): 77–118.

Böhm-Bawerk, E. von, 1959. *Positive theory of capital,* vol II, Book III. Trans. G.D. Huncke and H.F. Sennholz. South Holland, IL: Libertarian Press (original publication in German 1889).

Bork, R.H. 1978. *The antitrust paradox: a policy at war with itself*. New York: Basic Books.

Burns, A.F. 1934. *Production trends in the United States since 1870*. New York: National Bureau of Economic Research.

Bullock, C.J. 1901. Trust literature: a survey and a criticism. *Quarterly Journal of Economics* **15**(Feb.): 167–217.

Cassel, G. 1967. *The theory of social economy*. Trans. S.L. Barron from 5th German ed. 1932. New York: A.M. Kelley.

Chandler, A. 1977. *The visible hand: the managerial revolution in American business*. Cambridge, Mass.: Belknap Press, Harvard University Press.

Clark, J.M. 1923. *Studies in the economics of overhead costs*. Chicago & London: University of Chicago Press.

Cournot, A. 1960. *Researches into the mathematical principles of the theory of wealth.* Trans. Nathaniel Bacon from 1838 French ed., introductory essay Irving Fisher. New York: A.M. Kelley.

Cramèr, H. 1946. *Mathematical methods of statistics.* Princeton: Princeton University Press.

Creamer, D., Dobrovolsky, S.P., and Borenstein, I. 1960. *Capital in manufacturing and mining. its formation and financing.* National Bureau of Economic Research. Princeton: Princeton University Press.

Cowles, A. 1938. *Common-stock indexes 1871–1937.* Cowles Commission Mon. No. 3. Bloomington, IN: Principia Press.

Dasgupta, P., and Stiglitz, J. 1980. Uncertainty, industrial structure and the speed of R&D. *Bell Journal of Economics* **11**: 1–28.

Demsetz, H. 1968. Do competition and monopolistic competition differ. *Journal of Political Economy* **76**(Jan./Feb.): 146–8.

Demsetz, H. 1973. Industry structure, market rivalry and public policy. *Journal of Law and Economics* **16**(April): 1–9.

Derrick's hand book of petroleum. 1898. A complete chronological and statistical review of petroleum developments from 1859–1898. Oil City, PA: Derrick Publishing Co.

Edgeworth, F.Y. 1881. *Mathematical psychics.* London: Kegan-Paul.

Edgeworth, F.Y. 1925. The pure theory of monopoly. *Papers relating to political economy,* vol I. London: Royal Economic Society. (Republished 1970 by Burt Franklin, NY.)

Eis, C. 1969. The 1919–1930 merger movement in American industry. *Journal of Law and Economics* **12**(Oct.): 267–96.

Feller, W. 1957. *An introduction to probability theory and its applications,* 2nd ed., vol. 1. New York: Wiley. (Third edition, 1968.)

Galambos, L. 1975. *The public image of big business in America, 1880–1940.* Baltimore: Johns Hopkins University Press.

Gallman, R.E. 1966. Gross national product in the United States, 1834–1909. *Output, employment and productivity in the United States after 1800.* New York: National Bureau of Economic Research.

Goldstine, H.H. 1972. *The computer from Pascal to von Neumann.* Princeton: Princeton University Press.

Gort, M. 1963. Analysis of stability and change in market shares. *Journal of Political Economy* **71**(Feb.): 51–63.

Gort, M. 1969. An economic disturbance theory of mergers. *Quarterly Journal of Economics* **83**(Nov.): 624–42.

Graves, L.M. 1946. *The theory of functions of real variables.* New York: McGraw-Hill.

Gumbel, E.J. 1958. *Statistics of extremes.* New York: Columbia University Press.

Haney, L.H. 1914. *Business organization and combination.* New York: Macmillan.

Hirshleifer, J. 1971. The private and social value of information and the reward to inventive activity. *American Economic Review* **51**(Sept.): 561–74.

Hounshell, D.A. 1984. *From the American system to mass production 1800–1932. The development of manufacturing technology in the United States.* Baltimore: Johns Hopkins University Press.

Jones, A.H. 1980. *Wealth of a nation to be: American colonies on the eve of the revolution.* New York: Columbia University Press.

Kaldor, N. 1935. Market imperfection and excess capacity. *Economica* (n.s.) **2:** 33–50.

Kamien, M.I., and Schwartz, N.L. 1975. Market structure and innovation: a survey. *Journal of Economic Literature* **13**(March): 1–37.

Kendrick, J.W. 1961. *Productivity trends in the United States.* National Bureau of Economic Research No. 71. Princeton: Princeton University Press.

Knight, F.H. 1921. *Risk, uncertainty and profit.* Boston: Houghton Mifflin.

Kolko, G. 1965. *Railroads and regulation 1877–1916.* Princeton: Princeton University Press.

Lange, O. 1934. The determinateness of the utility function. *Review of Economic Studies* **1**(June): 218–24.

Letwin, W. 1965. *Law and economic policy.* New York: Random House.

Lloyd, H.D. 1894. *Wealth against commonwealth.* New York: Harper & Bros.

Luce, R.D., and Raiffa, H. 1957. *Games and decisions.* New York: Wiley.

MacAvoy, P.W. 1965. *The economic effects of regulation: the trunk-line railroad cartels and the Interstate Commerce Commission before 1900.* Cambridge, Mass.: M.I.T. Press.

McGee, J.S. 1958. Predatory price cutting: the Standard Oil (NJ) case. *Journal of Law and Economics* **1**(Oct.): 137–69.

McGee, J.S. 1971. *In defense of industrial concentration.* New York: Praeger.

Machlup, F. 1962. *The production and distribution of knowledge in the United States.* Princeton: Princeton University Press.

Mackay, C. 1852. *Extraordinary popular delusions and the madness of crowds,* 2nd ed. London: Office of the National Illustrated Library. (Reprinted New York: Harmony Books, 1980.)

Marshall, A. 1920. *Principles of economics,* 8th ed. London: Macmillan.

Myers, G. 1909. *History of the great American fortunes.* Chicago: C.H. Kerr & Co.

Nash, J.F., Jr. 1950. Equilibrium points in *n*-person games. *Proc. Nat. Acad. Sci. U.S.A.* **36:** 48–9.

Nash, J.F., Jr. 1951. Non-cooperative games. *Ann. Math.* **54:** 286–95.

Nelson, R.L. 1959. *Merger movements in American industry 1895–1956.* National Bureau of Economic Research No. 66. Princeton: Princeton University Press.

Nelson, R.R., and Winter, S.G. 1982. *An evolutionary theory of economic change.* Cambridge, Mass.: Belknap Press, Harvard University Press.

Neumann, J. von, and Morgenstern, O. 1947. *The theory of games and economic behavior,* 2nd ed. Princeton: Princeton University Press.

Peltzman, S. 1977. The gains and losses from industrial concentration. *Journal of Law and Economics* **20**(Oct.): 229–64.

Porter, R.H. 1983. A study of cartel stability: the joint executive committee. *Bell Journal of Economics* **14**(Autumn): 301–14.

Reynolds, L.G. 1940. *The control of competition in Canada.* Cambridge, Mass.: Harvard University Press.

Sahal, D. 1981. *Patterns of technological innovation.* Reading, Mass.: Addison-Wesley.

Schumpeter, J.A. 1954. *Capitalism, socialism and democracy,* 4th ed. London: Unwin University Books.

Seligman, E.R.A. 1887. Railway tariffs and the interstate commerce law. *Pol. Sci. Qtly.* Reprinted in *Essays in economics,* 1967. New York: A.M. Kelly.

Seligman, E.R.A. 1914. *The income tax: a study of the history, theory and practice of income taxation at home and abroad,* 2nd ed. New York: Macmillan.

Shapley, L.S. 1971. Cores of convex games. *Int. J. Game Theory* **1:** 12–26.

Shubik, M. 1959. Edgeworth market games. *Contributions to the theory of games,* vol. 4, Tucker, A.W., and Luce, R.D., eds. Princeton: Princeton University Press.

Smith, A. 1776. *An inquiry into the nature and causes of the wealth of nations,* 2 vols. London: W. Strahan.

Spahr, C.B. 1896. *The present distribution of wealth of the United States.* New York: Crowell.

Stigler, G.J. 1985. The origin of the Sherman Act. *J. of Legal Studies* **14:** 1–12.

Tarbell, I.M. 1904. *The history of the Standard Oil Company.* New York: Macmillan.

Taussig, F.W. 1931. *The tariff history of the United States,* 8th ed. Reprints of Economic Classics. New York: A.M. Kelley, 1967.

Telser, L.G. 1960. Why should manufacturers want fair trade? *Journal of Law and Economics* **3**(Oct.): 86–105.

Telser, L.G. 1972. *Competition, collusion & game theory.* Chicago: Aldine-Atherton.

Telser, L.G. 1978. *Economic theory and the core.* Chicago: University of Chicago Press.

Telser, L.G. 1980. A theory of self-enforcing agreements. *Journal of Business* **53**(Jan.): 27–44.

Telser, L.G. 1982a. A theory of innovation and its effects. *Bell Journal of Economics* **13**(Spring): 69–92.

Telser, L.G. 1982b. Voting and paying for public goods: an application of the theory of the core. *Journal of Economic Theory* **27**(Aug.): 376–409.

Telser, L.G. 1984a. Genesis of the Sherman Act. *Management under government intervention: The view from Mt. Scopus,* Lanzilloti, R.F., and Peles, Y., eds. Greenwich, CT: JAI Press.

Telser, L.G. 1984b. Innovation: its public and private aspects and some of their empirical implications for mergers. *Economic Inquiry* **22:** 634–59.

Telser, L.G. 1985. Cooperation, competition, and efficiency. *Journal of Law and Economics* **28:** 271–95.

Telser, L.G., and Graves, R.L. 1972. *Functional analysis in mathematical economics: optimization over infinite horizons.* Chicago: University of Chicago Press.

Thorelli, H.B. 1955. *The federal antitrust policy*. Baltimore: Johns Hopkins University Press.

Ulen, T.S. 1979. Cartels and regulation: late nineteenth century railroad collusion and the creation of the Interstate Commerce Commission. Unpublished PhD dissertation, Stanford University, University Microfilms International, 300 N. Zeeb Road, Ann Arbor, MI 48106.

Ulen, T.S. 1983. Railroad cartels before 1887: the effectiveness of private enforcement of collusion. *Research in Economic History* **8**: 125–44.

U.S. Senate. 1903. *Bills and debates in Congress relating to trusts*. 57th Cong., 2nd Sess. Senate Document no. 157, I. Washington, DC: U.S. Government Printing Office.

Veblen, T. 1899. *The theory of the leisure class*. New York: Macmillan.

Warburton, C. 1932. *The economic results of prohibition*. New York: Columbia University Press. PhD dissertation.

Index

Addyston case, 25, 43–7
  effect of, on cast-iron pipe prices, 44
  as form of collusion, 44
  mergers of defendents in, 47
age of self-enforcing agreement, 191
allocation, efficient, 136
Alt, F., 132
American Sugar Refining Company, 43
ancillary constraints in Addyston case,
  46
artificial intelligence (AI), 245
assembly line, 17–18
  auto, 72
assignment, optimal 65
Astor, J., 12
auction
  English, 44
  sealed bid, 44
auto industry, 72–3
avoidable cost, 147
Axelrod, R., 214

backward induction, 212
Bain, J. 270n6
Bank of England, 15
Baumol, W., 120n1
Bellman, R., 106
benefit, expected net, 55
  net, from shipping, 146
Bertrand, J., 220
Bittlingmayer, G., 45n5, 47
Böhm-Bawerk, E. von, 48, 51–2
bond as security for malfeasance, 200
book value, 252
Bork, R., 21n1, 41n4
break-even factor, 152
breeching contract, 194
Bryan, William Jennings, 20
Bullock, C. J., 36, 38
Bureau of Ordnance, 243
Burns, A. F., 287n12
buyers' gain, 156

cartel
  and cheating, 143

  as hypothesis, 30
  in imperial Germany, 5–6
  and prisoners' dilemma, 210
  railroad, 20–1
  self-enforcing, 30
Cassel, G., 132
Census Bureau, 255
Chamberlin, E. H., 5
Chandler, A., 47
characteristic extreme, 274
cheating
  by agent, 202
  and cartel viability, 216–7
  gain from, 201–2
  optimal, 216–7
  punishment for, 33, 216
Chicago Board of Trade, 14
Clark, J. M., 49
Cleveland, Grover, 23–4
coalitions
  extreme, 85
  grand, 74
  simple, defined, 153
  size of, 74
collusion, legal status of, in U.S.,
  England, and Germany, 5–6
commitments, long-term, 53
competition
  chaotic, 6–7
  as means, 45, 51
  and property rights, 49–50
  unrestricted, 68
competitive equilibrium
  and nature of property rights, 50
  resolves collision of interests, 65
competitive process, Böhm-Bawerk, 52
computer languages, 246
concave function
  superadditive, 108
  superhomogeneous, 108
constraints on shipments, 148
contract enforceability, 143
contracting restrictions, 4
convex, strictly, 85

301